THE DEADLY EMBRACE

The Impact of Israeli and Palestinian Rejectionism on the Peace Process

Ilana Kass
Bard O'Neill

National Institute for
Public Policy
and
University Press of America, Inc.
Lanham • New York • London

Copyright © 1997 by
University Press of America,® Inc.
4720 Boston Way
Lanham, Maryland 20706

3 Henrietta Street
London, WC2E 8LU England

All rights reserved
Printed in the United States of America
British Cataloging in Publication Information Available

Copublished by arrangement with the
National Institute for Public Policy
Fairfax, Virginia

Library of Congress Cataloging-in-Publication Data

Kass, Ilana.
The deadly embrace : the impact of Israeli and Palestinian rejectionism on the peace process / Ilana Kass, Bard O'Neill.
p. cm.
Includes bibliographical references and index.
1. Israel-Arab conflicts. 2. Insurgency--Israel. 3. Conflict management--Israel. 4. Palestinian Arabs--Political activity. 5. Judaism and politics. 6. Islam and pollitics. I. O'Neill, Bard E. II. Title.
DS119.7.K2996 1996   956--dc20   96-41463 CIP

ISBN 0-7618-0534-6 (cloth: alk. ppr.)
ISBN 0-7618-0535-4 (pbk: alk. ppr.)

∞™ The paper used in this publication meets the minimum requirements of American National Standard for information Sciences—Permanence of Paper for Printed Library Materials, ANSI Z39.48—1984

This book is dedicated to the memory of Israel's slain Prime Minister, Yitzhak Rabin, whom both authors knew and admired as a soldier and statesman. He has made the ultimate sacrifice for peace. "Blessed are the peacemakers, for they shall be called the sons of God."

CONTENTS

Preface vii

Introduction xi

Chapter I
On Internal Warfare 3

Chapter II
The Context of Israeli Rejectionism 61

Chapter III
Analytical Assessment of Israeli Rejectionism 115

Chapter IV
The Context of Palestinian Rejectionism 213

Chapter V
Analytical Assessment of Palestinian Rejectionism ... 249

Chapter VI
The Deadly Embrace: Implications
for the Peace Process 313

Index 341

About the Authors 347

PREFACE

Men will wrangle for religion; write for it; fight for it; die for it; anything but live it.

Charles Caleb Colton, *Lacon*

The Rabin assassination, the Hebron massacre, suicide bombings in Jerusalem and Tel Aviv which leave innocent people killed and maimed--equal outrages, but have they a common genesis? Yes, and at risk is much more than the lives of individuals. Indeed, the very existence of Israel as a secular democracy, as well the future of the newly-created Palestinian National Authority are threatened by the curious yet lethal interaction between Palestinians and Israeli zealots who reject any mutual compromise.

This book is about two nations, bound together by myriad of geographical, historical, political, economic, and cultural links, destined to fight over--or agree to share--the same piece of land. It also about two communities locked in a deadly embrace of primordial passions, feeding off and reinforcing each other's fears and enmities. Drawing on a wide array of primary sources, the book paints a sobering picture of mortal enemies, acting in the name of God to kill each other so as to kill the peace process. This deadly embrace poses a serious and immediate threat to regional peace and stability. Thus, it directly endangers enduring American interests in the Middle East.

Our overarching premise is that the currently ongoing peace process is a complex, fragile enterprise, taking place in one of the world's most volatile regions. Fond hopes and wishful thinking aside, progress can neither be taken for granted, nor considered an established fact. Given the stakes involved, serious, systematic analysis of not only the prospects for peace, but also of the organized forces that would subvert it is imperative.

For both of us, researching and writing this book has been as much about discovery as it has been about scholarship. For, like most specialists, we were quite familiar with the various components of the Palestinian resistance that have been active for almost three decades. What we discovered were not only new, multi-dimensional nuances among these traditional opponents of peace, but also the rapidly evolving, complex, and largely unexplored world of religious militants. Equally importantly, we found that this fundamentalist mutation has a mirror image on the Israeli side, where equally committed believers espouse remarkably similar--if mutually exclusive--agendas. These rejectionists are united in their near-term objective of destroying peace, but ultimately sworn to destroy each other.

Ours is the first known attempt at a comparative analysis of Israeli and Palestinian rejectionism. To this end, we apply a common framework, using explicit evaluative criteria to identify the strengths and weaknesses of each side, assess the dynamics of their interaction, and evaluate their future potential. On this basis, we offer a set of policy choices and recommendations which the U.S., Israel and the Palestinian National Authority should pursue in tandem to marginalize the rejectionist threat before it escalates to literally unimaginable levels of violence.

In our work, we have benefitted from the generous assistance of a number of individuals. First, we owe a debt of gratitude to the National Institute for Public Policy, under whose gracious auspices this book is published, especially to Dr. Keith B. Payne and Dr. Robert Rudney. We would also like to thank our students at the National War College for always asking the hard questions which stimulate undertakings such as this. The Commandant of the National War College, Rear Admiral M. A. McDevitt, provided us with unwavering encouragement and support. So did our respective Department Chairmen, Colonel Harry Rothmann and Dr. Terry Deibel. Special thanks for helpful comments on the early drafts of this manuscript go to Mr. Bruce Harris, of the Dynamics Research Corporation.

Invaluable editorial assistance was provided by Ms. Gwen Powell, whose professionalism, skill and dedication were

Preface

indispensable in preparing the book for publication. Special thanks should also go to Ms. Angela Parham, doctoral candidate at Howard University, who worked diligently to prepare the index and to Ms. Pam Adams, who always knew which buttons needed to be pushed to save us from the perils of the computer age.

Last but certainly not least, we wish to thank our spouses, Nancy O'Neill and Norm Kass, for their patience, understanding and encouragement. Most special gratitude is due to Norm, who read and read again the various iterations of this manuscript, offered many astute suggestions, and provided us with a much needed, critical sounding board.

The views expressed in this book are those of the authors alone. They do not necessarily represent the official position of the United States government, the Department of Defense, or the National Defense University.

INTRODUCTION

The Persian Gulf War of 1990-91 has ushered in a truly remarkable period in the contemporary Middle East. Almost a century of seemingly endless strife has given way to a series of limited agreements between two bitter foes, the Israelis and the Palestinians. There is even hope that a final, comprehensive peace accord will be concluded before the end of the millennium.

Safeguarding what has been accomplished thus far and actualizing the hopes for the future will not be easy. There are two reasons for this cautionary note. First, the existing agreements are hardly the product of some sudden surge of mutual good will. Rather, they reflect a recognition, by pragmatists on both sides, of the political realities facing them and the bleak future they foreshadow.

Israel, whose ultimate political objective is to live in peace with its neighbors, had to face the prospect of interminable threats to both its security and its democratic nature, in the context of irreconcilable political differences with the Palestinians. For the Palestinians, whose ultimate goal is the creation of an independent nation-state, there was the prospect of continued political stagnation and a stalemated armed struggle, in the context of decreasing support from past benefactors in both the Arab world and the former Soviet Bloc. More than anything, these grim realities led both sides to overcome their phobias and seize the opportunity for negotiations provided by the United States in the aftermath of the Persian Gulf War.

Yet, what has been achieved thus far rests solely on a foundation of mutual political interests, shared by notably distrustful adversaries. Stripped of lofty rhetoric, the peace process is basically the product of necessity, lacking a legacy of confidence and trust. Thus far, there has been only a modest accumulation of the psychological capital necessary to anchor--and thus stabilize-- the agreements, so as to guide them through the inevitable storms that lie ahead. To endure, the peace process will need careful nurturing, particularly in light of the second and most compelling reason for caution, namely, the entrenched opposition by so-called rejectionists--that is, groups in both Israel and the Arab world that struggle against political settlement and territorial compromise on religious/ideological grounds. The November 1995 assassination of Israel's Prime Minister, Yitzhak Rabin, is a sad reminder of this elemental fact.

Prior to this tragedy, there was a growing sense of complacency and undue optimism as to the future course and direction of regional processes. Simply put, peace was deemed to be irreversible. Although the peacemakers and their supporters recognized that many tough issues had yet to be tackled and that a sizeable opposition to the negotiations existed on both sides, they shared--and projected--a virtually unshakable faith that peace will prevail. The mantra was echoed by countless diplomats, propagandists and pundits, reinforcing the optimistic image of regional peace as a permanent, self-sustaining, indestructible trend. Fond hopes thus acquired the status of unexamined axioms. Left unanswered were such key questions as what "irreversibility" really means, whether it allows for temporary setbacks and, if so, what the impact and duration of these setbacks might be. Needless to say, no criteria were established to permit the continued validation of the assumption itself.

Yet, if the recent history counsels anything, it is that we keep an open mind when it comes to potential deviations from seemingly well-established patterns. Linear thinking is particularly precarious in the Middle East, where what is deemed unlikely by outsiders, might be viewed as quite plausible by regional actors. It is with good reason that the Middle East has been characterized--somewhat sardonically--as an area where there is a high probability that the low probability will occur. In this vein, instead of dismissing out of hand the possibility that the peace process could be derailed or eviscerated, we intend to spotlight the all-too-real threats looming on the horizon.

The purpose of this book is three-fold: First, drawing on a wide array of primary and secondary sources, it aims to compare and

Introduction

contrast the historical roots, goals, strategies, organizational structures, and current activities of Palestinian and Israeli opponents of any mutual compromise. Second, the book assesses the dynamic interaction of two rejectionist movements, espousing mutually exclusive political agendas and demonstrates how they feed off and reinforce each others enmities. Third, the book seeks to expose to public scrutiny a deeply-entrenched phenomenon that has continued to lurk in the shadows, while enjoying both tacit and direct support from segments within the American Arab and Jewish communities. Although such recent outrages as the Hebron massacre, the Rabin assassination and the spate of suicide bombings in Israel's cities have re-centered attention on Middle Eastern terrorism, the primary focus has been on lone actions of deranged individuals. In contrast, our thesis is that what we have witnessed thus far is merely the tip of the iceberg--overt manifestations of a deep-seated, festering problem, namely: increasingly militant insurgent movements, united in their near-term aim of destroying the peace process, but ultimately sworn to destroy each other. The book concludes with a set of policy choices and recommendations which the U.S., Israel and the Palestinian National Authority should pursue in tandem to marginalize the rejectionist threat, before it escalates to hitherto unimaginable levels of violence.

While the terms "rejectionism" and "rejectionists" have been associated primarily with Palestinian opponents of the peace process, we shall argue that they are equally applicable in Israel-- or, for that matter, elsewhere in the Middle East. Furthermore, we shall demonstrate that the mutual antagonism of Israeli and Palestinian rejectionists locks them in a deadly embrace, wherein both benefit from and are sustained by the violence that disrupts the peace process--regardless of who the actual perpetrators might be. Since innocent civilians are usually and deliberately the intended targets, this interaction amounts to a paradoxical convergence of evil. For, what can be more evil--or more paradoxical--than killing innocent people in the name of God?

Our admittedly ambitious agenda calls for a systematic comparative analysis of two distinct, yet related and interacting rejectionist movements which engage in acts of internal political violence. To this end, we shall apply a framework for analysis of terrorism and insurgency which has been extensively used by analysts and practitioners in both the Western national security community and academia.[1] Indeed, first-hand observers have spotted copies in such insurgent redoubts as the Pansjir Valley in Afghanistan and the jungles of Southeastern Angola, suggesting its use by actual practitioners of internal war.

In order to avoid any misunderstanding, it is important to note at the outset that the framework is not a macro-theoretical scheme that develops highly formalized, abstract relationships among variables. Nor is it a normative "model" that lays out behavioral patterns that all insurgent groups should manifest. This does not mean, however, that we are uninterested in relationships among the factors. To the contrary, the linkages and inter-connections will become quite evident, as we proceed with our systematic, comparative analysis.[2]

Our framework sets out a comprehensive series of generic questions that need to be asked about any insurgent group, at any time and in any place, in order to ascertain its current status and future prospects. In sequence, these questions are:

---What is the ultimate goal of the insurgent movement? Are there different factions with contradictory ultimate aims? What are the salient intermediate aims?

---What forms of warfare or violence (terrorism, guerrilla attacks or conventional combat) do the insurgents use? How extensive and effective are they?

---Does the insurgent movement have a grand strategy? If so, does it purport to follow currently existing strategic approaches or some variation thereof? Are there multiple strategies? A new strategy?

---Is the physical environment conducive to the forms of warfare and strategy chosen by the insurgents?

---What is the impact of human environmental factors like demography, race, ethnicity, religion, social structure and values,

Introduction

economic distribution, and the political culture and system on the genesis and progression of the conflict?

---How much active and passive support does the insurgent organization enjoy? What are the relative roles and importance of elites and mass components? What techniques are used to gain popular support?

---How well organized are the insurgents? Is their level of organization compatible with their objectives and grand strategy?

---Are the insurgents cohesive? If not, what are the causes and effects of disunity?

---What kinds of external support do the insurgents get and from whom? How important is it? How vulnerable is it to being curtailed or terminated?

---What is the nature of the government response? Does the government have a candid profile of its adversaries? Does it use appropriate measures for undermining the strengths and exacerbating the weaknesses of the insurgents?

These questions are not arbitrary. They derive from an extensive, multi-disciplinary survey of internal conflicts, political violence, terrorism, and the like. As such, the framework reflects the work of many scholars and colleagues. Its key concepts will be readily recognizable by students of internal wars. The approach has been validated, refined and modified as a result of over 200 past and present case studies, conducted by different study groups and individuals with extensive civilian and military experience from across the world. These cases include: Various urban terrorist groups in Europe, such as the Irish Republican Army, Basque Homeland and Liberty and the Red Brigades in Italy; insurgents in the Latin American countries of Guatemala, Uruguay, El Salvador and Peru; Asian groups like the Tamil Tigers in Sri Lanka and the New People's Army in the Philippines; Middle Eastern secessionist organizations such the PKK in Turkey and Polisario in Western Sahara; militant Islamic organizations like the Islamic Group in Egypt; and uprisings in Angola and Mozambique in sub-Saharan Africa.

We have organized our analysis of Israeli and Palestinian rejectionism around the same essential questions which--as suggested by both academic literature and empirical experience--should be asked about any group engaged in internal political violence. Naturally, the answers will vary considerably from case to case, a point that will become quite clear when we compare the two movements. Indeed, this diversity is inherent in the very nature of our inquiry, as well as in our purpose of highlighting similarities, differences, and patterns of interaction.

Lest the reader be left with just a series of questions, we have taken the time to discuss them in a systematic, yet concise manner in the next chapter where, for reasons of analytic clarity, they are presented as explanatory factors and evaluative criteria. This approach reflects our aim of giving the reader pertinent background on each factor, drawing on some of the best thinking of historians, political scientists, anthropologists and sociologists, as well as first-hand observers, especially journalists. Since key terms like "revolutionary war," "guerrilla warfare," "insurgency" and so on are often used interchangeably and defined in various ways in the general literature, we will offer our own operational definitions along the way.

In laying out the social, political, economic and military factors that help explain and anticipate the dynamics of insurgencies, we are also striving to be as comprehensive and comparative as possible. This should become evident in the chapters on the Israeli and Palestinian rejectionists, which are organized explicitly and sequentially around the same set of evaluative criteria.

We have deliberately devoted more time to Israeli rejectionism than to the better known Palestinian case. In our view, the vast and readily accessible literature on the latter contains many details that need not be repeated here. Accordingly, wherever possible, we have condensed our commentary on the Palestinians in favor of making more space available for the lesser known Israeli case. We fully recognize the asymmetry this creates, but believe it necessary and justifiable in this instance.

Moreover, as will become evident in subsequent chapters,

Introduction

Palestinian rejectionism is a fully articulated, entrenched insurgent movement. Because the Palestinians have been engaged in an armed struggle for decades, the framework is more obviously and extensively applicable to their case. Israeli rejectionism, in contrast, is an emerging, still evolving phenomenon. The commitment to violence is relatively new and far less sustained than its Palestinian counterparts'. Indeed, until very recently, the very terms "rejectionism," or "extremism"--veritable cliches when it comes to Western literature dealing with the Palestinians--were rarely even used in reference to Israeli opponents of territorial compromise. Yet, as we shall argue, the threat posed by Israeli rejectionism, if left unchecked, is potentially graver, since it imperils not only peace, but also democracy and the rule of law.

Consequently, our application of the framework to the Israeli case is necessarily more speculative and futuristic. Nonetheless, a sober analysis of Jewish rejectionism--in terms of its strengths, weaknesses, and probable future directions--calls for explicit concepts, grounded in a coherent methodology. By the same token, comparative analysis of Palestinian and Israeli rejectionism is impossible without the systematic application of common evaluative criteria. These, in turn, will serve to highlight the two movements' dynamic interaction, laying the groundwork for the development of rational approaches designed to marginalize and, thus, mitigate, their impact.

One final note. It is our hope that the application of a comprehensive framework will help the reader interpret and order the vast amount of data we have assembled on Israeli and Palestinian rejectionism--as well as set the baseline against which future developments could be judged. For, our purpose is not merely to describe a series of interesting episodes but, rather, to offer a road map for thinking the problem through with us. Hopefully, our effort will provide the analytical dimension against which informed judgments and prudent policy choices would be made. The fateful nature of the issues at stake, at this crucial juncture in Middle East history, demands nothing less.

Introduction

Notes

1. The framework is set forth in Bard E. O'Neill, *Insurgency and Terrorism: Inside Modern Revolutionary Warfare*, (New York, NY: Brassey's, Inc., 1990). For an application of the framework to several cases see, Bard E. O'Neill, William R. Heaton and Donald J. Alberts, eds., *Insurgency in the Modern World*, (Boulder, CO: Westview Press, 1980). For over a decade, the framework has been consistently applied in courses directed by the present authors at the National War College. It has also served as a basis for several doctoral dissertations and M.A. theses.

2. An excellent source for discerning the differences among such terms as paradigm, model, theory, conceptual framework, and the like is Lawrence C. Mayer, *Comparative Political Inquiry: A Methodological Survey* (Homewood, IL: The Dorsey Press, 1972). What we have done is somewhat beyond Abraham Kaplan's "concatenated theory," that is, we present a set of empirical generalizations that possess a common focus. Although our main concern is the impact of six critical factors on the progress and outcome of internal political violence, we have suggested a number of relationships between and among the factors (e.g., the nexus between popular support and organization, unity and external support, unity and government response, etc.). As indicated in the text, we by no means claim to have developed a "hierarchial theory" or a formal model. See, Abraham Kaplan, *The Conduct of Inquiry* (San Francisco, CA: Chandler Publishing Company, 1964), pp. 298 ff.

CHAPTER ONE

ON INTERNAL WARFARE

CHAPTER I

ON INTERNAL WARFARE

The Nature of Internal War

Insurgency is about the interplay of power, politics and violence. It is a high-stakes game, with few discernible rules, in which perceptions are as important as reality. It involves such primordial passions as hatred and enmity, deeply-felt grievances and core beliefs for which people are willing to kill and die.

Internal political violence begins with a crisis of legitimacy[1] and a breakdown in the social compact that binds people together. It involves a struggle between a non-ruling group and the incumbent authorities, in which the former consciously uses violence and political means to destroy, change, or preserve some aspect of politics--be it the political community, the political system, the authorities, and/or their policies. Insurgency can entail both the overt and covert use of force, supported by such non-violent measures as agitation, organization, propaganda, and demonstrations--all targeted at a political objective. What is at stake are issues of legitimacy and illegitimacy--that is, moral value judgments as to right and wrong--as perceived by the people at large, or by specific social groups.

Insurgency might involve a fundamental rejection of the **political community** as presently constituted. In the contemporary international system, this usually means a violent challenge to the integrity or composition of a nation-state. The ongoing war in the former Yugoslavia is an example of the destructive forces that might be unleashed by those rebelling against--and seeking to destroy--the social fabric that weaves diverse groups into a single political entity.

A second source of violent internal conflict may be discord over the **political system**, i.e., the salient values and structures which make up the basic framework within which people interact.

In recent times, this has been exemplified by groups as ideologically divergent as the Marxist Popular Front for the Liberation of Oman and the Islamic Group in Egypt, both of which seek to impose their own political values, structures and institutions on their respective societies.

On another level, some insurgent groups may grant legitimacy to the political system *per se*, but reject the **authorities,** that is, the specific individuals holding the reins of power. This is exemplified by coups in which insurgents seize key offices yet do not change the political system put in place by their predecessors. Besides the well-known Latin American cases of the 1950's, one could point to the 1970 overthrow of the Sultan of Oman, Said bin Taimur, by his son Qabus as an example.

Finally, violence may be used by non-ruling groups in an effort to change existing **policies** which they believe have prevented them from acquiring their fair share of the collective political and economic wealth. Recent examples of such insurgencies include the Miskito Indians in Nicaragua and the Zapatistas in Mexico.

The key point to bear in mind is that insurgency is essentially a political legitimacy crisis of some sort. To gain a further insight into the nature of that crisis, however, it is important to ascertain what is at stake--what are the core issues for which people are ready to fight and die. In other words, one needs to understand the long-term goals pursued by the insurgents.

Types of Insurgencies

When we inquire about the ultimate goals of insurgent movements and consider the aspects of politics they focus on, some very important distinctions emerge. Simply put, insurgencies differ widely in terms of the end-state they seek to attain and the ways and means by which they intend to arrive at their desired goals. Consequently, the first question that needs to be addressed is: What type of insurgency are we dealing with?

Research on the subject suggests seven types of insurgent

movements: anarchist, egalitarian, traditionalist, pluralist, preservationist, reformist, and secessionist. The first four are revolutionary in nature, because they seek to completely change an existing political system.[2] Without a doubt, the most far-reaching--or totalistic--goal is espoused by the **anarchist** insurgents, who wish to eliminate all institutionalized political arrangements because they view them as illegitimate. Various groups in Tsarist Russia and Europe near the turn of the century fall into this category.

Egalitarian insurgent movements seek to impose a new political system, based on the ultimate value of distributional equality and on centrally controlled structures, designed to mobilize the people and radically transform society. This type of insurgency has been a familiar part of the post World War II international political landscape. It is epitomized by violent Marxist groups, such as the New People's Army in the Philippines, the Viet Cong in South Vietnam, the PFLO in Oman, and the *Sendero Luminoso* (Shining Path) in Peru.

Traditionalist insurgents seek to restore a system that existed in the recent or distant past. The values they articulate are primordial and sacred--rooted in ancestral ties and religion. Political structures in a traditional system are characterized by limited, or guided, participation and low autonomy. The focus of political power is usually an autocratic leader and his family, supported by the nobility, army and clergy. While the majority of the population may enjoy some autonomy at the local level, widespread participation in national politics is discouraged. Recent and current traditionalist insurgents include those who supported the return of the Imam in the Yemen Arab Republic (North Yemen) in the 1960's and moderate Islamic groups in Afghanistan, such as Mohammed Gailani's National Islamic Front for the Liberation of Afghanistan.

Within the category of traditionalist insurgents one also finds more zealous groups, seeking to re-establish an ancient regime which they idealize as a golden age. We refer to this subtype as **reactionary-traditionalists**. The Muslim Brotherhood in Syria, the

Armed Islamic Group in Algeria, *Hezbollah* in Lebanon, and the *Hezb-i--Islami* in Afghanistan exemplify this category. All wish to establish Islamic political and social arrangements, in accordance with either Sunni or Shi'ite visions of what the ideal past was really like. That these visions are frequently distorted--reflecting more wishful thinking than historically accurate facts--is immaterial. Since reactionaries believe they are the sole repositories of the truth, their rhetoric is dogmatic and their approach intolerant towards those who do not share their views.[3] As we shall see, this subtype is particularly relevant and applicable to both the Israeli and Palestinian cases.

The **pluralists**, in contrast, wish to establish a political system in which the values of individual freedom, liberty and participation are emphasized and in which political structures are differentiated and autonomous. Although the history of Western civilization is marked by a number of such uprisings, in more recent times there have been few, if any, insurgencies that we could confidently classify as pluralist. Case studies of almost every major insurgency in the past fifteen years suggest that while many groups use pluralistic rhetoric, their ultimate goals and behavior are anything but pluralistic.

Even more far-reaching than the revolutionary goals espoused by the four types of groups we have just discussed is the ultimate aim of **secessionist**, or separatist insurgents. Secessionists renounce the political community of which they are formally a part. They seek to withdraw from it and constitute a new and independent political entity. Examples include the Front for the Liberation of Rio d'Oro and *Saguia el Hamra* (Polisario) in Western Sahara, the Sikhs of the Khalistan Liberation Front in India, the Tamil Tigers in Sri Lanka, the Quebec Liberation Front, and, more recently, several small Jewish groups seeking to establish an independent Judea in the West Bank.

The sixth type of insurgency, the **reformist**, is the least ambitious. Exemplified in the early 1980's by the Kurds in Iran and the Miskito Indians in Nicaragua, reformists aim at gaining greater political, social, and economic benefits for their constituencies, without rejecting the political community, the system, or the authorities. They are primarily concerned with the existing allocation of political and material resources, which they deem to be discriminatory and illegitimate. Insurgents who demand autonomy, as opposed to separation, fall within this category.

The seventh and final type of insurgent movement is **preservationist**. Insurgents in this category are essentially oriented toward maintaining the *status quo*, because of the relative political, economic and social privileges they derive from it. Basically, preservationist insurgents seek to conserve the existing political system and policies by engaging in illegal acts of violence against non-ruling groups and the authorities who are trying to effect change. The Ulster Defense Association in Northern Ireland today, the Serbs in Bosnia and, as we will demonstrate, mainstream Israeli rejectionists exemplify this type.

Although identifying types of internal wars might seem as a relatively easy task, three complications should be kept in mind. First, some insurgent movements go through goal transformation, either because new leaders--with alternate aims--gain control, or because existing leaders calculate that less ambitious objectives stand a better chance of success. The evolution of the Dhofar insurgency in Oman from a secessionist to an egalitarian movement as the result of a Marxist takeover illustrates the former case. The transformation of the Sudanese insurrection, carried out by blacks in the Southern area in the 1960's, from secessionism to reformism illustrates the scaling down of a movement's aims.

A second analytical problem is presented by situations wherein distinct groups or factions comprising an insurgent movement espouse different and, at times, mutually exclusive goals. Recent cases have been the uprising against the Marxist regime in Afghanistan, which involved reactionary, reformist and pluralist factions, and the Palestinian resistance, which contains egalitarian, traditionalist and putatively pluralist elements. As we shall see, Israeli rejectionism also suffers from this malady.

The third difficulty confronting a researcher is the frequent masking of ultimate goals by democratic rhetoric. Where such obfuscation is suspected, it is particularly important to examine carefully the insurgents' public and internal documents, as well as their manner of governing the movement. Only then can we render judgment as to their true aspirations. The democratic pronouncements of centrally controlled and authoritarian organizations, such as Marxist or religiously-inspired movements that claim monopoly over the truth, should be treated with great skepticism.

The Means: Organization and Forms of Warfare

To accomplish their goals, insurgent movements use political resources and violence against the ruling authorities. Political activity includes such things as: the dissemination of information (propaganda) through meetings, pamphlets, media broadcasts, and the like; arranging protest demonstrations; proselytizing government officials; training and infiltrating agents into the official establishment; persuading outside powers to extend various kinds of assistance; raising and managing finances; creating supportive groups (e.g., workers', farmers', women's, writers', and youth associations); providing services to the people; devising and implementing strategies and plans. The critical importance of such activities has led many analysts to characterize insurgency as primarily a political phenomenon and to attribute the success of individuals such as Mao Tse-tung and Ho Chi Minh more to their political acumen than to their prowess as military leaders.

Yet, as important as political skills may be, it is the use of violence which sets insurgency apart from political protest movements like Solidarity in Poland and the civil rights movement in the United States. The violent aspect of insurgency is manifested in different **forms of warfare**. Historically, three forms of warfare have been associated with internal conflicts: terrorism, guerrilla war and conventional warfare.

Terrorism is a form of warfare in which violence is directed primarily against unarmed civilians, rather than the uniformed military, police forces, or economic assets.[4] The operational units are normally small and organized covertly into cells. Their actions are all too familiar, consisting of such things as assassinations, bombings, tossing grenades, arson, torture, mutilation, hijacking, and kidnapping. While the targets of such violence might, at times, be arbitrary, they are often carefully chosen so as to maximize the political impact. Although terrorism has generally occurred within the borders of a political entity whose community, system, authorities, or policies have become the focus of insurgent violence, there has been an increasing tendency over the past fifteen years to strike at targets outside such boundaries. Since these acts are carried out by insurgent groups, they have been referred to as transnational terrorism, so as to distinguish them from similar behavior on the part of individuals or groups controlled by sovereign states (international terrorism).

Insurgent terrorism is purposeful violence, aimed at achieving specific long-, intermediate- and short-term goals. The long-term objective is, of course, to change the political community, system, authorities, or policies and, as indicated above, it may be specified in terms of the type insurgency being waged. The intermediate goal of terrorism is not so much to deplete the government's physical resources, as it is to erode its psychological support. To this end, terrorists seek to instill fear among state officials and unnerve the government's domestic and international supporters. Though the intermediate purpose of terrorism is to alter the behavior and attitudes of specific groups, this has not excluded the simultaneous pursuit of one or more proximate objectives, such as: extracting particular concessions (e.g., payment of ransom or the release of prisoners); gaining publicity; demoralizing the population through the creation of widespread disorder; provoking repression by the government; enforcing obedience and cooperation from those inside and outside the movement; fulfilling the need for revenge; or enhancing the political stature of specific factions within an insurgent movement. Exactly which goals are being pursued by the well-known terrorist acts of Palestinian and Israeli rejectionists is an important consideration that will be addressed later.

The upsurge in terrorism in the past decade or so notwithstanding, the most familiar kind of violence used by insurgents has been **guerrilla warfare**. The essence of guerrilla warfare is highly mobile hit-and-run attacks, carried out by armed groups, with the objective of harassing the enemy, thus gradually eroding his will and capability to resist. Although victories are always important, they consist of relatively modest engagements, followed by withdrawal, rather than large positional battles designed to seize and hold territory. Guerrilla warfare differs from terrorism in that its primary targets are the government's armed forces, police, or their support units and, in some cases, key economic targets--rather than unarmed civilians. As a consequence, guerrilla units are larger than terrorist cells and tend to require a more elaborate logistical infrastructure, as well as base camps. Moreover, the locus of guerrilla activity is normally in the rural areas.[5] Like terrorism, guerrilla warfare is a weapon of the weak. It is decisive only where the government fails to commit adequate resources to the conflict. In some cases it has been necessary to accompany guerrilla warfare with other forms of violence, or to transition into **conventional warfare**--that is, the direct confrontation of large units in the field--in order to achieve success. The decision to engage in this form of warfare depends on the strategy pursued by the insurgents.

Insurgent Strategies

Strategy is the systematic, integrated, coherently orchestrated use of various means to achieve specific goals. The kinds of objectives that are chosen, the types of means that are emphasized, and the nature of the plans that are followed differ considerably from case to case. To facilitate our analytical effort, we shall concentrate on four broad approaches which have provided guidance--if not inspiration--for many recent and contemporary insurgencies. These are: the conspiratorial, protracted popular war, military focus, and urban warfare strategies. Since a number of Palestinian insurgent leaders have studied and adopted one or another of these strategies, an understanding of their main features is important for the assessment of the quality of Palestinian strategic thinking. By the same token, such understanding will shed light on the still evolving Israeli case.

The Conspiratorial Strategy: Perhaps the oldest and least complicated insurgent strategy is the conspiratorial approach, which seeks to remove the ruling authorities through a limited but swift use of force. Conspiracies are basically coups led by either military officers, who are not part of the ruling elite, or by disaffected civilians. In many cases, the removal of the authorities is deemed necessary to achieve the real goal--that is, to change policies and/or to replace a political system deemed to be illegitimate. In other situations, the aim may be to replace the authorities, either because they are threatening to undertake major policy initiatives that will upset the existing distribution of social, economic and political privileges (preservationist insurgents), or because they are perceived to be corrupt and inefficient (reformist insurgents).

Whatever the ultimate goal, the crucial instrument for seizing power is a small, secretive, disciplined, and tightly organized group. The locus of insurgent activity is the major urban centers, especially the capital city, where political and economic power is concentrated. When the conspiracy is based on the military, little or no attention is paid to the organized involvement of the larger public. To the extent that popular views are taken into consideration, calculations center on assuring acceptance of the outcome. Popular support, mass organization and external support are not salient considerations. While environmental factors--e.g., economic regression and maldistribution, and/or political disorder, corruption and the like--might be the underlying cause of the insurrection, the defection of military officers is almost always the crucial variable.

Although military insurrections have occurred throughout history and are hardly uncommon in the present era, governments facing severe social, economic and political problems often manage to retain the loyalty of the military. When this happens, civilian-led conspiracies may be hatched. Since the military's continued loyalty to the governing authorities is a formidable impediment to the insurgents, a greater emphasis must be placed on substantial political activity and extensive preparations for using violence. This effort frequently involves attempts to infiltrate and subvert the military, particularly rank and file officers and enlisted personnel.

The most striking contemporary example of this particular approach is the 1917 Bolshevik insurrection in Russia, which popularized the conspiratorial strategy. In that context, a small vanguard of dedicated activists, whose behavior could be more easily controlled and coordinated, was key. Emphasis was placed on ideological, strategic and operational unity. Deviations were unacceptable. While a principal aim of the leadership elites and cadres was to exploit mass discontent, only segments of the population, mainly in the urban centers, became the targets of proselytization, infiltration, manipulation and, ultimately, control. Although scattered terrorist acts took place, violence was basically confined to the direct seizure of key government facilities.
Neither systematic terrorism, nor guerrilla warfare was accorded importance. In theory, there was little need for external support, because deteriorating social and economic conditions--as well as the government's political and military ineptitude--made it vulnerable to a quick, decisive and forceful move by the insurgents.

Lenin's historical stature is not overly diminished by the fact that the success of his strategy depended as much on events beyond his control as it did on his considerable conceptual, organizational and political skills. Thus, his strategy could not be easily replicated in other countries, especially in Europe, where the Bolsheviks had great hopes for sparking a wide-ranging proletarian revolution. The main problem was that the particular combination of political, economic and social factors which had created a vacuum of legitimacy and authority in Russia was absent elsewhere. Even in China, where the decay of the traditional regime, the diffusion of power to warlords, corruption, and socio-economic problems led some Marxists to believe they could seize power in the late 1920's, the authorities proved too resilient to topple. Consequently, the Chinese crafted a markedly different strategy for insurgency that emphasized a prolonged armed struggle, based on active mass support.[6]

The Protracted Popular War Strategy: The protracted popular war strategy, as articulated by Mao and codified by his disciples, is undoubtedly the most conceptually elaborate and widely emulated insurgent strategy. It is especially important for our purposes, since many of the Palestinian rejectionists have been captivated by all or part of it. The strategy consists of three sequential phases, each of which differs with respect to the correlation of forces. The first, the *strategic defensive*, is a time when the enemy is on the offensive and the insurgents must concentrate on survival, political organization and low-level violence. As the insurgents gradually gain support and achieve military successes, they enter the second and longest phase, the *strategic stalemate*, which is characterized by guerrilla warfare. Further escalation and victories, which lead to demoralization, lethargy and defections on the government side, usher in the *strategic offensive*. During this phase, the insurgents transition from guerrilla warfare to conventional attacks on a large scale. The cumulative political and psychological effects of the insurgent victories lead to a collapse of the government.

The three stages in Mao's scheme have specific objectives, involve different combinations of political and military actions, all dependent on the outcomes of preceding stages. The *strategic defensive* phase emphasizes political organization. Cellular networks are created; political organizers engage in propaganda activities to win popular support; and terrorists carry out selective acts of intimidation against recalcitrant individuals. At this point, fronts composed of various social segments--based on religious affiliation, occupation, age group, or gender--may be organized, along with pressure groups and parties. All are designed to facilitate the acquisition of popular support. Simultaneously, insurgents usually try to infiltrate enemy institutions, foment strikes, demonstrations and riots, and, perhaps, carry out sabotage missions. As part of their political effort, the insurgents stress appeals based on both ideology and material grievances, while attempting to provide some social services and engage in mutual self-help projects.

Guerrilla warfare is central in the ***strategic stalemate*** phase. The insurgent aim in the incipient part of this stage is to isolate the people from the incumbent government. The organizational apparatus established in the first phase begins to supply small guerrilla units. Full- and part-time personnel play a more prominent role. Yet, during the early part of stage two, there is still a lack of organization above the village level, and groups operate from shifting, remote bases. Militarily, actions undertaken early in stage two are small, hit-and-run attacks against convoys, military and economic installations, and isolated outposts. These scattered attacks are intended to force the enemy into a static defensive posture, wherein his forces are dispersed to protect numerous potential targets.

If there is satisfactory progress during the early part of stage two, insurgents normally move into the second half of that stage and expand their organization in the regions they control. During stage two, the parallel hierarchy is more visible than during stage one. Besides resembling the state apparatus, it also includes auxiliary organizations controlled by cells linked to the central political structure. Moreover, a government-in-exile may be created. The organizational evolution in late stage two includes the establishment of arsenals, arms production facilities and hospitals. The logistics operation encompasses activities ranging from procurement of basic foodstuffs and war supplies to acquisition of material aid from external sources.

In the military realm, recruitment of full-time guerrillas, establishment of an extensive reserve system, and the creation and training of regular army units are emphasized. Three operational levels often comprise the military organization in late stage two: regional, district, and local. The regional troops--the best armed and trained--form the strike forces. At the next level, the district battalion is led by full-time cadres, though the subordinate companies are themselves composed of part-time soldiers. Local forces are made up of both full- and part-time guerrillas, with the latter predominant. All three levels are coordinated by a central headquarters in pursuit of common military and political objectives. While military actions in late stage two are basically large-scale guerrilla attacks, carried out from secure base areas, attention is devoted to seizing territory and preparing the battlefield for conventional warfare.

The third and final stage of the protracted popular warfare strategy, *the strategic offensive*, is, as we have noted, characterized by the transformation of guerrilla forces into regular, conventional troops. Although regular units may engage in some positional warfare, the primary emphasis is on mobile operations, with small guerrilla bands supporting the main effort in an ancillary role. The salient military objective at this point is to destroy the enemy's main forces. The principal political aim is the displacement of the governing authorities.

It was, no doubt, inevitable that a number of variations on the protracted popular war strategy would emerge, as it was adopted and operationalized in places other than China. The Algerian insurgency against the French during the 1950's is a case in point. The goal of the Algerian insurgents--Arab nationalists and Muslims, rather than Marxists--was to achieve independence from France. To this end, they waged a protracted struggle which emphasized popular support and gradually escalating violence, i.e., guerrilla warfare, followed by conventional operations. Their so-called "oil spot" strategy was reminiscent of Mao's approach, in that it was based on the gradual expansion of their political control in the countryside surrounding the cities. Unlike the Chinese, however, the Algerians never transitioned to the conventional warfare stage, because the French had defeated the insurgents militarily. Yet, although the French won on the battlefield, the Algerians won the war. The reason for this apparent paradox was that the insurgents were able to sustain widespread popular support and to wear down French political resolve. They did so by posing the prospect of a costly, interminable struggle, as well as through skillful propaganda at home and abroad (especially in Paris), specifically exploiting such French excesses as torture and terror.

In the final analysis, the Algerian war showed that victory is possible without the structured phasing and military progression associated with Mao's strategy. The key to overcoming military regression was the acquisition and maintenance of popular support by means of good organization and astute psychological warfare campaigns.

Whatever the variations in specific cases, the protracted popular war strategy is quite demanding. It relies on extensive popular support and a complex organizational apparatus--the construction of which requires considerable time and effort, as well as secure base areas for the insurgents. By the same token, the strategy calls for directly or indirectly engaging increasing numbers of people in a long-term conflict with the government, in order to control the countryside and, thereby, isolate the urban centers so as to erode the government's will to resist. Such an undertaking is vulnerable at many points to determined psychological, organizational and military-police countermeasures--as the British demonstrated in both Malaya in the 1950's and Oman in the 1960's.

Moreover, many groups currently following a protracted popular war strategy find it more difficult to rally popular support than was the case for the Chinese or the Algerians, because they have a narrower base. Whereas the Chinese and Algerians transformed resentment of political, social and economic discrimination by foreigners into a widespread surge of nationalism directed at imperial and colonial ruling authorities--the Japanese and the French, respectively--many of today's insurgents represent smaller segments of the population, such as class, ethnic, racial, or religious groups. Similarly, they often face an indigenous government, rather than a foreign colonial power. Under such circumstances, it is far more difficult to galvanize nationalist sentiments, even when an effort is made to depict the powers that be as tools of neo-imperialist, foreign interests.

The successful application of a protracted popular war strategy by contemporary insurgents may also be impeded by unfavorable environmental factors and enhanced government capabilities. In China, Vietnam and, to a lesser extent, Algeria, the insurgents were able to secure bases, consolidate and then expand their organization, and nurture popular support in the relative security accorded by favorable topographical and demographic patterns. In today's world, several insurgent movements that subscribe to a protracted popular war strategy operate in physical and human settings that are less than desirable, to say the least. Another burden which insurgents must confront and neutralize is the enhanced firepower, mobility and intelligence capabilities often available to government forces as an outgrowth of technological developments in transportation, weaponry, detection systems, and information processing.[7]

The Military Focus Strategy: The military focus strategy is different from the protracted popular war strategy in that it accords primacy to military action rather than politics. Though fully aware of the value of popular support, the insurgents make no systematic, sustained effort to acquire it through extensive, politically-focused organizational efforts in the rural areas. Instead, proponents of the military focus believe that popular support either already exists or will emerge as a by-product of military victories. Moreover, widespread support may be unnecessary, if the government's forces are defeated on the battlefield.

Thus, for example, in the American civil war, the South emphasized the military as a means to its goal of secession. Since a political organization was already in place, extending down to the local level, the Confederacy did not have to worry about creating an entire array of political institutions to gain popular support. The Confederates' main focus was on the military dimension of the conflict because, in contrast to insurgents who adopt a protracted popular war strategy, they saw a need neither to mobilize and gradually expand popular support, nor to engage in prolonged guerrilla warfare and/or terrorist operations.[8]

Not all insurgents who adhere to a military focus strategy

engage in conventional military operations. Where the balance of military force favors the opposition, immediate action is often manifested in lesser forms of violence, such as terrorism and/or guerrilla warfare. The most notable example in recent times is the Cuban insurrection, which came to be viewed as an alternative to the protracted popular war strategy.

Che Guevara, a veritable icon in insurgent folklore, opened his book *Guerrilla Warfare* with the following comments: "We consider that the Cuban Revolution contributed three fundamental lessons to the conduct of revolutionary movements in America. They are: (1) Popular forces can win a war against the army. (2) It is not necessary to wait until all the conditions for making revolution exist; the insurrection can create them. (3) In underdeveloped America, the countryside is the basic area for armed fighting."[9]

Guevara's strategy bears some similarities to Mao's thinking. In addition to situating the conflict in the countryside, Guevara stressed the importance of bases in inaccessible terrain, the need for popular support, and the requirement to establish civil organization after key areas have been seized. Moreover, like Mao, he argued that complete victory would only be achieved when the guerrilla army is transformed into a regular army. While it is tempting to interpret this as little more than a reiteration of Mao's strategy, a closer look at the Cuban case reveals noteworthy divergences from the protracted popular war strategy.

Guevara contended that insurgent leaders did not have to wait for the preconditions of insurgency to appear. Rather, they could act to catalyze existing grievances, thus spurring positive action. He contended that thirty to fifty men would suffice to start an armed rebellion in Latin American countries, given such favorable conditions as suitable terrain for operations, hunger for land and widespread abuse of power and injustice. In other words, Guevara suggests that the mere fact of taking up arms could spark a revolution, particularly in situations where grievances are deeply felt. One of the major characteristics of the Cuban revolution, according to Regis Debray, is its rejection of the communist idea of subordinating the guerrilla force to the party, in favor of placing primary emphasis on the army as the nucleus of the party. Putting it another way, he argued that the guerrilla force is a political embryo from which the party can arise. Whereas Mao and Lenin stressed the leading role of the party and the need for substantial political preparation before the military struggle, Debray touted the Cuban success as proof that military priorities must take precedence over politics.[10]

For insurgents who see the Cuban experience as analogous to their own situation--or those operating in environments where the protracted popular war strategy is inappropriate, due to unfavorable physical conditions--the military focus strategy provides a viable alternative approach. It relies on violence--in the form of small to moderately sized guerrilla attacks--buttressed by limited organization and popular support. While a weak government is not a critical strategic assumption, nor the *sine qua non* of success, it is important to the Guevera version of the military focus strategy. Indeed, it is questionable whether Castro could have achieved his aims if the Batista government had not been in a state of profound decay.

As is the case with the conspiratorial and protracted popular war strategies, practitioners and sympathetic analysts see the military focus strategy as widely applicable, especially to Latin America. In fact, it was the belief that the Cuban experience could be replicated in Bolivia which led Che Guevara to a fateful end in that country. His failure and the ensuing recognition that not all governments are as fragile as Batista's, led to a reassessment of strategic approaches by radical intellectuals in Latin America. The soul-searching and the lessons-learned were soon reflected in a new insurgent strategy: urban warfare in which terrorism is prominent.[11]

The Urban Warfare Strategy: Terrorist acts in support of political objectives are hardly a new phenomenon. Although assassinations, kidnappings and the slaughter of innocent people can be traced back to antiquity, our concern at this point is the systematic articulation of a contemporary, urban-centered terrorist strategy. Its emergence as an alternative to the strategies discussed thus far is attributable not only to the relative strength and resilience of incumbent governments, but also to the increased urbanization that has taken place in many parts of the world.

Although their ultimate goals may vary, insurgents engaged in urban violence all pursue the intermediate aim of eroding the government's will to resist. Like the protracted popular war and military focus strategies, eventual mass support is considered important; the manner of achieving it is different, however. The essential strategy of the urban terrorist, according to the late Carlos Marighella, one of its foremost proponents, is to "...turn political crisis into armed conflict by performing violent actions that will force those in power to transform the political situation of the country into a military situation. That will alienate the masses who from then on will revolt against the army and police and thus blame them for the state of things."[12]

To bring about this transformation, urban insurgents engage in various actions, including: armed propaganda, strikes and work interruptions, ambushes, assassinations, kidnapping, temporary occupation of schools, factories and radio stations, sabotage of economic assets, and assaults on fixed targets, such as banks, businesses, military camps, police stations, and prisons. In addition, there is usually a desire to infiltrate police and military units, in order to foster a breakdown from within. The purpose of the cumulative acts of violence is to wreak havoc and insecurity, which will eventually produce a loss of confidence in the government. The emphasis on violence, it should be noted, is a key factor differentiating the urban warfare strategy from the conspiratorial strategy which down-plays violence.

For Latin American theorists like Marighella and Abraham Guillen, the actions in the cities are crucial but not decisive, since the struggle must eventually be transferred to the countryside. As Marighella saw it, the function of urban terrorists was to tie down the government forces in the cities, so as to permit the emergence and survival of rural guerrilla warfare, "...which is destined to play the decisive role in the revolutionary war." Accordingly, the key determinant is how effective urban terrorism is in undermining the government and in gaining popular support, not whether urban warfare alone can be successful. The perceived need to transfer the conflict to the rural areas stems from the belief that widespread popular support will be required to defeat those controlling the state apparatus--i.e., adversaries who are unlikely to remain passive in the face of challenge to the political community or the political system.[13]

Initiating an insurgency by means of urban warfare and eventually transferring it to the countryside is, for the most part, a Latin American notion. In contrast, such urban insurgents as the Provisional Irish Republican Army (IRA) leaders have long believed that violence in the cities and abroad, directed at British officials and military personnel, as well as unarmed civilians, will eventually wear down London's will and lead to a withdrawal from Ulster. Likewise, organizations like Direct Action in France, the Red Brigades in Italy, the Fighting Communist Cells in Belgium, the Japanese Red Army, and Basque Homeland and Liberty (ETA) in Spain have pursued their goals through urban violence, giving no indication of plans to eventually carry out a rural struggle. In effect, this means that there are really two variations on the urban warfare strategy theme: one calling for a move to the countryside and one solely centered on the cities. As of this writing, the urban warfare strategy has proven to be ineffective. Although the *Tupamaros* in Uruguay and the *Monteneros* in Argentina succeeded in provoking a heavily militarized response by the incumbent governments, the brutal repression associated with it crushed the insurgent movements. Thus, it is not altogether surprising that insurgents in places like El Salvador, Guatemala, Peru and elsewhere have returned to either the rural-based protracted popular war or the military focus strategies. Others, like the previously mentioned European groups, continue to carry out urban terrorist actions, but appear to have little prospect of achieving their ultimate goals.

None of this is to suggest a presumption on our part that all insurgents adopt a clear, defined strategy. To the contrary, many insurgents espouse only disjointed strategic concepts; others have no strategy at all. A telltale sign here is the proclivity of insurgent leaders to state lofty goals, while paying scant attention to the ways and means of achieving them--let alone being able to clarify how, precisely, those means are to be integrated and coordinated. As we shall demonstrate, such strategic incoherence is prevalent among both the Israeli and Palestinian rejectionists. This qualification aside, most insurgent movements do adopt one of the four approaches. The question then is: what modifications they make to the original theme and how effectively they implement their own variant.

To gauge the effectiveness of the four strategies (or, for that matter, even *ad hoc* approaches), we must first identify the factors that are crucial for success and then assess how the insurgency is progressing with respect to each. This leads us directly to the criteria we use to evaluate insurgencies.

The Evaluative Criteria

The Environment: The initial criterion for evaluating an internal war, the environment, has two general components: the ***physical aspect***, that is, the nature of the terrain, the transportation-communications system, etc., and the ***human dimension***, that is, demography, social-economic conditions and the extant political culture and system. Both the physical aspect and the human dimension are critical determinants because they yield opportunities for--and place constraints on--insurgent strategies.

The physical environment plays a key role in places where the government is assumed to enjoy political-military supremacy at the beginning of hostilities and the insurgents adopt either a protracted popular war or military focus strategy that emphasizes guerrilla warfare. Difficult terrain--mountains, jungles, swamps, forests, and the like--is usually conducive to successful guerrilla operations, because it hinders movement by government troops and provides inaccessible hideouts for the guerrillas' main bases. The triple-canopy jungles of Indochina--an invaluable asset to Ho Chi Minh's forces in two wars--and the rugged mountains of Afghanistan are examples of terrain suitable to guerrilla operations.[14]

In contrast, open spaces, like deserts, are normally unfavorable for guerrillas. Especially since the advent of air surveillance and attack, such terrain makes insurgents susceptible to detection and destruction. It is important to keep in mind, however, that where effective air power is lacking, vast expanses of desert might be exploited successfully by insurgents who are intimately familiar with the terrain. The activity of the Polisario guerrillas in the Western Sahara from 1977-1984 is a case in point.[15]

Even when the makeup of the terrain is favorable for guerrilla warfare, its effects may be limited by considerations of size. Small areas can be cordoned off, isolated, turned into free fire zones, and penetrated by government forces. By contrast, where guerrillas are able to exploit favorable terrain to expand their operations, the government will find it more difficult to maintain and defend its civilian administration, supervise the populace, and concentrate troops and firepower.

Often, seclusion of base areas is key. Bases are necessary for guerrilla warfare, particularly in the earliest phases when, as Che Guevara points out, the guerrilla fighter's most essential task is to survive. This is best accomplished by staking out inaccessible positions, out of the enemy's reach. Concealed permanent base areas enable insurgents to plan, train, rest, recuperate, marshall equipment, and organize the people--all in relative security.[16] A case in point is the network of bases set up by one of Afghanistan's most notable guerrilla leaders, Ahmed Shah Massoud, in the mountains overlooking the Panjshir Valley. On the other hand, the absence of permanent bases inside the country means the insurgent units cannot generate a steadily increasing level of guerrilla warfare. The experience of the Polisario guerrillas in the Western Sahara--once the government got its act together in the late 1980's--is instructive here.

The specific issue of bases underscores the more general connection between insurgent success and topography. However, this does not imply that favorable topography is necessary in all insurgencies,--as demonstrated by such exceptions as the Jewish and Cypriot revolts against the British, and Lenin's seizure of power in Russia. In these cases topography played little, if any, role. The insurgents succeeded because they had popular support and the government was weak and wavering. However, when governments evince a strong commitment and are able to prevent a deterioration of morale in the military and police forces--as is often the case--topographical features and base areas are vital for insurgents who emphasize rural guerrilla warfare.

As far as urban areas are concerned, their role thus far has been non-decisive in situations where governments show a reasonable commitment to the struggle. Although urban centers yield tempting targets and provide concealment for terrorists, groups which have relied almost exclusively on terrorism, such as Baader Meinhof in Germany and the Red Brigades in Italy, have not come close to achieving their long term aims. Indeed, in most cases, they have been dealt severe losses. One reason for this is that police and military forces are usually concentrated in or near cities. Thus, unless the insurgents command the loyalty of most of the urban population and have the sympathy of the security forces--a rare set of conditions--they are easily contained and dispersed, if not defeated.

Another aspect of the physical environment that can have an important bearing on the fortunes of an insurgency--especially in large countries experiencing rural guerrilla warfare--is the transportation-communications system. Under such circumstances, the responsibility of government forces to provide security for many areas--i.e., cities, towns, military installations, and so forth-- puts great strain on manpower and resources. To compensate for shortcomings generated by the need to provide sufficient defense throughout the country, there is usually an emphasis on mobile-reaction units. Naturally, if the transportation and communications systems are highly developed, the missions of mobile-reaction teams can be carried out more easily and expeditiously. Conversely, poor roads, rail networks, or river transport systems and inadequate communications render mobility difficult and, therefore, favor the insurgents.[17]

Although students of internal political violence have devoted substantial attention to the physical attributes of the environment, the human dimension is equally important. Of primary interest here are demography, social structure, economics, and the political culture and system. Demography, for instance, can have a major impact on the course of events. Where the population is small and concentrated, it is easier for the government to control the people and sever their links with the insurgents.

Urbanization seems less favorable to insurgent movements than a primarily rural structure, although some contemporary insurgent strategists believe otherwise. As suggested earlier, if a society is highly modernized, the government can control and monitor the people more easily, thus minimizing the role and effects of rural guerrilla bases. When the authorities demonstrate both the resolve and competence to combat political violence, compelling the insurgents to opt for protracted warfare, an urban environment, while conducive to terrorist activities, hardly suffices. A rural, underdeveloped society holds greater promise.

Looking beyond the basic demographic attributes of a population, one needs to assess the impact of its social structure--both vertically, in terms of race, ethnicity and religion and horizontally, by class. Societal divisions along racial, ethnic and religious lines are frequently among the root causes of an internal war. They can be either helpful or detrimental with respect to the progression of an insurrection. Where one segment of society enjoys disproportionate political and economic power and benefits, insurgents often find an opportunity to gain support from the disadvantaged groups. If the relatively deprived group constitutes a majority, the potential for support is naturally greater. Colonial governments, as the French found out in Algeria and Vietnam, are especially vulnerable. The same is true of minority-based governments--like Ian Smith's regime in Rhodesia (now Zimbabwe)--that exclude the majority from political participation and practice economic discrimination. Even if disadvantaged groups do not constitute a majority, they can still provide the foundation for a serious insurrection if they are sizeable: witness the Ovimbundu people in Angola, the Kurds in Iraq and Iran, and the Eritreans in Ethiopia.

Yet, not all situations where minorities experience political and economic deprivation are advantageous to insurgent movements. In circumstances where the disenfranchised constitute small minorities, governments may galvanize support against them by emphasizing ancient antagonisms and/or by highlighting the threat to the majority's privileges. When this transpires, insurgents--such as those in north and northeast Thailand, or the Moros in the southern Philippines--find it very difficult, if not impossible, to attract wide popular support. Their identification with minority groups undercuts their appeal to the majority. Reliance on minorities is especially precarious for insurgents in conditions permitting the isolation of such groups in particular geographic areas.

Societal divisions and rivalries might have a deleterious impact on an insurgent movement, on the government, or on both. Where more than one disadvantaged group is incorporated into insurgent ranks, the size and capability of the movement could increase. Such expansion, however, often creates problems with respect to cohesion. In Afghanistan, for instance, all ethnic and religious groups were engaged in the struggle against the Soviets and the Moscow-sponsored Afghan government. At the same time, however, the ancient animosities among the groups, most notably Hazara, Tajik, Uzbek, and Baluchi resentment of the Pushtuns, was a source of disunity, fragmenting political-military strategies and fuelling internecine strife. Such rivalries also present the government with opportunities to infiltrate insurgent ranks and play one group off against another. But, as the Afghan case also shows, the government can suffer the same malady--witness the endemic strife inside the People's Democratic Party of Afghanistan, caused, in no small way, by the different ethnic composition of its Khalq and Parchamite wings. (The former is Pushtun-based; the latter is composed largely of Tajiks and other minorities).

As our brief discussion of societal factors should make clear, it would be a mistake to simply focus on the more familiar economic and political dimensions of the human environment. Although the relationships between societal divisions and the fortunes of insurgent movements are varied and complex, they cannot be passed over lightly. For, often, they hold the key to explaining insurgent success or failure. In many cases, moreover, their impact is an outgrowth of the interplay among societal and economic factors.

As even a cursory look at insurrections makes clear, in most cases economic factors play a key part in the outbreak of political violence. While both stagnation or sudden downturns in the economy--particularly when following a period of growth--have been associated with insurgencies, violence occurs also during periods of prosperity. Thus, one needs to relate economic indicators to popular expectations and ascertain whether or not social groups and/or classes have come to see themselves as victims of institutionalized discrimination in respect to such socio-economic benefits as income, jobs, education, housing, health services, etc. Many conflicts which, on the surface, seem to be based soley on communal rivalries, upon closer scrutiny turn out to have significant economic dimensions. No serious commentator, for example, would deny that the Provisional IRA's ability to take advantage of Catholic-Protestant differences in Northern Ireland is related to actual and perceived economic discrimination against the Catholics.

Analysts should also examine the political culture and system to ascertain if political grievances are a key issue. Since this is a broad subject which cannot be adequately treated in this brief summary, we shall limit ourselves to the issue of political participation as an example of the difficulties involved. The key questions here are as follows:

- Is there a strong tradition of inter-personal and inter-group trust that encourages and sustains cooperative behavior and participation?

- Is there an increased demand for participation in the policy process?
- Which groups wish to participate and how do they wish to participate?
- To what extent are the political institutions accommodating these and other demands?

Not surprisingly, where socio-economic grievances merge with demands for political participation, the challenge to the government is greater. Since the potential responsiveness of a government is related to the calculations of political elites, it is important to assess their ideologies and the internal structure of power which can affect their range of choices.

To sum up, a careful assessment of the physical and human dimensions of the environment is a good starting point for the assessment of movements engaged in internal political violence. Analysis of topography and the transportation-communications system can be quite revealing as to the potential or actual effectiveness of the forms of violence used by insurgents, particularly guerrilla warfare. A careful look at demography, social groups, economic conditions, political culture, and the political system will shed light on the causes underlying and sustaining insurgencies. Of course, no matter how favorable the physical milieu might be--and no matter how bad the social, economic and political conditions--a serious insurgent threat will not emerge in the absence of determined leaders who have the requisite skills to organize at least some popular support. What that consists of and how it is acquired is the subject to which we now turn.

Popular Support: For many insurgent leaders, popular support is an overriding strategic consideration. In the words of Mao: "the richest source of power to wage war lies in the masses of the people."[18] The significance attributed to civilian support can be understood by viewing it as a means to offset advantages the government possesses by virtue of its control of the administrative apparatus of the state, most specifically, the army and police. Since insurgents know they would risk destruction by confronting the government forces in direct conventional engagements, they opt instead to erode their adversary's strength and will through the use of terrorism or guerrilla warfare. Thereby, they seek not only to increase the human and material cost to the government, but also to demonstrate its failure to maintain effective control and protect the citizenry. Eventually, according to insurgent logic, the government will grow weary of the struggle and try to cut its losses by either capitulating, or negotiating a settlement favorable to the insurgents.

Popular support is divided into two categories: passive and active. Passive support includes individuals who merely sympathize with the aims and activities of the insurgents, while active support encompasses those who are willing to assume personal risks on behalf of the insurgents. In the active support category are individuals who provide insurgents with supplies, information, shelter, concealment, liaison agents, and who, in some cases, carry out acts of disobedience or protest--all of which might entail severe punishment by the government. Although most discussions of popular support tend to emphasize active support, passive supporters are important in the sense that, at a minimum, they are not apt to betray or otherwise deliberately impede the insurgents.

In focusing on the need for active and passive support from the masses, insurgents do not neglect the vital role of the intelligentsia, which, in most Third World countries, roughly equates to the professional middle class. The intelligentsia is the principal source for recruitment of both high- and mid-level leadership positions, e.g., commanders of guerrilla units and terrorist networks, as well as political cadres. Indeed, some analysts believe that the intellectuals' desertion of and alienation from the government has been repeatedly a harbinger of revolution.[19] If so, this is a key point to bear in mind with respect to the Israeli rejectionists, who seem to be making significant inroads among the national elites.

It has been argued that community support and security are "safeguarded best when the native population identifies itself spontaneously with the fortunes of the guerrilla movement."[20] However. since spontaneity is usually lacking, the insurgent movement must actively proselytize the people. Generally, insurgents will employ one or several of the following methods to gain the desired support and recruits: charismatic attraction, esoteric appeals, exoteric appeals, terrorism, provocation of government repression, demonstrations of potency, and coercion.

In certain cases, assertive individuals emerge as the clearly identifiable leaders of insurgent movements. When such persons are either perceived to have supernatural qualities and/or manifest oratorical skills and a dynamic, forceful personality, they might be able to motivate others to join the cause by virtue of their example and persuasiveness. This is especially true in communities where a tradition of heroic leadership is highly valued, as is the case in both Israeli and Arab cultures. While the process of "great men" inspiring the people to follow their lead might, at times, unfold naturally or even subliminally, in many instances the insurgent movement deliberately exaggerates the prowess and attributes of its leader to attract support. Whatever the case, the individual leader becomes the principal reason drawing people to back the movement. This phenomenon, which we refer to as **charismatic attraction,** has been exemplified by Mao, Fidel Castro and, more recently, Jonas Savimbi--to name but a few.[21] Although, in the absence of reliable survey data, it is impossible to ascertain how many people joined these causes because of charismatic attraction, we do know from many direct and indirect accounts that the force of their personality was important. Therefore, in investigating insurgencies, both the analyst and the decision maker must be alert to the possible impact of charismatic attraction.

Another way to obtain popular support--frequently, though not invariably, associated with charismatic leadership--is to play up **esoteric appeals**. Directed primarily at the intellectual strata (broadly defined), esoteric messages seek to clarify the situation by placing it in an ideological or theoretical context--be it secular or religious--that orders and interprets political complexities. In the words of Gabriel Almond: "An ideology imputes a particular structure to political action. It defines who or what the main initiators of action are, whether they be individuals, status groups, classes, nations, magical forces, or deities. It attributes specific roles to these actors, describes their relationships with one another, and defines the arena in which actions occur."[22]

Many revolutionaries, for example, have found that Lenin's thesis on imperialism as the last stage of capitalism holds a powerful intellectual attraction in Third World countries, because it provides a coherent, logical, all-encompassing explanation of the poverty, illiteracy and oppression that characterize the political and social milieu.[23] Furthermore, by pointing a finger at indigenous feudal or capitalist classes and their links to external imperialist elements, the theory provides an identifiable target for the frustrations of the intellectuals, may of whom are either unemployed or underemployed. Although Almond has suggested that ideology is rarely crucial at the point of admission to political movements, one must still account for those few who do respond to ideological incantations. This is especially important in circumstances where members of the educated elite choose to join an insurgent group--in preference to its rivals--because it is more ideologically appealing and, thus, intellectually compelling.

Even though esoteric appeals are primarily directed at the intellectuals, they are also key to mass support. Specifically, such appeals respond to the often-felt need for an object on which to focus popular discontent, so as to galvanize the masses for action. One of the key functions of secular or religious ideology--the identification of friend and foe--fulfills this requirement. Indeed, identifying the source of frustration and grievances is important because "...discontented people act aggressively only when they become aware of the supposed source of frustration, or something or someone with whom they associate frustration."[24] This point, as we shall see, is dramatically illustrated by the Palestinian and Israeli religious extremists' demonization of each other's communities.

Exoteric appeals focus on concrete grievances of both the intelligentsia and the masses. These involve such things as unemployment, underemployment, corruption, and repression by local officials, as well as the need for food, land reform, social services, schools, and physical security. If they are successful in achieving their ultimate goal, the insurgents promise that such needs will be met.[25]

In situations where foreign powers impose their authority directly (imperialism), exert influence through international economic networks (neo-imperialism), or intervene in support of the local authorities, the insurgents will frequently merge nationalist themes with esoteric and exoteric appeals. Relying on formulations such as Lenin's theory of imperialism, they will identify the external enemy as the source of national deprivations. For many intellectuals this provides both a cogent explanation of and a target for their frustrations. For the masses, the message is presented in such a way as to provide a simplified explanation of grievances and an object on which to focus animosity.

Where esoteric and exoteric appeals prove insufficient, the insurgents might turn to **terrorism**. In this context, the purpose of terrorist acts is to obtain popular support by demonstrating the government's weaknesses *vis-a-vis* the insurgents' strength. Success or failure depend, in large measure, on two factors: the target of terror and the duration of terrorist campaigns.

With respect to the target, if terror is aimed at individuals or groups disliked by the people, it can facilitate the identification of the insurgents with oppressed and exploited elements. By manipulating resentment, playing up grievances, and employing selective terror against hated individuals and groups, the insurgents may well be able to increase popular support. On the other hand, if, at the outset, potential support is low, terror can only generate hostility toward the insurgents. In any case, as the *Sendero Luminoso* experience in Peru shows, terrorism that becomes indiscriminate or unduly prolonged can easily backfire and, thereby, alienate potential domestic and international supporters.[26] Parenthetically, this is something to bear in mind as we enter the age of more readily accessible weapons of mass destruction, since their lethality would appear to diminish their utility as a means of gaining popular support. Unhappily, however, this in no way guarantees they will not be used.

Another tool used by insurgents to win popular support is "catalyzing and intensifying counter-terror, which further alienates the enemy from the local population." In other words, the insurgents seek to **provoke arbitrary and indiscriminate government reprisals** against the population which, in turn, will increase resentment and win the insurrectionary forces more adherents and support.[27] The success of such a stratagem--widely employed by, among others, Palestinian rejectionists--will be determined largely by the nature of the government response. A widespread violent reaction by the government, similar to that of the Pakistani Army in Bangladesh in 1971, would appear to cause more resentment and hatred than, say, such nonviolent actions as curfews and resettlement. While ruthless methods by the government might restore law and order in the short run, the long-term effect may be to foster insurgency.

The sixth technique often employed to establish popular support, **demonstration of potency**, has two dimensions: (1) meeting the needs of the people through social services and a governing apparatus; and (2) gaining the military initiative. Insurgent political operators normally seek to meet some of the people's basic needs and cooperate with them in such affairs as harvesting crops, building schools, and so forth. Quite often, the extension of such aid will be the first step in involving the populace with the insurgent movement, either actively or passively. This would seem to be especially true in those situations where the regime has been delinquent in responding to popular grievances, a reality that has not been lost on Islamic militants. Likewise, as we shall see, the Israeli rejectionists have gathered significant support among secular settlers, who rely on them to provide a wide array of goods and services.

Potency can also be demonstrated through military success, thus creating the impression that the insurgency has gained the initiative and is moving forward toward victory. A number of writers have stressed the importance of action to the guerrillas because, in addition to winning adherents for the movement, it boosts and sustains morale within insurgent organizations. "Units that are active and successful in the accomplishment of assigned missions build up a high *esprit de corps* and attract followers; success is contagious." Putting it another way, "no guerrilla movement in the field can afford to remain inactive for long; by so doing, it loses its morale and sense of purpose."[28] The same can, of course, be said of terrorist groups. Despite their best efforts, insurgents may still find major segments of the population unresponsive. When this happens, there is a great temptation to turn to the final technique for gaining support, **coercion**. The plain fact is that coercive measures are rarely effective. Usually, they engender little more than resentment and weak commitment.

To summarize, popular support is often crucial for the success of an internal war. To attain it, the insurgent movement may rely on charismatic attraction, esoteric and exoteric appeals, terrorism, provocation of government repression, demonstrations of potency, coercion--or some combination thereof. The orchestration of such a campaign is quite complex, with success dependent on the insurgents' organizational dexterity.

Organization: Organization is a major factor enabling insurgents to compensate for the material superiority of their opponents. Indeed, when analysts claim that insurgency is more a political phenomenon than a military one, they usually have in mind the effort devoted to organization. Looking at organization, three structural dimensions--scope, complexity and cohesion--and two functions--provision of instrumental services and establishment of channels for expressing protest--are of primary interest.[29] Given the particular salience of cohesion in so many cases, it will be treated in a separate section below.

Scope refers to the number of people who either play key roles in the movement--as terrorists, guerrillas, or political cadres--or provide active support. How many will be controlled by the insurgent movement is partially a function of complexity and cohesion. If an insurgent organization perceives a need to augment its membership, it will normally increase its level of differentiation or complexity and, through the efforts of its political cadres, penetrate hamlets, villages and cities especially in contested areas (i.e., areas in which neither the government nor insurgents have firm control). Insurgents often create what Bernard Fall called "parallel hierarchies" to compete with government institutions. The parallel hierarchy can take two forms: penetration of the existing official administrative structures by subversive agents, or creation of autonomous insurgent structures, designed to take over full administrative responsibility when military-political conditions are deemed appropriate. The importance of this type organization is well-known to students of the two Vietnam conflicts.

To further broaden its support base, the insurgent organization may go beyond the government structures it seeks to imitate and set up functional auxiliaries, such as youth groups, peasant organizations, workers' groups, and women's organizations. It could also create tactical alliances with other independent groups that oppose the government. When this is done, the new entity is frequently referred to as a "front." The effectiveness of winning adherents by increasing the differentiation of the organization is exemplified by the Huk movement in the Philippines, where many joined front organizations, often without even knowing--or caring about--the party's aims.[30]

In addition to the differentiation of political structures, insurgents--especially those engaged in a protracted armed struggle --may diversify their military organization by creating logistics units, terrorist networks and guerrilla forces, with the last-mentioned divided between full-time and part-time fighters. The full-time guerrillas, operating from secure bases, attack government military units and installations on a continuous basis and constitute a nucleus for a regular force in the event the movement transitions to conventional warfare. The part-time or local guerrillas, on the other hand, stay in their communities and provide such invaluable services as collecting intelligence, storing supplies and protecting the political organizers. In addition, the local guerrillas can attach themselves to main force units in support of local attacks--either as full-fledged combatants or as scouts and guides.

The effective functioning of both parallel hierarchies and military units may itself convert people to the cause, by demonstrating the insurgent's ability to control an area in defiance of the government. Such a development--linking demonstration of potency with organization--is particularly important in situations where the government is reasonably strong, as is the case in Israel.

Although most insurgents strive to establish a complex organizational apparatus in order to increase and maximize the use of human and material resources, there are some who place little emphasis on this. Yet others aspire to popular support, but seem to believe that a secretive cellular structure can somehow suffice. We shall see all three variations on this theme in our coverage of Israeli and Palestinian rejectionists.

Cohesion: The extent to which insurgents are united around the cause can have a profound effect on the development and outcome of their quest. As Mao pointed out in *The Strategy of Partisan Warfare*, "without centralized strategic command, the partisans can inflict little damage on their adversaries, as without this, they can break down into roaming, armed bands, and then find no more support by the population."[31]

Although unity is usually important for insurgent movements, its absence has not always resulted in failure. Other factors might serve to offset the problems diversity so often creates. Disunity need not preclude eventual success by insurgents where the governing authorities: lose the will to persevere, as the French did in Algeria; see their advantage being undercut by widespread popular support for the insurgents, as happened in Afghanistan in early 1980's; or face severe, long-term geographic and demographic asymmetries in favor of the guerrillas, as was the case in Rhodesia. But, if offsetting conditions such as these do not exist and if the government is strong, insurgents court disaster by fighting among themselves and failing to coordinate their efforts, a point that, as we shall later see, the Palestinian rejectionists have learned the hard way. This being the case, it is important to take a closer and more specific look at the effects of discord.

First of all, disunity can lead to an inability to agree on grand strategy and cause a lack of coordination between political and military policies. Typically, this is reflected in either inadvertent or deliberate military actions which undercut political undertakings. A case in point would be an attack by one insurgent faction or group that occurs while negotiations are taking place between the government and the top leadership of the insurgent movement.

Second, disunity aggravates deficiencies in combat support. As the Afghan guerrillas discovered, where insurgent groups insist on autonomy and distrust one another, intelligence collection, analysis and dissemination are fragmented and unsatisfactory. Worse, the flow of logistical supplies is generally unbalanced, training is inadequate, unstandardized, or both, and systematic communications are difficult to establish and sustain.

Inability to plan, orchestrate and integrate multiple military operations is a third disadvantage disunity may cause. When this happens, the potential for sizeable campaigns, involving attacks in many areas, is seriously eroded, if not foreclosed altogether. Again, the experience of Afghan guerrillas illustrates the point. Disunity also tends to cause unnecessary loss of personnel and equipment--through both poor combat performance and fratricide. The consequences of internecine violence which has plagued Kurdish groups in northern Iraq illustrate the point.

Disunity also undermines external support. The reluctance of outside states to commit themselves to fragmented insurgents can be seen in the Afghanistan case, where the Islamic Conference Organization made it quite clear that greater largesse depended on the unification of the various groups.

Perhaps even worse, lack of cohesion increases the potential for outside interference. When insurgent leaders are engaged in internal conflicts, they open the doors to undesirable involvement on the part of both their adversaries and the states which support their cause. Slack discipline and competition for recruits among insurgent factions often presents governments with opportunities to infiltrate the groups and sow the seeds of greater dissension. Last, disunity leads some insurgents to provide information about their rivals to the government, in the hope that the authorities will apprehend or attack them. Even the venerable Ho Chi Minh was reputed to have done this in the early, formative stages of his resistance to the French. Similarly, Israel's struggle for independence was marred by betrayals and fratricide, to the benefit of the British Mandatory Authorities.

As the foregoing discussion makes clear, discord can be a source of difficulties for an insurgent movement. Accordingly, where disunity is apparent, a careful analysis of its specific effects is imperative. Often, it is key to understanding the course and outcome of internal political violence. Moreover, since most insurgent leaders recognize the profound consequences of disunity, they try to ameliorate--if not prevent--its impact through organizational, coercive and other political measures. However, such efforts are usually futile, particularly if the causes of disunity are too deeply ingrained or, conversely, ignored or misunderstood.

Our studies of insurgent movements suggest seven causes of disunity: social, political-cultural, personal, teleological, theoretical, strategic, and tactical. Social and cultural causes of disunity are rooted in the environment. The former involves group cleavages based on race, ethnicity, religion, and, sometimes, regionalism. Where these exist, where they are marked by acrimony and, particularly where they are cumulative, it is very hard to create and sustain broad-based insurgent movements. The political culture, as noted previously, may also be a source of fissiparous tendencies in an insurgent movement. This is especially true of countries where there is low inter-personal and inter-group trust and aversion to centralized authority.

Personal ambitions--manifested in struggles among individual leaders vying for control--often undermine cohesion, particularly when resources are fragmented and no single group is strong enough to eliminate its rivals. As time goes by, competing leaders become even more convinced that they, rather than their rivals, should become first among equals, if not sole authority figures. The bitterness and hatred which characterize such infighting are recognizable to all analysts of politics. As the Palestinians and Israelis could attest, it is recognizable to practitioners as well.

Disunity may also be caused by teleological, theoretical, and/or strategic differences. Although often intertwined, the three are distinct. Teleological differences--that is, discord over the ultimate political goal the insurgents ought to be pursuing--can be profoundly unsettling, as the uneasy mixture of reactionary-traditionalists, moderate-traditionalists and egalitarians in the Afghan resistance has shown. In later chapters, we will have occasion to revisit this phenomenon and demonstrate its impact in both the Israeli and Palestinian cases.

Where goal dissensus exists, it is frequently an outgrowth of theoretical disagreements involving ideology or theology. The problem is, of course, that different ideological and theological assumptions about man and society can yield quite different prescriptions as to the required actions, potential friends and enemies, and desired outcomes. For example, the Marxist ideology of the Popular Front for the Liberation of Palestine (PFLP) led it to view the Jordanian regime as a reactionary class enemy that should be overthrown, whereas the traditional outlook espoused by *Fatah* permitted cooperation with Amman. One grave consequence of this ideological divergence was the Jordanian civil war of 1970, provoked by PFLP subversive acts, but ultimately engulfing the entire Palestinian Liberation Organization (PLO).

Insurgent disunity may also be caused by conflict over which strategies to adopt in the conflict. For purposes of illustration, the contrast between the protracted popular war and military focus strategies is useful. The former emphasizes careful political preparation and the consolidation of a strong party prior to initiating hostilities, whereas the latter calls for the immediate initiation of violence, with political consolidation left for later. Where strategies diverge as much as these, their simultaneous adoption by different groups results in quite different and, often, contradictory operations. A group committed to clandestine organizational activity can find its efforts undercut by the premature violence initiated by groups following the military focus strategy. Worse, such violence might alert the government and cause it to crack down on those insurgents who are keeping a low profile and engaging in political undertakings.

Discord over strategy may also center around more specific

issues, such as the forms of violence deemed advisable at various points in time. Decisions about whether--and, if so, when, where, and against whom--acts of terrorism should be carried out have often been a cause of internal strife.

The sources of disunity are many. While each may be quite damaging in and of itself, their combined effect is usually devastating. Worse, although insurgents generally acknowledge the problem and the need to address it, effective remedies are hard to come by.

Cohesion rests on a combination of effective socialization, organizational schemes and sanctions. Socialization involves inculcation of loyalty and a common sense of purpose through propaganda and political education programs. Where social and political-cultural factors pose a potential threat to cohesion, insurgents will normally emphasize one or more of the following: the need to close ranks against the common enemy; an ideology or theology which transcends group differences and distrust; and the equitable, mutual benefits to be derived from success.

Organizational approaches are also important in the establishment of unity. In one scheme, the politicians are in charge. This was frequently the case in communist movements, with two variants. One may be a chain of command that derives from the Politburo, through the Central Executive Committee, which exercises control over State, District and Branch committees. These, in turn, will control the military units within their jurisdiction. The other possibility is separate chains of command for the military and the civilian organizations. The latter was the case in the Greek civil war, where the stationary civil administration--a parallel hierarchy--ran the liberated base areas, while the guerrilla bands, under separate command, moved from sector to sector.

In the second scheme, the political and military arms exist independently of one another. Such was the situation in the World War II Italian Resistance, wherein military operations were in the hands of the Corps of Volunteers for Liberation, while civil resistance and local administration were handled by the Central

Committee of Liberation. In more recent times, the relationship between the civilian Democratic Revolutionary Front (FDR) and the military Farabundo Marti National Liberation Front (FMLN) in El Salvador serves as an example of this format.

The third organizational approach allows the military element to take charge.[32] An example--to which we'll return later--would be the Jewish *Irgun* which operated in Palestine during the British Mandate. Another approximation of this scheme is the one described by Regis Debray.[33]

When socialization and organizational formats fail to curb factionalism, obedience may be imposed by insurgent security forces, assuming, of course, that they are loyal and effective. The recourse to coercion may succeed if recalcitrant individuals or groups are relatively small and impotent. However, if dissident groups are sizeable and have enough resources to threaten prolonged and costly fighting, the use of coercion to ensure unity will usually be avoided.

The reluctance to use force against rival factions can dissipate quickly once a particular group perceives that it has gained preponderant strength. For instance, in Sri Lanka, the Tamil Tigers emerged as the most important insurgent group by either eliminating or silencing their opponents through brutal force and intimidation.

Disunity may not be amenable to forceful resolution. The fact of the matter is that once divergent groups gain autonomy and strength, they are difficult to discipline. In order to mitigate the effects of rivalries and to foster a modicum of cooperation, insurgent leaders may create a unified command for a particular operation, agree on a division of labor among various groups, or establish a permanent unified command. Of the three options, the idea of a unified command is most conducive to giving the insurgents a sense of strategic direction, thus ameliorating at least some of factors which divide the movement in the first place. As we shall see, both the Israelis and Palestinians have opted for this approach. Yet, success hinges on the rival organizations' ability to subordinate their parochial interests to the overall cause, as defined by the unified command. If the unified command's decisions are to be considered authoritative and legitimate, the rival groups must reach consensus on the mechanics of the decision-making process and on the methods for disciplining dissenters. This, of course, resurfaces the question of who will wield dominant power and who will invoke sanctions. Since groups are generally unwilling to make major concessions on these vital matters, the effectiveness of unified commands tends to be marginal and their durability limited.

To sum up, no analysis of internal political violence would be complete, or meaningful, without an assessment of the scope, complexity and cohesion of the principal groups involved. A careful look at the structures and functions of insurgent organizations can reveal a good deal about the progress of an insurrection, as well as the type and magnitude of the threat confronting the government. Several questions are key in this regard. What organizational requirements are associated with the strategy and forms of violence adopted by the insurgents, and are those requirements being met? In particular, if a sophisticated parallel hierarchy is deemed necessary, has it emerged? Where is it located? How extensive it is? Does it provide effective command, control and coordination? Is the insurgent movement unified? If not, what are the causes and effects of disunity? As one proceeds to answer such questions, relationships between organization and the other evaluative criteria should be readily apparent, particularly those involving the acquisition of popular and external support.

External Support: There are four types of external support: moral, political, material, and sanctuary. Moral support is least costly and risky for a donor, for all it involves is public acknowledgment that the insurgent movement is just and admirable. Political support advances a step further, since the donor nation actively promotes the insurgent's strategic goal in international fora. From the insurgents' perspective, political support is clearly more desirable: Its payoffs are more immediate and concrete, with the added bonus of encouraging additional uncommitted nations to render support.

In contrast, material assistance is more tangible and risky for an outside power. Consisting of money, weapons, ammunition, medical supplies, food, and training--and, perhaps, even the provision of military advisors, fire support, or combat units--such assistance becomes particularly important as the insurgents increase the scale and intensity of violence, thus necessitating greater logistical inputs.[34] Otherwise, the insurgents would have to make do by relying on the populace and such uncertain resources as arms merchants, or materials seized from the government.

When insurgents conclude that external logistical inputs are essential, the role of sympathetic major powers can be very important. Accordingly, insurgent leaders often go to great lengths to persuade potential patrons to provide material assistance. Yet, success in this endeavor is not the end of the story, for in some cases the provision of aid may be dependent on third parties, who control overland or air transportation routes. In light of this, the attitude of states contiguous to the contested area is vital. A positive response on their part will facilitate the flow of materials; a negative reaction may neutralize the entire effort--as demonstrated by the land-locked Bosnian Muslims' dependence on Croatian good-will and cooperation, as well as by Syria's role in the conflict between Israel and the Palestinians.

Besides facilitating the supply flow or actually making materials available to the insurgents, external states may be important as sanctuaries in which guerrillas can be trained, arms stockpiled, operations planned, leadership secured, and perhaps a provisional government established. While both sanctuaries and material aid are usually more critical in the terminal stages of an insurgency, there are circumstances which can make them indispensable early in the struggle. Such may be the case where the insurgents lack popular support and are unable to establish a secure base in the target country. With such an inauspicious start, the insurgents are literally forced to rely on adjacent countries, for, at a minimum, security and freedom of movement must be guaranteed if the insurgents are ever to establish bases, organize the people and obtain popular support. The Polisario base at Tindouf in Algeria is a striking example here.

While the types of external support discussed thus far are very often important to the fortunes of insurgent movements, there have been cases where only low-level outside help proved sufficient. In these instances one usually finds the insurgents benefiting from a favorable position *vis-a-vis* other major factors, e.g., a weak regime, or substantial popular support. A case in point would be the Castro revolution, during which the insurgents did not have a contiguous friendly country to function as a sanctuary or logistics area, although they did receive some arms via flights from Mexico, Venezuela and the United States. Since the government was inept, corrupt and indecisive, with a demoralized army, this level of aid was sufficient to topple the Batista regime and to obviate the need for a protracted guerrilla war, along the lines of the Chinese and Vietnamese experiences.

Government Response: Contrary to romantic myths, strong governments can eliminate or marginalize insurgent threats. Thus, it is not surprising that many experts have argued that the government's response to an insurgent challenge is the major variable determining the outcome of an insurrection: "As soon as the challenge is in the open, the success of the operation depends not primarily on the development of insurgent strength, but more importantly on the degree of vigor, determination and skill with which the incumbent regime acts to defend itself, both politically and militarily."[35]

Carrying this argument a step further, one might suggest that the nature of the government and its responses to incipient insurgent actions largely determine whether a given insurgency can succeed by confining itself to low-level activity, or will it have to take on the dimensions of a protracted internal war. Thus, the counterinsurgency aspects merit closer examination, particularly given our focus on--and enduring U.S. interests in--the ability of both Israel and the Palestinian National Authority to counter threats to peace, stability and democracy.

Governments facing an insurrection may confront one or more of the political challenges, or forms of violence, discussed earlier, namely, propaganda-organizational activity, terrorism, guerrilla warfare, and conventional warfare. Since each type of threat involves different techniques and poses a unique problem for the government, effective and appropriate countermeasures are predicated on its will and ability to differentiate among them. This is so because each type of threat compels the government to emphasize a particular facet of counterinsurgency. To cope successfully with the organizational challenge, the government will have to stress civic action, administration and low-level police activity. Whereas a terrorist threat necessitates intensified police work, guerrilla warfare calls for a low-level military response, and conventional warfare requires full-scale conventional military operations. An undifferentiated, inconsistent approach is fraught with peril.

The design and execution of a coherent counterinsurgency program is further complicated by the fact that, in practice, insurgent threats are not only overlapping and cumulative but, often, variable. Consequently, an effective government response is associated not with a single-purpose strategy applied indiscriminately in all sectors but, rather, with the adoption of a flexible policy that coordinates a variety of countermeasures, reflecting the diverse nature of the threats. For example, it would be a mistake for a government facing a substantial conventional threat in one sector and low-level guerrilla activity in another to extend its search and destroy operations to the guerrilla area. Such a move would constitute a costly and, perhaps, counterproductive overreaction. For, as history has repeatedly shown, guerrillas can easily blend back into the population and, thus, raise the possibility of regular military units striking out against the people, many of whom may be quite innocent. Past experience suggests that under such circumstances it is more appropriate to conduct search and destroy operations in one area and patrols in the other.

The execution of a sophisticated counterinsurgency program obviously requires coordination of political, administrative, military, police, and intelligence efforts. Such careful orchestration is essential, if the various counterinsurgency agencies are to avoid working at cross purposes. The problem here, however, is that optimal organizational conditions--i.e., an effective administration, a tradition of civilian primacy and an adequate number of good leaders--are often missing. In fact, their very absence may be one of the reasons for internal political violence.

A critical ingredient for an effective government organizational effort is the provision of a common purpose and policy guidelines to its officials. This, in turn, places a premium on the articulation and communication of an overall strategy for the future. Since the national program is also instrumental in gaining the support of the population, an honest attempt to ascertain the people's aspirations--which vary from one insurrection to another, or from one region to another within the same country--becomes important. Land reform, for instance, may provide the answer to a basic grievance in some circumstances, but be quite irrelevant in others. As a general matter, however, the historical record demonstrates that benevolent treatment of the population and reforms designed to meet the people's basic needs can go a long way toward undermining support for insurgents.

A classic case of the government regaining popular support would be the actions of the Philippines' regime against the Huks. In that instance, Ramon Magsaysay's election to the presidency led to a number of social and military reforms. These, in turn, mobilized popular support for central authorities, reinforcing their military effort against the insurgents and, ultimately, bringing victory.

Devising a program to satisfy the grievances of the population is, of course, no easy undertaking, especially for a poor, developing nation. Therefore, it is frequently necessary for the government to seek economic assistance from external sources to provide for basic needs. Demands for redistribution of existing economic or political power, on the other hand, are largely internal matters that must be accommodated by the government from within, often at the risk of political--or even military--resistance from privileged classes or groups.

The most difficult demand for a government to meet is abdication in favor of insurgent rule. Nevertheless, since popular support for an insurgent organization with such a totalistic objective is often predicated on socio-economic needs, the government can seek to undercut such support by attenuating the masses' concrete grievances. In other words, the material demands of the people are distinguished from the political power aims of the insurgent leadership. While the government cannot accommodate the latter, it might well be able to deal with the former and, by so doing, deprive the insurgent movement of its main source of strength and resources--the people. This is exactly what transpired in Oman under Sultan Qabus in the early 1970's.

Clearly, it is more difficult to design an effective counterinsurgency program in colonial situations, where not only the insurgent leadership, but also the people, are motivated by the nationalist aim of independence. Faced with such circumstances, some regimes have sought to contain the situation by improving the standard of living, in the hope that the people would support the existing political order in return for short-term benefits. Where the population is divided into rival ethnic or religious groups, the government may also seek to sustain or exacerbate societal cleavages in order to keep the insurgent movement fragmented. This strategy of divide-and-rule dates back to the Roman Empire.

An effort to address the needs of the people depends upon effective administration, preferably staffed by local personnel. History is replete with cases wherein governments forfeited their presence to insurgent forces, which were quick to exploit the administrative vacuum by establishing their own organizational apparatus--however rudimentary.

It is also essential to forge a sense of loyalty between the government and the people. To facilitate this task, potential groups and leaders that can serve the government, or provide personnel for auxiliary police and militia forces, should be identified and organized. The role of the police and militia is to isolate the people from infiltrators, reduce insurgent pressure on the people, and provide security against terrorism and low-level guerrilla operations. Since humans tend to value individual security, the government's success in gaining cooperation is closely related to its ability to provide personal protection.

Along with the political and administrative actions outlined above, effective counterinsurgency invariably involves a number of security measures--detention without trial, resettlement of sections of the population, control of the distribution of food, curfews, restrictions on movement, the issuance and checking of identification cards, and the imposition of severe penalties for the carrying of unauthorized weapons--all designed to separate the population from the insurgents. While such sanctions may be undesirable from an ideal or moral standpoint, they have proven effective, especially when applied consistently, fairly and judiciously.

Whenever the government invokes security measures, it can expect the insurgents to use existing legal structures and the media, in an attempt to portray the regime as a violator of civil and human rights. This ploy, which makes it even more difficult for the government to avoid alienating the population--and, potentially, tarnishing its international image, as happened to Israel during the *Intifada*--is another argument in favor of a judicious and limited resort to such steps.

By the same token, fair security measures facilitate collection of accurate information about the insurgent organization, including the identification and location of its members and intended activities. Traditionally, the easiest way for the government to obtain the necessary information has been the creation of effective rapport with the people by means of good administration and prudent, diligent police work. This, in turn, has required well-trained interrogation experts, who can minimize violence by knowing the right questions to ask, and skilled, loyal agents who can penetrate the insurgent apparatus.

Since insurgents themselves are a potentially valuable source of intelligence, their treatment by government forces is important. While it is unlikely that members of the hard core will defect, it is quite possible that less dedicated insurgents may be induced to surrender, especially if their prospects appear to be waning. Psychological warfare efforts, designed to increase the number of defectors by promising them amnesty, security and material benefits, have often been used to exploit such situations.

As far as military measures of dealing with internal political violence are concerned, there is a number of prescriptive propositions, based on past experience. To cope with an insurgent organizational threat and the low-level terrorism and sporadic guerrilla attacks which often accompany it, the military must interact with the population. Armed units should be positioned in a large number of posts, allowing for protection of and close contact with the local people. If there is a small-scale guerrilla threat, the government forces must make extensive use of ambushes and patrols, in an effort to intercept insurgent bands. Moreover, the government ordinarily needs to provide back-up mobile air, naval and ground forces, to assist patrols that engage the enemy, as well as to carry out harassment operations against insurgent units in underpopulated hinterlands.

Where the insurgent movement has been able to mount a substantial internal terrorist campaign, the government must consolidate its own areas and then, operating from secure bases, seek to destroy the insurgents' political-military structures by locating and detaining its members. Police forces, having received quasi-military training for operations in the contested areas, can concentrate on these tasks, while lesser duties are performed by the auxiliary police.

If terrorism becomes a threat to officials and civilians abroad, the government may resort to a combination of defensive and offensive measures. Defensively, the government can enhance the security of embassies, consulates, airline offices, airliners, and the like by such simple steps as the assignment of armed guards. It may also cooperate with national and international police and intelligence agencies, and inform its citizens abroad as to personal security measures. Offensively, it can undertake intensive diplomatic efforts to acquire international support for anti-terrorist sanctions. In the event such steps prove unsatisfactory, the government may consider punitive military attacks against countries that provide sanctuary for terrorists, as well as special operations against insurgents located in such countries.

When insurgents have begun to conduct large-scale guerrilla actions, the government normally faces a more serious threat. In response, it must first consolidate the areas if does hold and gradually expand therefrom. Such an effort is aimed at gaining control of the population, food and other resources, while inflicting losses on guerrilla units and defending vital lines of communication. An essential component of the anti-guerrilla campaign is a mobile territorial defense that emphasizes the use of sophisticated detection technology, patrols, attacks, and ambushes by small, dispersed units operating around the clock. Once an area has been cleared of guerrilla bands, experience counsels that the government should establish an administrative presence, if only initially by civic action teams.

To further deprive the guerrillas of the initiative, the government can employ commandos, air power, and artillery to harass insurgents in remote and thinly populated hinterlands, where they are likely to have established bases. Eventually, this area should also be organized by the government. If free-fire zones (i.e., areas that can be fired into at will) are to be created, great care should be taken to assure the safety of innocent civilians. Otherwise, such indiscriminate military actions may risk creating more insurgents than are eliminated.

If the government finds itself confronted by conventional warfare, it might be on the verge of defeat. Herein, the options are quite limited: fight till the bitter end, surrender, or call for outside assistance. The first countermove by the government should be to consolidate base areas, even if this means sacrificing large portions of the country. Having secured and expanded these areas, mobile strike forces can be used against insurgent strongholds--as was done during the Greek civil war. If the government is lucky, the insurgents may choose to defend their bases, thus violating a cardinal guerrilla principle which warns against engaging a superior force. In the event insurgents decide to revert to guerrilla warfare, the government should respond likewise, taking the appropriate steps noted above.

If the government concludes that sanctuaries across the border are playing an important role in sustaining the insurgent activities, it can attempt to create a *cordon sanitaire*. Should jungle and mountainous terrain make this task impossible or difficult, the government might opt for free-fire zones, conduct mobile territorial operations, implant detection devices, build barriers, infiltrate counter-guerrillas across the border, or directly strike the sanctuary country. Since the last-mentioned tactic could become a *casus belli* that will widen the conflict, the government must carefully weigh its aims, their potential costs and associated risks.

Although the insurgent threat is largely a political-administrative challenge, military success is important to the government. Besides inflicting material and personnel damage on the insurgents--and, in some cases, forcing them out of familiar operating terrain--victories enhance government morale, undermine insurgent resolve and impress the population. A key point to bear in mind is that the insurgents are trying to project an image of strength, in order to convince the people they are bound to succeed. When most of the victories go to the government, the insurgents' credibility and, thus, strength, suffer.

One caveat is in order here. If, as seems to have been the case in El Salvador and Guatemala, military victories are achieved at the expense of the local population--in terms of casualties and material losses--they often prove counterproductive. For, the alienation they engender may increase the ranks of the disaffected, or unite an otherwise fragmented foe. This leads to the inexorable conclusion that all military operations must be planned and executed in such a way as to minimize civilian losses. One misplaced bomb or artillery shell can eviscerate countless hours of political effort. This is a lesson that the Israelis ruefully relearned in Lebanon in the Spring of 1996.

In summary, a government faced with an insurgency must combat four different types of threats with four different types of responses. Insurgent organizational and propaganda efforts must be countered by both government counter-organization and psychological warfare actions, as well as by police operations designed to uncover insurgent political cadres. Terrorism must be countered by security measures and intensified police and intelligence operations. Guerrilla warfare must be dealt with by low-level offensive and defensive operations that put a premium on small unit patrolling, mobile operations against hinterland guerrilla bases, and the defense of vital lines of communication. Conventional warfare must be neutralized by conventional military operations carried out by the government's armed forces, with or without external support. Furthermore, the government must be prepared to deal with each of these threats simultaneously.[36]

Clearly, the effort required by a counterinsurgency program is substantial. The demands in terms of morale, patience and determination become greater as the insurgent movement progresses. To be successful, the counterinsurgency forces need the firm backing of their government and people. Whether or not such support is forthcoming will be partially determined by the strategy the regime uses and the ways in which it is implemented. Indicators that things are not going well are: serious dissent, to include explicit or implicit support for the insurgent objectives; large-scale desertions from government forces; general lack of combativeness; poor performance by local law enforcement; guerrilla operations carried out by increasingly larger units; lack of information from the people; and a low insurgent surrender rate. Conversely, the opposite of each of these indicators would suggest the government is succeeding.

When all is said and done, an effective counterinsurgency effort depends primarily on the political and military adroitness of the government. Although moral, political and material support from friendly states may be an important asset in specific cases, there is always a danger--as the United States found in Vietnam--of over reliance and, thus, a failure on the part of indigenous authorities to fulfill their responsibilities. When this occurs, the outside power may end up assuming the major burden of the conflict, especially in the military area, while the essential political tasks necessary to undercut the insurrection are performed poorly, if at all.

Where threatened governments eschew an inordinate reliance on external powers, moving, instead, to devise and apply the types of programs suggested above, insurgents will have little chance of success. Moreover, even if the government does a mediocre job, it might still carry the day, depending upon how insurgents perform with respect to the other major criteria for successful insurgency. With this firmly in mind, we are ready to assess the current status and future prospects of Israeli and Palestinian rejectionism.

Notes

1. The centrality of legitimacy in insurgencies is noted by Harry Eckstein, "On the Etiology of Internal Wars," *History and Theory 4*, No. 2 (1965), p. 133. On the question of legitimacy and parts of the political system see Charles F. Andrain, *Political Life and Social Change*, 2d ed. (Belmont, CA: Duxbury Press, 1974), pp. 150-179. A recent discussion of legitimacy and internal wars may be found in Courtney E. Prisk, "The Umbrella of Legitimacy," in *Uncomfortable Wars*, Max G. Manwaring, ed. (Boulder, CO: Westview Press, 1991), pp. 69-91.

2. The term revolution as used in this chapter refers primarily to political revolution. Whether it will be followed by a social revolution that drastically changes the class stratification system depends on many things, not the least of which are the actions by the new revolutionary elite and the response to those actions. On the question of revolutionary change see Chalmers Johnson, *Revolutionary Change* (Boston, MA: Little, Brown, and Co., 1965). For a critique of Johnson see Waltraund Q. Morales, *Social Revolution: Theory and Historical Explanation* (Denver, CO: Denver University, 1973).

3. For a discussion the utopian conceptions of Islamic groups see Gilles Kepel, *Muslim Extremism in Egypt* (Berkeley, CA: University of California Press, 1984), pp. 226-240.

4. A cogent analysis of political terrorism is Paul Wilkinson, *Political Terrorism* (New York, NY: John Wiley and Sons, 1974), pp. 14-18.

5. For an excellent distillation of the essence of guerrilla warfare see Mao Tse-tung, *On Guerrilla Warfare*, Samuel B. Griffith, trans. (New York, NY: Fredrick A. Praeger, 1962, p. 46.

6. On the conspiratorial strategy as developed by Lenin see V. I. Lenin, *What Is to Be Done*, S. V. Utechin and Patricia Utechin, trans. (London: Oxford

University Press, 1963; Robert H. McNeal, The Bolshevik Tradition (Englewood Cliffs, NJ: Prentice Hall, 1963, p. 4; Robert C. Tucker, ed., *The Lenin Anthology* (New York, NY: W. W. Norton Co., Inc., 1975), p. 602; David Shub, *Lenin*, abridged ed. (New York, NY: Mentor Books, 1950, pp. 76-139; Alan Morehead, *The Russian Revolution* (New York, NY: Bantam Books, 1959), pp. 132-260; and Bertram D. Wolfe, *Three Who Made a Revolution* (New York, NY: Delta Books, 1948).

7. The following are useful for gaining an insight into the protracted popular war strategy: *Selected Military Writings of Mao Tse-tung* (Beijing: Foreign Language Press, 1967) pp. 92-98, 210-219 and 228; Benjamin I. Schwartz, *Chinese Communism and the Rise of Mao* (Cambridge, MA: Harvard University Press, 1951), pp. 189-204; John J. McCuen, *The Art of Counter-Revolutionary War* (Harrisburg, PA; Stackpole Books, n.d.), pp. 31-33; John S. Pustay, *Counterinsurgency Warfare* (New York, NY: The Free Press, 1965. The last two are especially helpful in summarizing the progression of the protracted popular war strategy.

8. On the southern strategy during the civil war see Clement Eaton, A History of the *Southern Confederacy* (New York, NY: The Macmillan Company, 1958), pp. 124-125. A recent and perceptive examination of this, which emphasizes vacillation between a defensive strategy, favored by Jefferson Davis and an offensive one, favored by Robert E. Lee, is Steven E. Woodworth, *Davis and Lee at War* (Kansas: University of Kansas Press, 1995).

9. Che Guevara, *Guerrilla Warfare* (New York, NY: Vintage Books, 1961), p. 1.

10. Ibid., pp. 3-12, 80-86; Regis Debray, *Revolution in the Revolution?*, Bobbir Ortiz, trans. (New York, NY: Monthly Review Press, 1967, pp. 20-21, 83-84; 95-105.

11. On the failure of the guerrilla foco in Latin America see Douglas S. Blaufarb, *The Counter-insurgency Era* (New York, NY: Free Press, 1977), pp. 280-286; John Pimlott, ed., *Guerrilla Warfare* (New York, NY: Bison Books, 1985, pp. 108-115.

12. Carlos Marighella, "On Principles and Strategic Questions," *Les Tempes Modernes*, November 1969.

13. For further insights regarding the urban warfare strategy see Robert Moss, *Urban Guerrilla Warfare*, Adelphi Paper, No. 79 (London: The International

Institute for Strategic Studies, 1971. On the urban-rural linkage see Abraham Guillen, *Philosophy of the Urban Guerrilla*, Donald C. Hodges, ed., and trans. (New York, NY: William Morrow, 1973), pp. 229-300. An incisive critique of the urban strategy may be found in Anthony Burton, *Revolutionary Violence* (New York, NY: Crane, Russak, 1978), pp. 130-144.

14. A. H. Shollom, "Nowhere Yet Everywhere," in Franklin Mark Osanka, ed., *Modern Guerrilla Warfare* (New York, NY: The Free Press of Glencoe, 1962), p. 19.

15. Arthur Campbell, *Guerrillas* (New York, NY: The John Day Company, 1968), p. 283.

16. Guevara, *Guerrilla Warfare*, p. 9. On the importance of bases see Osanka, ed., *Modern Guerrilla Warfare*, pp. 45, 90, 197, 312, 406.

17. Ted Robert Gurr, *Why Men Rebel* (Princeton, New Jersey, NJ: Princeton University Press, 1970), pp. 263-264.

18. *Selected Military Writings of Mao Tse-tung*, p. 260.

19. Gurr, *Why Men Rebel*, p. 337.

20. Osanka, ed. *Modern Guerrilla Warfare*, p. 34.

21. On the psychological foundations of the leader-follower relationship see Bruce Mazlish, *The Revolutionary Ascetic* (New York, NY: Basic Books, 1976), especially pp. 22-43 and E. Victor Wolfenstein, *The Revolutionary Personality* (Princeton, NJ: Princeton University Press, 1967).

22. Gabriel A. Almond, *The Appeals of Communism* (Princeton, New Jersey: Princeton University Press), p. 62. On the basic distinction between esoteric and exoteric appeals see Almond, pp. 65-66 and Morris Watnick, "The Appeal of Communism to Underdeveloped Peoples," in John H. Kautsky, ed., *Political Change in Underdeveloped Countries* (New York, NY: John Wiley and Sons, 1967). The same distinction is implicit in Peter Van Ness, *Revolution and Chinese Foreign Policy* (Berkeley, CA: University of California Press, 1970), pp. 118-119. On the functions of ideology see David Apter, *The Politics of Modernization* (Chicago" University of Chicago Press, 1965), pp. 354-370.

23. V. I. Lenin, Imperialism: *The Highest Stage of Capitalism* (New York, NY: International Publishers, 1969), pp. 1-128.

24. Gurr, *Why Men Rebel*, pp. 119.

25. The masses rarely show interest in or comprehend the ideological theorizing of insurgent leaders. See Almond, *The Appeals of Communism*, p. 65. The failure of the masses who support insurgencies to perceive the ideological aims is a major conclusion of Haim Gerber, *Islam, Guerrilla War, and Revolution* (Boulder, CO: Lynne Reiner, 1988). Recognition of this led Mao to instruct his cadres to solicit the grievances of the people and then replay them to the people. See Mao Tse-tung, "On Methods of Leadership," in *Selected Works*, Vol. 4 (New York, NY: International Publishers, 1958), p. 113.

26. A number of experts have called attention to the counterproductive effects of prolonged and/or indiscriminate terrorism. On this general point and specific cases in point see Jerry M. Silverman and Peter M. Jackson, "Terror in Insurgency Warfare," *Military Review*, October 1970, pp. 64-67; Richard L. Clutterbuck, *The Long, Long War* (New York, NY: Fredrick A. Praeger, 1966), p. 63; Julian Paget, *Counter-Insurgency Campaigning* (New York: Walker and Co., 1967), pp. 22-23; and, Otto Heilbrunn, *Partisan Warfare* (New York, NY: Fredrick A. Praeger, 1962). p. 89.

27. The impact of government ruthlessness on popular support is noted in Clutterbuck, *The Long,Long War*, pp. 178-179 and T. David Mason and Dale R. Krane, "The Political Economy of Death Squads: Toward a Theory of the Impact of State-Sponsored Terror" *International Studies Quarterly*, 1989, pp. 175-198.

28. George B. Jordan, "Objectives and Methods of Communist Guerrilla Warfare," in Osanka, *Modern Guerrilla Warfare*, pp. 404, 409.

29. Gurr, *Why Men Rebel*, pp. 274-316 contains a good discussion of the structural and functional aspects of organizations.

30. On parallel hierarchies see Bernard B. Fall, *The Two Viet-Nams*, 2d ed. (New York, NY: Fredrick A. Praeger, 1967), pp. 130-138; McCuen, The Art *of Counter-Revolutionary War*, p. 31; Clutterbuck, *The Long, Long War*, pp. 22, 56, 87-88; Douglas Hyde, The Roots of Guerrilla Warfare (Chester Springs, PA: Dufour Editions, 1968), pp. 92, 126; and Roger Trinquier, *Modern Warfare* (Fredrick A. Praeger, 1966), pp. 30, 70. A particularly good treatment of auxiliary organizations may be found in Douglas Pike, *Viet Cong* (Cambridge, MA: MIT Press, 1966), Chapters 6 and 10.

31. Cited in Jordan, "Objectives and Methods of Communist Guerrilla Warfare," p. 403.

32. Heilbrunn, *Partisan Warfare*, p. 39.

33. Debray, *Revolution in the Revolution?*, pp. 95-116.

34. Edward E. Rice, *Wars of the Third Kind* (Berkeley, CA: University of California Press, 1988), pp. 79-80.

35. Walter C. Sonderland, "An Analysis of Guerrilla Insurgency and Coup d'Etate as Techniques of Indirect Aggression," *International Studies Quarterly*, December, 1970, p. 345.

36. A more detailed discussion of all the points raised in the government response, which integrates the thinking of John J. McCuen, Richard Clutterbuck and others, is found in Bard E. O'Neill, *Insurgency and Terrorism* (Washington, DC: Brassey's, Inc., 1990), pp. 125-154.

CHAPTER TWO

THE CONTEXT OF ISRAELI REJECTIONISM

CHAPTER II

THE CONTEXT OF ISRAELI REJECTIONISM

> *The villain from Hebron put a mark on all of us, even though we are not to blame. That despicable man may not have been deranged in the clinical sense of the term when he pulled the murderous trigger, but the ghastly act was that of a mentally ill person, and in our hearts we feel only deep contempt for his vile deed. That murderer surfaced from within a small, limited political framework. He grew up in a morass whose sources exist here and overseas. They are foreign to Judaism; they do not belong to us. To him and those like him, we say today: You are not part of the people of Israel; you are not part of the national democratic camp in which all in this House are partners. Many among us despise you. You are not partners to the Zionist effort. You are wild weeds. Sane Judaism vomits you out from its midst. You are an alien element. You have alienated yourselves from the community.... You are a shame to Zionism and a disgrace to Judaism. One direct line links all the lunatics and racists of the world, a single line of blood and terror from the Islamic Jihad that shot at Jewish worshippers at prayer in synagogues in Istanbul, Paris and Amsterdam and including the Jewish Hamas member who shot at Ramadan worshippers.*
>
> Yitzhak Rabin, February 28, 1994

The above-cited public excommunication--pillorying Baruch Goldstein's February 1994 rampage at the Tomb of the Patriarchs in Hebron, which left 29 Palestinian worshipers dead--gave voice to a sentiment long held by many Israelis, namely, that Jewish extremism has contaminated the humanist heritage of Zionism and stained the nation's democratic record. If nothing else, Rabin's assassination less than two years later provides incontrovertible proof that the pernicious "wild weeds" had, indeed, taken root in Israel's body-politic.

Israel stands at a critical crossroads. The mounting rejectionist challenge is not just an academic issue, or an interesting partisan contest to be decided at the ballot box. At stake are Israel's civic culture, its international standing, particularly its relations with the U.S. and, ultimately, regional peace. Indeed, the course and outcome of the struggle between secular, liberal Zionism and the ascendent religious right might well determine Israel's very survival as a functioning Western democracy.

Israel is usually described as a homogeneous, consensual society, united by shared beliefs, goals and fears. This popular perception is particularly common in the United States, where a more differentiated analysis of the Israeli polity remains limited to a fairly narrow circle of area specialists.

Contrary to this idealized view, however, Israel is riven by deep--and deepening--societal, economic, political, cultural, and ethnic cleavages. Stated briefly and in broad categories, these rifts include divisions between the secular majority and Orthodox minority; between the political right, currently led by Likud (Union), and the Labor-led political left; between Ashkenazi Jews, i.e., those who trace their heritage to Eastern and Western Europe, and the *Sepharadim*, who originate from Africa and the Middle East; between native born and veteran Israelis and new immigrants, particularly those from the former Soviet Union; and the deep, enduring socio-economic and political cleavages between Israeli Jews and the Palestinian population of the occupied West Bank and Gaza, as well as Israel proper.

Insofar as all these divisions cut across social strata and shape divergent views on virtually every aspect of Israel's policy, their impact on and implications for the national security consensus are fundamental. That is, the polarizations affect both national goals and the alternative ways of attaining these goals. Moreover, these divisions are deeply rooted in both Jewish history and culture. Consequently, they are reflected in the nature of the political system, in daily decision-making and in the ends, ways and means of Israel's strategy.

To function properly, all societies require a minimal common structure of shared symbols and values. In their absence, political, social and economic conflicts could, ultimately, lead to internal war. As a newly created society--and one whose right to exist has

The Context of Israeli Rejectionism

not always been taken for granted by its neighbors and the international community at large--Israel appears to have a greater need for a unifying vision and a collective sense of mission. For almost a hundred years, Zionism fulfilled both roles, becoming not only Israel's state ideology but its citizens' secular religion, effectively supplanting Judaism as the primary source of self-identification and focus of allegiance. Yet, the very success of Zionism resulted, almost inevitably, in disenchantment, because reality has fallen short of the founding fathers' utopian vision of a just, moral society--"a light unto the nations." The disillusionment, in turn, spawned a host of alternative ideological approaches, ultimately crystallizing into a serious challenge to the very essence of Israel's national ethos.

Historical Overview

Understanding the historic origins of this mounting challenge to the basic premises upon which Israel was founded is key to grasping both its current nature and future directions. As the following analysis will demonstrate, contemporary Israeli rejectionism springs from two distinct sources: Jewish theology and Zionist revisionism. A brief review of the evolution of Zionism as both a national liberation movement and a political ideology will provide a good starting point for a comprehensive assessment.

The Religious Roots: Zionism arose in 19th century Europe in response to "the problem of the Jews"--namely, their persecution and insecurity as stateless refugees in an alien, often anti-Semitic diaspora--and as a reaction to the "problem of Judaism," that is, the concern that enlightenment and assimilation would undermine authentic Jewish culture. From its inception, Zionism rejected both cultural assimilation, characteristic primarily of West European Jewry, and the passivity of waiting for messianic redemption, typical of the more traditional Jews of Eastern Europe.[1] Instead, the movement advocated a "return to Zion" and creation of a Jewish homeland in the historic Land of Israel--then Palestine under the rule of the Ottoman Empire.

The idea of renewing Jewish statehood has been a central tenet of Judaism ever since the Great Revolt against the Romans and the resultant destruction of the Second Temple in 70 A.D. However, the task of ending the exile and reinstating Jewish sovereignty--the redemption--was relegated to God and his Messiah. Insofar as the exile, with its attendant miseries, was perceived as having been divinely ordained, any attempt to alter it without divine sanction was, *ipso facto*, sacrilegious and futile. The core belief, then, inspired passivity: avoiding action until God, in his own good time, sends the Messiah to redeem his chosen people and the world at large.

As a modern national liberation movement, Zionism derived its power and legitimacy from reinterpretation of and, ultimately, deviation from these traditional tenets. Its most radical innovation was the call for immediate political action to attain national renaissance.

Zionism assigned the task of renewing Jewish statehood to humans, rather than to divine providence. Israel's secular founding fathers did not intend to reinstate a Jewish theocracy, nor to pave the way for the kingdom of heaven on earth. Rather, they saw an independent state as a refuge from persecution and a cure to the societal pathologies associated with the diaspora. Their focus has always been on the historic process, not a millennial end of history. Their vision was a national--vice religious--redemption, to be realized through reclaiming, working and defending the land.

Orthodox Jews, almost uniformly, perceived these innovations as blasphemy. In practice, however, their reaction to the challenge of Zionism took several forms, ranging from a total rejection of both the ideology and its product--a modern, secular state of Israel--to pragmatic accommodation and cooperation with the Zionist enterprise.

The basic contradiction between Zionism and Jewish theology has never been fully reconciled, resulting in one of the deepest of the many rifts dividing contemporary Israeli society. Its practical manifestations, however, have been quite diverse, ranging from a

The Context of Israeli Rejectionism

total boycott of all state institutions--typical, for example, of the primarily Jerusalem-based *Neturei Karta* (Guardians of the City)--to full-fledged participation in the political process. As a group, however, most ultra-Orthodox Jews--referred to in Hebrew as *Haredim* (literally, the fearful, or the God-fearing)--have effectively opted out of Israeli society and its collective pursuits. In a sense, theirs is the ultimate rejectionism.

Segregation between ultra-Orthodox and secular Israelis--in terms of residence, education, military service, and daily life--is almost absolute. The *Haredim*'s key objective is to isolate their way of life from the state--much as Jews have done for centuries in the diaspora. Given the close quarters and daily frictions of life in Israel, however, clashes between the secular majority and the ultra-Orthodox minority are inevitable. But, while these outbursts are often violent and attract a good deal of sensationalist press attention, their main focus is on such matters as traffic on the Sabbath, the operating hours of restaurants and theaters, and the sexual content of billboards, rather than issues of national security.

In contrast, the neo-Orthodox and national religious movements--the former represented by *Agudat Israel* (Congregation of Israel), the latter initially associated with the *Mizrahi* (Eastern) faction in the Zionist Congress and subsequently represented by *MAFDAL* (National Religious Party, hereafter NRP)--opted for varying degrees of cooperation with mainstream Zionism. The more traditional *Aguda* saw the Jewish homeland as a much needed refuge--a haven from persecution. In the wake of the Holocaust, *Agudat Israel* shifted its attitude from being actively anti-Zionist to what can best be described as a non-Zionist posture. To its leaders, Israel as a modern state had little theological significance: It "was the place for the body but not the soul of Jewry."[2]

Nonetheless, in 1948, *Agudat Israel* struck a bargain with the dominant Labor Zionists and the National Religious Party to establish a *modus vivendi* in matters of church and state. Specifically, the accord gave Orthodox rabbis exclusive control over such matters as marriage, divorce and religious conversion, and obligated the supposedly secular State of Israel to observe the

Sabbath and Jewish dietary laws, at least in its public institutions. Moreover, the agreement deferred the question of the official status of religion in the newly-founded State by dispensing with a written constitution. In return, *Agudat Israel* consented to join the ruling coalition, effectively employing its new political clout to sustain-- and, often, expand upon--the religious *status quo*. Until the 1970s, however, the *Aguda*--like the *Haredi* community at large--tended toward moderation in national security matters. Its main focus was on the domestic agenda, specifically on such issues as religious legislation, patronage for its social and educational institutions, as well as a self-styled guardianship over the "Jewishness" of Israel.

In contrast, *Mizrahi* and its post-1948 successor, the NRP, opted for a different path, attempting to bridge the gap between Jewish tradition and secular Zionism. The movement's leaders sought to endow the Zionist idea with religious content, while integrating observance of Jewish law (*halacha*) with full participation in the Zionist enterprise and modern Israeli society. Some rabbis, most notably, Abraham Isaac Kook (1856-1935), went as far as to argue that, by restoring Jewish sovereignty, secular Zionists were carrying out the divine plan of redemption, thus hastening, even if unwittingly, the coming of the Messiah. While few Orthodox rabbis shared Kook's tolerance of the often loudly-proclaimed atheism of many young Israelis--or his "sanctification" of Jewish manual labor and military valor--the endorsement facilitated the emergence of a symbiotic relationship between the two camps.

The readiness of at least some religious leaders to cooperate with and see positive value in secular Zionism was a critical source of legitimacy for the movement, particularly before the 1948 declaration of independence. But, while mainstream Zionism sought to use individuals like Rabbi Kook in its efforts to gain credibility among observant Jews throughout the diaspora, Kook and his followers, in turn, intended to exploit secular Zionism as a tool of their own brand of nationalism.

The early political links between religious Zionism and its secular counterpart--led by David Ben Gurion's Labor Party--soon solidified into a seemingly permanent alliance, based on shared interests and pragmatic needs. As Labor's dominance over the emerging Israeli society, culture and political system crystallized, the NRP played an important--albeit clearly supporting--role.[3] This situation was to change dramatically after the spectacular victories of 1967 and the near defeat of 1973, which catapulted the National Religious Party to the opposite end of the political spectrum--into an alliance with the right-of-center Likud.

Zionist Revisionism: Unlike the ideological schism between Jewish theology and secular Zionism, the rift **within** the Zionist movement initially centered around alternative courses of action to attain shared objectives. Paradoxically, however, it was the latter that evolved into a bitter and, sometimes, bloody contest, actually bringing the fledgling state of Israel to the brink of civil war.

The Revisionist Movement was formed by Vladimir Ze'ev Jabotinsky in 1925, largely as a reaction to the 1921 British decision to separate Transjordan (i.e., the Eastern Bank of the Jordan River) from the Palestine Mandate and, thus, from the area in which the Jewish national home, promised in the 1917 Balfour Declaration, was to be established. Ten years later, amidst bitter acrimony, the Revisionists withdrew from the World Zionist Organization, vowing unswerving commitment to Jewish sovereignty over the entire Land of Israel. Thereafter, Revisionism developed and operated completely outside the Zionist mainstream.

Since its inception, the Revisionist Movement had a dual--if not contradictory--nature. On the one hand, its conservative socio-economic agenda put it at odds with Labor's socialism. On the other hand, its radical nationalism--in terms of both totalist ends and militant ways and means--had little to do with conservative pragmatism. Revisionism called for an immediate armed revolt against the British authorities, aimed at establishing exclusive Jewish control over both Western and Eastern Palestine (that is, on both banks of the Jordan River). Its key emphasis was on military action, rather than on the laborious, gradual creation of national infrastructure espoused by Labor. Given the inherent fragility of the Zionist enterprise in Palestine and its narrow base of international support, the military focus strategy advocated by the Revisionists was, by any objective measure, highly risky, if not irresponsible.

The leaders of the Revisionist Movement, most notably Jabotinsky, were clearly aware of the virtues of liberal democracy, pluralism, political tolerance, and reasoned discourse.[4] Yet, they remained skeptical of their value in the struggle for national liberation. Militarism, determination and discipline--encapsulated in Jabotinsky's motto "blood and iron"--were the tenets upon which the movement was founded. Political power was clearly to come from the barrel of the gun, and the quicker the better. Thus, the rivalry between Labor Zionism and the Revisionists was soon to encompass conflicting visions, divergent strategies and irreconcilable approaches to such fundamental issues as relations with the British Mandatory authorities, attitudes toward the Arabs and territorial compromise.

The intensity of the ideological clash between the two camps was reflected in both words and deeds. The bitter rhetoric escalated to the point of Ben Gurion calling the Revisionists "fascists," and referring to Jabotinsky as "Il Duce" (Mussolini) and "Vladimir Hitler." Responding in kind, the revisionists labelled Ben Gurion a "British agent" and his party "Bolsheviks."[5] Tensions reached a peak on June 16, 1933, with the assassination of Chaim Arlosoroff, a prominent Labor leader. Three members of an extremist Revisionist faction were charged with the murder. Although evidence proved insufficient for conviction, the incident marked a point of no return. More bloodshed was soon to follow.

To the Brink of Fratricide: Within less than a decade, the military auxiliaries of the two camps--Ben Gurion's *Hagana* (Defense), on the one hand, and the Revisionists' *Irgun Zvai Leumi* (National Military Organization, better known by its Hebrew acronym *ETZEL*, or *Irgun*) and the even more extremist *Lohamei Herut Israel* (Israel's Freedom Fighters, also known as *LEHI* or the Stern Gang), on the other hand--came precariously close to open warfare.

Whereas the *Hagana* suspended its anti-British activities for the

The Context of Israeli Rejectionism

duration of World War II, in order to jointly face the Nazi menace, *ETZEL* and especially *LEHI* refused to follow suit. Their escalating campaign of terrorist strikes against British and Arab targets throughout Palestine and their steadfast refusal to submit to the authority of elected Jewish institutions ultimately led Ben Gurion to declare war on the opposition. In "Operation *Saison*" (as in hunting, or open season), *Hagana*'s elite strike units were sent on a virtual search and destroy mission against key elements of *LEHI* and *ETZEL*. Dissidents were tracked down, abducted and interrogated. Many were handed over to the British authorities, to face trial and, often, the gallows.

If the *Saison* was the darkest hour in Israel's struggle for national liberation, an even darker period was to follow the May 14, 1948 declaration of independence. The Provisional Government and Constitutional Assembly were faced with the twin missions of repelling a four-front Arab invasion, while melding the various partisan organizations into an integrated, national army. The legal tool to accomplish both objectives was Order No. 4, issued on May 26, 1948, establishing the Israel Defense Forces (IDF) as the sole armed force of the new state. The *Hagana*, led by the authors of Order No. 4, and the *PALMACH*--its ostensibly subordinate elite commando organization--complied immediately. *LEHI*, under the leadership of Yitzhak Shamir, rejected the order, denying its legitimacy. *ETZEL*, led by Menachem Begin, who had taken over after Jabotinsky's death in 1940, agreed to turn itself into a political party. Yet, while *ETZEL* platoons and companies were being integrated into IDF battalions, the organization attempted to smuggle weapons into the country to outfit its own combatants.

On June 11, 1948, a UN-sponsored truce between Israel and the invading Arab armies went into effect, giving the Provisional Government a much needed, if only temporary, respite from the war. Ben Gurion seized the opportunity to deal with the equally urgent problem of the rival militias. *ETZEL* was the first target: Its arms-carrying ship, the *Altalena*, was bombarded and sunk off the coast of Tel Aviv, in full view of thousands of bewildered citizens. Fourteen *ETZEL* fighters and one *PALMACH* soldier died in the fire-fight. Dozens were wounded. In an ironic twist of history, the assault was led by a 25-year-old battalion commander named Yitzhak Rabin.[6]

In the acrimony that followed the bloody confrontation, it became clear that Ben Gurion feared that the dissidents would use the weapons from the *Altalena* to stage an armed revolt against his government and, perhaps, secede from the newly-founded state to create their utopian, purely Jewish "Kingdom of Israel." Yet, it was Begin who chose to retreat from the brink of civil war and submit to the state's supreme authority--in spite of *LEHI*'s pressure to the contrary.[7] On June 29, 1948, eight days after the *Altalena* went down, the remaining *ETZEL* brigade was dismantled and the IDF took its oath of allegiance to the state.

The much smaller *LEHI* continued to function as an armed underground organization until the September 17, 1948 assassination of UN mediator Count Volke Bernadotte. While the Israeli Provisional Government was not necessarily sorry to see the termination of Bernadotte's mission, *LEHI*'s outrageous defiance gave Ben Gurion the needed pretext for a relentless clamp-down. A massive manhunt was launched and, within days, *LEHI* ceased to exist as an armed organization. This left the *PALMACH*'s three brigades as the only semi-independent outfit within the IDF.

Unlike the Revisionist organizations, the *PALMACH* was a prestigious elite corps affiliated with Labor Zionism, that is, with Ben Gurion's own camp. Yet, its independent ethos, loose chain of command, thorough disregard for military order and discipline, and the association of many of its officers with a Marxist, *kibbutz*-based political movement made the organization a threat to central authority. With the War of Independence drawing to a close--and the IDF growing exponentially in terms of both force structure and combat experience--the *PALMACH*'s vaunted expertise in infantry assaults and long-range reconnaissance was no longer deemed vital to success. This allowed Ben Gurion to move against the last remaining vestige of armed factionalism.

Although some of its officers resigned in protest, the *PALMACH* was absorbed into the IDF without the much-feared

The Context of Israeli Rejectionism 71

mutiny. Yet, even though Israel could ill-afford the loss of battle-earned experience, the organization's top commanders were placed on a slow promotion track for the next decade. Indeed, the first IDF Chief of the General Staff with a prominent *PALMACH* background was Yitzhak Rabin. He took office in 1964, after Ben Gurion's retirement.[8]

The single-minded and often brutal suppression of armed factionalism described above is important for three reasons:

First, in large measure, it insulated the Israeli Defense Forces from politics, fostering an ethos of apolitical professionalism and subordination to civilian authority, without which democracy and military success might have been impossible. This is a lesson that Arafat and the fledgling Palestinian National Authority can ignore only at their own peril. Equally importantly, this is an achievement that Israel can ill afford to fritter away. For, as we shall argue, Israel's current leaders are faced with the grave consequences inherent in politicizing and, thus, potentially fragmenting the Armed Forces. Their skill and resolve in dealing with the danger--that is, their ability to keep the IDF united and out of politics--will define Israel's future as a functioning democracy.

Second, the experience demonstrates how a relatively small, but determined and well-organized minority can shape political processes. Given that, in 1948, the Revisionists commanded the support of only 10-15 percent of the population, the implications of their ability to bring an emerging nation to the brink of disaster are significant. If nothing else, these implications suggest that politicians and analysts should be wary of underestimating the import of contemporary militant minorities on both the Israeli and the Palestinian sides.

Third, and perhaps most critically, the experience provides a useful example of the vision, leadership and political will necessary to overcome rejectionism. As the analysis that follows will demonstrate, these are important lessons for both Israel's current leadership and the Palestinian National Authority to learn and apply.

Marginalization and Resurgence: Following the establishment of a firm civilian authority, Israel could have attempted to heal the fratricidal wounds. Instead, the suppression of armed factionalism was followed by a deliberate, concerted effort to delegitimize and isolate the opposition. Ben Gurion's famous dictum that he will accept any party as a coalition partner except the Communists and Begin's *Herut* (Freedom), effectively placed the latter outside the pale of political legitimacy.

The sustained campaign to marginalize the right-wing reflected more than power politics and an effort to consolidate Labor's dominance. It appears to have been driven by a genuine fear that, should the Revisionists ever come to power, "Begin will replace the army and police with his thugs and rule the way Hitler ruled Germany, using brute force to suppress any opposition. This will destroy the state."[9]

Whatever combination of personal, ideological and practical considerations underpinned *Herut*'s effective delegitimization, the process was facilitated by the fact that the territorial issue--a key plank in the Revisionist platform--had become moot. As the 1949 armistice lines crystallized into Israel's internationally-recognized, permanent borders, maximalist territorial objectives and visions of Greater Israel came to be perceived as irrelevant pipe dreams. This changed dramatically in the wake of the Six Day War.

In the anxious, gloomy period leading up to the war, Israel faced its worst fears. Frightened, isolated and surrounded by vastly superior opponents, it was acutely aware of the fragility of its very existence. On June 5, 1967, Israel initiated an audacious offensive with the sole objective of assuring its survival. It emerged, six days later, a changed nation--in psychological, political, military, and territorial terms. A twenty-year-old national security paradigm seemed to have been smashed in one bold stroke.

The immense sense of national vulnerability, personal insecurity and memories of the Holocaust were replaced, within a week, with the euphoria of unprecedented victory. The ever-present threat to the nation's survival lay in ruins. For the first time since its inception, Israel was no longer David facing the Arab Goliath. Militarily at least, it was--and saw itself as--the strongest regional

The Context of Israeli Rejectionism

power. The unification of Jerusalem, the capture of the Sinai, West Bank and the Golan Heights--territories three times larger than Israel proper--gave the nation unprecedented strategic depth. With the military significance of the territories magnified still further by Israel's traditional siege mentality, the land soon came to be perceived in existential terms--as a critical ingredient of national survival, rather than as a bargaining chip for peace.

The scope of the paradigm shift is neatly summed up by A. B. Yehoshua, one of Israel's foremost poets and publicists: "Since the Six Day War...we have come to realize that questions we thought decided were not decided.... The political debate on the future of the [occupied] territories became the chink through which the depths of controversy and interpretation, intention and fantasy...were exposed once again."[10] Put more succinctly, in 1967 Israel inflicted a quick and decisive defeat on the Arabs and a protracted political and ethical crisis on itself. For, the war bestowed a "poisoned gift: One million stunned, frightened and potentially hostile Palestinians in the West Bank and Gaza, whose very presence posed a permanent security threat and whose frustrated aspirations would soon challenge Israel and the democratic values upon which it was founded."[11]

The war and its outcome produced many of the political, military and psychological conditions for the reemergence of the radical right, albeit in a new, more militant incarnation. The Six Day War could be--and was--portrayed as a glorious event of biblical proportions, involving blood, valor, land, and folk--all traditional Revisionist values. Greater Israel was no longer an irrelevant dream. The fact that Begin and his party were now legitimate political players--having been invited to join in a National Unity Government during the pre-war crisis--lent credibility to their maximalist territorial claims, couched, as they were, in seemingly compelling security terms.

The Six Day War could also be--and was--interpreted as a message from God, reinstating his "chosen people" to their biblical patrimony. As a result, redemption, sanctity of the land, the coming of the Messiah, and national salvation "in the Kingdom of

Israel as the Kingdom of Heaven on Earth" were no longer seen as purely eschatological precepts, to be discussed only in the relative obscurity of theological seminaries. In the eyes of the reawakening religious right, these concepts acquired both practical relevance and the force of divine commandments. The basis for Jewish reactionary traditionalism was thus created.

Yet, elated as Begin was by the resurrection of his territorial dreams, he was careful not to undermine his growing public legitimacy with premature militancy. Similarly, the future rejectionists--a new breed of territorial maximalists, calling themselves The Land of Israel Movement, and the Zionist religious nationalists who joined them--were, for the time being, relatively open, democratic and full of pioneering zeal and optimism. Thus, a critical element was missing for the consummation of a revisionist-religious alliance as a fully articulated rejectionist movement: the negative syndrome of bitterness and alienation.[12]

This impetus was provided by the trauma of the 1973 Yom Kippur War, by the resultant popular resentment towards and disenchantment with Labor's leadership, and by the post-war emergence of a broad range of popular protest movements. The bitterness was reinforced by the Camp David Accords and then-Prime Minister Begin's apparent readiness to consider granting autonomy to the Palestinians, while trading land for peace with Egypt. The frustration with Begin's "betrayal" and the ugly confrontation between settlers and IDF troops during the evacuation of the Sinai settlements, particularly Yamit, provided the final push toward radicalization.

Goals and Strategies

To the extent that they even considered such things as Jewish rejectionism, most Western analysts tended to dismiss it as an insignificant fringe, whose rantings and ravings had little impact on Israeli society or policy. Even in the wake of Prime Minister Rabin's November 1995 assassination, Western commentary remains focused on the actions perpetrated by individuals, rather than on the phenomenon as a whole. In contrast, following the pioneering work of Yehoshafat Harkabi, Ehud Sprinzak and Ian Lustick,[13] we shall argue that Israeli rejectionism constitutes a deeply rooted and increasingly active insurgency, complete with a unique world view and a fully-fledged action program. Far from being an inconsequential handful of militants, they have already changed Israel's society and its political discourse, perhaps irreversibly. While their actual influence has waxed and waned over the years--reaching a new low amidst the outrage and recriminations that followed Prime Minister Rabin's slaying--the rejectionists remain a well-organized, dedicated and militant political group, with a significant base of popular support. Given the volatility of the Israeli electorate and the existential nature of the issues at stake, the rejectionists' enduring ability to shape policy and impede the peace process warrants serious analysis.

The Six Day War and the ensuing occupation transformed both Israel's political landscape and its national agenda. The territorial issue and its colloraries--peace and security, law and civil rights, relations with the Arab world in general and the Palestinians in particular, and Israel's status as a Western democracy--became the dominant focus of political discourse. Traditional political platforms and party ideologies were realigned to reflect increasingly more divisive postures on these core values. New single-issue parties--such as *Tehiya* (Revival), *Moledet* (Motherland), *Tzomet* (Crossroads), and Rabbi Kahane's *Kach* (Thus!)--as well as extra-parliamentary movements--e.g., *Shalom Achshav* (Peace Now) on the left and *Gush Emunim* (Bloc of the Faithful) on the right--emerged with the sole objective of influencing policies in regard to the occupied territories.

Within the context of this novel constellation, Israel's future frontiers became the demarcation line of the nation's politics. "Right" and "Left" were no longer defined by competing socio-economic agendas (conservative-capitalist versus socialist-trade unionist, respectively), but, rather, in terms of increasingly polarized positions on the territorial issue.

Along the traditional left-to-right political spectrum, the Israeli Left became identified--at least rhetorically, if not always in practice--with territorial compromise, alleviation of the inevitable hardships of occupation, observance of democratic norms, and protection of civil rights. The Right favored, as a minimum, preservation of the territorial *status quo*, with annexation--*de facto*, through settlement, and *de jure*, through legislation--its longer term goal. The Right also tended to deny the very existence of the Palestinians as a *bona fide* nation, entitled to self-determination, emphasizing, instead, the PLO's terrorist nature in the context of the Arabs' implacable hostility toward Israel. Consequently, democracy, civil rights and the rule of law were perceived as secondary to the exigencies of sustaining the occupation. Increasingly frequent human rights' violations were treated with leniency, if not impunity, as long as they could be justified in terms of the overriding goal of holding on to the occupied territories.

While both the Right and Left supported Jewish presence in the territories as a matter of principle, the former advocated a more comprehensive colonization, to include settlements in close proximity to Palestinian population centers. In contrast, Labor's policy has been driven primarily by considerations of security--as well as economic viability--with settlements largely limited to the Jordan River Valley, or clustered astride such strategic points as the approaches to Jerusalem and Tel Aviv, and the high ground in the Golan. In contrast to its right-wing rivals, Labor also sought to avoid settlement of the densely populated Samaria region.

Thus, over time, the refusal to trade land for peace has crystallized as the key unifying goal--and public trademark--of contemporary Israeli rejectionism. Yet, while the territorial issue remains the touch-stone of Israeli politics--axiomatically defining "Right" and "Left" on the political spectrum--there is more to Israeli rejectionism than its overarching commitment to keep the Land of Israel, in its post-1967 boundaries, under undivided Jewish control. Indeed, as is the case with the Palestinians, the centrality of the shared strategic objective tends to obscure the deep

The Context of Israeli Rejectionism

cleavages within the rejectionist camp.

With an eye toward a more differentiated analysis of Israeli rejectionism, we should note several dividing lines, distinguishing, at a minimum, among:

(1) The **religious** core and its **secular** counterpart, with the former further subdivided along the fundamentalist-to-progressive spectrum.

(2) The **pragmatic right**--that is, those loyalists of Greater Land of Israel who recognize the constraints of political, economic and demographic realities and understand that Israel is not an independent actor in the global arena--versus the **radical right**, i.e., those who tend to ignore considerations of *realpolitik* and assert Israel to be free of the norms and pressures circumscribing other nations' behavior. Many, but not all, proponents of the radical right agenda are also religious fundamentalists.

(3) **Actual settlers**, who have a personal stake in the territorial issue and their much more numerous **sympathizers** who remain within the Green Line. The settler community is further subdivided in terms of its members' actual rationale for living in the occupied territories--religious, ideological, or purely socio-economic, i.e., cheaper housing, cleaner environment and better quality of life than readily available within Israel proper.

In terms of goals and strategies, Israeli rejectionism is comprised of three distinct, yet interdependent branches:

(a) **The national religious camp** is politically identified with the NRP Knesset faction, as well as with some elements of the more orthodox *Agudat Israel.* Its activist component, *Gush Emunim* (Bloc of the Faithful), was created in 1974 as an extra-parliamentary, grassroots movement with the express purpose of expanding the borders of Zionism through settlement in all parts of the biblical Land of Israel. *Bnei Akiva* (the Sons of Rabbi Akiva), the well-established religious Zionist youth movement, serves as the Bloc's strategic reserve and recruitment base. Both organizations share an unvarnished commitment to the messianic teachings of Rabbi Kook, the elder, and his son, Zvi Yehuda Kook; a pioneering spirit; and a rejection of secular materialism. In addition to their obvious appeal to Israel's religious minority, these movements elicit a significantly broader popular support through identification with such cherished national values as labor and defense, selfless patriotism and return to the ancestral land. Thus, by wrapping itself in--if not effectively usurping--Labor's Zionist mantle, *Gush Emunim* could bestow genuine legitimacy on and mobilize popular support for the entire rejectionist camp. In terms of our analytical framework, the religious wing of Israeli rejectionism falls into the traditionalist category, with the curious admixture of some egalitarian rhetoric and reactionary-traditionalist symbols.

(b) **The secular-nationalist camp** is politically identified with several right-wing parties, most notably, *Likud, Moledet, Tehiya and Tzomet*. In contrast to the natural cohesion of the religious core, the secular camp is both larger and more diverse. It ranges from right-of-center former Laborites, wary of the security implications of territorial compromise, through *Likud*-based Revisionists, with their traditional territorial aspirations, to ultra-nationalist advocates of a purely Jewish empire, stretching to the banks of the Nile and Euphrates. What unites this camp is distrust of the Arabs, a xenophobic attitude towards the world at large, and a conviction that strategic depth and defensible borders are indispensable to national survival. These postulates were tested and significantly reinforced in the crucible of the October 1973 surprise attack and ensuing war, leading to an unshakable belief that the territorial *status quo* saved Israel from certain annihilation. *Ergo*, according to this view, any territorial compromise would place the nation's very existence at grave peril. In terms of our analytical framework, the secular rejectionists fall into the preservationist category, with some elements closer to the reactionary-traditionalist subtype.

(c) **The reactionary-traditionalist faction** comprises the now-outlawed *Kach* and its assorted offshoots--e.g., *Kahane Chai* (Rabbi Kahane Lives), *Herev David* (the Sword of David),

The Context of Israeli Rejectionism

EYAL (Irgun Yehudi Lohem, or Jewish Fighting Organization*), Zu Artzenu* (This is Our Land), and *Bereshit* (Genesis). While undoubtedly a small element of and, often, an embarrassment to the national-religious establishment from which it springs, this group deserves attention for three reasons: its fully articulated political agenda; its ultra-radical strategy, to include an explicit commitment to violence; and its significant--albeit largely covert--base of support overseas.

Shared Goals, Divergent Visions: The strategic thinking of the religious rejectionists is predicated on seven mutually reinforcing core beliefs.[14] Taken together, these axioms provide the key to understanding their current agenda and future pursuits.

    a. **The cardinal importance and sanctity of the Land of Israel**, as a integral element of a "holy trinity"--to borrow a concept--of God, His Chosen People and their Promised Land. This divine unity--and triple commitment--are clearly expressed in *Gush Emunim*'s slogan: "The Land of Israel, for the People of Israel, according to the Torah of Israel." Furthermore, insofar as the Land of Israel, in its biblical entirety, is believed to belong exclusively to the Jews, no other nation may be recognized as having a legitimate claim to any portion of it. These tenets make it incumbent upon all believers to "inherit the land," as per Numbers 33:53, sacrificing life and limb, if necessary, on the altar of territorial integrity. By the same token, ceding Jewish land to non-believers is considered a sacrilege, tantamount to violation of the biblical covenant with God. Such an apostasy is deemed to be a capital offense, punishable by death.

    b. **The eternal uniqueness of the Jewish people**, as a nation endowed with a divine destiny and a special mission. The notion here is that Jews, as "the chosen people," are both qualitatively different from and intrinsically superior to any other nation. As such, Israel is not bound by laws that circumscribe the behavior of "normal" states. The very concept of "chosenness" sanctions unequal and discriminatory treatment of non-Jews, who are, by definition, inferior. This tenet is, of course, diametrically opposed to both the traditional Zionist axiom that the Jews are a nation like all others, with identical rights and obligations, and to the explicit pledge of equality, regardless of gender, race, religion, and national origin, contained in Israel's Declaration of Independence.

    c. **Israel's international isolation is proof of its "chosenness"** and, thus, an intrinsically positive status. In contrast to the traditional Zionist belief that anti-Semitism will gradually disappear as a result of Jewish "normalization," the religious view holds that the inherent antagonism between Jews and Gentiles will continue until the coming of the Messiah. By the same token, efforts to integrate Israel into the global community are considered to be both futile and unnecessary, because Israel cannot and should not become a nation like all others. In the context of these basic assumptions, instances of Gentile good will--e.g., U.S. support for Israel--are perceived as the direct result of divine intervention, rather than rational behavior which Israel should strive to reinforce. Seeing the Jewish people as beholden only to God, this tenet also provides an *a priori* absolution for actions likely to be condemned by the world community. This, in turn, removes the onus of consequences from the believers.

    d. **The conflict with the Arabs is not a "normal" struggle** between hostile nations but, rather, the latest phase of the eternal battle between good and evil. This belief lends an uncompromising character to the Arab-Israeli conflict, especially when coupled--as it is for the reactionary-traditionalists--with a literal acceptance of the biblical injunction to "mercilessly expel" all non-Jews from the Land of Israel, lest they become, as per Joshua 23:13, "snares and traps unto you, and scourges in your sides and thorns in your eyes, until ye perish from off this good land which the Lord your God hath given you." Given the assumption of implacable Arabs hostility toward Israel and the metaphysical nature of the struggle being waged, any attempts at a negotiated compromise are perceived, *ipso facto*, as futile and doomed to failure.

e. **Current history is God's means of communicating with His people.** In the context of this belief, historic events--such as the Holocaust, the establishment of the State of Israel, the Six Day War, the Yom Kippur War, or the *Intifada*--are all perceived as divine messages, signalling the schedule of the redemption. Thus, "correct" political and historic analysis amounts to interpretation of God's will, providing instructions, reprimands and rewards.[*] More than anything, it is this belief in the possession of a special and direct access to a transcendental truth--that is, a unique understanding of the future course of events and the actions required to bring them about--that accounts for our classification of the Israeli religious right as a fundamentalist movement.

f. **Faith and personal dedication are decisive factors.** Despite the dominant role ascribed to God as the ultimate designer of history, there is little fatalism in this world view. To the contrary: Individual and collective faith, commitment and self-sacrifice are perceived as the turbines of a divinely-inspired process, propelling it forward to its preordained culmination in the establishment of the messianic kingdom. This approach, in turn, places a premium on mobilization and direct action, with the believers assuming personal responsibility for the successful realization of God's plans and the imperatives of Jewish destiny. This intimate connection between what is believed to be celestially ordained and what is perceived as one's personal duty is another distinguishing mark of a fundamentalist political vision.

g. **The Messiah's arrival is imminent.** While the expectation of an eventual messianic redemption is an article of faith to every observant Jew, what distinguishes the fundamentalist approach is its transformation of a belief into a political ideology.

---

[*] It is this belief that allowed several Orthodox rabbis to assert that Prime Minister Rabin was responsible for the deaths of 21 Israelis in the January 22, 1995 suicide bombing in Beit Lid, because he met with his economic advisors on the preceding Saturday--in violation of the Sabbath. It should be noted that this was not the first time that religious leaders proclaimed terrorist attacks to be "God's punishment" for similar transgressions.

In this view, the Messiah is not a distant dream, a symbol of a better world, or an ideal but, rather, a means to an end and a sanction for political action. The vision of a Jewish millennium comes complete with such reactionary-traditionalist hallmarks as: the restoration of the Kingdom of Israel in its biblical borders; state enforcement of Jewish law (*halacha*); and reconstruction of the Temple in Jerusalem. Insofar as the process of redemption is believed to be already underway, the believers' sacred duty is to hasten its culmination by laying--and preserving--the foundations of Judaism's renewed Golden Age. Significantly, both successes and failures along the way are seen as evidence of progress--the former heralding gains in the redemptive process, the latter "the birth pangs of the Messiah" himself. The idea is thus immutable, self-perpetuating and irrefutable.[15] As an article of faith, it justifies action with little regard for actual consequences.

The secular nationalists within the Israeli rejectionist movement share the fundamentalists' core beliefs as to: the uniqueness of the Jewish people; the existential nature of the Arab-Israeli conflict; and the cardinal importance of the Land of Israel. Consequently, the two factions are united in terms of the basic, preservationist ends of their strategy: keeping the Land of Israel whole, settled and, thus, under full Jewish control.

The secular world view, however, is predicated less on divine commandments and more on seemingly rational considerations, derived from the political, economic and military exigencies of national survival. For example, many of the secular rejectionists view basic democratic norms in a relativist manner, questioning not so much their intrinsic value as their applicability to Israel's "unique" security situation. In their perception, the State of Israel was established with the sole purpose of providing a safe home for the Jews, and no abstract democratic principles should be allowed to supplant this over-riding *raison d'etre*.[16] Thus, albeit based on different premises and a distinct logic, the secularist approach is consistent with the fundamentalist view that insofar as democracy is not a true Jewish value, it is secondary to religious or national imperatives.[17]

The Context of Israeli Rejectionism

Nonetheless, in terms of actual behavior, the secularists tend to be more circumspect in their actions, operating primarily within the broadly defined confines of the Israeli legal system. As a general matter, few secular Israelis--regardless of political affiliation--share the reactionary-traditionalist axiom that duties to the Bible supersede duties to the State. Consequently, at least in their public discourse, the secular nationalists demonstrate a higher degree of respect for democratic norms and the rule of law than does the religious core.

The secular nationalists do not attempt to legitimize their aims or justify their actions through literal interpretation of sacred texts or the exegeses of revered rabbis. Although hardly anti-religious, they draw inspiration from contemporary role-models and heroes (e.g., *LEHI* commander, Yair Stern). Instead of quoting the Bible, they tend to invoke the epic visions of such modern nationalist poets as Uri Zvi Greenberg, or the lyrical longings for "the old Land of Israel" of Naomi Shemer's ever-popular ballads. In short, for the secularists, it is Israel's security and national grandeur-- rather than a mission from God--which guide strategy and operations.

Likewise, the secular nationalists do not share the fundamentalist belief that the Israeli polity is likely to be transformed any time soon into a theocracy, governed by strictly interpreted Torah laws. That said, few secularists openly question the ultimate desirability of restoring the ancient Golden Age of Jewish kings and prophets. This critical dissonance between the religious traditionalists and the secular preservationists might, at some point, fracture the movement's integrity. For the foreseeable future, however, the two groups' shared objectives--as well as pragmatic political imperatives--are likely to sustain their symbiotic relationship, allowing both sides to continue glossing over their core differences.[18]

The third and most extremist branch of the Israeli rejectionism evolved from Rabbi Meir Kahane's New York-based Jewish Defense League (JDL). With its leader under FBI investigation for terrorist activities, the organization was transplanted to Israel in the

1971 and recreated as *Kach* (Thus!). From the outset, its strategy focused on provoking headline-grabbing confrontations: with the Palestinians, with Christian missionaries and with the small community of Black Hebrews. Without a local support base and lacking the credibility enjoyed by well-established, home-grown organizations, however, it languished in almost total obscurity till the 1978 Camp David Accords. Then, amid the political disarray caused by Begin's "betrayal"--and with many future rejectionists too stunned to directly confront the man who had only recently been their hero--*Kach* stood out as a viable alternative to Likud's frustrating pragmatism. Yet, in the span of a decade, the outfit's reactionary-traditionalist goals and strategy would make it a nightmare to many Israelis, ultimately leading to its 1988 disqualification by the Central Elections Committee from participation in the electoral process--a decision unprecedented in Israel's history.

Unlike the essentially constructive orientation of *Gush Emunim* and the secular nationalists, whose initial focus has been on Jewish settlement of the biblical patrimony and rejuvenation of pioneering Zionism, *Kach* was and remains an insurgent movement par excellence--"a politically organized right-wing backlash."[19] In both its American and Israeli incarnations, it tends to attract bitter, insecure social misfits. Thus, it shares little of the youthful optimism, self-confidence and success radiated by the Israeli-born religious and secular nationalists. Instead, *Kach* activists--and supporters--seem to project a sense of failure and alienation: failure in the Israeli economy, failure to identify with the nation's traditional symbols of legitimacy, failure to advance constructive projects, and, consequently, alienation from society at large.

The organization's style is declaredly anti-establishment, thoroughly negative and destructive. Its exoteric and esoteric appeals are largely emotional and predicated on simplistic, catch-all solutions (e.g., "evict all the Arabs from the Land of Israel and purify the congregation to help the Messiah along."). Hence its initial popularity among the poorest, least educated, most disenfranchised--and predominantly Sepharadi--segments of the

The Context of Israeli Rejectionism 85

Israeli electorate.[20] Even after Kahane's 1984 election to the Knesset, the movement continued to suffer from inadequate political content and organization. Its local branches were successful in stimulating street demonstrations and protests--as well as in carrying out several well-publicized acts of urban terrorism--yet the movement remained totally dependent on Kahane's personal ideology, leadership, and zeal. It was very much a one-man show.

Kahane may not have gone as far as Georges Sorel or Francis Fanon in believing that violence is a moral force which sets nations and individuals free, but he shared many of their ideas. In Kahane's view, an independent Jewish state was but a partial solution to the misery of the exile. Sovereignty alone could not remedy the damage caused to the Jews' collective psyche by centuries of persecution and, ultimately, by the Holocaust. That trauma could be redressed only through concrete revenge against and reciprocal humiliation of the Gentiles. Consequently, Kahane, like Fanon, was not satisfied with peaceful national liberation. What was needed, in his view, was "a military force that astonishes the world, a fist in the face of the gentiles."[21] In fact, this ideology remains encapsulated in *Kach*'s logo: a clenched fist bursting through the Star of David. Accordingly, violence, militancy and radical action <u>are</u> the movement, in terms of both its ethos and *raison d'etre*.

Kahane's very personal perception of the Jews' historic suffering and his hostility toward the Gentiles in general and the Arabs in particular have been the dominant force in the movement's political psychology. In a sense, *Kach* has transferred the JDL's anti-Black radicalism to the Palestinians. Yet, this new racist mutation is also anchored in a fundamentalist application of ancient biblical injunctions and augmented by the militant nationalism typical of 20th-century politics.

Kach's position is that aliens in general and Palestinian in particular are inherently vicious, dangerous and ought to be expelled from the Jewish state by any means--the sooner the better. In this world-view, the Palestinian people have no *a priori* rights whatsoever. They hardly even exist--except as "dogs," "thorns in our eyes" and "a cancer which must be excised." The Palestinian problem, then, boils down to individual Arabs, who happen to live in the Land of Israel: "They must go, or remain humble and low, under strict restrictions."[22]

It should be noted that *Kach* and its offshoots are alone among the Israeli rejectionists in their advocacy of expulsion and overt dehumanization of the Arabs. However, the idea of "transfer"--a more civilized and "politically correct" version of that same general idea--does crop up periodically in mainstream rejectionist discourse.[23] Moreover, the ultra-right *Moledet* (Motherland) party ran in the 1992 elections on a platform explicitly advocating "transfer." It won 3 Knesset seats--one more than it had in 1988, carrying over 44,000 of the 2.65 million votes.[24]

Kach's unvarnished racism is coupled with and reinforced by an overtly anti-democratic posture. Like many religious traditionalists, Kahane saw democracy as both alien and irrelevant to Judaism. Yet, his--and his followers'--repeated, vitriolic attacks on the norms, politics and culture of democracy in general, and Israeli democracy and duly elected leaders in particular, set him apart from most indigenous rejectionists. The vilification of democracy, coupled with espousal of classical fascist principles-- such as the legitimization and use of violence; a virtual cult of personality associated with the Leader; racism, xenophobia and social Darwinism; and reliance on propaganda and terror as political tools--make *Kach* as textbook case of a neo-fascist political movement.[25] In terms of our framework, *Kach* and the myriad splinter groups it has spawned constitute a reactionary-traditionalist insurgency, with a military focus strategy, espousing terrorism as the key means of warfare.

Whatever social, cultural, or psychological explanation might be given to Kahane's personality, it is clear that *Kach* was created specifically to fulfill his ideas. His 1990 death in midtown Manhattan, at the hands of a Muslim assassin, dealt a huge blow to the movement.[26] However, the evil seed has been planted. The tenor--if not the nature--of Israel's political discourse has been changed by *Kach*, perhaps for ever.

While *Kach* can be "credited" with importing political violence into post-independence Israel, the organization did not establish a monopoly on direct action and terrorism. Others were quick to follow. And, as the next chapter will demonstrate, Kahane was much more successful in instilling the spirit of Kahanism in Israel's political culture than in securing the long-term viability and cohesion of his own organization. Thus, ironically, the New York Rabbi's often-repeated assertion that "I'm only saying what you're thinking" has proven to be much closer to the mark than most progressive Israelis were ready to believe at the time.

It is important to note that many of the hundreds of thousands of Israeli citizens who share the rejectionists' basic ideas remain blissfully unaware of the fundamentalist, anti-democratic doctrines of *Gush Emunim* or the reactionary principles espoused by *Kach*'s offshoots. Even fewer follow their religious practices. Yet, they support their broadly stated preservationist objectives, because they feel unsafe in a small Israel, are deeply suspicious of the Arabs and mistrust both the pragmatism and complex liberalism that underpin Labor's policy agenda. Consequently, Israeli rejectionism continues to thrive on the broad popular appeal of its esoteric and exoteric messages--with their unique blend of chauvinism, militarism, ethnocentricity, egalitarian demagoguery, and Jewish traditions--coupled with a minimal recognition of its true nature among the uninitiated. This, in turn, lends a decidedly conspiratorial cast to its strategy, wherein only a small vanguard has access to and grasp of the movement's real objectives.

There are, of course, good reasons why Israeli rejectionism has not been well understood outside its own circles. First, there is no single book or coherent body of literature to provide a systematic presentation of its goals, strategies and preferred forms of warfare. Indeed, as we shall demonstrate, the movement's leaders have engaged in at least a measure of deliberate obfuscation--if not outright deception--with the apparent aim of facilitating internal cohesion and sustaining a broad base of popular support. Second, the very essence of the reactionary-traditionalist ideology--with its eschatological thrust and focus on Jewish uniqueness--discourages explication to non-believers. Third, there has been a natural reluctance on the part of both Israeli and American intellectuals to call attention to the rejectionists' true nature, lest they provide ammunition to Israel's enemies and, thereby, fuel anti-Semitism.[27]

The storm of revulsion and outrage that followed Rabin's murder has already lifted some of the many veils covering the rejectionists' agenda. Yet, as long as public scrutiny remains focused on the despicable actions of individual conspirators--or, conversely, as long as blame is diluted through blanket indictments of entire social strata--the sober analysis of the rejectionist menace that must precede an effective counter-strategy is unlikely to emerge.

Any analysis of the forms of warfare pursued by the Israeli rejectionists is, by necessity, a study in contrasts. In a sense, the very term "warfare" has been--thus far--a misnomer, with few within the rejectionist camp overtly advocating an armed struggle and even fewer actually engaging in organized violence against either an external opponent or the incumbent government. As we shall demonstrate, however, Israeli rejectionism has been--well before Rabin's November 4, 1995 assassination--in the midst of a fundamental shift: away from primarily political activity and towards an ever more pronounced military focus strategy.

Most Israeli rejectionists do not perceive themselves as being at war--as distinct from being under siege and compelled to defend themselves. In this sense, their views are consistent with the self-perception typical of the vast majority of Israeli citizens. Consequently, rejectionist activists and spokesmen tend to describe the violence that does occur as isolated incidents, motivated by legitimate self-defense, or as sporadic reactions to "unbearable" provocations on the part of well-meaning, if misguided, individuals. Direct action thus becomes legitimized as a last resort, with the movement as a whole gaining plausible deniability, to wit: "An abnormal government created an abnormal situation in which, unfortunately, some people behave abnormally."[28] In a similar vein, speaking immediately after Rabin's murder, right-wing leaders sought to cast the blame on a "lone, deranged assassin," denying any complicity in Israel's first post-independence politicide.[29]

Yet, this public posturing has long been belied by the all too memorable images of gun-totting settlers, firing indiscriminately into crowds of stone-throwing Palestinians.[30] Similarly, the rejectionists' self-righteousness contrasts sharply with the verbal venom they have spewed at Israel's elected leaders, or at IDF soldiers and policemen who sought to prevent yet another anti-Arab rampage. The half-hearted retractions that often followed such confrontations did little to dispel the impression that Israel might be inching toward an internal war. To illustrate the point, it is worthwhile to quote at some length the "apology", published on July 15, 1994 in the settlers' influential paper *Nekuda* in the wake of particularly vitriolic confrontation with the IDF:

> With all the pain (and it is great) that we feel about what is happening around us, we absolutely must not lose our senses and curse people in uniform, even if they are carrying out a totally mistaken policy dictated to them by a wicked government. People who shout 'traitor' and 'Nazi' at IDF and police officers have apparently lost all sense of proportion and judgment. Beyond that, they are bringing about irreparable damage to the cause for which they are demonstrating and which they want to

save. Even though the organizers are not responsible for them and their shouts, or the destruction that some of them caused...the leaders must identify those that cannot control themselves and remove them from our protest activities and demonstrations.[31]

By the same token, the protestations of "self-defense" and "last resort" have long rung hollow against the backdrop of attempts to seize control of the Temple Mount--which led, in October 1990, to a bloody clash in which 21 Palestinians died and hundreds of Jewish worshipers at the Wailing Wall came under a barrage of stones--or the escapades of the so-called Jewish Underground, uncovered in 1984 and indicted for terrorist attacks on West Bank mayors, Islamic institutions and public transportation. Similarly, calls to assassinate Prime Minister Rabin as "a tyrant and a traitor," published in a leaflet signed by the avowedly terrorist group *Herev David* (The Sword of David) 14 months before the shots were actually fired, have long mocked the rejectionists' self-portrayal as law-abiding, loyal citizens, motivated by a genuine concern for their nation's well-being.[32]

These contradictory images and postures are, nonetheless, all real. Together, they add up to a complex, multifaceted picture of a unique, dynamic and still evolving phenomenon. In a sense, the contradictions reflect the inherent diversity of Israeli rejectionism, divided, as it is, between zealots and pragmatists, between religious fundamentalists and secular preservationists--with *Kach* offshoots' reactionary-traditionalism marking its most extremist fringe.

Concurrently, the movement's multi-dimensional nature mirrors the coupling of strategic rigidity with tactical flexibility characteristic of Israeli rejectionism. The resultant dissonance between a totalist ideology--with its apocalyptic visions, militant chauvinism, and religious zealotry--on the one hand, and the many examples of genuine pragmatism, political savvy and outright opportunism, on the other hand, is confusing at first glance. The point to bear in mind, however, is quite simple: In the rejectionists' world-view, the end justifies the means. The movement's leaders and activists are totally committed to the over-arching objective of "possessing" the entire Land of Israel. Yet, to facilitate the attainment of this goal, they have been ready to maneuver in many directions, employing a variety of tactics: legal, quasi-legal and illegal.

As the analysis that follows will demonstrate, the rejectionists' activities evolved along three distinct--but, often, intersecting--tracks: lobbying and outreach; settlement; and direct action, vigilantism and terrorism. Within this context, the resort to politicide is an ugly, grotesque, yet, unfortunately, natural mutation of an absolute commitment to sacred goals.

Lobbying and Outreach: The *modus operandi* adopted by any organization reflects the political environment within which it functions. Insofar as the Israeli rejectionists operate within the framework of a vibrant--if often fractious--democracy, they enjoy all the civil rights and freedoms accorded to other citizens. Thus, they can avail themselves of multiple channels of access to decision-makers and to the public at large. They, like anyone in a democracy, can get their message across through the media, through educational or political outreach, through lobbying and grass-roots organization, or through civic disobedience, protests and demonstrations. Given the relative ease with which any Israeli interest group can organize and finance a political campaign to compete for the popular vote, one would expect the rejectionists to center their activity in the parliament--rather than in the streets, or outside the parameters of the law.

Indeed, over the years, the rejectionists have evolved a most effective lobbying system, targeted at both the administrative/operational and top political echelons of the Israeli government. Their lobby was instrumental in securing budgets, gaining timely and accurate information and, thus, in influencing key decisions.[33] Following Likud's victory in the 1977 elections, the rejectionists became an integral part of the ruling coalition, gaining unprecedented access to and influence over the Begin government. By the time Shamir succeeded Begin in 1986, the rejectionists' ability to set the national agenda, influence legislation and shape decision-making had increased exponentially.

While initially small, young and relatively poor--and, thus,

The Context of Israeli Rejectionism

hardly a match for the established political parties--the movement drew its strength from the exceptional determination of its members, its sophisticated penetration of key political institutions and the strategic location of its constituency. It also benefited from the fact that Israeli coalition governments tend to be deeply divided in peacetime, making it easy for outsiders to manipulate ambitious cabinet members and, through them, the government as a whole. In such an environment, a dedicated cadre--with an appealing message, a sense of timing and political savvy--could and often did work miracles, capitalizing on a culture where "bending the rules for a good cause" has always been a common practice.

In the 1970's, the rejectionists exploited the political weaknesses and internal rivalries of two Labor governments to expand their foothold in the occupied territories. Following Labor's 1977 electoral defeat, they capitalized on Begin's perceived need for legitimacy to cast the settlers as Likud's Zionist vanguard--a role traditionally played by Labor's *kibbutz* movement. The ensuing symbiosis could not but enhance the rejectionists' ability to impose their territorial agenda on the incumbent authorities. In 1984, an official parliamentary caucus was set up to represent settlers' interests to the Israeli legislature. Chaired by a Likud Knesset member and run from the faction's central party offices, by 1987 the caucus commanded the votes of some fifty parliamentarians (out of a total of 120). Henceforth, the rejectionists could approach the government with parochial demands based on power politics, rather than ideological appeal.[34]

Paradoxically, having penetrated the Likud establishment, the rejectionists kept outflanking it on the right, maneuvering it into increasingly intransigent positions and, thus, eventually, contributing to its 1992 downfall. Specifically, their single-minded obsession with colonization of the West Bank pushed the Shamir government onto a collision course with the Bush Administration, undermining, in the process, Israel's international standing, its economic well-being and its ability to absorb the influx of immigrants from the former Soviet Union. The inevitable outcome was a growing public disenchantment with right-wing postures, culminating in a defeat of the pro-settlement government and Labor's return to power.

The rejectionists' cultural and educational outreach was equally well-coordinated and skillfully executed--albeit without the self-defeating consequences incurred in the political arena. The many excellent writers and publicists associated with the movement were particularly instrumental in creating and sustaining a positive public image. Countless op-ed pieces, songs, poems, feature films, and journal articles portrayed control over Greater Israel as both a birth right and a civic duty. Throughout, the publicity blitz underscored such widely attractive messages as patriotism, valor, national grandeur, and revival of ancient glories and traditions, while successfully playing down the more divisive, fundamentalist-chauvinist themes.

The popular appeal was reinforced by slick pamphlets and advertisements, extolling the virtues of life in the territories in both lofty Zionist terms--with the settlers cast in the role of latter-day pioneers, reclaiming the ancestral land--as well as an opportunity to fulfil the more mundane aspirations, shared by most Israelis: a house with a garden, good schools, clean air, and a sense of community. Clearly, the irony inherent in this fusion of Zionist egalitarianism with outright materialism was lost on the thousands of secular Israelis who flocked to the territories in search of a better life, at low cost and within easy commuting distance from Tel Aviv or Jerusalem.

Yet, in a society where traditional symbols remain important--and where conspicuous consumption is still frowned upon--the dual message was important. It bestowed legitimacy on and accorded special status to all settlers, regardless of their actual motivation. Personal choices could thus be justified in altruistic, patriotic terms. The predictable consequence was that society at large--through the nation's elected officials--became responsible for the settlers' security and well-being: After all, they were there for the greater good.

Even such innocuous activities as nature hikes and volks marches were exploited for propaganda purposes. Settlers often

The Context of Israeli Rejectionism

acted as guides for military units, youth groups and ordinary citizens on the ever-popular outings, skillfully combining love of land and nature with the more subtle message of ownership. The target audience reached by that message was significantly expanded through such tactics as: hosting soldiers and civilians--as well as Jewish tourists--in the settlements; volunteering speakers for high schools, community centers and military educational institutions; organizing cultural or social get-togethers with troops deployed in the territories; and opening archeological excavations, adult education classes and nature centers to attract both visitors and potential future settlers. These and countless other, similarly innocent activities fostered increasingly stronger bonds between the rejectionists and mainstream society, effectively erasing the divide separating Israel proper from the occupied territories.

Perhaps the clearest indication of how successful these outreach efforts have been is the fact that the very terms "occupied territories" and "Green Line" gradually disappeared from the Israeli lexicon. In their stead, the biblical, value-laden words *Yehuda* and *Shomron* (Judea and Samaria) became a part of everyday language, from media coverage, to school textbooks and personal conversations. The dictum attributed to Stalin that "he who controls the dictionaries, controls history" is quite relevant in this context. Language not only reflects values and attitudes, it shapes them-- often for the long term.

It is important to emphasize that the above-described lobbying and outreach campaign did not evolve willy-nilly. Rather, it proceeded according to a comprehensive, systematic action program developed as early as July 1982. It involved not only a massive, well-targeted propaganda effort, but also such spurious political activities as:

- Clogging the legal system, particularly the Supreme Court, with "dozens of appeals, filed repeatedly," so as "to shake the system which presently operates undisturbed against us;"
- "Demanding civil and criminal legal action for slander for each and every smear publication," be it Palestinian or Israeli;

- Flooding the media with letters to the editor and complaints to managers of broadcasting corporations, so as to "force a more balanced and fair" representation of the rejectionist point of view.[35]

Theoretically, all the actions delineated above are legitimate venues for expressing dissent within the context of a pluralistic political system. However, their actual objectives--and consequences--have been quite insidious. For one, they kept the rejectionists' agenda at the center of public attention, while consistently reinforcing and expanding the invisible network of sympathizers without whom the lobbying effort could not succeed. For another, by effectively making a mockery of the Israeli legal system, the rejectionists could create and sustain an atmosphere within which their specious operations could flourish with little effective opposition.

Settlement: While fully exploiting the rights and freedoms of the Israeli democracy to mobilize popular support, the rejectionist movement engaged in extra-legal actions from its very inception. Indeed, the skillful combination of highly effective political organization with attention-getting illegal operations quickly became the movement's hallmark, forcing the authorities into a reactive mode.

Veteran members of *Gush Emunim* began creating *fait accompli* on the ground long before they formed the movement and became its leaders. The tactic was used in early forays into the West Bank to establish what can only be termed squatters' colonies. It proceeded along four distinct stages, planned and executed with military precision:

1. The surprise establishment of a temporary presence, usually overnight, with the ostensible purpose of worship at some sacred site;

2. An uncompromising, public refusal to vacate the area, coupled with equally well-publicized declaration of interest in "constructive" solutions and alleviation of "unnecessary" tensions with either or both the IDF and the local population;

The Context of Israeli Rejectionism 95

3. With the authorities reluctant to use force against fellow-citizens, a compromise agreement is reached whereby a small yeshiva (religious seminary) is established at the controversial site, and/or the squatters are allowed to stay at a nearby military installation;

4. Finally, a few months or even years later and usually with little fanfare, a permanent settlement is established on the site of the original initiative.[36]

The pattern was set in Hebron, in 1968, and remained basically unchanged until the 1977 election of a pro-settlement government obviated the need for illegal colonization. It was resurrected in 1994, with the express objective of forcing the new government to renege on its deal with the PLO. As a result, despite Labor's officially declared policy of freezing construction in the occupied territories, hundreds of new houses and miles of roads were built throughout the West Bank. Most of this construction was private--i.e., it was carried out without public funds--"but with the approval of the local authorities and local government officials."[37]

Additional activities designed to circumvent the Labor government's territorial policy included: (1) "Squatting organized by local councils, which assist occupancy of houses without the approval of the Housing Ministry;" (2) "Massive sales" of empty apartments; and (3) Extensive--as well as expensive--infrastructure work in supposedly frozen neighborhoods, to include roads, electricity, water and sewage networks. According to a study commissioned by Dedi Zucker, a liberal Knesset member, "by the time this private construction is completed, the settlers' population will have increased by 3,000 to 4,000 people," making the government's decision to freeze construction in the settlements a worthless piece of paper."[38] As of this writing, residential construction is proceeding apace--spurred, in large measure, by Peres' last-ditch effort to appease the settlers on the eve of the May 1996 elections--with a significant acceleration likely as Likud begins to repay campaign debts to its supporters.[39]

Direct Action, Vigilantism and Terrorism: Undoubtedly,

these are the most controversial--and internally divisive--activities pursued by the Israeli rejectionists. As indicated above, until 1993, the <u>overt</u> advocacy of organized violence was largely limited to the far-right fringe associated with *Kach* and its offshoots, with the mainstream adhering to a "see no evil, hear no evil" attitude. This posture reflected a complex set of religious and cultural imperatives, most notably: the biblical injunction against the shedding of blood; the Israeli self perception as a victim--rather than actual, or even potential, perpetrator--of terrorism; and the strict taboo placed on armed factionalism and fratricide after the War of Independence.

It is these imperatives and perceptions that account for the genuine surprise with which most Israeli citizens greeted the 1984 discovery and subsequent indictment of the so-called "Jewish Underground," which intended to blow up the Dome of the Rock in Jerusalem and was held responsible for car bombings that killed or maimed several West Bank mayors. That same perplexity was reflected, ten years later, in sworn testimony by Major General Danny Yatom, acting Commander in Chief, Central Command, delivered to the Commission of Inquiry convened after the February 1994 Hebron massacre:

> The IDF had not prepared for the possibility of Jewish terror because past experience had not led anyone to believe this was a problem....Hundreds of attacks by Arabs against Jews--that's the history of the past few years. I look at the overall picture of Arab attacks against Jews and Jewish attacks against Arabs, and on the one side there are hundreds, while on the other, a few isolated incidents....A crazy act like this isn't something we expected in light of our accumulated experience....There have been no intelligence warnings of planned attacks by Jews, only of planned attacks by Arabs.[40]

Assuming that General Yatom was not being disingenuous, his testimony seems to reflect the very same bias which led other, equally astute observers to miss--or misjudge--the implications of rather obvious trends. These trends--some deeply ingrained, some new, most still evolving--combined to subvert the traditional

The Context of Israeli Rejectionism

inhibitions and create a climate in which violence was increasingly likely, if not inevitable. Key among these interlinked factors are:

1. **The primacy accorded in Israeli culture to strength and resolve.** What's at issue here is not mere *machismo*, but, rather, a deep-seated reaction to centuries of persecution and a collective determination not to be, ever again, "led like sheep to slaughter." This attitude is inculcated early on in every Israeli child and fostered through the entire education and socialization process. To wit, in Hebrew slang, the term for "wimp" is "soap"--the insult evocative of the fate of many Jews during the Holocaust. That same posture is reflected in the primacy IDF doctrine has always placed on quick and effective retaliation--with the punishment, designed to reestablish deterrence, often disproportionate to the actual provocation.

The determination to stand up for oneself and "teach the bullies a lesson" is quickly adopted--sometimes in extreme form--by new immigrants, especially those who come from societies where Jews are not immediately associated with either a martial spirit or the profession of arms, as well as by many Orthodox Jews, who otherwise shun military service. This attitude accounts for much of the deliberately provocative, "in your face" behavior of the settlers, as well as for the ensuing cycle of attacks and counter-attacks that swept the territories before, during and after the *Intifada*.

2. **The general atmosphere prevalent in the occupied territories**, wherein basic laws, norms and standards of conduct, generally observed inside the Green Line, did not seem to apply. The settlers' overt defiance and the government's unwillingness or inability to clamp down on violators eroded still further what little respect there was for established authority. The inevitable consequence was a "Wild West" milieu, in which every Israeli carried a weapon and where taking the law into one's hands was a daily occurrence. The absolute advantage--by any measure of power save relative numbers--enjoyed by the occupiers could not but lead to abuse and reciprocal resentment.

The settlers' self-image as latter-day Zionist pioneers was

equally instrumental in this regard. For, it revived the pre-statehood days, where outwitting and subverting the British Mandatory authorities was considered a legitimate strategy in the struggle for independence. The fundamental difference--largely ignored by the rejectionists--was that, this time, it was the credibility and legitimacy of their own, democratically elected government that was being undercut on a daily basis. The inevitable consequence was a general increase in lawlessness and criminal activity, both in the territories and inside the Green Line, and a concomitant weakening of central authority.[41] This, in turn, created and perpetuated a vicious circle, wherein the settlers reacted violently to their self-generated view that the government was unable or unwilling to deal effectively with the *Intifada* and that, therefore, they had no choice but to use force to provide for their own defense.

3. **The overall polarization and brutalization of Israeli society**, reflecting deepening political, ethnic, religious, and social cleavages, as well as the frustrations born of the 1982 Lebanon fiasco and, subsequently, the *Intifada*. As a result, the whole tenor of national discourse--never entirely "civilized" by Western standards--started to change for the worse in the 1980's, leading many intellectuals to voice concern with the "Levantinization" of Israel. Noisy street demonstrations, heckling of elected officials and seditious statements in both the media and the Knesset became a regular occurrence, with political opponents accusing each other of high treason.

Extremist rhetoric led to physical violence and, ultimately, to fratricide: During a February 10, 1983 confrontation between Peace Now and a street mob, incited by *Gush Emunim* activists, a grenade was thrown, killing one Peace Now demonstrator and severely wounding several others. Like the bloody clash between settlers and IDF troops during the evacuation of the Sinai settlement of Yamit, the fratricide marked the crossing of a Rubicon: The long-standing taboo on politically-motivated murder was shattered. The President of Israel--the largely ceremonial, but highly respected symbol of national unity--had to intercede to prevent further bloodshed. But, the damage had already been done: The brutality prevalent in the occupied territories had been transferred to Israel proper. The cycle of violence thus became deeply embedded and self-perpetuating. In this sense, the shots that felled Prime Minister Rabin were but a dramatic flare-up of a long smoldering fire.

4. **The religious rejectionists' core beliefs invalidate the bonds of civic law**, effectively sanctioning violence to promote their cause. With the believers quite literally seeing themselves as being on a mission from God, answerable only to the Almighty, there is little room for restraint or respect for legal niceties. In this view, the rule of law is irrelevant: Contemporary Israel is an "illegitimate state of sin" and, thus, "merely a challenge that we must confront." Therefore, instead of "succumbing to the temptation of the foreign logic of democracy," Jews are duty-bound to follow their own "code of zealotry," which compels them to "reject and circumvent any decree, obstacle, or impediment to Israel's redemption."[42]

It is this mind-set that produced the spectacularly provocative actions designed to change the *status quo* on the Temple Mount, to include at least three abortive attempts to blow up the Al Aksa Mosque, as well as numerous, albeit less dramatic efforts to wrest control of the site from the Muslim religious authorities.[43] Ultimately, the gospel of violence led to the Hebron massacre[44] and, within a two-year span, to Rabin's death. Against this background, it should have been difficult to discount the extremists' threats to assassinate both Israeli and Palestinian leaders. Indeed, leaflets stating that Prime Minister Rabin "is a traitor who deserves to die," just like "the arch-murderer Arafat," have been circulated throughout the West Bank since at least 1994, cropping up also during political demonstrations in Israel proper.[45] Nonetheless, when the three shots that changed Israel were fired on November 4, 1995, the universal reaction has been nothing but shock and surprise.

5. **The legitimization of violence on religious grounds**, with some rejectionist rabbis effectively providing an *a priori* exculpation to future terrorists. A ruling issued in 1989 by Rabbi

Ginsburg, head of the Joseph's Tomb Yeshiva in Nablus, is a case in point: Responding to reports of his students' rampages in neighboring villages, the Rabbi averred that "there's blood and there's blood. Jewish blood is not the same as Arab blood. He who is not a Jew, and throws stones, or threatens Jews, comes under the [biblical injunction] 'you should kill him first'."[46]

Not surprisingly, that same Rabbi praised Baruch Goldstein's Hebron massacre as "the sanctification of God's name," reiterating the position that "God favors Jewish blood, which is therefore redder and the Jew's life more important than a gentile's, even if said gentile does not mean the Jew any harm."[47] In a similar vein, Rabbi Israel Ariel, a combat veteran and former chaplain of the Northern Command, decreed that "the commandment 'thou shall not kill' does not apply to Arabs, only to Jews." Moreover, "when Jews kill Jews, they should be tried in courts on earth, but anyone who murders an Arab will only be tried in heaven."[48] Rabbi Ido Elba went even further, "ruling" that "it is a *mitzvah* [a religious duty and a good deed] to kill all gentiles, even women and children," because, even when they pose no direct danger, "they help the enemy continue the war."[49] Rabbi Elba was subsequently indicted for participating in a new "Jewish Underground."

Reliable statistics establishing the patterns of Jewish terrorism are hard to come by. According to Lustick, between 1980 and 1984--that is, before the *Intifada*--there were 380 assaults against Palestinians, in which 23 individuals were killed, 191 injured and 38 abducted. Hundreds of attacks were directed at property--cars, homes and shops.[50] The April 1984 arrest of 25 members of the so-called Jewish Underground did not dampen the cycle of violence. Prime Minister Rabin reported 69 Palestinians killed by Israeli civilians (presumably, settlers) during the six-and-a-half years of the *Intifada*--this in addition to 99 killed in "unknown circumstances," 1045 killed by the IDF and security services, and 922 killed by their own people--for a total of 2156. Some 2500 were wounded. The comparative figures for Israel are 219 killed, 151 of them civilians.[51] But, the numbers do not even begin to tell the full story. Glenn Frankel's impassioned prose comes closer to

The Context of Israeli Rejectionism 101

expressing the raw emotions and the stakes involved:

> A sizable core of hotheads and ideologues exploited the Intifada as an excuse to wage vigilante war on their Arab neighbors and political war on their own government....The original two-way game between soldiers and youths, brutal as it was, had a certain symmetry and a set of rules. But once the settlers were drawn in, the new conflict was more volatile and vicious. A struggle between the occupier and the occupied rapidly disintegrated into something rawer and more atavistic-a blood feud between two entangled communities. Decent men did merciless deeds. The young died on both sides. And both groups, Arabs and Jews, inevitably turned on themselves, focusing on purported traitors and collaborators within their own fractious ranks, identifying the hideously distorted face of the enemy in their own cracked mirrors....There were souls on fire in the West Bank.[52]

That such primordial passions--once unleashed and stoked with ever more inflammatory invective should traverse the invisible Green Line was only natural. That religious leaders who sanctioned murder of innocent Arab civilians would proceed to cast curses upon and offer prayers for the death of elected officials was a similarly linear evolution. Against this backdrop, the slain Prime Minister's words reverberate as a prophecy: "There is a great deal of anger and incitement among the extremist fringe....Thousands, or, perhaps, tens of thousands on the right-wing hold radical views which could lead less sophisticated people to murder."[53]

Implications for the Future: What this book is all about is two communities locked in a seemingly unbreakable cycle of violence, wherein rejectionists, on both sides, feed off and, thereby, reinforce each other's visceral hatreds. The current tenor of discourse on the Israeli side leaves little room for optimism as to what the future might hold. None of the above-delineated factors-- nor the overall climate--which allowed terrorism to fester has been ameliorated. If anything, the accord with the PLO, the ensuing *Hamas* terror campaign and the outcome of the May 1996 elections have stiffened the Israeli rejectionists' resolve to oppose the peace process, by force if necessary. This, in turn, could lead to a dramatic transition from episodic violence to a systematic internal war, particularly were Likud to renege on its campaign promises and follow Labor's land-for-peace course. The following evidence would support this admittedly pessimistic conclusion:

- **Contingency plans to thwart evacuation from the West Bank and Gaza have been developed.** According to Israeli press reports, the plans involve a military-style layered defense, with the inner core comprised of "hundreds of settlers" who will barricade themselves in houses, some filled with fresh cement. The roads to the settlements will be blocked with rocks, concrete and the shells of heavy vehicles. Some settlements will be "surrounded by minefields and rings of fire." The outer perimeter will include human chains around settlements "to physically block the movement of soldiers and bulldozers. In order to make it more difficult for the Army, crowds will be instructed to invade neighboring Arab houses and barricade themselves inside." Call-up lists have been prepared by regional headquarters to recruit, mobilize and deploy thousands of activists from around the country. "They will hole up in houses, chain themselves and physically prevent the evacuation. Some will commit suicide."[54]

- **Settlers are stockpiling additional weapons and ammunition**, in preparation for the next phase of the struggle against the peace process.[55] Whether these weapons will be turned on the Palestinians, or the withdrawing IDF--or both--remains to be seen. Either way, the potential for violence is high, particularly if the settlers make good on their threat to form "armed militias."[56] The settlers are already well armed and trained, having been made, since 1979, an integral component of the IDF's territorial defense system. Each settlement has a full-time resident security officer, with ready access to arms, equipment and communications gear. Many adults have served in the military and are, therefore, well trained in basic offensive and defensive operations. Thus, the issue is not settlers' capability, but their intent and resolve to push Israel into an internal war.

- **The likelihood of clashes with the IDF is similarly high.** While most rejectionists leaders continue to state for the record that

The Context of Israeli Rejectionism

"shooting at soldiers is forbidden under any circumstances,"[57] it is difficult to see how fratricide could be avoided. For one, some extremist settlers have already begun openly to incite a "civil revolt now," suggesting that IDF soldiers who carry out "the illegitimate government's illegal orders" are "criminals, to be regarded as violent hooligans and cossacks."[58] Furthermore, as indicated above, the Rubicon has been crossed in Yamit and in countless shouting matches and fist fights between enraged settlers and IDF troops. In this context, the following statement by a settlement Council Chairman is worth quoting:

> This government is in for a surprise. Yamit will not fall again. This time soldiers will have to confront thousands of people who will physically prevent any evacuation....There are people who sleep with their guns under the mattress and are prepared to go much farther than us. It really scares me. I'm afraid that some people's patriotism may know no limit.[59]

- There is little sympathy--but plenty of resentment--for the settlers among IDF troops serving in the territories. This can only increase the potential for violence. According to an August 1994 survey conducted by the General Staff's Behavioral Sciences Unit, "one of the preeminent factors contributing to low morale are the confrontations with the settlers." Commenting on the poll results, a senior General Staff officer explained that:

> There are two factors which converge to produce this reality. There is the natural fatigue that erodes soldiers' morale and diminishes motivation, resulting from carrying out such demeaning duties as escorting settlers' children to drama classes. Soldiers feel that this is not what being a paratrooper or a tank commander is all about. Then there is a minority of extremist settlers who regularly harass, insult, and offend soldiers. They deliberately ask to be escorted to the synagogue at 3 a.m., or alert patrols knowing that nothing had happened.[60]

Thus, the climate is ripe for a serious clash--either during a scheduled withdrawal from populated areas and hand-over to the

Palestinian National Authority, or as a result of spontaneous combustion. A related danger is that IDF units could split, with some religious soldiers rallying to the settlers, while others seek to execute their mission. In this context, public appeals and religious injunctions calling on soldiers, officers and policemen to "disobey such manifestly illegal orders as the uprooting of settlements" are particularly portentous.[61]

- **The September 1994 discovery of a new "Jewish Underground"** should have been treated as a clear warning sign. In addition to several high-profile settlers, the new "Underground" was reported to include two serving IDF officers: Lieutenant Kobi Pinto, a deputy company commander in the elite Golani Infantry Brigade and Lieutenant Oren Edri, a paratrooper. The two were indicted for transferring weapons, ammunition and explosives, stolen from IDF depots, to extremist settlers and participating in several attacks against Palestinian civilians. Amazingly, instead of the expected universal condemnation--on the order of the public outcry that followed the 1984 arrest of the original Underground--this time the right-wing opposition has been much more circumspect. Indeed, according to media reports, there were "serious divisions within the Likud leadership as to how to deal with the case," with some officials more concerned with Labor's ability to garner political capital from the plot than with its actual significance and ramifications.[62]

The very participation of active duty personnel in illegal, subversive activities is a cause for serious concern. First, it suggests that the rejectionists have evolved a complex network of active and passive support, spanning the Green Line and involving such Israeli elites as the armed forces. Second, it reveals a worrisome breakdown in military order and discipline. Third, it demonstrates the sophisticated penetration of the IDF officer corps by religious fundamentalists, who, until recently, tended to avoid military service altogether--a trend we will analyze in greater detail in the next chapter. Last, it reflects the widening gap between, on the one hand, the democratically elected government of Israel--be it Labor or Likud--with its stated commitment to the peace process and, on the other hand, militant rejectionists bent on its destruction. This, in turn, raises the specter of an internal war.

To sum up: Contemporary Israeli rejectionism is a curious amalgam of preservationists, traditionalists and reactionary-traditionalists, united in their unequivocal opposition to peace based on territorial compromise. While the small--but growing--reactionary-traditionalist fringe rejects democracy as both a cherished value and a desirable political regime, the preservationist majority seeks a change to specific policies rather than to the political system *per se*. Consequently, until the May 1996 elections, their efforts were focused on the incumbent authorities and aimed, in the immediate term, at torpedoing the Labor coalition's political agenda. The longer-term goal was to topple the incumbent leadership, thus clearing the way for a government more congenial to the rejectionist platform. How might these objectives change, now that Likud is back in power, would depend, in large measure, on the latter's policies toward the peace process in general and the occupied territories in particular. Indeed, given the level of expectations associated with Likud's return--and the universal perception that Netanyahu owes his victory to the religious right--the potential for confrontation would increase exponentially should their hopes and prayers go unfulfilled.

When it comes to strategy, the picture is considerably more complex. First, in contrast to the movement's explicitly stated--if not always consistent--goals, the strategy by which these aims might be attained is yet to be fully articulated. In a sense, this failing is understandable. For, with a sympathetic government in power between 1977-1992, there was little need to evolve anything more comprehensive than a sustained--and highly effective--political lobbying-*cum*-organization effort. The right-wing's 1992 electoral defeat and the ensuing progress in the peace process galvanized the movement, providing it with a tangible target to attack. Moreover, insofar as rejectionism is, by its very nature, focused on a negative aim--i.e., refusal to accept the polity, the political system, the authorities, and/or their policies--rejection of the land-for-peace agenda effectively became both the movement's *raison d'etre* and key organizing principle. With Likud back in power as a result of the 1996 vote, rejectionist strategy could evolve in one of two directions: return to the earlier lobbying/organizational mode, with the goal of preserving and expanding Israel's hold on the territories or--should the new government follow its predecessor's peace policies--resumption of subversive actions aimed at preventing any further territorial compromises.

Thus, while a full-fledged strategy remains elusive, emerging trends point toward a military focus approach, with a growing emphasis on violence against both Palestinian and Israeli opponents, and an increasing reliance on terrorism. Indeed, as the analysis that follows will demonstrate, the militant drift--away from episodic, low-level violence and toward a systematic internal war-- is a key source of disunity, threatening to fragment the rejectionists over the longer term. In the interim, however, the radicalization poses a clear and present danger to both the rule of law in Israel and regional stability overall.

Notes

1. Myron J. Aronoff, *Israeli Visions and Divisions* (New Brunswick: Transaction Publishers, 1989, pp. xviii-xix. There is a voluminous body of both English and Hebrew language literature delineating the origins and historic evolution of Zionism. Among the best are: Shlomo Avineri, *Varieties of Zionist Thought* (Tel Aviv: Am Oved, 1980 - Hebrew), Shlomo Avineri, *The Making of Modern Zionism* (London: Weidenfeld and Nicholson, 1981), Harold Fish, *The Zionist Revolution: A New Perspective* (Boston, MA: Little, Brown and Co., 1968), Dan Horowitz and Moshe Lissak, *The Origins of the Israeli Polity* (Chicago, IL: University of Chicago Press, 1978), and Howard M. Sachar, *The History of Israel: From the Rise of Zionism to Our Time* (New York, NY: Knopf, 1976). For a more personal perspective, see David Ben Gurion, *Rebirth and Destiny of Israel* (New York: The Philosophical Library, 1954), David Ben Gurion, *Israel: Years of Challenge* (New York, NY: Holt Rhinehart and Winston, 1963), Abba Eban, *My People: The Story of the Jews* (New York, NY: Behram House Inc. and Random House, 1968) Golda Meir, *My Life* (New York, NY: Putnam, 1975) and Menachem Begin, *The Revolt* (New York, NY: Dell Publishing Company, 1977).

The Context of Israeli Rejectionism 107

2. Bernard Reich and Gershon R. Kieval, Editors, *Israeli Politics in the 1990's* (New York, NY: Greenwood Press, 1991) pp. 72-73. See also, Yehoshafat Harkabi, *Israel's Fateful Hour* (New York, NY: Harper and Row Publishers, 1988), pp. 70-83. For a superb overview of religious, ethnic and social cleavages in Israel see, Dan Horowitz and Moshe Lissak, *Trouble in Utopia: The Overburdened Polity of Israel* (Albany, NY: State University of New York Press, 1989).

3. Aronoff, pp. 1-17, provides an excellent summary of Labor's dominance before and after 1948. See also, Eban, pp. 308-340 and 430-466.

4. Shlomo Avineri, *Varieties of Zionist Thought* (Tel Aviv: Am Oved, 1980), pp. 210-215. For a comprehensive depiction of revisionist ideology see also Ya'acov Shavit, *Jabotinsky and the Revisionist Movement* (London: Frank Cass and Company, Ltd., 1980).

5. Michael Bar Zohar, *Ben Gurion: A Biography* (Jerusalem: Steimatzki,1978 - Hebrew), p. 73. For a thorough review of Israel's origin's and early years of strife see, Amos Perlmutter, *Israel, The Partitioned State: A Political History Since 1900* (New York, NY: C. Scribner's Sons, 1985).

6. Glenn Frankel, *Beyond the Promised Land* (New York, NY: Simon and Schuster, 1994), pp. 115-116. See also, Menachem Begin, *The Revolt*, in particular, pp. 60-284.

7. Aronoff, pp. 22-23. See also, Bar Zohar, p. 171, Begin, pp. 189-213, and Yitzhak Shamir, *Summing Up* (Tel Aviv: Edanim Publishers, 1994 - Hebrew), pp. 25-67.

8. Avner Yaniv, *National Security and Democracy in Israel* (Boulder, CO and London: Lynne Riehner Publishers, 1993), pp. 83-87. See also, Yehuda Slutzky, *The History of the Hagana* (Tel Aviv: The Ministry of Defense, 1973 - Hebrew), particularly Volume II.

9. Ben Gurion's Knesset Speech, May 13, 1963, quoted in Bar Zohar, p. 303.

10. Quoted in Aronoff, p. 26. See also, Ehud Sprinzak, The *Ascendence of Israel's Radical Right* (Oxford: Oxford University Press, 1991), pp. 35-38. For a personal insight on this dramatic period see, Yael Dayan, *Israel Journal, June 1967* (New York, NY: Mcgraw-Hill, 1967).

11. Frankel, p. 33.

12. Keith Kyle and Joel Peters, Editors, *Whither Israel* (London: The Royal Institute of International Affairs, 1993), pp. 120-123.

13. Yehoshafat Harkabi, *Israel's Fateful Hour* (New York, NY: Harper and Row Publishers, 1998), Ehud Sprinzak, *The Ascendence of Israel Radical Right* (Oxford: Oxford University Press, 1991) and Ian S. Lustick, *For the Land and the Lord* (New York, NY: The Council on Foreign Relations, 1988) all provide superb analyses of the origins and early activities of the Israeli radical right. This chapter draws upon their ground-breaking research,as well as on the present authors' own review of original Hebrew-language texts, especially such anthologies as *Morasha* (Tradition), *Artzi* (My Land), *Eretz Nahala* (Land of Heritage), and,most notably, the settlers' key mouthpiece *Nekuda* (Point). The Israeli Internet provides another important window on the extremists' current thinking.

14. This section draws primarily on Lustick, pp. 72-90 and Sprinzak, pp. 109-124, to establish the baseline for our own research.

15. Harkabi, pp. 165-167.

16. Sprinzak, p. 293.

17. *Identity Card*, (Tehiya's Elections Platform, Jerusalem, 1988 - Hebrew).

18. Sprinzak, pp. 181-183. See also, Yossi Klein Halevi, *Memoirs of a Jewish Extremist* (Boston, MA: Little Brown and Company, 1995), for a personal account of a JDL member.

19. Sprinzak, p. 211.

20. *The Jerusalem Post*, April 11, 1986.

21. Sprinzak, pp. 219-220 and Klein Halevi, pp. 159-162.

22. Ibid., pp. 225-227. See also, Meir Kahane, *Thorns in Our Eyes* (New York, NY: Druker Publishing Company, 1980 - Hebrew), especially pp. 244-245.

23. See, for example, *Nekuda*, Number 115, November 1987, p. 16 and Yuval Ne'eman in *Yediot Ahronot*, April 14, 1984.

24. *Jerusalem Post*, July 16, 1992. *Moledet* lost one of its three seats in the 1996 elections. Still, it carried at least 50,000 votes.

25. Sprinzak, pp. 231-250. See also, Klein Halevi, pp. 180-182.

26. Ibid.

27. See Harkabi, pp. 179-182 for a candid discussion of the misgivings and moral dilemmas he has faced in writing *Israel's Fateful Hour*.

28. Settlers' Regional Council leader Tzvi Katzover, quoted in *Ha'aretz*, 15 July 1994, JPRS-NEA-94-045, 18 August 1994, p.40

29. See, for example, Likud Chairman's CNN interview, November 4, 1995, *The Jerusalem Post*, November 5, 1995 and *Israel Radio* broadcast of interviews with religious and secular-nationalist leaders, November 5, 1995, FBIS-NES-95-214-S, November 6, 1995, pp. 18-19.

30. For an excellent description of the visceral rage with which the Palestinians and the settlers confronted each other during the *Intifada*, see Frankel, pp. 91-111.

31. Printed in JPRS-NEA-94-045, August 18, 1994, p. 39.

32. *Ma'ariv*, September 21, 1994. For a similar contrition, published after Rabin's assassination see *Ma'ariv*, November 7, 1995, *The Jerusalem Post*, November 9, 1995 and *Ha'tzofe*, November 5, 1995.

33. See Sprinzak, pp. 141-149 for a detailed description of *Gush Emunim*'s lobbying efforts.

34. Sprinzak, p. 147.

35. *Nekuda*, Number 45, July 16, 1982, pp. 4-6, JPRS-82023, October 19, 1982, pp. 101-111.

36. Sprinzak pp. 139-140.

37. *Ha'aretz*, January 17, 1995.

38. Ibid.

39. *Ha'aretz*, April 5, 1995. See also, *The Washington Post*, June 26, 1995, *Ma'ariv* May 28, 1996 and Likud's *Issues Platform*, all available on Internet.

40. *The Jerusalem Post*, March 9, 1994.

41. See *Davar*, August 15, 1980, for an insightful analysis of the risks inherent in the "deterioration of state authority in the territories." See also, *Yediot Ahronot*, June 23, 1995, FBIS-NES-95-124, pp. 43-44 for an unusually candid description of the lawlessness still prevailing in the West Bank.

42. *Nekuda*, July 1994, pp. 26-29, FBIS-NES-94-165, August 25, 1994.

43. Lustick, pp. 68-69. For details on the Israeli investigation of the October 8, 1990 Temple Mount events see *Summary of the Zamir Commission Report* (Jerusalem: Government Printing Office, October 26, 1990).

44. See Aviva Shabi and Zvi Singer, "The Mentors," *Yediot Ahronot*, March 18, 1994 for a comprehensive review of Baruch Goldstein's "sources of inspiration" and spiritual "mentors."

45. *IDF Radio*, January 2, 1995, FBIS-NES-95-002, January 4, 1995, p. 56. Earlier, settlers' leader Aharon Domb sent a personal letter to Prime Minister Rabin to warn him of "plans by the extreme fringe right wing to carry out a political assassination." *Ha'aretz*, June 19, 1994.

46. Quoted in Sprinzak, p. 165.

47. *Ha'aretz*, September 4, 1994, JPRS-TOT-94-038-L, September 15, 1994, p. 32.

48. These and other, equally vile statements are quoted in *Yediot Ahronot*, March 18, 1994, FBIS-NES-94-061, March 30, 1994, pp. 36-39.

49. *Ma'ariv*, September 30, 1994, FBIS-NES-94-193, October 5, 1994, pp. 32-33.

50. Lustick, p. 86.

51. Yitzhak Rabin, Speech to the Knesset, April 18, 1994.

52. Frankel p. 92.

53. Rabin's interview with *The Jerusalem Post*, September 24, 1995.

54. *Ma'ariv*, November 16, 1994, FBIS-NES-94-223, November 18, 1994, p. 29. See also, *Ma'ariv*, September 25, 1994, FBIS-NES-94-186, September 26, 1994, p. 36 and *Israel Radio*, 8 June, 1995, FBIS-NES-95-110, June 8, 1995, pp. 39-40.

55. *Ma'ariv*, September 9, 1994, FBIS-NES-94-175, September 9, 1994, p. 38.

56. *Ha'tzofe*, December 18, 1994, FBIS-NES-94-244, December 20, 1994, p. 28 and *Israel Radio*, June 8, 1995 interview with Knesset Members Tzahi Ha'negbi and Moshe Peled, FBIS-NES-95-110, June 8, 1995, pp. 39-40.

57. *Ma'ariv*, November 16, 1994, FBIS-NES-94-223, November 18, 1994, p. 29.

58. *Ha'aretz*, August 31, 1994, FBIS-NES-94-170, September 1, 1994, p. 35. See also, *The Jerusalem Post*, April 4, 1995.

59. *Ha'aretz*, August 31, 1994.

60. *The Jerusalem Post*, August 4, 1994. Similar sentiments were expressed by a senior Israeli officer, with extensive experience in the West Bank, in informal conversations with the present authors.

61. *Nekuda*, December 1994, pp. 46-48, FBIS-NES-95-016, January 25, 1995, p. 34. See also Likud Knesset Member Uzi Landau's statement that were he a soldier, he would disobey "as manifestly illegal" any orders to evacuate settlements, *Israel Radio*, May 28, 1995, FBIS-NES-95-104, May 31, 1995, p.41. A religious edict, prohibiting soldiers from obeying orders to evacuate, was issued in July and reaffirmed in September 1995 by the "Organization of Land of Israel Rabbis" at its rally in Hebron. According to Israeli press reports, the gathering was attended by "hundreds of religious leaders, from Israel and abroad," as well as by "senior reserve officers who are active in right-wing causes." *Ha'tzofe*, September 21, 1995, FBIS-NES-95-183, September 21, 1995,

p. 42.

62. *Israel Radio,* September 24, 1994, FBIS-NES-94-186, September 26, 1994, p. 36.

CHAPTER THREE

ANALYTICAL ASSESSMENT OF ISRAELI REJECTIONISM

CHAPTER III

ANALYTICAL ASSESSMENT OF ISRAELI REJECTIONISM

Environment and Popular Support

The threads which still join our people together as one entity are beginning to unravel, if not tear. Territorial concessions--a policy many consider to be flagrantly illegal--may lead Israel to constant unrest, chaos and chronic instability, if not worse....The tendency toward division and insurrection [is] spreading all over the country....Those who feel with all their being that they are being abused and humiliated, because that which is most sacred to them is being handed over to their sworn enemy, will soon become sick and tired of a democracy that exploits its power to bring all this upon them. And when this rumbling volcano erupts, the molten lava may wash away everything in its path.

The Jerusalem Post, August 8, 1995

This is not only an assassination of the Prime Minister. This is a threat to the very foundations of democracy. These cancerous cells, consisting of thousands of people who believe that God speaks to them and orders them to kill, affect the entire political system.

Amnon Rubinstein, Israel's Education and Culture Minister, November 8, 1995

To facilitate analysis of the Israeli rejectionist movement--and to set out a persuasive case--we have included a fairly thorough characterization of the milieu within which Israeli extremism operates in our discussion of its history, goals, strategies, and forms of warfare. Similarly, we will integrate the analysis of popular support into our examination of the political environment, since, in a democracy, much of the effort to mobilize the masses takes the form of competition for the popular vote. We shall return to this point in our analysis of cohesion, so as to distinguish between the rejectionists' popular message and the platform they promulgate within their own ranks. Additionally, this chapter will highlight those unique features of Israeli society, political culture and economic conditions which will determine the future of rejectionism, and define the scope, thrust and ultimate success of efforts to marginalize its impact. The nature and implications of the ongoing Arab-Israeli and, more specifically, the Palestinian-Israeli conflict, set the backdrop for this analysis.

Of Geostrategy, Democracy, and Risk-taking: Both the Israeli and Palestinian rejectionists operate within the same physical environment--a small, open, relatively flat area, with a modern transport and communications system. While Israel proper and the occupied territories differ in terms of urbanization and population densities, neither offers the vast stretches of wilderness necessary for concealment, secure bases and large-scale guerrilla operations. As the Palestinian insurgents have learned over the years, the nature of the physical environment effectively dictates reliance on terrorism and hit-and-run guerrilla attacks as the only suitable forms of warfare.

For all practical purposes, both the Israelis and the Palestinians operate on home turf. Consequently, while control over territory defines the nature of their conflict, neither side has a clear advantage in terms of the terrain itself, or familiarity with its peculiar features. The fundamental distinction is in the relative freedom of action that the two sides enjoy. As indicated in the preceding chapter, the Israeli rejectionists function within--and, often, against--the established framework of an open, pluralistic, democratic society. Consequently, they operate with the clear advantage of civil rights and freedoms--especially in respect to movement, assembly, access to media, due process, and possession of arms--which the Palestinians do not have. Often, the Israelis can also count on leniency, if not impunity and outright support, on the part of the central authorities.[1] Thus, the personal risk and sacrifice involved in participation in insurgent activities--in terms of the price one might be expected to pay if apprehended--are highly differentiated in favor of the Israelis.

Throughout its 48 years, Israel has managed to retain its democratic nature, while successfully dealing with threats to its survival. This is no trivial matter: Israel is unique among 20th century democracies in that it has fought more wars than any other and has been in a state of national emergency for the better part of its existence. Specifically, Israel faced a war in each decade since independence: 1948, 1956, 1967, 1973, 1982, and 1991. In between, it was engaged in grinding wars of attrition, sporadic low-intensity conflicts, continuous terrorism and, since 1987, a civil rebellion, the *Intifada*. More than anything, this accounts for the war-weariness and a genuine desire for "normalization" permeating most segments of society. What is at stake, however, is the price of democracy, peace and normalcy. Herein, divisions are wide and antagonisms deeply entrenched.

The Israeli democracy is not perfect--neither in concept nor in implementation. Absent a Constitution and a clear separation of powers among the executive, the legislature and the judiciary, it has often relied on *ad-hoc* decrees, rules and regulations. This is particularly true in the occupied territories, where two distinct legal systems are in effect: one for the indigenous Palestinian population, the other for the Israeli settlers.

Each system is rooted in a different set of values, principles and norms. Essentially, the Palestinians, as residents of territories occupied through war, are under martial law, subject to the military court system. In civil matters, they are under a cumbersome--and often contradictory--code incorporating Ottoman, British, Jordanian and Israeli legislation. The settlers, in contrast, are subject to the same judicial system as are citizens residing within the Green Line. Concurrently, however, the settlers are also an extension of the military authorities administering the territories. They are provided with weapons, military training and ample opportunity to use both. Claude Klein, a professor of law at the Hebrew University of Jerusalem, compared the situation prevalent in the territories to the colonization of the American West under the protection of federal troops. In cases of conflict between settlers and the native population--be it Indian or Palestinian--the former always had the undisputed advantage and protection of the law.[2] Put even more succinctly, "there are two laws in the territories: one against the Palestinians and one for the settlers."[3]

Israel's inability to fully solve the Palestinian problem poses a long-term challenge to its democratic nature--as well as to its security. Having effectively drawn a Green Line of democracy, while permitting, since 1967, the routinization of extra-legal behavior beyond it, Israel now faces the risks inherent in fragmenting an essentially indivisible concept. Insofar as there is no such thing as selective or situational democracy, the inevitable outcome has been a progressive erosion of the very values that anchor the nation's existence and assure it of continued Western support.

The nature of the conflict Israel has been engaged in further exacerbates its basic dilemma. The strategic balance and geopolitical relations between Israel and its neighbors are perpetually asymmetric. The Arab world--heterogeneous and fractious as it is--has at its disposal infinitely greater material and human resources than Israel. Therefore, any Israeli military victory, over any combination of opponents, will forever be strategically inconclusive. Conversely, any Arab victory will be, by definition, strategic and decisive, because it would pose the threat of annihilation--to both sides, if weapons of mass destruction were to be employed. While these circumstances make the quest for a comprehensive peace all the more important, they also highlight the very real dangers inherent in ceding hard-won territorial gains.

This existential nature of the Arab-Israeli conflict accounts for the primacy Israel accords to security as both the overriding national interest and the defining aspect of its political culture. It also explains the apocalyptic, uncompromising tenor of the currently raging internal debates on the peace process. The point to bear in mind is that, in Israel, "security" is not only the ultimate rallying cry, but also the trump card in any political argument. Furthermore, security is the prism through which every issue is looked at and the touch-stone against which it is analyzed. Insofar

Analytical Assessment of Israeli Rejectionism

as all Israeli leaders--and, indeed, most citizens, regardless of political affiliation--feel personally responsible for the nation's survival, these basic realities make the risk-taking, necessary for any political settlement, all the more difficult. Concurrently, from the Israeli rejectionists' perspective, these attitudes provide the ultimate legitimization for direct action. For, in their eyes, their efforts are aimed at nothing less than national salvation, that is, at forestalling the mortal danger inherent in any change of the territorial *status quo*. Another peculiarity of the Arab-Israeli conflict is that the Palestinian minority under Israel's control is an integral part of the outer Arab majority encircling the Jewish state. The external threat--comparatively easier to cope with and prepare for--is, thus, merged with the less manageable internal peril.[4] This factor shapes attitudes towards and procedures pertaining to the treatment of the Palestinians, both those living in the occupied territories and those residing in Israel proper.

The complexity of the Israeli case is rendered even more vexing by the fact that the territories it is holding--having conquered them in a defensive war--are immediately adjacent to its porous borders. In this sense, the French experience in Algeria, or the British experience in India, often touted as analogies, have but a limited value. The *sui generis* nature of Israel's situation, in turn, lends credibility to the rejectionists' argument that relinquishing the territories would be tantamount to "the tearing off limbs from a live body," and accounts for its resonance even among those segments of the public who do not buy into the "biblical inheritance" reasoning.

These and the many other dilemmas facing present-day Israel are reflected in its political system and culture. Since a significant portion of the rejectionists' activity takes place within the broad confines of Israel's parliamentary democracy, the next segment will analyze the salient features of this system and the ways in which it shapes--and is shaped by--the rejectionists' political behavior.

The Imperatives of Coalition Politics: To paraphrase the late Tip O'Neill's famous dictum that "all politics are local," in Israel, all politics are coalition-based. Given Israel's multi-party system and its uniquely complex voting practices, it is virtually impossible for any faction to gain the parliamentary majority necessary to form a ruling cabinet.

In Israel, there is only one, nation-wide constituency which elects all 120 members of the Knesset every four years via direct, proportional representation. Although the citizens vote directly, not through electors, they cast the ballot for a party slate, rather than for individual candidates for office. A candidate's place on the slate and, consequently, his/her future cabinet and/or parliamentary committee position are decided through inter- and intra-party horse trading, with no voter input. Consequently, elected officials bear primary allegiance to their political faction, rather than to their constituents, as is the case in the U.S.

By law, each party that passes the modest parliamentary threshold of 1.5%,[5] is eligible for a number of plenary and committee seats proportionate to the number of votes cast in its favor. To complicate matters further, however, the total number of valid ballots--e.g., 2,657,327 in 1992 and 2,972,589 in 1996--is divided by 120 (the number of available Knesset seats) to determine what is called the "index", that is, the "price", in ballots, of each parliamentary seat. The remaining "fractions"--representing thousands of votes--are traded among potential coalition partners, through a complex and highly charged bargaining process, until they add up to the index necessary to accord the winner an additional seat.

Following elections, the President, as part of his largely ceremonial duties, tasks the leader of the winning party--normally the Prime Minister-elect--to proceed with forming a ruling cabinet, to be backed by a parliamentary coalition of at least 61 representatives. Needless to say, the majority faction would attempt to gain as broad a plurality as feasible, lest it be toppled by a non-confidence vote (which requires only a simple majority of the parliamentarians physically present on the floor when such a vote is called). What follows, therefore, is a new and even more laborious round of bargaining, wherein ministerial portfolios and key committee positions are allocated--again, behind closed doors.

Analytical Assessment of Israeli Rejectionism 121

Often, assignments go to the highest bidder, based on factional exigencies rather than on personal qualifications or the Premier's wishes.

Ever since Israel's first parliamentary elections of 1949, every cabinet has been a coalition, cobbling together representatives from several political parties and reflecting diverse--and, at times, irreconcilable--positions. This has been true both when the objective was to incorporate as wide a representation as practicable--as was the case with the early post-independence coalitions, headed by Ben Gurion, or the subsequent national unity governments, formed at times of major crisis--and when it was impossible to garner more votes than the bare minimum needed to govern--as has proved to be the case for the Rabin-Peres Administration.[6]

While the coalition system constitutes an important check and balance in the Israeli political context and reflects the ideological diversity of the voting public, it tends also to favor small, often single-issue parties, upon whose support the cabinet rises and falls. Combined with procedures that make it quite easy--and low cost-- for any interest group to set up a new political faction, gain campaign financing and compete in nation-wide elections, this system breeds a multitude of parties, splinters the popular vote and effectively dictates compromise at the lowest common denominator. Indeed, the 1996 electoral reform, designed to reduce the weight of small parties by allowing voters to cast separate ballots for the Prime Minister and Parliament, achieved precisely the opposite effect: a 22 seat increase in the representation of small parties, at the expense of Labor's and Likud's combined loss of 18 seats, for a historic low of 34 and 32 seats, respectively.[7]

Elaborate pacts are negotiated between potential coalition partners before, during and after the electoral campaign, often complete with bank deposits to guarantee good faith and adherence to the agreed-upon party line. The validity of the old adage that "politics makes strange bedfellows" is fully demonstrated in this sometimes painful, always painstaking process. The resulting patchwork of crisscrossing--and, at times, very fragile--alliances of convenience effectively locks the participants into a conservative, "don't rock the boat" mode. Bold policy initiatives and timely decision making are often avoided, so as not to unhinge the coalition and topple the government. The net result is that sustaining the coalition becomes a goal in and of itself, rather than a means to an end.

Moreover, the coalition agreements are concluded in proverbial smoke-filled rooms, away from public scrutiny. This process accords the swing-vote parties undue power to dictate policies. Consequently, for the next four years, the entire government--and the nation at large--are held hostage to narrowly-based, parochial interests.

Israel's religious parties, both the Zionist NRP and the non-Zionist *Agudat Israel* and *SHAS* (Sepharadi Guardians of the Torah) are a case in point. Although only 20% of Israel's Jewish population describes itself as "religious" or "traditional," these factions have been most successful in translating their leverage into ever-expanding privileges, subsidies and exemptions. This power, perceived by many members of the secular majority as effective blackmail, enabled the non-Zionist segment of the Orthodox population to flourish and grow, while remaining largely outside the normal economic system and enjoying *de facto* exemption from otherwise obligatory military service.[8]

The Politics of Ethnicity and Religion: As we have noted in the introductory chapter, social structures and economic grievances are, often, crucial factors shaping the dynamics of rejectionist movements. In the Israeli case, ethnic and religious cleavages--and their overlap and interplay with issues of politics and socio-economics--are salient considerations indeed.

During the past decade, the religious parties have been expanding their sphere of influence, venturing into the national security arena and away from their more traditional concerns with financial patronage, domestic legislation, or, in the case of *SHAS*, an agenda tuned to the feelings of discrimination among lower-income Sepharadim. Insofar as their constituencies tend to espouse "hawkish," uncompromising and, often, anti-Arab positions, this

Analytical Assessment of Israeli Rejectionism

trend is likely to impact <u>any</u> incumbent government's maneuver room and, consequently, the peace process.

This conclusion is reinforced by several additional factors. First, the religious public's parliamentary representation has been growing steadily over the past decade. Thus, the percentage of the Israeli electorate that voted for the four religious parties competing in the 1988 elections was 50% higher than in 1984. Consequently, they surged from 12 seats in 1984 to 18 in 1988--a record high. Although the 1992 elections showed a net loss of two seats--down to 16--and a redistribution of the religious vote among the contending factions, the upswing resumed in 1996, with religious representation reaching an unprecedented high of 23 Knesset seats. Throughout, the growing strength of *Haredi*, that is, non-Zionist parties, was unmistakable. Most notably, *SHAS*, established in 1984 to represent the predominantly traditional Sepharadi constituency, garnered six seats in both 1988 and 1992, soaring to 10 in 1996. As the largest religious party (and third largest overall), its support would be vital to any future coalition.

Second, *SHAS*'s consistently strong showing is reflective of other, wider socio-political and economic trends, most notably: the resurgence of ethnicity on the part of Israel's Sepharadi community; its concomitant rejection of Israel's melting pot policies; its disenchantment with unfulfilled promises of equal opportunity; its simmering resentment toward new immigrants in general and Jews from the former Soviet Union in particular-- perceived as unfairly pampered competitors at the public trough; and its discontent with both Likud's and Labor's socio-economic ventures, as well as with the Ashkenazi-dominated religious establishment.

Looking to the future, *SHAS* has real growth potential precisely because it plays to the pent-up frustrations of an already highly politicized constituency--comprising more than 40% of Israel's Jewish population--whose legitimate needs have been, thus far, largely ignored. Indeed, commenting on the 1996 election results, Israel's popular daily, *Ma'ariv*, noted: "The new composition of the Knesset shows that the upheaval is not only political, but also social. Not only did Netanyahu defeat Peres, but the mostly Middle Eastern, national-religious world view defeated the mostly Ashkenazi, liberal world-view."[9]

More importantly for our purposes, *SHAS*'s national security agenda--while somewhat fuzzy on such key details as the priority to be accorded to and the price to be paid for peace--nonetheless articulates the visceral anti-Arab--and, often, anti-democratic--postures held by many lower-income, less-educated Sepharadim.[10] Insofar as *SHAS* has acquired the leverage necessary to make or break a ruling coalition, its potential impact on the future of the peace process is clear. Simply put, its actual political power exceeds its showing at the ballot box.

Third, as the *Haredi* parties grew more politically assertive and less reluctant to throw their weight into national security debates, they have also become more radicalized in their postures. This "ultra-Orthodox awakening" has led some Israeli observers to conclude that: "The street struggle against the [Labor] government has shifted from the knitted yarmulkes' [i.e., NRP's] exclusive domain to a joint front with the much larger ultra-Orthodox public, resulting in a vastly expanded circle of active opposition to government's policies."[11] While the century-old divisions between the Zionist religious camp and its ultra-Orthodox counterpart might prove too wide to bridge, the rapprochement is important and bears watching.

Fourth, and related, is the fact that the national-religious establishment, apparently unwilling to cede its traditional lead position, has grown correspondingly more active. Indeed, it has begun to reinvent itself. Starting with a 1994 appraisal to the effect that "the national religious public enjoys tremendous power in some sectors, but has failed to translate that strength into tangible achievements in three key fields: political leadership, the media, and the rabbinate," the NRP has embarked on a long-range effort to consolidate and enhance its positions.[12] The entire process is based on the faction's self-perception as Israel's "moral majority, now that secular Zionism has exhausted itself." Hence, the party's mission is to "offer the public a political alternative with a firm and cohesive ideology" and, thus, respond to "the public's yearning for a new and refreshing message of national revival on the basis of Jewish traditions, values and dignity."[13]

While some of the NRP's new-found activism was centered on internal reorganization and articulated through such legitimate venues as lobbying, media campaigns and the establishment of "political action committees," other proposed moves were far less benign. Specifically, some rabbis and activists maintained that "displays of strength and organizational power are not enough" and that only by "shaking the political foundations, or, in other words, making the government fear for its continued rule, can we force it to refrain from further concessions [to the Palestinians] and unleash the full power of the IDF and other security forces."[14] To this end, the self-proclaimed "zealots" should "vow to reject the democratic laws of the Gentiles and the idolatry of Western humanism, while circumventing any decree or decision of the corrupt Israeli government."[15]

Tempting as it might be to dismiss such sedition as the rantings and ravings of a lunatic fringe, the genuine rage they articulate would suggest otherwise. The growing alienation of the NRP's traditionally Zionist constituency from the Israeli political community was further symbolized by its 1994 decision to refrain from offering prayers to the state and its officials' well-being, as has been the practice for almost 50 years.[16] While in practical terms this move brought the NRP closer to the ultra-Orthodox position that prayer for the secular state of Israel is sacrilegious, its real significance lay elsewhere. For, together with the reactionary-traditionalist postures noted above, it demonstrated the depth of the cultural chasm dividing present-day Israel. In this context, it is worthwhile to quote at some length a most insightful--and worrisome--analysis published in the July 7, 1994 issue of *Ha'aretz*:

> A great deal of anger and a great deal of enmity are building up on the secular and religious right against what they see as a dominant, secular, liberal, permissive, and leftist culture that has taken over the state and the spirit of its people. Not surprisingly, the assertions against this

culture...are similar to the assertions that ultra-nationalist, right-wing circles in Europe voiced in the 1920's and 1930's against the Jewish culture: that it is degenerate, cosmopolitan, corrupting, hedonistic and sick. Opposed to it is a healthy, traditional, national culture that is linked to the land and to religion....The bad news is that the religious, nationalist right is really alienated from the dominant culture in Israel, scorns it and envies it a bit....The cultural alienation is what frightens more than the political antagonism, for the former, more than the latter, is what negates the legitimacy of the other side, defines it as despicable and abhorrent, and prepares the ground for acts of violence of Jews against Jews.

Could Labor Have Survived Peace?: While the May 29, 1996 election results provide a conclusively negative answer, it is important to note that, until then, the very question of Labor's political survival would have been considered frivolous and the answer obvious, if not self-evident. After all, the conventional wisdom in the West was that the right-wing's defeat and Labor's landslide victory in the 1992 elections secured the latter's position for the long term and that, consequently, its mandate for peace would remain unchallenged. Whether these assumptions stemmed from mirror-imaging--that is, applying American standards to the analysis of a different culture--or wishful thinking --i.e., a genuine desire to see the peace efforts succeed--is less relevant than the fact that they failed to adequately reflect the complex realities of Israeli socio-politics. The unvarnished fact is that the Labor government's position has been quite precarious since at least 1993. Consequently, neither its survival until the 1996 elections, nor its subsequent electoral victory should have been taken for granted. The following points would support this conclusion, as drawn by the authors in Summer 1995, when this chapter was first drafted:

The perils of a narrow plurality: While Labor defeated Likud in 1992 by a decisive margin--44 to 32 Knesset seats--a majority of at least 61 is needed to govern. This reality forced Rabin into an inherently fragile coalition with, on the one hand, the left-wing *Meretz* (Vigor), whose 12 seats represent Israel's most liberal, dovish constituency and, on the other hand, the hawkish Sepharadi Torah Guardians (*SHAS*), all for the narrow majority of 62.

Analytical Assessment of Israeli Rejectionism 127

Although Labor could also count on the tacit support of two Arab parties--the communist *Hadash* (New) with three seats and the Arab Democratic Party (ADP) with two, adding up to a more comfortable margin of 67--Rabin had initially foresworn depending on "non-Zionist" (read, non-Jewish) votes, particularly as far as national security issues were concerned.[17]

The inevitable result of this attempt to bridge the irreconcilable differences between the outspokenly anti-clerical *Meretz* and *SHAS*'s traditionalist agenda has been a flurry of crises and public vitriol. Rabin was thus compelled to deal with intra-coalition squabbles and personality conflicts--most notably, clashes between the fiery Minister of Education, Shulamit Aloni, on the left and the Orthodox Minister of the Interior, Aryeh Deri, on the right--at the expense of his clearly articulated desire to focus on the peace process. Not surprisingly, after a series of shaky compromises, transfers and resignations, the entire arrangement unravelled, forcing Labor to bid for *SHAS* support every time a vote was called.

The precarious nature of Labor's position was further accentuated when the two Arab parties reacted to the government's May 1995 decision to expropriate 131 acres of Arab-owned land by submitting a no-confidence motion--with full support of the entire right wing. That Likud would take part in a charge against construction in the Jerusalem suburbs--thus not only betraying its own cherished principles, but also undercutting a hitherto unshakable national consensus as to Israel's sovereignty over united Jerusalem--was bizarre enough. What made this chain of events even more outlandish, however, was that the Israeli rejectionists linked forces with Palestinian representatives, in a desperate bid to topple the very government they have consistently accused of selling out to the PLO.[18] While the government had little choice but to suspend the expropriations, thus rendering the opposition's power-play a dismal failure and a serious blow to Likud's credibility, the bewildering spectacle of short-sighted, partisan considerations overriding the imperatives of basic rationality was sure to set the tone for the then-evolving election campaign.[19]

The ill-fated expropriation decision brought about a rare--and, in retrospect, wasted--U.S. veto in the United Nations Security Council, costing Israel a blue chip it might desperately need at some later point. Equally importantly, having showcased Labor's weakness and the fragility of its support base, the right wing could capitalize on the momentum to further erode Labor's tenuous hold on power. As an additional, albeit probably unintended consequence, the two Arab parties scored an unprecedented victory: "Following years of sharp insults, total disregard for their demands and positions, and a feeling of degradation and deprecation on the part of their constituency, the Arab parties have become an element that can tip the balance and therefore cannot be ignored....The Israeli Arabs joined the democratic process not only in words, but in fact....Rabin gave his Arab supporters a grenade with the safety pin removed. If he wants to remain in power into the next elections, he has exactly four seconds to obey their commands."[20]

The challenge from within: To make matters worse, the parliamentary infighting took place against the backdrop of repeated challenges to Rabin's leadership from within his own party and the concurrent disclosure of widespread corruption in the Labor-dominated trade union *Histadrut*.

The longer-term repercussions of the extensive police probe, underway since September 1993, into alleged campaign fraud, diversion of funds, wire-tapping, and influence peddling could only be surmised. However, to quote Trade and Industry Minister and former Labor Secretary General, Mikha Harish, "Labor could be dealt a grave blow should the investigation drag on and involve an increasing number of officials. The longer the police examine Labor's affairs, the greater the danger to the party....Lengthy investigations and additional revelations of wrongdoing could hurt Labor so much that its electoral prospects would be further eroded."[21]

Labor's initially panicky reaction did not inspire confidence. For one, while publicly acknowledging that, "this is a serious storm, liable to wreak havoc" on the party's support base and appealing for "a quick and thorough cleansing, lest the disease

Analytical Assessment of Israeli Rejectionism 129

spread," the party failed to close ranks behind its embattled leadership. The unavoidable impression thus was of the proverbial rats abandoning the sinking ship.[22]

Worse, amidst the ensuing bickering, finger pointing, accusations of cover up, and intra- and inter-party mud slinging, a self-styled "octet" of second-tier Labor officials, led by Abraham Burg, the powerful Chairman of the Jewish Agency, attempted to exploit the scandal to engineer an anti-Rabin palace coup.[23] Concurrently, a splinter faction calling itself "The Third Way" mounted an internal challenge to Labor's cohesion, with some members threatening to break party discipline and abstain from, or support the opposition in crucial parliamentary votes.[24] Ultimately, Third Way broke away to run as an independent party in the 1996 elections, winning 4 Knesset seats which, otherwise, might have gone to Labor.

The impact of the domestic agenda: While the Arab-Israeli conflict permeates every aspect of Israel's life and choices on security issues play a central role in its political campaigns, it is misleading to present either the 1992 or the 1996 vote as a referendum on the future of the occupied territories. By the same token, it would be a mistake to portray either electoral outcome as a final popular verdict on issues of war and peace.

The reality is that, in 1992, Labor rode to power on a wave of socio-economic discontent and disaffection with Likud's bungling that extended far beyond the peace process, to involve such matters as relations with Washington, budgetary priorities, unemployment (particularly among new immigrants), discriminatory policies vis-a-vis the Sepharadim, intra-party squabbles, and charges of widespread corruption.[25] Similarly, the ultra-Orthodox parties--particularly *Agudat Israel*--suffered a popular backlash, as voters expressed their frustration with the religious minority's undue political power, excessive patronage and economic perquisites, as well as with the overt meddling by American rabbis in the electoral process, complete with a bizarre campaign of curses and blessings.

Labor was, thus, the beneficiary of a protest vote. It was charged with a domestic agenda packed with issues where action has been long overdue--items ranging from the absorption of over 500,000 immigrants from the former Soviet Union, through lackluster economic performance, health, education and electoral reform, to relations between church and state. Consequently, its success or failure in the 1996 ballot depended, in large measure, on its perceived ability to provide for both Israel's well-being and its security.

Judging by 1993-1996 public opinion surveys, there was a yawning gap between popular expectations and Labor's performance, particularly as far as domestic issues were concerned. The disenchantment was particularly acute among immigrants from the former Soviet Union, whose votes were critical to Labor's success in 1992. Indeed, some Israeli commentators predicted that these immigrants, accounting for 11% of the electorate, or some 13 Knesset seats, were likely to return Likud to power in 1996.[26] As things turned out, the so-called "Russian vote" succeeded in both solidifying Benjamin Netanyahu's victory and gaining 7 Knesset seats for an independent immigrants' faction, *Israel B'Aliya* (a Hebrew play on words that means both "Israel with Immigration" and "Israel in Ascendence")

More broadly, a public opinion poll conducted by the respectable Shelakh Institute in July 1994 found only 4% of the respondents rating the government's "general handling of Israel's problems" as "very good"--as against a 65% rating of "not so good" and "very bad." Thirty percent thought that "a right-wing/religious government headed by Likud" would do better, with an almost equal percentage (27%) expecting little positive change. In contrast, 45% of the citizens polled rated "the government's performance in promoting the peace process" as successful, with 51% depicting it as a failure.[27]

These results have remained remarkably consistent in similar polls conducted in 1993 and 1995, indicating a bifurcation among the voters and, consequently, a virtual dead heat between the two principal contenders for leadership. This, in turn, suggested that the 1996 elections might turn as much on the domestic agenda as on progress in the Arab-Israeli arena.[28] In that case, the opposition

Analytical Assessment of Israeli Rejectionism

was bound to benefit from the outsider's advantage, particularly since Labor frittered away the opportunity for national reconciliation afforded by Rabin's murder. That said, Likud is vulnerable to a similar backlash. Should it fail to meet voters' expectations, it would be returned to the opposition benches.

The growing power of small parties: Politics is rarely a zero-sum game, wherein one side's loss automatically counts as the rival's gain. This is particularly true in the Israeli context, where a multitude of parties competes for and splinters the public vote. Moreover, to the extent that opinion polls faithfully reflect actual attitudes, Israel is gripped by a general malaise, born of enduring frustration with "politics as usual." Unfulfilled expectations of quick, tangible results in both the domestic and international arenas and an overall disenchantment with the ability of either Labor or Likud to deliver on their sweeping campaign promises, in turn, could not but enhance the already considerable power of smaller parties.

The trend was readily apparent in the 1992 vote. While Likud lost 8 Knesset seats, its two smaller, yet more extremist allies--*Tzomet* and *Moledet*--gained 6 and 1, respectively. The NRP gained an additional seat (growing from 5 in 1988 to 6 in 1992). Together with *Agudat Israel's* 4 seats, this more than made up for Likud's own loss, while according the far-right opposition proportionately greater influence. The trend carried over to the 1996 vote, wherein Likud, now allied with *Tzomet*, lost 8 seats. In contrast, the NRP gained 3 seats, *SHAS* won an additional 4, *Agudat Israel* retained its four-seat representation, and such new factions as Third Way and *Israel B'Aliya* won 4 and 7 seats, respectively.

The left wing of the political spectrum was shaped by a similar set of factors. The resultant change was significant, albeit less dramatic, with the liberal *Meretz* winning two additional seats (for a total of 12) in 1992. The 1996 ballot reversed the trend, costing *Meretz* three seats and reducing its ability to tilt Labor to the left. In contrast, the two Arab parties gained a total of 4 seats, increasing their representation from 5 to 9 in the 1996 Knesset.

Were these trends to continue, decision-making would move even further away from the center of the political spectrum. This, in turn, would tend to accentuate ideological schisms, fractionalize policy and accelerate the drift toward the political extremes.[29]

Far-reaching corrosion of the political culture: As a general matter, Israelis are prone to more extreme forms of political expression than are citizens of most other Western democracies. Even the most detached observer of the Israeli scene cannot but be struck by the intense emotionalism, brutal directness and uncompromising conviction which seem to permeate virtually every aspect of discourse--from parliamentary debates, through media coverage, to casual conversations. These common impressions were recently validated in a series of surveys conducted by Gadi Wolfsfeld in Austria, Finland, Germany, Great Britain, Israel, Italy, the Netherlands, Switzerland, and the United States. According to his findings, compared to all other Westerners, Israelis were significantly more inclined to view street demonstrations as "the best way of doing something about an urgent political issue," and much less sanguine as to the value of such "soft" forms of political expression as signing a petition.[30]

The reasons underpinning these trends are easy to explain: They are rooted in the overall intensity of life on the edge, in the all-pervasive sense of a constant national emergency and the imperatives of an extremely narrow margin for error. What is more important for our purposes, however, are not the causes but their long-term, pernicious effects. For, given that the ingrained tendency toward extreme expression is now coupled with growing popular discontent, disrespect for the rule of law and declining credibility of key political institutions, the probability of turmoil is correspondingly high. To wit, assorted "Action Committees" and "circles," spanning the religious-secular divide and unifying settlers with such Israeli elites as university professors and reserve officers, were debating the exigencies of "popular insurrection" and "civil revolt" months before Israel's first politicide.[31] Once that threshold was crossed, the potential for a dramatic flare-up of internecine violence increased exponentially. To quote Israel's Attorney

General: "Rabin's assassination has broken a psychological barrier. We can now anticipate another political murder with a high degree of probability."[32]

Implications for the Peace Process: The analysis offered above leads to the inescapable conclusion that, far from enjoying a solid, popular mandate, Labor's hold on power was in decline well before the voters rendered their May 29, 1996 verdict. Thus, a realistic assessment of emerging trends should have alerted both analysts and policy-makers as to the probability of a Likud victory, with a comfortable plurality for a right-wing coalition.

That said, Labor's departure does not, by itself, spell the end of the peace process--at least not any more than its continued tenure could have guaranteed a successful conclusion. For one, it was Likud, with Begin at the helm, that signed the Camp David Accords, endorsed a Palestinian autonomy and executed an extensive withdrawal from the Sinai--to include the uprooting of settlements. The new, Likud-led coalition might prove equally capable of a bold, "peace through strength" strategy. For another, Rabin was no dove when it came to issues of war and peace. His life-long, deeply held and very personal commitment to the nation's security translated into readiness to compromise on the ideology of Greater Israel, but not on the fundamentals of Israel's survival. Peres was likely to have been an equally tough negotiator in spite of--or, perhaps, because of--his dovish reputation and his lack of a warrior's aura. Regardless, the inevitable ascendancy of Labor's "young guard"--particularly retired Generals Shahak, Sneh and Barak, with their impeccable security credentials--would have militated against quick compromises or high-risk decisions, even if Labor remained in power.

More than anything, the 1996 vote demonstrates that the Israeli polity is in the throes of one of the most difficult, emotionally-charged and, potentially, revolutionary debates in its history. In this context, cherished Zionist axioms inexorably linking settlement, security and sovereignty are being challenged.

The implementation of Palestinian self-rule in the West Bank and Gaza--indeed, the entire peace process--is predicated on two unstated assumptions: that a generation of settlers has failed in its mission to transform the territories into an integral part of Israel and that, consequently, the IDF, deployed in the territories since 1967, has remained an occupation army. This, in turn, has placed the price of sustaining the *status quo*--as measured in blood and treasure, as well as in dwindling morale, declining readiness and diminished international stature--at the top of the national agenda.

Thus far, the rejectionists have been quite effective in exploiting the Labor government's weakness, the fragility of the peace process, the impact of *Hama*s' terror campaign, and the overall lack of consensus--all to mobilize public support for their cause. Most notably, they have managed to polarize society by setting the national agenda in binary terms: as a choice between the safety of a Greater Israel and the mortal danger inherent in ceding the territories and creating, thereby, "a spring-board for terrorism and a hot-bed for Islamic fundamentalism."[33]

The simplicity of the exoteric message--especially relative to how complex reality actually is--has an obvious public appeal, as well as political utility. First, it neatly divides society into "us" and "them," while defining "right" and "wrong" in stark, contrasting terms. Second, by keying off the basic survival instincts of a naturally insecure society, the message resonates with a wide range of audiences--bridging societal disparities and crossing the secular-religious divide. Third, by seemingly calling for little more than preservation of the *status quo*, it offers an easily acceptable common denominator. Concurrently, the message puts all proponents of territorial compromise on the defensive, challenging them to the obviously more difficult task of demonstrating to an increasingly skeptical public that the sacrifice is both necessary and beneficial. More than anything, it is these sentiments that are so clearly reflected in the May 1996 prime-ministerial elections--with Netanyahu leading Peres by a solid 11% margin among Israel's Jewish voters.

Clearly, the likelihood of a further rejectionist ascendence would decrease were the new Likud government to pursue territorial compromise, cooperating--either formally, through a national unity government, or tacitly, via parliamentary support--with the traditional, left-of-center "peace constituencies." The systemic shock of Rabin's death accords his successors a golden opportunity to unite the nation behind his legacy and build an enduring, non-partisan consensus for peace. Yet, neither Likud's ability to rise to the task nor the rejectionists' longer-term quiescence should be taken for granted. Indeed, conciliatory rhetoric to the contrary, the chance to heal the wounds of fratricide and reestablish unity might have already been lost in campaign acrimony--assuming such an opportunity was ever more than a fond wish.[34] On a more practical level, Likud faces a painful dilemma, as it moves from electoral rhetoric to the imperatives of policy-making. On the one hand, its leadership is well aware that paralysis or, worse, regression on the Palestinian and Syrian negotiating fronts would undermine the rapprochement with the Arab world, particularly with Egypt and Jordan, sour Israel's relations with Washington and, potentially, re-ignite the *Intifada*. On the other hand, were Likud to renege on its campaign promises, break ranks with its allies on the far-right and follow Labor's land-for-peace agenda--with or without the latter participation in a governing coalition--the nation could split, with all the festering wounds of century-old ideological schisms inflamed still further by contemporary grievances and a sense of betrayal. Indeed, the rejectionists are already on record warning Netanyahu to make good on his campaign promises, or else face "harassment even harsher than what we have gone through until now."[35]

Given the societal bifurcation and the existential nature of the issues at stake, the threat of internal war is real. Indeed, prior to Rabin's assassination, public opinion polls indicated fairly high levels of popular anxiety in this regard. For example, in September 1995, 56% of the respondents believed that the confrontation between the government and the "right wing" was likely to escalate "to the point of the use of firearms."[36] Two months later, this general sense of foreboding would become a painful reality.

Undoubtedly, both Labor and Likud have long understood these imperatives. Hence, the Labor government's unprecedented pledge to hold a referendum before ceding "even one centimeter of the Golan" and its election eve promise to submit all future peace accords to a plebiscite.[37] Hence also a Likud-sponsored bill, supported by some Labor parliamentarians, that would require a special majority of 70 Knesset votes and a 60% plurality in a nation-wide referendum, before the Golan could be returned to Syria.[38] One can only surmise that, were the precedent to be established, it would fully apply to the even more emotionally-charged issue of uprooting Jewish settlements and relinquishing additional portions of the West Bank to Palestinian sovereignty.[39]

Regardless, the mere presence of some 140,000 settlers in the West Bank and Gaza, with another 15,000 on the Golan Heights, does not bode well for a peaceful resolution and quick marginalization of militant rejectionism. Indeed, recent polls suggest that a full 65.8% of West Bank settlers "totally oppose" territorial compromise, another 10.6% "somewhat oppose it" and only 19.3% agree with the principle of trading land for peace.[40] Significantly, rejection of the peace process appears to span the religious-secular divide. The above-noted poll indicates that, "by their own definition," settlers are split into "31.4% who are religious [presumably, NRP], 30% who are secular, 24.8% who are observant [a term commonly used by Sepharadi Jews, regardless of political affiliation] and 12.6% who are ultra-Orthodox."

Clearly, public opinion surveys can, at best, gauge the level of passive support--as distinct from readiness to engage actively in the struggle. Nonetheless, a plurality of 65.8% (for a total of 92,120 settlers) is simply too significant to dismiss. Stated differently, the threat of internal war would be real enough even if only a fraction of that plurality--say, 25%, or some 23,000 settlers--were to translate their declared "total" rejection of territorial compromise into active support of and direct participation in political violence. To make matters worse, as the analysis that follows will demonstrate, the rejectionists already have in place the necessary organizational structures and leadership to pose a serious challenge to both Israeli and Palestinian authorities.

Organization

Given that the rejectionists are engaged in an extensive, multi-dimensional range of activities, it is not surprising that they have evolved, over the years, a comprehensive and highly complex network of organizations, each supporting a specific operational facet. Thus, for example, most of the parliamentary activity is carried out by the political parties representing the nationalist and religious right-wing. When these parties are in power--as they were between 1977 and 1992--their ideology effectively becomes state policy, manifested in such difficult to reverse acts as the 1981 annexation of East Jerusalem, followed, within a year by the extension of Israeli sovereignty to the Golan Heights and the creeping annexation of the West Bank. It remains to be seen whether Likud's 1996 victory will reinstate unconstrained settlement and the massive, heavily-subsidized public construction programs which have made the venture attractive to thousands of middle-class Israelis seeking affordable housing.

Parliamentary Opposition: When the rejectionists are relegated to the opposition, as they have been in 1992-96, their actions mirror the endeavors of most out-of-power political parties, with one added dimension: Insofar as the concept of a "loyal opposition" remains alien to the Israeli milieu, these right-wing factions engage in undercutting the incumbent government's policies, subverting its domestic and international standing and otherwise forestalling the implementation of its agenda. Two recent examples, involving the long-stalled negotiations with Syria, illustrate this point:

- Likud Chairman, Benjamin Netanyahu, was reported in April 1995 to have sent several "private" messages to Syrian President Assad, via the U.S. Secretary of State, warning Syria that Likud does not intend to abide by any withdrawal agreements negotiated by the Labor government.[41]

- Likud and the NRP have also attempted to orchestrate a

wide-ranging campaign in the U.S. against the stationing of American troops as peacekeepers on the Golan. This has involved, *inter alia*, direct approaches to legislators, American Jewish organizations and the public at large, as well as presentations, lectures, op-ed pieces, and scholarly papers by opposition strategists--all with the objective of derailing the very idea of a U.S.-backed deal.[42]

Whatever one might think about the actual merits of negotiating a withdrawal from the Golan and/or interposing American soldiers between the Syrians and the Israelis, such interference in highly sensitive, tripartite negotiations clearly stretches the bounds of legitimate opposition. Whether the Likud leadership has actually engaged in a separate correspondence with Damascus is immaterial; the public spat of accusations and half-hearted denials was harmful in and of itself. Similarly, the specifics of the campaign against deployment of American peacekeepers are less relevant than the longer-term consequences of unseemly foreign meddling in what ought to be the prerogative of democratically elected administrations--in both Jerusalem and Washington. If nothing else, the above-cited examples demonstrate the pernicious effects of allowing partisan politics to extend "beyond the water's edge."

The political factions' parliamentary and extra-parliamentary activities are accompanied by and reinforced through an array of specialized, skillfully administered and flexibly employed organizations. Key among them are *Gush Emunim*, its formal settlement arm, *Amana*, and the settlers' council-*cum*-lobbying group, *YESHA*.

Gush Emunim - It's not a Bloc, It's a Web: The Bloc of Faithful is rightfully seen as the most "effective, charismatic, messianic, religious, political revitalization movement" to emerge in Israel since 1948.[43] It is responsible for lobbying and outreach, as well as for extensive fund-raising, conducted both in Israel and overseas, to finance its multifaceted operations. The organization's popular appeal, power and position stem from a unique combination of its members' common socio-cultural roots and

Analytical Assessment of Israeli Rejectionism 139

experiences, a deeply held ideology, charismatic leadership, and more than twenty years of proven political success. "People become part of *Gush Emunim* because they grow into it. The long process of socialization often starts at home, and continues through kindergarten, religious elementary school, high school yeshiva, *Yeshivat Hesder* [a special field college combining military service with religious study] or advanced yeshiva."[44] Association usually presupposes a general commitment to Rabbi Kook's messianic ideology, an actual or clearly intended residence in the occupied territories, and a close relationship with one of the movement's many leading rabbis.

The majority of *Gush* activists hail from middle-class Ashkenazi families. They tend to be better educated and more politically astute than the average citizen. Women play a key role in both the movement's political activities and spiritual life, and are granted a much higher degree of representation (and respect) than is the case in traditional Orthodox communities. This, in turn, tends to attract well-educated, articulate and dedicated women-- many of them born and raised in the U.S.--who often become the movement's most extremist spokespersons and, thereby, its image overseas. The attention-grabbing and largely independent activities of Miriam Levinger, the wife of Rabbi Moshe Levinger, who came to symbolize *Gush Emunim*'s method of creating facts on the ground in the occupied territories, as well as the 1985 election of the outspoken Daniela Weiss--then a forty year old mother of four --as *Gush Emunim*'s Secretary General, illustrate the point.[45]

The evolution of *Gush Emunim* from a small group of dreamers, struggling to gain a foothold in the West Bank, into an established, powerful institution, with significant assets and resources is, in large measure, due to its members' extraordinary dedication, savvy and ability to tap into and capitalize on public sentiments. As a result, the movement now controls much of the regional and municipal infrastructure in the occupied territories. Its actual power, far outweighing its numerical strength, derives from decisive influence over--if not outright control of--hundreds of lucratively paid positions, huge development budgets, schools, roads, health clinics, and, consequently, the daily lives of some 140,000 settlers, most of whom are not active *Gush* members.

The movement's character and public profile are defined by a small, tightly knit, hard-core leadership, as well as by the homogeneity and intense personal involvement of its rank-and-file. Yet, appearances of wholesome egalitarianism to the contrary, the *Gush* is distinctly undemocratic, elitist and highly hierarchial. It sees itself as a vanguard--"a small missionary order" duty bound to show the way to the entire nation.[46]

While its loudly-professed religious fervor and reactionary-traditionalist agenda might make the characterization odd at first glance, *Gush Emunim* bears close resemblance to Lenin's model of the Communist Party as the committed elite, leading the masses to a better future. To extend the analogy still further, the *Gush* has drawn tremendous strength from its ability to rejuvenate itself through yearly infusions of young, enthusiastic and dedicated cadre, graduating from the *Bnei Akiva* (Sons of Rabbi Akiva) youth movement. The similarities between *Bnei Akiva*'s role as the rejectionists' recruitment pool and the Komsomol's heyday as the Communist Party's shock troops should not be exaggerated. That said, the youth movement's contributions have been a critical ingredient of *Gush Emunim*'s success.[47]

Named after the spiritual leader of the disastrous second Jewish revolt against the Romans (132-135 A.D.), *Bnei Akiva* was established in the 1920's as the pioneering arm of the *Mizrahi* faction and its successor, the NRP. Like the other Zionist youth movements, its primary missions have been to spearhead Jewish immigration to and agricultural settlement in Palestine and post-independence Israel, while instilling the ethos of service to the nation, patriotism and collectivism. These cherished Zionist tenets were combined, in *Bnei Akiva*'s doctrine, with religious study and inculcation of traditional Jewish values. Through the years of Labor's alliance with the NRP, *Bnei Akiva* remained in the shadow of the much larger, Labor-sponsored and *kibbutz*-supported youth movements, often the loser in the competition for scarce resources and the allegiance of increasingly more cynical, individualistic

Analytical Assessment of Israeli Rejectionism   141

youth. Its metamorphosis, in the 1970's, into Israel's largest, most politicized and best endowed youth movement is a story that remains to be told. For our present purposes suffice it is to say that, after the Six Day War, *Bnei Akiva* has turned its considerable energies away from the traditional values of "Torah and labor" to the pursuit of millennial redemption in Greater Israel.

What ensued was a symbiotic relationship between two messianic organizations, predicated on shared backgrounds, goals and beliefs. Insofar as most *Gush Emunim* activists were also *Bnei Akiva* alumni--as well as graduates of the NRP-sponsored school system--the natural affinity quickly evolved into a mentorship, followed, quite logically, by preferential treatment for and recruitment of the youth movement's rising stars. Yet, while initially it was *Gush Emunim's* esoteric message that galvanized the younger generation--with charismatic settlement leaders like Hanan Porat and Rabbi Levinger cast in the role of idols--the relationship soon became a two-way street: As the *Gush* became increasingly institutionalized in the late 1970's-early 1980's, it was *Bnei Akiva* that continued to sustain the entire religious camp with its zeal, spontaneity and youthful enthusiasm.[48]

Although only a small minority of Israel's religious youth actually moved to the occupied territories, they provided the rejectionists with an indispensable source of manpower, as well as with political, moral and financial support. Effectively, they--as well as their extended families and friends--became the movement's foot soldiers and ever-ready reserve. The inspiring image of a small, dedicated vanguard, backed by a popular movement of many thousands was thus reinforced.

In this context, the prestigious *Merkaz Ha'rav* (Rabbi's Center) yeshiva played a central role, becoming the juncture at which *Gush Emunim* and *Bnei Akiva* converged. Not only was the religious seminary the fount of both organizations' reactionary-traditionalist doctrines, but its leader, Rabbi Zvi Yehuda Kook, effectively turned the Jerusalem yeshiva into *a Gush Emunim* command post. The students who lived under his spell were unequivocally ordered to settle in the biblical lands and otherwise do their utmost to spread the fundamentalist gospel. Because *Merkaz Ha'rav* aimed to convert the entire nation to the new, messianic theology of "the Judaism of the Land of Israel," it effectively became the headquarters of a missionary order, with outposts spanning the Green Line. Funding was clearly not an issue, as the seminary's growing fame attracted huge contributions from both Israeli and foreign donors.[49]

For their part, Rabbi Kook's many disciples harnessed their considerable talents to the promotion of his teachings. In so doing, some tended towards ever growing rigidity in the interpretation of Jewish law, purity of observance and mysticism[50]-- in short, towards an ever more reactionary outlook and esoteric message. This, in turn, as we have posited earlier, facilitated the rapprochement between the nationalist-religious camp and its ultra-Orthodox counterpart, while adding considerable clout to both groups.

The close association with *Bnei Akiva* kept the *Gush* young--both literally and figuratively--preventing the ossification process that often corrodes grass-roots protest movements. This allowed its activists to move adroitly between, on the one hand, spontaneous, seemingly uncoordinated acts of defiance and, on the other hand, well-planned, carefully orchestrated, professionally executed, and mutually reinforcing operations--all backed by a structured, yet flexible organization and targeted at a singular strategic objective: to secure Jewish control over the occupied territories.[51]

***Amana* and *YESHA* - Legitimacy and Power through a United Front**: To guide its massive colonization drive, *Gush Emunim* took advantage of Likud's 1977 victory and established its own, officially recognized and state-supported settlement arm. The organization's very name, *Amana,* was a stroke of marketing genius. Literally meaning "covenant" or "pact," it is also a clever play on words: It derives from the same root as "faith" (*emuna*). Indeed, in Hebrew, only one diacritical mark separates the two words. Thus, in its literal meaning, *amana* connotes trust and promise, while keying off and playing to religious sentiments. Concurrently, it clearly evokes the parent institution's own name

Analytical Assessment of Israeli Rejectionism 143

(*Gush Emunim*), thus suggesting a direct linkage while maintaining a semblance of independence.

Amana's 1978 official recognition as a full-fledged settlement movement entitled it to large state budgets and World Zionist Organization (WZO) donations. The status also accorded it access to such perquisites as: secure positions for its members in Israel's sprawling bureaucracy; a voice in decision-making fora hitherto dominated by Labor; and the paid assistance of the very best experts in areas like irrigation, horticulture, land management, urban and rural planning, industrial development, etc. Concurrently, "recognition meant that *Amana*'s activities were considered essential for the nation, part of state-sponsored Zionism. In the past such recognition has been accorded only to [Labor-sponsored] pioneering settlement organizations....Therefore it was extremely important for the extralegal zealots of *Gush Emunim* to become legitimized as partners in this exclusive club."[52]

Once *Amana*'s ambitious plan to settle a 100,000 Jews in the West Bank was adopted as official policy by the Likud government, the organization focused its efforts on establishing settlements in less attractive, but politically important areas: away from the Green Line and Israel's urban centers, but in close proximity to densely populated Palestinian towns. By 1992, it was marketing 66 different settlements--out of a total of 142--ranging from small communities of only a handful of families to booming towns of 15,000.[53]

Additionally, *Amana* has been instrumental in attracting industry and high-tech enterprises to the occupied territories, thus creating jobs, solidifying patronage and facilitating further development. It has also enticed thousands of new immigrants--primarily well-educated and highly motivated Americans, Canadians and South Africans, as well as some new arrivals from the former Soviet Union--to join its existing and planned settlements. Perhaps the clearest measure of *Amana*'s success and marketing skills is the fact that although it remains a religious organization and most of its settlements adhere to Jewish traditions, some 60% of the settlers it sponsors are secular Israelis, who, nonetheless, identify with the movement's goals and are able to pass its sophisticated battery of suitability tests.[54]

The close collaboration between religious and secular settlers was further solidified in the daily workings of local and regional councils. A true example of *Gush Emunim*'s united front strategy, these councils were established by the Likud government between 1979 and 1981, with the explicit objective of strengthening Israeli rule over the occupied territories and ensuring the permanence of the settlements. Yet, for all intents and purposes, the councils gave the *Gush* a singularly effective tool with which to control the entire program. A takeover from within was, thus, only a matter of time.

Even though *Gush Emunim* represented only some 20% of the territories' Jewish population, its leaders were appointed to key executive positions in most of the newly created municipalities and county governments. Consequently, "former illegal settlers and candidates for arrest were now state officials with large budgets, powers and responsibilities. *Amana*'s small staff and budget were supplemented by hundreds of paid official jobs in its control."[55]

With the Likud government pouring huge sums of money into the West Bank regional councils--in what amounted to a clear preferential treatment, particularly relative to allocations given to similar local governments in depressed areas within Israel proper-- *Gush Emunim* leaders were provided with a formidable financial and political base.[56] Consequently, when the *YESHA* Council was created in 1980, ostensibly to represent all Jewish communities in the West Bank and Gaza, the list of its founding members read like the *Gush* "Who's Who."[57]

Similar to *Amana*'s, the Council's name was tailor-made for public appeal. *YESHA* is the Hebrew acronym for *Yehuda, Shomron, Aza*--Judea, Samaria and the Gaza Strip--thus connoting the Council's territorial span of control. The word *yesha* also means "salvation," thus encapsulating its self-generated political mission. Functionally, just like *Amana*, *YESHA* is an implementing framework, headed by settlers for whom these organizations are a source of livelihood, as well as a means to accumulate--and exercise--power and influence. As a local government and, thus, a political representative body, *YESHA* deals with such practical matters as water and land distribution, security, contacts with military authorities, as well as lobbying on the settlers' behalf.[58] Insofar as these activities affect the daily lives and welfare of the entire Jewish population of the West Bank and Gaza, success becomes a common, vital interest.

Consequently, the fundamentalists continue to dominate key institutions in the occupied territories because the entire settler community, regardless of political or religious affiliation, benefits from the arrangement. Simply put, *Gush Emunim*, *Amana* and *YESHA* have proven that they can bring home the "Kosher bacon." Through their tireless lobbying efforts, the settlements have been accorded the privilege of being considered, at once, "development towns," "pioneering settlements," and "confrontation settlements." This combined status, conferred by the government and confirmed by the Knesset, makes them eligible for huge subsidies, concessions and incentives. Furthermore, to quote Meron Benvenisti, "it is politically impossible to revoke their status, only to change the entire system of Israeli subsidies. The powerful pressure groups which rely on continued preferential treatment would not allow that, even if they are opposed to settlements in the West Bank."[59] The system is, thus, self-sustaining and self-perpetuating.

Having enmeshed virtually the entire settler population, as well as key sectors of the general public, in an elaborate, interlocking web of symbiotic relationships and mutual dependencies, *Gush Emunim* holds some very powerful levers with which to influence --if not shape--Israel's policies. Its skillful manipulation of esoteric and exoteric appeals, reinforced by a track record of proven success, makes it a formidable political challenge to any administration. Indeed, as subsequent sections will demonstrate, throughout its tenure, the Labor government has proven unable, or unwilling, to curb its activities and wrest power from what, after all, is a minority constituency.

The Far-right Splinter Organizations: As we have noted earlier, the outbreak of the *Intifada* brought concerns with physical security to the forefront, causing further radicalization among the settlers. Many grew increasingly frustrated with what they saw as the government's "tepid" reaction. Some were equally angry with the perceived "impotence and incompetence," supposedly demonstrated by established local structures, in coping with the escalating violence. In particular, *Gush* and *YESHA*--as well as the IDF--were seen as too "soft" and "restrained" in their response.[60]

Frustration soon spurred action, with sporadic acts of settler vigilantism spawning a panoply of splinter groups, all committed to terrorist violence. The Oslo process and the ensuing "surrender agreements" only reinforced these trends, imparting an even greater urgency to the imperative to "stop crying and start acting."[61] Evidence about these splinter groups' make-up, organization, leadership, and membership is largely anecdotal. Thus, their inter-relationships and allegiance, if any, to the outfits from which they all sprang--e.g., *Gush Emunim* and *Kach*--can only be surmised. Similarly, it would appear that some individuals belong to more than one organization and that the same cells use different names in their media contacts--presumably for clandestine purposes.[62] The clearly overlapping, yet highly conspiratorial nature of at least some of these groups, as well as their public self-aggrandizement and obviously exaggerated claims to popular support, further complicate analysis. With these caveats in mind, however, an assessment of at least the most prominent splinter groups is both valid and--given their explicit commitment to terrorism--vital.

The self-proclaimed **Republic of Judea**, also known as the **State of Judea**, was established in 1988 as a joint religious-secular group. Its founding members included *Kach* activists, *Gush Emunim* members and secular nationalists identified with Likud and *Moledet*. Some Israeli analysts attribute the group's success to the decline of *Gush Emuni*m and the outlawing of *Kach*, whose activists "were thrown into the market" after Rabbi Kahane's parliamentary list was disqualified. Yet, perhaps paradoxically, the group is also reported to be gaining strength in settlements known to be relatively moderate.[63]

In any event, the organization's support base currently extends

Analytical Assessment of Israeli Rejectionism 147

well beyond the settler community: cells are reported to be active throughout Israel proper, with membership--allegedly in the thousands--including such diverse religious and secular representatives as university professors, rabbis, school teachers, physicians, reserve officers, and blue collar workers. Their views are regularly aired on Internet's "Judean Voice" and via the settlers' independent radio station, the so-called "Channel 7." There is also speculation that the organization "serves as an umbrella for other subgroups, probably without the leadership's knowledge."[64]

The organization's goal is to stir up the territories, polarize settlers' positions and, thus, torpedo the peace process. Terrorist violence, against both Palestinians and Israeli "traitors," is the means of choice. Secession, in the sense of declaring "independence" and remaining in the West Bank after the IDF is withdrawn, is a stated option--presumably, a last resort.[65]

The July 1995 emergence of *SHAY* (acronym for *Shomer Israel*, or Guardian of Israel) could provide the proponents of "Judean" separatism with a major boost. Ostensibly established to patrol and safeguard West Bank roads, *SHAY*'s true purpose is to subvert the Palestinian self-rule and, potentially, to underwrite secession with an independent para-military force. Moreover, insofar as the IDF and the PNA have been planning to patrol the area jointly, the organization appears to be set on a collision course with both Israeli and Palestinian authorities. Equally ominous is the fact that *SHAY* is reportedly backed by 500 senior reserve officers and their association *Aharai* (Follow me).[66] If true, this would increase the already significant probability of a split within the IDF, with tragic consequences for Israel's future. By the same token, the creation of independent para-military units raises the specter of a major escalation in rejectionist violence: from terrorism to guerrilla warfare against regular military and/or police forces.

Another broad-based umbrella organization is the self-styled **Joint Action Committee** (JAC), established in 1994 to "coordinate the struggle against the Rabin government." It is made up of representatives of the Settlers' Council, *Bnei Akiva* and *Betar* (the

Likud-sponsored youth movement) members, and the Endeavor group (another *Gush*-based splinter faction). Functionally structured, JAC is broken down into five committees: political, infrastructure, security, economic, and operational. Cells, or "commands," are said to be active in 98 towns, spanning the Green Line, and connected via a telephone and computer network.[67]

Activities range from setting up and manning roadblocks, through organizing protest rallies, to distribution of propaganda materials. Yet, JAC's declared objectives are far more ambitious: "Foil the withdrawal process and generate public momentum against the government's policies.[68] Its preferred means are direct action, terrorism and assassinations, targeted at both Israeli and Palestinian leaders:

> Whoever becomes a friend of a murderer and sells parts of the homeland for a mess of lentils is a traitor, and, more precisely, carries out an act of treason. The red line is not human lives. We have to disrupt the agenda of the prime minister and his band of ministers. Rabin and the members of his government and their wives should be worried about what is being done to them, just as our families and wives are worried about what this government is imposing on us.[69]

In early 1995, the Israeli media exposed six additional extremist groups: **Terror Victims' Command** (TVC), *EYAL* (*Irgun Yehudi Lohem*, or Jewish Fighting Organization), **United Zionist Command**, also known as **Endeavor**, *Zu Artzenu* (This Is Our Land), *DOV* (*Dikuy Bogdim*, or Suppression of Traitors) and *Bereshit* (Genesis). Like their above-noted counterparts, these new (or revamped) organizations were dedicated to direct action, aimed at overthrowing the government and stopping the withdrawal from the territories. What distinguished them, however, were the added objectives of "putting the state back on the Jewish-Zionist track," "engineering a cultural and political revolution" and "provoking the right-wing, so as to get it into the streets to fight."[70]

Moreover, in contrast to both mainstream rejectionists and the other splinter groups, whose target audience were those segments of the population that remained ambivalent toward the peace process, TVC, *EYAL*, Endeavor, *DOV*, Genesis, and *Zu Artzenu* aimed at those who were already convinced. Their primary tactic was to consolidate, rather than broaden the support base. Similarly, they did not share the mainstream's professed "respect" for the IDF and state police. To the contrary, they perceived the military and law enforcement organizations as tools of a government that has lost its legitimacy and, thus, as a fair target for attacks. The following excerpt from a TVC leaflet encapsulates its unbridled fanaticism. It also constitutes an unambiguous warning which should not have been ignored:

> The season of threats, gimmicks and public relations stunts has passed. If you want to live and are interested in the continued existence of the state as a Jewish entity, do not return home....Take to the streets.... Devote every moment to the struggle. Think of our dead and severely wounded comrades, who would be very willing to switch places with each of us.... God Almighty gave us life and commanded us to save our people, and our country, and the spirit of our Bible.[71]

Throughout the summer and early fall of 1995, Israeli media focused on the disruptive activities of *Zu Artzenu* (This is Our Land)--a previously unknown and still fairly obscure settler group. Reportedly headed by Rabbi Beni Elon and Moshe Feiglin, its main activities centered on staging noisy protests around government installations, as well as on blockading highways and key road junctions within the Green Line, often bringing traffic to a standstill and tying down significant police forces. It is unclear whether *Zu Artzenu* is a new rejectionist group or a an existing organization operating under a different name. In any case, its agenda encompassed such political issues as precipitating new elections and denying the legitimacy of decisions taken by Labor with the sole support of Arab parliamentarians. At least in their public statements, its leaders professed to support democracy and oppose terrorism as "counterproductive." At the same time, rank and file members--particularly the younger generation--have been reported to "declare that they no longer recognize the legitimacy of the state and its laws."[72]

EYAL deserves special attention because Rabin's assassin, Yigal Amir, is a confessed member of this self-proclaimed successor to the pre-independence Jewish fighting organizations *Irgun* and *LEHI*. Clearly conspiratorial in its nature, *EYAL*'s members operate under aliases in a highly compartmented organization--complete with an internal security section. They are urged not to allow themselves to be photographed, not to engage in political arguments, not to stand out, and not to express radical opinions in public--all to assure security. Members are trained in such military skills as "sabotage, surveillance, reconnaissance, navigation, first aid, street warfare, and shooting practice with a handgun and an Uzi."[73] While *EYAL* has engaged in provocations and harassment of Arab civilians throughout the West Bank, its main objective was clearly far more ambitious: Force a shift of policy, "torpedo" the accord with the Palestinians and preclude any territorial compromise.[74] To this end, EYAL members were committed to "use all means to fight the Rabin government--the most ruthless enemy the Jewish nation has ever faced--to the very last drop of blood."[75]

We should emphasize that all these organizations coexist--and, presumably, collaborate with--such still active *Kach* off-shoots as *Kahane Chai* (Rabbi Kahane Lives) and *Herev David* (David's Sword), whose commitment to terrorism predates both the *Intifada* and the peace process.[76] Indeed, yet another newly-discovered group--the Meshulam Sect, headed by a religious "guru similar to David Koresh"--has been assessed by senior police sources to make "Kahane's men appear like small-time hoodlums and bleeding heart leftists in comparison. These guys fear nothing and will devotedly and blindly carry out any order given to them by their admired leader." Senior government officials, including Prime Minister Peres, several cabinet members and police officers were reported to be on the Sect's hit list.[77]

Thus, the outlawing of *Kach* did little to prevent the emergence--and still-ongoing proliferation--of a new crop of equally insidious zealots, whose sedition and overt advocacy of

Analytical Assessment of Israeli Rejectionism 151

violence pose a serious threat to both Israel's future as a secular democracy and the peace process. For, in terms of both their rhetoric and, increasingly, in terms of actual operations, these organizations constitute an active insurgency that has declared war on Israel's democratically elected government.[78]

Cohesion

Our depiction of the Israeli political map and the forces arrayed on it highlights some far-reaching divisions among the various groups comprising the rejectionist movement. Similarly, we have noted several socio-economic and ethnic cleavages, which are mirrored within the rejectionist camp, as they are in society at large. With these findings in mind, our focus here is on a more differentiated assessment of the crisscrossing alignments and fractures, as they shape the movement's current actions and impact its longer-term viability. The analysis that follows is predicated on three inter-related premises:

- There is a clear trade-off between mass appeal and internal cohesion, wherein unity is, often, the price of expansion.
- Unity is not a *sine qua non* of success. Indeed, diversity can be a source of strength, but only as long as the component parts reinforce each other in an effective synergy, rather than working at cross purposes.
- Action is the only true test of unity and commitment.

In a political culture where consensus is both elusive and fleeting, solidifying only during--and for the duration of--a true national emergency, cohesion is bound to be a rare commodity. This is particularly true with respect to a rejectionist movement that runs the gamut from legitimate parliamentary factions to clandestine cells of conspirators, and seeks to mobilize a broad segment of an inherently diverse, fractious society.[79] Consequently, cohesion must also be assessed in relative terms: To be successful, the rejectionists need to be either less fragmented than their opponents, or, simply, more capable of ameliorating the effects of disunity. As we shall demonstrate, thus far they have held the comparative advantage--on both scores.

Overall, the rejectionists have been most effective in their effort to polarize society by setting the national agenda in binary terms: as a choice between the safety of a Greater Israel and the mortal danger inherent in ceding the territories. The simplicity of this exoteric message is as useful in building internal cohesion as it is in mobilizing popular support. First, it neatly divides society into "us" and "them," with the obvious suggestion that "those who aren't with us are against us." Second, the message is easy to identify with, precisely because it keys off the basic survival instincts of a naturally insecure society. Third, by seemingly calling for little more than preservation of the *status quo*, it offers a readily acceptable common denominator. Thereby, it helps bridge--or, at least, gloss over--the very real differences among the various rejectionist factions, as well as between them and the uncommitted public.

Posturing and lowest common denominators aside, however, the rejectionists have been more successful in bifurcating Israeli society than in establishing unity within their own ranks. Absent a universally revered, charismatic leader and an agreed upon agenda, the deep divide between, on the one hand, the reactionary-traditionalist core and, on the other hand, the far more diverse "nationalist camp," does not bode well for long-term unity of purpose. The two wings are yet to evolve a truly joint ideology, strategy and tactics. Theirs is an alliance of convenience--or, more accurately, of political necessity--united in its visceral opposition to the peace process, but fragmented in virtually every other respect. Even their slogan of "going together"--coined during the 1982 elections campaign and reiterated since then in countless speeches, songs and essays--suggests short-term expediency rather than long-term cohesion. Indeed, whether intentionally or coincidentally, both the slogan and the alliance it represents evoke the Bolsheviks and their "fellow travellers."

Analytical Assessment of Israeli Rejectionism 153

Clearly aware of the negative consequences of open discord, the rejectionists have tended to accentuate unifying--if not universally acceptable--themes in their public discourse and propaganda, with the twin objectives of building and sustaining internal consensus, while expanding the base of popular support. Accordingly, they tended to play down the scope and depth of dissent on such core issues as:

- **The future nature and make-up of the Jewish state**, that is, a secular, modern, Western-style democracy, versus a theocracy based on a strict application of religious laws. Within this context, the relative importance of duty to the state and its laws, as opposed to duty to the Bible and its commandments, has been a key bone of contention. Here the divide between religious fundamentalists and secular nationalists has been most apparent, with some Sepharadi supporters leaning toward the reactionary-traditionalist view that democracy is a Western construct of little immediate relevance to Israel's unique circumstances.[80]

- **Attitudes towards and eventual status of the Palestinian minority**, with views ranging from their immediate expulsion, through negotiated "transfer," to the granting of varying degrees of civil rights. Herein, discord has crisscrossed the religious-secular divide, with some secular nationalists clustering around proponency of transfer and some religious activists urging tolerance, based on biblical injunctions which define the proper treatment of resident aliens.[81]

- **The territorial boundaries of the "Whole Land of Israel"**, with the range of opinion spanning the Western Land of Israel--i.e., the area between the Jordan River and the Mediterranean Sea--as the irreducible minimum, through maximalist claims to significant portions of present day Lebanon, Jordan, Syria, Egypt, and Iraq, to even more totalist exhortations to "fight wars of liberation to take possession of this entire land, in its holy borders, as commanded by the God of Israel."[82] Here again attitudes traverse the religious-secular divide, with some leading secular nationalists espousing the most maximalist views, albeit on the basis of *raison d'etat*, rather than biblical commandments.

- **The acceptability and suitability of violence** towards both the Palestinians and Israeli "traitors." As we have noted earlier, discord on this issue also transcends the religious-secular divide, with vocal proponents of direct action clustered on both sides. Within this framework, attitudes toward the IDF--viewed by the vast majority of Israelis as an inviolable national asset--stood out as the most intractable schism,[83] only to be overshadowed by the even greater divulsion caused by Rabin's murder.[84]

In ideological terms, the discord reflects a fault-line between the more cautious "protracted war strategy" and the "military focus" approach, with the latter predicated on the assumption that the gravity of the situation dictates immediate actions against a government--and Armed Forces--which have lost legitimacy and, thus, their rightful claim to the citizens' allegiance. In tactical terms, the split pits proponents of "armed revolt now" as against advocates of "civic disobedience," whose agenda encompasses such traditional forms of passive resistance as refusal to pay taxes, appear in court, or fulfill military reserve service obligations.[85] It should be noted that the more militant postures remain, thus far, a minority view. However, their proponents are among the movement's most charismatic, dedicated and respected leaders. Given the depth of emotions involved and the volatility of the overall situation, their ability to spark violence should not be underestimated.

Clearly, then, the range of disagreement among the rejectionists encompasses the desired end-state, as well as the ways and means of attaining it. Thus, the issues at stake go to the very heart of what the entire effort is about. There are obvious risks involved in deferring resolution, particularly given that few, if any, of these matters are easily negotiable or amenable to compromise. Moreover, if dissension is allowed to fester, each and every one of these issues is significant enough to cause an irreparable schism.

We can only speculate as to the true motivation driving the ongoing efforts to gloss over such fundamental differences.

Analytical Assessment of Israeli Rejectionism 155

Undoubtedly, pragmatic considerations and political exigencies dictate consensus building, at least for the short term. As a minority group, the true believers have little choice but to link their political fortunes to and ride the coattails of factions that have a reasonable chance of legitimately taking the reins of power. In this sense, the lack of internal cohesion actually accords an advantage, granting the movement as a whole greater tactical flexibility, adaptability and maneuverability. As a diverse organization, they can, indeed, try to be all things to all people, presenting different public personae to fit changing circumstances, while reaping the benefits of an expanding base of support. Moreover, tactical compromise at the lowest common denominator might be deemed sufficient if the initial objective is to defeat an equally--if not more--fractured opposition.

Nonetheless, available evidence would suggest that there is at least an element of premeditated deception in the united front strategy espoused by the fundamentalist core. Thus, several *Gush Emunim* spokesmen are on record urging a "low public profile" and deliberate obfuscation as to the movement's ultimate goals, so as to avoid alienating potential allies and supporters: "It is very important to educate the people, especially the youth. But the transmission of the truth must be gradual. In order to acclimate the public to our ideas, we should refrain from expressing them in their fullness...the ear cannot hear too great a noise."[86] Even more explicitly, such ideologues as Yosef Ben Shlomo, chairman of the Jewish philosophy department at Tel Aviv University, advocate "elaborating a manifesto highlighting only those objectives that the people of Israel agree with deep in their soul and then launching a comprehensive educational, ideological, and cultural campaign for the final defeat of secular Zionism."[87] The similarities between this approach and the tactics followed by both Soviet and Chinese communists are hard to miss.

Clearly, strategic deception and obfuscation of teleological aims do not add up to a good basis upon which long-term collaboration can be built. In the mid-to-short run, however, their practical utility is equally obvious. Simply put, the two sides need each other, because neither can attain its goals by itself. For the secular nationalists, the alliance with the fundamentalists, uneasy as it might be, serves the dual purpose of anchoring their agenda in a broader popular mandate and legitimacy than they could attain on their own, while permitting sufficient independence to gravitate back to the center, should political circumstances so dictate. For the religious component, steeped as it is in the belief that it is carrying out God's will--and seeing its own role as merely helping along a preordained millennial process, while returning errant Jews to the fold--the end literally sanctifies the means.

Moreover, each side appears quite confident that its preferred approach would ultimately prevail, because its counterpart is bound to see the light--either through divine intervention, as the reactionary-traditionalists tend to believe, or due to the imperatives of what is rational and feasible in the last decade of the 20th Century, as the secularists apparently suppose. Thus, as long as the symbiosis allows each side to thrive, while producing synergistic results, there is little to be gained from forcing the issue in the name of ideological purity.

Several additional reasons might also account for the reluctance to bring the discord into the open. First, the long-term, teleological nature of at least some of the contentious issues does not seem to warrant urgent solutions, particularly given the potentially high costs to be incurred in addressing the disagreements head on. Second, within the context of the necessary trade-off between cohesion and broad-based support, the latter is clearly deemed to be the more important, especially as long as disunity is manageable--in the sense that it does not impede progress or disrupt joint action. Third, as we have already suggested, each of the two main rejectionist wings is divided internally, with the range of dissent spanning both the above-noted cluster of issues, as well as rifts along ethnic, political and theological lines. Aware of these divisions, each side might have weighed the limited gains that could accrue from honest debate, as against the obviously damaging effects of exacerbated internal discord, and concluded that it is too weak to suffer the stress of open polemics.[88]

Analytical Assessment of Israeli Rejectionism 157

When evaluated against each other, the naturally more homogeneous religious core seems to hold a clear advantage over its more diverse secular counterpart. The former also appears better equipped to cope with and adjust to the impact of internal disunity.[89] For one, insofar as much of the discord stems from divergent exegeses of sacred texts, it is seen as an acceptable outcome of devout study and, thus, as a continuous testimony to the richness and vitality of the Jewish heritage. For another, in traditional Judaism, unanimity is not the expected norm. Indeed, in light of the assumed limits on human ability to divine the word of God, debate and disagreement are anticipated, with the resolution of all pending "questions, puzzles and mysteries" deferred to the end of times, when the Messiah will adjudicate them once and for all.

Furthermore, since no single rabbinical authority could claim the mantle of unique access to the transcendental truth, competition among independent schools of thought has been traditionally tolerated, if not encouraged. While not always friendly--as some rabbis have not only enjoyed greater authority and a larger following than others, but, often, turned these into power centers to be used against rival sects--such competition continues to be accepted as a natural and, therefore, healthy tension. Rabbi Tzvi Yehuda Kook is a case in point: While he was widely revered as the spiritual leader of *Gush Emunim*, his writings and homilies were treated as little more than a point of departure for varying interpretations. After his 1982 death, these statements--like the hermeneutics upon which they were based--became tools to support the contradictory positions openly advanced by his students.[90]

By the same token, although Rabbi Kook's departure left an obvious leadership vacuum, the organization could recover fairly smoothly, as his disciples stepped in to fill the void. Through their efforts, alternative rabbinical centers--headed by some of Kook's best students and located throughout the occupied territories, as well as in Israel proper--quickly gained prominence, ultimately coalescing into a flexible, polycentric structure. Perhaps more importantly, this younger generation of leaders has been able to outdo the master in combining active political involvement with their religious and educational duties, thus solidifying still further the movement's scope, reach and influence.[91]

In contrast, the secular rejectionists have long been buffeted by the twin forces of internal disarray and ongoing power struggles. As ambitious politicians vied for status, finger-pointing and open quarrels continued to aggravate the general malaise born of electoral defeat. For example, throughout 1995 and the early part of 1996, Likud has been in the throes of an ugly--and quite public--rivalry between its elected leader, Benjamin Netanyahu, and the equally ambitious former Foreign Minister, David Levy. Netanyahu's reputation as a power-hungry, slick, yet sophisticated and elitist "prince," on the one hand, and, on the other hand, Levy's readiness to cast the competition in ethnic terms, highlighting his own blue-collar, Sepharadi roots to mobilize support, lent a particularly distasteful tinge to the pre-election strife.[92]

The appearance of moral complicity in Rabin's death--reinforced by both Mrs. Leah Rabin's highly publicized refusal to accept Netanyahu's condolences and media insinuations of culpability--could have also weakened Likud, at least in the immediate term. Yet, as demonstrated by the 1996 election results, sentiments tend to be, by their very nature, volatile, if not fleeting. Moreover, Netanyahu has mastered the art of the "political spin"--perhaps better than any other Israeli politician. Thus, his media skills and reputed "teflon coating"--aided by *Hamas'* terror campaign and Labor's bungling--were clearly enough to shield both him and his party from longer term damage.

Further to the right, *Tehiya* has never recovered from the 1992 loss of its entire parliamentary representation. While its core leaders--former Knesset members Geula Cohen, the fiery former *LEHI* fighter, Yuval Ne'eman, one of Israel's foremost physicists, and settlement activist Dr. Israel Eldad--remain in the public eye, their political future is uncertain at best. *Tzomet*, headed by the charismatic--though highly controversial--former Chief of the General Staff, Raphael Eytan, seems to be enjoying a renaissance

Analytical Assessment of Israeli Rejectionism 159

at *Tehiya*'s expense. Having quadrupled its strength in the 1992 ballot, *Tzomet*'s unabashedly anti-Arab, yet also anti-clerical, pro-reform, clean-government agenda is likely to continue attracting young voters, allowing the party to capitalize on the public's disenchantment with the "business as usual" of mainstream politics. Likewise, *Tzomet*'s unique ability to link rejectionism with widely-appealing socio-economic planks, borrowed from the left-wing's platform, is bound to aggravate the already significant polarization within the nationalist camp particularly now that *Tzumet* is integrated with Likud. In contrast, *Moledet,* led by Rehavam Ze'evi, another colorful and highly controversial retired general officer, is unlikely to experience significant growth. Yet, while its extremist agenda and open advocacy of "transfer" have but a limited following among the secularists, both the party *per se* and its maverick leader are likely to act as spoilers, accentuating the overall discord.[93]

Party politics and philosophical polemics aside, the bottom line is quite simple: Action is the only true test of cohesion. There is a qualitative difference between casting a ballot and firing a bullet --as there is between carrying an anti-government placard and actually carrying out an act of terrorism. By the same token, there is a critical distinction--in terms of the depth of commitment to the cause and the personal risk involved--between violence against unarmed civilians and guerrilla attacks against the security police or the military. The former is basically a criminal act, risking, at worst, a long jail sentence. The latter requires, quite literally, having the courage of one's convictions, for it entails the readiness to make the ultimate sacrifice. Thus, while the overall slide toward extremism is unmistakable, the rejectionists' ability to muster--and sustain--the cohesion, will and fire-power necessary to engage the authorities in open warfare has yet to be proven. Coincidentally, the government itself is yet to demonstrate its own readiness to use all necessary means against the rejectionist challenge to legal authority.

Assuming that neither side fundamentally revamps its stated postures, the rejectionists' capability and resolve could be put to the test as soon as the new Likud government attempts to deliver on its predecessor's commitments to the Palestinians. The course and outcome of this initial confrontation would be crucial: Anything less than their outright, undeniable defeat would, likely, feed the rejectionists' determination, enhance their cohesion and spawn additional clashes. The resultant escalatory spiral would be difficult to stop.

External Support

Following the intersecting trails of moral, political, material, and sanctuary support is, usually, an effective way of investigating a rejectionist movement's activities and longer-term prospects. In the Israeli case, however, any attempt to ascertain the scope, level and nature of external support is hampered by several factors peculiar to both the rejectionists themselves and the environment within which they operate.

First, the Israeli rejectionists function within a nation that has been, virtually since its inception, the recipient of huge amounts of Western material assistance, as well as significant moral and political backing. Second, they benefit, both directly and indirectly, from the unique set of relationships that ties Israel to the Jewish diaspora in general and to the six-million-strong, politically active American Jewish community in particular. Third, the rejectionists have developed a sophisticated, overt and covert network of fund-raising organizations in the West--primarily in the U.S., but also in Europe, Australia, Canada, and South Africa--parallel to but independent from the long-established Jewish charities. Combined, these factors make it exceedingly difficult to disentangle the intermeshed lifelines of external support and distinguish those that sustain the State of Israel from those that feed the internal opposition.

U.S. Assistance: The special relationship between Israel and the U.S. is literally in a class all of its own. One would be hard-pressed to find an analogue in the international arena that

Analytical Assessment of Israeli Rejectionism   161

demonstrates a similarly intricate web of moral, religious, ideological, political, geostrategic, economic, and military-technical ties between a superpower and a tiny, embattled, yet fiercely independent nation. Equally unique is the fact that the unwritten alliance has weathered almost five decades of global and regional turmoil, to include six local wars, political transitions and the vicissitudes of the peace process. It remains robust and largely unchallenged--sustained by more than $10 million per day in American aid--even after such revolutionary changes as the end of the Cold War and the collapse of the Soviet Union obviated erstwhile geostrategic verities.

While initially outpaced by both France and Germany, U.S. material assistance to and political support of Israel increased steadily in the wake of the spectacular victory in the 1967 Six Day War. The surge of Soviet involvement in the Middle East and the ensuing superpower competition for regional influence further solidified the U.S.-Israeli alliance, adding a critical strategic dimension to a relationship originally predicated primarily on shared values and moral considerations. By the mid-1970's, and, particularly after the fall of the Shah and the conclusion of the Camp David Accords, Israel moved, together with Egypt, to the top of the list of U.S. aid recipients. Concurrently, the bilateral strategic alliance flourished, as relations between Moscow and Washington continued to deteriorate in the wake of the Soviet invasion of Afghanistan. With Israel increasingly portrayed as an indispensable bulwark against Soviet aggression, and, thus, a vital U.S. interest, political, military and economic assistance became an almost unconditional entitlement.[94]

Politically, Israel could count on U.S. support in key international fora, to include a virtually automatic veto of--or, at least, an abstention from--adverse UN Security Council resolutions. Atmospherics varied with the personalities at the helm in Jerusalem and Washington, reaching a zenith, for example, during the second Reagan Administration, when Israel was elevated to the status of a non-NATO ally,[95] and plummeting precipitously when Prime Minister Shamir and President Bush sparred over practically every point of mutual interest.[96] Nonetheless, the overall relationship remained solid, with the U.S. rarely availing itself of the considerable leverage inherent in its position as Israel's sole international sponsor.[97]

In terms of material support, the actual figures tell the dramatic story: During the first two decades of its existence, Israel received less than 3% of U.S. foreign assistance--averaging $6 million per annum. This share increased exponentially during the seventies, peaking at 35% in 1978, then settling down at a consistent 20%-25% range. Since 1985, the regular U.S. aid program for Israel has been straight-lined at about $3 billion per year--$1.8 billion in military assistance and $1.2 billion in economic aid, not counting special aid enhancements, supplementals, grants, non-aid programs, and emergency military transfers, like the ones provided to offset losses resulting from the Persian Gulf War. While the quantity, type and monetary value of these enhancements tend to fluctuate, making a precise assessment quite difficult, reliable estimates suggest an annual boost of as much as $850 million.[98]

The cumulative figures are equally impressive: Between 1951 and 1991, the U.S. provided Israel with well over $51 billion in economic and military assistance. Assessed in constant 1991 dollars and adjusted for inflation, the aid totaled about $81 billion.[99] According to official Israeli data, in 1994, U.S. assistance amounted to 6.5% of Israel's Gross Domestic Product (GDP) of $66 billion--or roughly $700 per capita.[100]

Undoubtedly, the extremely generous annual aid package, earmarked for Israel, was never intended to sustain rejectionism. The undeniable fact, however, is that money is a fungible resource. To wit, the 15 years of Likud rule saw a massive colonization of the occupied territories. Effectively, this translated into a tremendous investment in the very growth medium in which extremism could thrive. And, although the build-up was financed primarily through internal appropriations, the necessary shifting of capital would have been difficult, if not impossible, without the ability to use overseas funds to plug the resultant budgetary holes. Thus, in real terms, the yearly infusion of U.S. assistance relieved at least some pressing defense and domestic needs, freeing resources for the government's territorial priorities.

This practice continued until 1991, when President Bush linked the approval of Israel's request for $10 billion in loan guarantees--intended to defray the cost of absorbing the influx of Russian immigrants--to Jerusalem's readiness to freeze construction in the occupied territories.[101] The ensuing spat contributed to the 1992 downfall of the Shamir government and created a serious rift within the American Jewish community. Yet, its monetary impact was marginal at best: The overall assistance program remained intact, with the penalty provision that dollars spent on projects in the occupied territories would be deducted from the loan guarantees.[102]

What is remarkable about this dispute is not so much the bold challenge posed by the Bush Administration to both the Shamir government and the Israeli lobby in Washington, nor the sometimes ugly overtones that crept into the debate, with charges of anti-Semitism rebuffed with counter-charges of undue power and influence, if not disloyalty.[103] Rather, the most noteworthy aspect of the squabble is that it happened at all. For, while the dissonance between Washington's consistent position that the settlements impede a peaceful resolution of the Arab-Israeli conflict and its equally consistent support of Israeli governments committed to an expansionist agenda has been long apparent, it was rare indeed that the U.S. sought to bridge the gap by translating the linkage into actual policy.

The 1992 change of administrations in both Jerusalem and Washington, coupled with unprecedented progress in Arab-Israeli negotiations and the Rabin government's commitment to freeze construction in the occupied territories, rendered the dispute moot--at least for the time being. Yet, the inescapable reality is that by effectively shielding Israel from the consequences of its actions, over the long-term the U.S. has contributed, however indirectly or unwittingly, to the creation of serious obstacles to the very peace process it has been seeking to promote. The inevitable--albeit equally unintended--result is a much more robust, more deeply-entrenched rejectionist threat to the negotiations Jerusalem and Washington have attempted to forge together.

Support from the American Jewish Community: In many respects, American Jewish support for Israel and the Washington-Jerusalem alliance evolved in tandem, with the former not only fuelling the latter but also gaining strength from and, thus, further reinforcing the interaction. By the same token, although each relationship was shaped by a distinct set of determinants, both were buffeted by similar tribulations, as they tried to adjust to and account for the often turbulent nature of Israel's policies.[104]

American Jewry's concern for Israel's safety and well-being dates back to at least 1948, reflecting collective guilt over its generally passive role during the Holocaust and a determination to help secure a haven from future persecution. However, overt, organized political activity on Israel's behalf did not begin in earnest until after the 1967 war. Thereafter, basking in the reflected glory of Israel's military success and buoyed by the opening of American society to minorities, the Jewish community plunged into active political participation, with Israel the unifying *cause celebre*. New organizations were born and existing support groups expanded. By the end of the 1980's, more than 70 political action committees have been organized, raising and contributing millions to pro-Israel legislators. Concurrently, the American-Israel Public Affairs Committee (AIPAC) evolved into one of the most formidable lobbies in Washington--envied, feared and emulated by friend and foe alike.[105]

The U.S. government and the American Jewish community have always been united in their unequivocal commitment to Israel's survival. Where the two tended to differ, at times, was in their respective assessments of and readiness to contribute to what each saw as essential for Israel's security. Accordingly, the Jewish lobby took on the mission of reconciling the differences and shaping Washington's Middle Eastern policies to Israel's advantage. It has done so by promoting a dual--and, sometimes, contradictory--image of a beleaguered, vulnerable Israel, in dire need of U.S. support, and a strong, militarily advanced, vibrant

Analytical Assessment of Israeli Rejectionism 165

democracy, capable of securing America's broader regional interests.

As a general matter, the American Jewish community has been far more restrained than official Washington in challenging--or seeking to leverage--Jerusalem's policies. For, as much as Israel needed the diaspora's support, the want was mutual. In the U.S., Israel was perceived as the glue that holds the American Jewish community together: an antidote to assimilation and a "psychological safety net for a people conditioned by bitter experience to keep their bags packed."[106] Solidarity with Israel was reflexive and unconditional. It was rooted in kinship, pride, guilt, and lingering insecurities and shaped more by ideals, hopes and Hollywood legends than by a sophisticated understanding of the realities of Israeli life and politics.[107]

American Jews have traditionally adhered to the tenet that the Israeli government knows best what is--and what is not--important to its well-being: Concerned outsiders should be unequivocally supportive, or, at the very least, refrain from airing their objections in public. In fairness, this natural inclination to abstain from second-guessing Jerusalem's policies has been reinforced over the years by the thinly veiled Israeli attitude that those who would rather avoid the risks and hardship of life in Israel, while sharing, however vicariously, in its achievements, ought to keep their checkbooks opened and their mouths shut.[108]

Consequently, despite their traditional liberalism, concern with human rights and positions generally far more dovish than those espoused by Begin or Shamir, American Jews largely abstained from openly questioning such controversial Israeli ventures as the invasion of Lebanon, the colonization of the West Bank, or the brutal suppression of the *Intifada*.[109] Internal discord was quashed quickly and, sometimes, heavy-handedly. The few vocal heretics who refused to promote policies at odds with their own, deeply held convictions were shunned, delegitimized and virtually excommunicated. As a result, by the end of the 1980's, "American Jewry has become a blunt instrument of Israeli policy,"[110] operating within the self-imposed limits of what one Jewish leader termed "dissent as pillow talk: You whisper in the ears of Israeli politicians when you visit Israel but you never say it in public."[111]

The moral and political support granted to Israel by the Jewish diaspora has been accompanied by equally generous infusions of material assistance, averaging $600 million a year. In the U.S., these donations are collected and distributed through an elaborate, multi-tiered, nationwide network of charitable organizations, most notably the United Jewish Appeal (UJA), the United Israel Appeal (UIA) and the Joint Distribution Committee, as well as such more specialized philanthropies as Women's International Zionist Organization (WIZO), Hadassah, The Organization for Rehabilitation and Training (ORT), etc., each with a myriad of local chapters and federations.[112] In addition, virtually every Israeli political party, youth movement, university, hospital, museum, or religious seminary is served by its own, no less elaborate fund-raising mechanism. These organizations funnel money directly to the sponsored group in Israel--all perfectly legally and in a tax-exempt status.[113]

None of the mainstream Jewish charities directly supports rejectionism--in word or in deed. In fact, the UJA expressly prohibits allocations for activities beyond the Green Line--excluding Jerusalem.[114] Yet, their dollars--just like the $3 billion in annual U.S. government assistance--have been fungible, contributing, however inadvertently, to the unconstrained growth of forces inimical to the very values the vast majority of American Jews wholeheartedly supports, namely peace and democracy. If nothing else, the Jewish community's massive moral, political and material assistance allowed successive Israeli governments to avoid making painful choices among competing priorities.

Without the diaspora's largesse, the fledgling State of Israel might not have been able to develop and sustain its universal, cradle-to-grave welfare system, its world-class educational, cultural and research-and-development institutions, or its overall standard of living, while allocating almost a quarter of its budget to defense. Whether present day Israel, with a per capita GDP of $12,610--on par with Hong Kong and well ahead of some members of the

European Community--should continue to ask for and receive cash donations from the 9 million Jews who live outside its borders is, of course, a different question altogether.

As demonstrated by the firestorm of protest which followed an Israeli official's candid remark that "Israel is too rich a country to be acting as a beggar," the core issue is not money but a symbiotic relationship gone awry.[115] For, while Israelis might feel that they can do without contributions that barely approach 1% of their current GDP and resent being patronized by their wealthier American brethren, the latter simply need Israel to need them. A strong, prosperous, secure Israel, at peace with its neighbors, might be less reliant on external support. The American Jewish establishment could thus lose its key rallying cry.

More than anything, this last point might explain why some American Jewish organizations have been undercutting the Labor government's pursuit of regional peace, even though 78% of the Jewish public favors its progress.[116] The still evolving coalition of Conservative and Orthodox religious leaders, Likud allies, journalists, and conservative political activists--backed by a bipartisan caucus of traditionally sympathetic legislators--has taken on the mission of "protecting" Israel from the perils inherent in territorial compromise. While these groups' apparent presumption that the State of Israel lacked the maturity, wisdom, or strategic vision to weigh properly the costs and risks of its own actions could have been initially dismissed as interesting but irrelevant, by 1994 their activities escalated well beyond mere nuisance.

The Effort to Save Israel from Itself: Operating under the guise of "helping" Israel, American Jewish activists enlisted Congressional support for several initiatives which the Labor government perceived as ill-timed, misdirected and harmful to the delicate, multi-track peace process. Thus, for example, the already noted public campaign to highlight the risks involved in deploying U.S. peacekeepers to the Golan was an abortive, but quite detrimental effort to derail the trilateral U.S.-Israel-Syria talks. Similarly, in May 1994, a bipartisan Congressional "Peace Accord Monitoring Group" was set up, with the stated aim of "exposing

Palestinian violations and non-compliance" which Jerusalem would have rather disregarded as immaterial in the overall context of the peace process. The group's attempts to discredit the Palestinian National Authority seemed to mirror the efforts of a Likud-sponsored organization operating in Israel under the name Peace Watch.[117] The U.S. caucus, which numbers 15 Senators and 31 House members from both sides of the aisle, supported legislation that would link U.S. aid to the Palestinians with an end of the Arab boycott. To quote one irate Israeli diplomat: "This would make the urgent repair of the Gaza sewage system hostage to a symbolic issue that will go away sooner or later."[118] More importantly, insofar as economic progress is key to the Palestinian moderates' success, denial of material assistance sabotages the peace process, thus playing into the hand of extremist elements like *Hamas*.[119]

The introduction of legislation to transfer the U.S. Embassy from Tel Aviv to Jerusalem was an equally damaging and ill-timed attempt to tamper with the peace process. The bill placed both the Clinton and the Rabin administrations in an untenable--and highly embarrassing--position. With the PLO and Jordan threatening that such a move would kill the peace process, Israeli and American officials were compelled to speak out against what for the former has been an enduring article of faith and, for the latter, an explicit campaign pledge. Secretary of State Warren Christopher went on record warning that "few actions would be more explosive and harmful to the peace efforts than for the U.S., as the key sponsor of this process, to be pushing the Jerusalem issue forward."[120] In a similar vein, Israel's Communications Minister, Shulamit Aloni, denounced the bill as "disruptive" and censured AIPAC as "a disaster, serving the domestic interests of the United States and the Jewish community at Israel's expense."[121]

The spats over Jerusalem, the Golan and financial assistance to the Palestinian National Authority reflected a broader discord between the Israeli government and the American Jewish establishment. At stake were issues of ideology and policy--as well as a legacy of 15 years of unwavering American-Jewish support for positions fundamentally at odds with those traditionally espoused

Analytical Assessment of Israeli Rejectionism 169

by Labor. According to an unusually candid public statement by Labor's Secretary General, Nisim Zvilli, "when Labor came to power, its leaders were shocked to discover that key positions in the American-Israel Public Affairs Committee and other organizations were held by right-wing figures, forming a right-wing nucleus which makes it difficult for the government and its positions to gain a foothold in these organization."[122]

Clearly, the above delineated attempts to undercut the Israeli negotiating posture could not but exacerbate an already strained relationship. Yet, grating as Israel might have found the second-guessing and meddling from afar, it could ill afford to alienate the Jewish lobby. AIPAC is simply too powerful to bypass or ignore. Whether it can be co-opted--and at what price--is, of course, a different matter altogether, bound to impact the peace process as it enters its most critical phase.

Significantly, the Washington-based lobbying efforts have been accompanied by--and, apparently, coordinated with--a massive fund-raising effort, designed to underwrite the campaign against Labor's land-for-peace agenda. For one, many Orthodox and Conservative congregations have begun to funnel money directly to selected West Bank settlements, primarily through an adoption program akin to the ever-popular "sister city" arrangement, as well as through dedicated grants, collected and transferred outside mainstream philanthropic channels. The fact that some 15% of the settlers--among them quite a few prominent religious and civic leaders, with friends, relatives and loyal followers--hail from the U.S., only reinforced the already strong bonds of kinship and communal responsibility.[123]

For another, several new American Jewish foundations have been set up to promote the right-wing's agenda. Key among them are Pro Israel, One Israel Fund, Americans for a Safe Israel, and American Friends of Yesha--all paralleling and, thus, purposefully competing with the long established, mainstream organizations.[124]

Their activities range from direct material and political support of *YESHA* and *Gush Emunim*, through sponsorship of anti-government propaganda and demonstrations in Israel and in the

U.S., to physical harassment of Israeli diplomats and visiting Labor officials.[125] Available evidence suggests that a significant portion of the money raised by these foundations have gone to compensate the settlements for subsidies cut by the Israeli government, thereby effectively sabotaging Labor's policy of making life in the territories less attractive to both current and future residents.

It is important to underscore that U.S. federal law prohibits tax-exempt organizations from financing partisan political activity of any kind, at home or abroad. It is also illegal to use tax-exempt funds to purchase or improve real estate in order to promote a manifestly political program. Yet, these organizations' blatantly anti-Rabin ads were published in *The New York Times*, in numerous Jewish newspapers and in assorted bulletins on Internet, while their dollars have been overtly allocated to West Bank settlements, as well as to land acquisition in such politically sensitive areas as Jerusalem's Muslim Quarter.[126] Indeed, the "endangerment" of the settlements and the UJA's alleged "discrimination" against "needy" Jews living in the occupied territories have been at the center of these organizations' deliberate effort to "tug at the heartstrings of American Jews," rallying them to the right-wing cause.[127]

Further, American Jews have been donating as much as $10 million a year to purchase real estate from Arabs in the occupied territories, with money flowing from "famous American Jewish businessmen, including Michael and Lowell Milken, through the Milken family foundation, the Reichmann family, Canadian owners of Olympia and York Developments Ltd., one of the largest privately owned real estate companies in the world, and from tens of thousands of people of more moderate means whose commitment to the Biblical Land of Israel is no less intense."[128]

The aggregate numbers tell a dramatic story: According to data compiled by the Bank of Israel, in 1994, "private" donations to specific projects, often beyond the Green Line, amounted to $675 million, as against $425 million raised by the mainstream Jewish-American charities. The longer-term trend is equally telling: Over a nine year period, donations to mainstream organizations grew by

Analytical Assessment of Israeli Rejectionism 171

$25 million, a 6% increase from $400 million in 1985 to $425 million in 1994. During the same time frame, the "private" philanthropies saw a growth of $500 million, a 386% increase from $175 million in 1985 to $675 million in 1994. Stated differently, in 1994, donations dedicated to specific--often political--causes in Israel and the occupied territories outstripped the mainstream charities by $250 million, for a complete reversal of the 1985 situation, when the latter enjoyed a $225 million lead.[129]

The net effect of this redistribution of the Jewish dollar has been a $60-80 million shortfall in the WZO's 1995 budget, cuts in *bona fide* charitable programs like day care centers, schools and hospitals, and some serious soul-searching within the Jewish establishment. More importantly, to the extent that monetary contributions reflect political loyalties, the communal consensus has been shattered, perhaps forever. If nothing else, American Jewish alignment with and blanket support of Israel's national priorities--as enunciated by its democratically elected governments--can no longer be taken for granted.[130]

Furthermore, elements within the American Jewish community have been providing material assistance to far right organizations, including *Kach* offshoots. The elaborate--and largely covert--network channeling money and military equipment to Jewish extremists was exposed in 1994 by Robert I. Friedman.[131] The organizations and their American backers were also the subject of Lawrence Cohler's investigative reporting in *The Jewish Week*.[132] The Anti-Defamation League of B'nai B'rith followed suit with a 53-page paper titled "Extremism in the Name of Religion: The Violent Legacy of Meir Kahane." Together, these reports add up to a powerful indictment of organized Jewish activity on behalf of terrorist groups, explicitly dedicated to subversion of peace and democracy. And, while *Kach* currently claims only 8,000 American members--with U.S. law enforcement officials estimating the support base at no more than 150[133]--its consistent commitment to violence would militate against its dismissal as an insignificant fringe.

President Clinton's February 3, 1995 decision to freeze the

assets of 12 Middle Eastern terrorist organizations, including *Kach* and *Kahane Chai*, might make their fund-raising efforts more difficult. However, given these groups' history of clandestine operations, there is little room for optimism. *Kach* and *Kahane Chai* have long functioned through front organizations, under a variety of names, to include such seemingly innocuous charities as "American Friends of Yeshiva Ha'rav Meir" [Rabbi Meir's (Kahane?) religious seminary] or "American Friends of the Yishuv."[134] The new legislation still permits transfer of funds for religious, charitable, literary, or educational purposes--the very covers most often exploited by both *Kach* offshoots and by the less extremist groups noted above.[135] Indeed, *Kahane Chai* spokesmen are already on record stating that the Omnibus Counterterrorism Act of 1995--like Israel's decision in March 1994 to oulaw the organization--will have little practical impact on either its activities or its fund raising efforts.[136]

Rabin's assassination has prompted an official accounting of the funds blocked since the legislation went into effect. The total catch, according to the U.S. Treasury Department was "a whooping $203," making the Presidential decrees to shut down the cash flow from Americans to Jewish terror groups "a dismal failure, long on symbolism but short on teeth."[137]

In addition to material assistance, *Kach* offshoots seem to be enjoying at least a semblance of sanctuary in the United States. First, because Washington and Jerusalem permit dual citizenship, U.S.-born activists can enter both countries freely, without visa requirements. Moreover, they enjoy the worldwide freedom of movement accorded by an American passport, while benefiting from the cover provided by Israeli documents--usually under an assumed Hebrew name. To wit, several American *Kach* activists were arrested by Israeli authorities for attempted smuggling of military equipment, including gun silencers, telescopes, training manuals, and tools for the production of weapons.[138] Equally ominously, *Kahane Chai* has been operating a training camp in the Catskill Mountains, with the stated purpose of "preparing a Jewish army to defend the settlers from the menace of armed Palestinian

Analytical Assessment of Israeli Rejectionism 173

police."[139] While even Michael Guzovsky, "the supreme commander" of this self-styled "Jewish reaction force" could not boast of being able to muster more than 200 trainees for the 45-day para-military program,[140] this nascent use of U.S. territory as a sanctuary is significant and bears watching.

To sum up: For five decades, the American Jewish community has been Israel's primary political, moral and material benefactor, effectively underwriting its security and well-being. Since 1993, however, key elements within this community have moved away from a virtually instinctive alignment with the incumbent government's policies, toward the promotion of their own agenda. This shift of allegiance involves, most notably, support for and sponsorship of activities opposed by the Israeli government as inimical to the peace process. Moreover, as we have demonstrated, a number of Jewish organizations, philanthropic foundations, and religious congregations--as well as some sympathetic and well-intentioned legislators--have been working at cross-purposes with the Israeli government's and the U.S. Administration's joint effort to forge a regional settlement.

Thus, at least to an extent, the threat to peace comes not only from Israeli rejectionists, but also from their American supporters. Naturally, this further complicates the already formidable task faced by any Israeli government, as it strives to cope with the all-too-real risks inherent in territorial compromise, with its own fears and internal divisions, and with the destabilizing influences of domestic and external opposition--all while attempting to sustain the delicate balance between hard-won independence and necessary reliance on the U.S. government, legislature and the Jewish community at large.

Government Response

As we have noted in our opening chapter, the principal and, often, painful lesson to be drawn from the historic record is that government response to the insurgent challenge is the key variable determining the course and outcome of internal war. To be effective, counterinsurgency must begin with a recognition that a threat exists, followed by an honest assessment of what it would take to eliminate--or, at least, ameliorate--its impact. Consistency, perseverance, flexibility, and resolve are crucial, as is the readiness to make though choices and accept their consequences.

Measured by these criteria, until November 1995, the balance sheet was weighted in favor of the rejectionists. The Rabin government's response fell short of the mark in terms of both initiatives undertaken and results achieved. Its hallmarks have been a lack of focus, inability to set and pursue coherent objectives, and a marked preference for rhetoric over actions.

Worse, even after Rabin's assassination, Labor failed to fully internalize the notion that Jewish rejectionism posed an immediate threat to both its authority and its peace agenda. Absent a clearer threat perception, there was little chance that a consistent, proactive counter-strategy would emerge to replace the traditional *ad hoc* approach. Insofar as momentum is crucial, the Rabin-Peres administration's most serious failing has been its inability to wrest the initiative from the opposition and move away from its generally reactive mode. The following evidence would support this pessimistic assessment of Labor's political program:

Missed opportunities: The Rabin government failed to capitalize on the nearly universal revulsion that followed the February 1994 Hebron massacre to move decisively against the rejectionists. While the public excommunication of Jewish "wild weeds" was unprecedented in its vehemence--and the security services were swift in closing down *Kach*'s offices, detaining its officials and banning the organization in accordance with Israel's Counter-Terrorism Act--there was little effort to expand the focus beyond the ultra-radical fringe. Strong public and coalition support for more vigorous measures--e.g., disarming the settlers and evacuating them from such high-friction areas as Hebron and Gaza --went unheeded. Instead of a concerted effort to build upon the emerging consensus to excise the "cancer ravaging Israel's body-politic," the government chose to limit itself to dealing with its symptoms.[141]

The coalition's hesitation gave the opposition time to recover and recapture the initiative. With the Knesset literally swamped with non-confidence motions, seeking to shield the settlers from further "maltreatment," and with West Bank activists officially proclaiming the onset of a "civil uprising," the government was placed on the defensive.[142] The opportunity to evolve a comprehensive political program--or, at least, solve the festering Hebron problem, thus setting a precedent of decisive response--was lost.

The pattern of failure to exploit the rejectionist's mistakes was repeated in the wake of a rabbinical ruling instructing the IDF to disobey orders to evacuate West Bank military installations. Despite a firestorm of protest--including condemnations from retired general officers currently associated with the right wing-- and contrary to wide-ranging public appeals to indict the offending "ayatollahs," the Attorney General declined to press charges.[143] Likewise, coalition leaders' warnings that, as a result of this "illegitimate challenge to state authority," Israel was "on the brink of civil war, if not anarchy, were quickly overshadowed by equally unequivocal statements belittling the threat as "bizarre" behavior by a "negligible minority."[144]

The government's vacillation was epitomized by Premier Rabin's statement to the effect that: "We must realize that we are headed toward a confrontation between two world views. This is not about declarations or definitions. In this conflict, we need to act wisely and intelligently."[145] As far as rhetoric goes, this was as true then as it is now. In practice, however, Labor has never managed to strike the proper balance between risky over-reaction to the rejectionist threat and an equally dangerous complacency.

Inconsistent policies vis-a-vis the settlements: Throughout the 1992 electoral campaign, Labor emphasized its intention to freeze construction in the settlements and do away with fiscal incentives that hitherto made residence in the territories both attractive and convenient. Upon taking office, the government specifically promised to "dry up the flow of all state and public funds" not only to the West Bank, but also for the purchase of properties in Old Jerusalem's Muslim and Christian Quarters.[146] Subsequently, Rabin and his coalition partners repeatedly characterized the settlements as an "obstacle to peace" and an "unjustifiable burden," detrimental to both Israel's socio-economic well-being and the IDF's combat readiness.[147] In March 1995, the Prime Minister went as far as to link the existence of "minuscule settlements in the midst of dense Arab populations" with escalation of *Hamas* terrorism, effectively blaming Likud for collusion with Palestinian rejectionists.[148]

The stated intent "to starve the settlements" elicited an angry response from the opposition, to include a petition to Israel's Supreme Court.[149] Yet, its practical impact was quickly marginalized. First, as we have already noted, the settlers mobilized political and material support in the U.S. to offset the budget cuts, effectively sabotaging the government's plan and forestalling its desired impact.

Second, apparently responding to domestic and external pressures, the government diluted its own policy by moving away from a blanket ban on all construction to a more differentiated approach, allocating public funds to specific "strategic settlements," (e.g., those located in the greater Jerusalem metropolitan area, in the Jordan Valley and in Gush Etzion) and authorizing "private" development in others. The inevitable result of this inconsistency, if not appeasement, has been a 15% increase in the West Bank's Jewish population since Labor came to power, with a 10.3% spurt in 1994 alone.[150]

The case of Efrat is instructive in this regard: Populated primarily by immigrants from the U.S. and jokingly referred to a "Scarsdale-East," Efrat has been at the forefront of efforts to defy the construction freeze. Its leaders vowed to disobey orders to evacuate illegal squatters "even if this means confrontation with the army."[151] After a prolonged standoff, the government caved in. The permission to continue construction was granted personally by the Prime Minister, even as Efrat leaders pledged to continue their struggle "to keep the Palestinians from taking the land over."[152]

The government further undermined its own credibility--thus

Analytical Assessment of Israeli Rejectionism 177

emboldening the opposition--by tolerating *YESHA*'s massive, well-publicized campaign to expand roads, infrastructure and settlement boundaries. While the actions were duly denounced as "violations of the law" and threats were made "to bodily remove" illegal squatters, little was done to punish the blatant insolence. Initially, security forces merely stood by, "awaiting clear orders," while the settlers walked around the military roadblocks to continue their work.[153] Consequently, when the IDF and police were finally ordered in, they literally had to haul away hundreds of settlers, many of whom used toddlers and infants as shields. The ordeal was so wrenching for the soldiers that the government decided to leave future evictions to the police, calling upon the IDF only *in extremis*.[154]

While the government's desire to protect the Armed Forces from the emotional toll involved in confronting enraged fellow-citizens--particularly women and children--was understandable, its noble intentions could not withstand the test of reality. For, the approach left the authorities with little choice but to embroil the IDF in the escalating violence--or else to concede defeat--should Israel's already thinly stretched police prove unable to deal with West Bank unrest, while simultaneously quelling right-wing riots within the Green Line and preventing protesters from blockading key road junctions.[155] Thus, Labor effectively ceded the initiative, allowing the rejectionists to set the rules of the game and determine the outcomes.[156]

Tough talk, kid-glove treatment: There has been an equally wide gap between official rhetoric, promising to "get tough" with the rejectionists' challenge to legal authority, and practical steps to weaken their power.[157] Thus, government spokesmen went on record pillorying the extremists not only as a "threat to the very foundations of the rule of law," but also as "enemies of the people, who must be treated as enemies."[158] However, legal measures to end the sedition and punish repeat-offenders have been rare and, until November 1995, halfhearted.

To wit, criminal charges--when filed at all--languished in Israel's notoriously slow civil courts. Explicit recommendations by the Attorney General to subject the rejectionists to the much stricter--and swifter--Uniform Code of Military Justice have not been heeded, due, in large measure, to the General Staff's opposition.[159] Understandably, the IDF leadership was concerned that the settlers would use the military courts "as a stage for political agitation against the army and drag the IDF into the political struggle."[160] However, the impasse effectively condoned criminal behavior, thus making a mockery of the entire legal system and raising serious doubts as to the government's overall resolve.

Likewise, despite warnings of settler anti-Arab violence, issued as far back as 1993, the IDF continued to operate with dual--and thoroughly confusing--rules of engagement regarding the use of force against Israeli and Palestinian civilians. In general, troops were instructed to do all they could to avoid confrontations with settlers, using "reasonable" force only on order and as a last resort. Even handcuffs were not to be used "except in extreme cases, against settlers resisting arrest." Lethal force was "strictly prohibited, but could be considered permissible under extraordinary circumstances, such as during the Hebron massacre."[161] As of this writing, the policy remains unchanged.

Against this backdrop, it is difficult to give credence to pledges that "it is the IDF's supreme duty to enforce law and order on Arabs and Jews alike."[162] Even a thoroughly neutral, United Nations' peacekeeping force would be hard-pressed to sustain such splendid impartiality. To expect more than a semblance of even-handedness from the IDF--brutalized by the bitter experience of the *Intifada*, comprised of thousands of religious soldiers whose sentiments, if not loyalties, are with the settlers, and, in general, brought up to believe that its sacred mission is to defend Israel against its Arab enemies--is simply unrealistic. No wonder that eighteen-year-old conscripts and their only-slightly-older officers quickly become jaded as to both their duties and their chain of command.[163] This, in turn, only impedes the military's necessary adjustment to the new, highly ambiguous environment, wherein the distinction between friend and foe needs to be based on more fine-

Analytical Assessment of Israeli Rejectionism 179

grained considerations than nationality or religion.
Ineffectual law enforcement: Like the IDF, the Police and Security Services have been severely constrained in their ability to deal with Jewish extremism. The scope of problems is bewildering, ranging from shortages of manpower, equipment and financial resources, through inadequate intelligence, to insufficient cooperation--if not outright competition--among the various law enforcement agencies. Israel's Attorney General characterized the situation as "shocking," with hundreds of cases of settler violence--to include "murders of Arabs by extremist settlers known to the legal authorities"--never solved, let alone brought to justice. According to his grim assessment, most cases are closed "due to failure in the investigation stage, for lack of evidence, documentation, or absence of plaintiff: Arabs do not report crimes because they distrust the Israeli system and fear retaliation from the settlers; the Jews are not prepared to 'rat' on their friends; and the policemen and IDF officers look the other way."[164]

Service in the occupied territories has never been considered career-enhancing. With few upwardly mobile military and police professionals seeking assignment to the West Bank, the ranks have been filled with lower quality personnel, as well as with those who are sympathetic to the settlers' cause.[165] Regardless, the authorities have been unable to penetrate homogeneous, tight, ideologically closed organizations, which are, to boot, well equipped with modern communications gear and "more familiar with the Security Services and their methods than are most Israeli citizens." We can only surmise that the recent expansion of the rejectionist circle to include such elites as university professors, reserve officers and successful businessmen would compound the law enforcement problem, particularly since the extremists "increasingly view all state officials as the enemy."[166]

While the soul-searching that followed the Hebron massacre resulted in a reordering of priorities and increased allocations for actions against Jewish militants, "operational paralysis" continued to plague the Security Services. For one, the frustrating reality was that "the addition of resources and manpower can, perhaps, deter subversion and make it more difficult to carry out, but it cannot change the atmosphere that breeds and encourages the mad attacker of the day."[167] For another, "the strong linkage between the extremist groups and the core of the Israeli right-wing establishment" exposed law enforcement officials to intolerable political pressures--pressures that can only be expected to escalate now that Likud is back in power.

Worse, officers were often left in a lurch, with little top-level backing to shield them from the inevitable public fallout, which was bound to accompany any aggressive moves against fellow Israelis. Having had "the rug pulled from under them" on numerous occasions, the Security Services "got the message: What counts is the appearance of law enforcement, rather than real law enforcement."[168] Thus, in the all-too-real game of "cops and robbers," played daily throughout the West Bank, the "robbers" have been clearly outwitting the cops.[169]

As of this writing, the embattled Security Services are yet to recover from allegations of incompetence, if not outright complicity in Rabin's murder. What they need is a breathing space, an opportunity to regroup and time to adjust to the new mission of "protecting democracy against right-wing religious terror, while continuing to confront the traditional threat of Arab terrorism."[170] Whether and, if so, how this dual mission might evolve under Likud's rule--shaping the Services' future structure and operations-- is, of course, an open question.

Embedded problems, painful solutions: Few administrations enjoy the luxury of starting with a clean slate, unencumbered by the consequences of past successes and failures. The Labor government was no exception: Upon taking office in 1992, it faced a broad array of long-festering problems, all in dire need of attention. At a minimum, the new cabinet had to deal with--all at once--a divided, impatient society, in the throes of a seemingly perpetual crisis; a smoldering Palestinian uprising; a sputtering peace process; an aggressive, deeply entrenched and increasingly reckless settlers' movement; and a powerful right-wing, committed to a quick reversal of the elections' results. Labor also inherited a

Analytical Assessment of Israeli Rejectionism 181

general atmosphere of lawlessness, wherein the single-minded preoccupation with the *Intifada* overshadowed any concerns with Jewish extremism.

To a large extent, the range of options available to the Rabin-Peres administration has been severely circumscribed by past policies. Pivotal decisions--like the incorporation of West Bank settlements into Israel's territorial defense system, or the establishment of the *Yeshivoth Hesder*--are inherently difficult to reverse. Complicating matters still further was the fact that, over the past three decades, Labor--and Rabin personally--have played a key role in the design of at least some of the very actions they were now seeking to undo.

Yeshivoth Hesder (literally, "Arrangement Yeshivas," or religious field seminaries) predate the Six Day War, although the concept flourished in the early 1970's. The "arrangement" refers to a deal struck between the Ministry of Defense and the Orthodox establishment, wherein observant high school graduates were permitted to combine religious study with military service, in six-month-long, on again, off again cycles. The set-up followed the model of the venerable *NAHAL* (Pioneering Fighting Youth) Brigade, in which graduates of the Zionist youth movements could combine combat training with agricultural work, serving a part of their tour of duty in a front-line *kibbutz*. Even though the "arrangement" effectively shortened the student-soldiers' service to two years, instead of the obligatory three, it was applauded by the IDF leadership as an alternative to the draft evasion which was, up till then, quite prevalent among the Orthodox. By the late-1980's, there were 14 *Yeshivoth Hesder*, with an annual enrolment of 3,500 students.[171]

The *Hesderniks*, as they came to be called, were expected to complete their tour of duty and remain as settlers in the occupied territories. Many did not, preferring to pursue educational and career opportunities elsewhere. This trend accelerated in the wake of the Lebanon War, in which, for the first time since 1948, a significant number of yeshiva graduates and students were killed in combat.[172] Yet, while the system failed to produce the expected stream of dedicated settlers, it had other, unintended consequences.

First, the overwhelming majority of the teachers were closely associated with *Gush Emunim*--often with its most militant branches. Not surprisingly, the seminaries quickly became strongholds of and breeding grounds for virulent religious chauvinism. The siege mentality born of such incitement, combined with the daily friction typical of life in the occupied territories, could not but feed mutual animosities, thus further tightening the deadly embrace that locked both Israelis and Palestinians into a vicious circle of violence.

Second, the establishment of the *Yeshivoth Hesder* exposed new segments of Israel's religious population to military training and combat skills. What was clearly neglected, however, was the inculcation of the basic values and norms that, in a democracy, strictly delimit the use of force. Among the consequences of this critical failing have been: excesses perpetrated against civilians during the *Intifada*; ongoing acts of vigilantism, many involving shooting incidents; and the emergence of a new "Jewish Underground," with two of the indicted active duty officers directly associated with the seminaries. Rabin's assassin, Yigal Amir, is a product of this very system, having followed his religious studies with service in the elite Golani Brigade. At least one other co-conspirator is an active duty soldier *cum* rabbinical student.[173]

Third, the "arrangement" introduced into the Armed Forces soldiers and officers whose world view and, consequently, conduct, were often at odds with IDF traditions and doctrine. To wit, it was the religious troops' "clamoring for guidance from their rabbinical mentors" that brought about the infamous ruling prohibiting soldiers from following orders to withdraw from the territories.[174] Regardless of who initiated the action, the inescapable reality is that the religious edict injected an external--and extraneous--factor into the chain of command. This, in turn, raised the specter of dual loyalty, violated such critical military principles as unity of command and unity of effort, and created a situation wherein legal orders could be countermanded, or disobeyed, based upon literal interpretations of biblical injunctions.[175]

That the military leadership was seriously concerned with potential insubordination and a split in the ranks was readily apparent from the reported establishment of a new, special unit whose task would be "to confront the settlers in Judea, Samaria and Gaza, if a decision to evacuate settlements is reached." The three requirements for acceptance into the unit were similarly telling: Candidates were expected to "hold political views widely different from the settlers'; have no friends or relatives in the territories; and have no religious friends and relatives."[176] The story was officially denied by the IDF Spokesman, with the revealing comment that: "The IDF does not examine the political opinions of its recruits and does not select soldiers according to their beliefs. The only prerequisite is that the soldier follow legal orders."[177] Evidently, such respect for the chain of command could no longer be taken for granted. Indeed, many Israeli observers believe that the Orthodox troops' allegiance to civilian authority is questionable and their behavior in time of crisis unpredictable.

Whereas the *Yeshivoth Hesder* involved only a relatively small number of soldiers, their impact has been magnified many times over by the incorporation of the settlements into Israel's territorial defense system. The process began shortly after the Six Day War, when the territories were placed under a military government and Jewish residents were authorized to use lethal force in self-defense. Ultimately, it entailed the establishment of quasi-independent military units in the settlements, directly engaging thousands of civilians in security matters that, in a democracy, should have remained the exclusive domain of regular military and police forces.

Clashes between settlers and the Palestinian population occurred as early as 1967, escalating significantly after 1977, in tandem with Likud's colonization drive. In 1978, then Chief of the General Staff, Lieutenant General Raphael Eytan, assigned the settlers a partial responsibility for their own security. Each settlement was required to have a set number of fit combatants, including active duty officers. The latter were allowed to perform their military service on a part time basis--effectively as soldiers on extended leave. Additionally, reservists were reassigned from their regular units to the territorial defense formations. For both categories of personnel, the settlements thus became a duty station, as well as a home. Large quantities of weapons, including sophisticated equipment, were stored in the settlements under the control of local commanders and security officers. Regional mobile forces, equipped with armored personnel carriers, were set up to keep the Palestinian population at bay, while also serving as a strategic reserve.[178]

Evidently, the General Staff saw this system as an efficient, cost-effective way to secure the settlements. Moreover, territorial defense had an obvious ideological appeal in that it harkened back to the venerable Zionist tradition of a nation in arms, wherein frontier *kibbutzim* were Israel's first line of defense. The obvious difference was that the new system was targeted at internal security, guarding against the surrounding Arab population, rather than against cross-border incursions.[179]

Serious problems arose almost immediately, as the new units failed to follow standard military procedures and directives. Some, like the Judea Company, comprised of militant settlers from the Hebron area, became notorious for being trigger-happy and for brutally mistreating the local population. In other instances, grenades, heavy weapons and explosives--as well as jeeps and communication gear--were taken from regular army depots and stored in the settlements.[180] The military government of the West Bank, whose officers were often *Gush Emunim* supporters, was neither capable of dealing with the problem nor particularly interested in doing so.[181]

The Hebron massacre, perpetrated by an IDF reserve captain, and the subsequent indictment of two active duty officers as members of the "Jewish Underground" should have served as a rude awakening for the Israeli government in general and the military leadership in particular. By the same token, the widely reported participation of several reservists and at least one active-duty soldier in the plot to assassinate Rabin should have confirmed

Analytical Assessment of Israeli Rejectionism 185

earlier warnings that the IDF was not immune to subversion. Yet, in its four years in power, Labor did nothing to marginalize the *Yeshivoth Hesder*. Instead, it chose to enhance the territorial defense system with new, settlement-based units.[182]

The extent to which the militant minority could have a broader impact on the IDF--in terms of its overall discipline, cohesion, combat readiness, and mission effectiveness--can only be surmised. The fact is that, since early 1995, cases of insubordination have been proliferating among religious reservists. For example, a reserve battalion commander has been relieved of command after he publicly referred to Baruch Goldstein as "a soldier fallen in battle"--thus effectively glorifying the Hebron rampage. In response, soldiers serving in his battalion--all fellow Hebron settlers --returned their identity cards and declared themselves "discharged from reserve duty."[183] Similarly, five reserve captains and majors, including a fighter pilot, called a press conference to announce their "refusal to serve in a military that proposes to implement the policy of evacuating Judea and Samaria.[184] And, in a new departure, an active duty Warrant Officer was court martialled for refusing to follow orders to evict settlers.[185]

While the Armed Forces' long-term ability to withstand such corrosive influences is debatable, the danger of a more extensive contamination is real, particularly in view of the IDF's heavy reliance on the reserve components to augment its small standing force.

As a professional soldier and a former Chief of the General Staff, Prime Minister Rabin could not but have been acutely aware of the threats posed to the IDF--both immediately and in the longer term. Indeed, he rarely missed an opportunity to voice his dismay with attempts to "delegitimize," "splinter," and otherwise "subvert" the IDF's apolitical professionalism.[186] Yet, the noble--and necessary--effort to preserve the Armed Forces' status as the nation's cherished icon required more than good intentions. The root of the problem, namely militant rejectionism, had to be dealt with.

This begs the obvious question: If the authorities were, indeed, cognizant of the dangers facing the IDF and the nation as a whole, why weren't more aggressive steps taken to counter them? The answer is as clear as it is complex. For one, as long as the irreducible requirements of peace remained uncertain, Israel was reluctant to cede more than it might ultimately have to. Specifically, given the Israel-PLO agreement to defer the uprooting of settlements to a later stage of the peace process, any unilateral steps in that direction might have been construed as a preemptive surrender, inviting pressure for additional unrequited concessions.[187] Yet, as long as the settlements remained in place, they had to be safeguarded. This reality, in turn, constrained the government's negotiating posture, to the detriment of the peace process. The IDF was thus trapped in a quandary of Israel's own making.

For another, the fragility of Labor's coalition and its internal disunity dictated caution: Bold actions could have solidified the opposition around a *cause celebre*, potentially toppling the government. By the same token, Labor's weakness accounted for its consistent--and, ultimately, futile--attempts to appease the rejectionists through dialogue and actual concessions.[188] The problems inherent in this approach were obvious: It merely postponed the inevitable confrontation, while inviting additional pressure from the opposition and alienating Labor's more liberal coalition partners.

Moreover--assuming that Labor actually believed its own warnings that Israel was on the brink of internal war--its reluctance to take steps that could precipitate bloodshed was both natural and understandable. The risk, of course, was that the rejectionists would be far less scrupulous, misreading prudence for impotence.

Last, but certainly not least, were Rabin's own, deep-seated misgivings as to both the price to be paid for peace and the Palestinians' sincerity. These attitudes were reflected in his apparent preference for incremental, reversible actions and his more general tendency to defer rather than to charge ahead. The naturally more cautious Peres chose to follow a similar course.

Thus, initial vows to "crush those who raise their hand against the Israeli democracy" and to "outlaw racist, radical right-wing

Analytical Assessment of Israeli Rejectionism 187

organizations which harm democracy"[189] quickly gave way to a quest for dialogue and accommodation. Moreover, while the cabinet ordered the establishment of "a special task force to handle Jewish terror and the incitement and sedition by the radical right,"[190] only the most visible--and vituperative--leaders have been detained. And, to foster the *rapprochement* with the right, Peres promised to examine the possibility of authorizing further construction in the territories, and "keeping the settlements under Israeli sovereignty in the framework of the permanent arrangement."[191]

The need to heal the national rift and reestablish consensus was clear. Equally obvious were the risks involved in any attempt to bridge insurmountable political, ideological and strategic differences. At the very least, Labor was faced with a tough balancing act, made all the more difficult by the requirement to mobilize public support during an election year. These imperatives, in turn, could not but paralyze the Peres government at a critical juncture in the peace process, eventually leading to its electoral defeat. Yet, as our final chapter will demonstrate, what was--and is--necessary to marginalize the rejectionist threat is precisely the kind of bold action that both the Israelis and the Palestinians have been, up till now, hesitant to take.

Notes

1. For an exceptionally candid description of Israeli police attitudes towards and treatment of settlers' violence see *Yediot Ahronot*, June 23, 1995.

2. *The Washington Post*, February 5, 1984.

3. Palestinian geographer Khalil Tufakji, quoted in *The Washington Post*, June 26, 1995.

4. Edy Kaufman, Shukri B. Abed and Robert L. Rothstein, Editors, *Democracy, Peace, and the Arab Palestinian Conflict* (Boulder, CO. Lynne Rienner Publishers, 1993), pp. 77-81.

5. According to *The Jerusalem Post* of July 16, 1992, the threshold in the 1992 elections was 39,227 votes. According to the Israeli Foreign Ministry's Information Service, available in Internet, the corresponding number for 1996 was 45,774, with each Knesset seat "worth" 24,775 votes.

6. For a thoughtful, concise analysis of the Israeli political system and its party politics see Aronoff, especially pp. 19-64; Reich and Kieval, particularly pp. 1-53; and Sprinzak, pp. 71-80. For a more comprehensive review of the historic evolution and current tribulations of the Israeli polity, see Dan Horowitz and Moshe Lissak, *The Origins of the Israeli Polity* (Tel Aviv: Am Oved, 1988 - Hebrew), Shlomo Yuval, *The Political System of the State of Israel* (Tel Aviv: Am Oved, 1982 - Hebrew), Don Peretz, *The Government and Politics of Israel* (Boulder, CO: Westview Press, 1978), and Samuel J. Roberts, *Party and Policy in Israel: The Battle between Hawks and Doves*, (Boulder, CO: Westview Press, 1990).

7. *The New York Times*, May 31, 1996; *The Christian Science Monitor*, May 31, 1996; Israeli Ministry of Foreign Affairs Information Service, Internet, June 3, 1996.

8. Kyle and Peters, pp. 246-247.

9. *Ma'ariv*, Editorial, June 2, 1996.

10. See Reich and Kieval, pp. 14-17 and 72-93 for an excellent review of Sepharadi political attitudes. See also Frankel, pp. 140-162, for a revealing portrayal of the fusion of ethnicity, religion and politics typical of the Sepharadi community.

11. *Ha'aretz*, July 4, 1994, FBIS-NES-94-129, July 6, 1994, pp. 44-45, emphasis added.

12. *Nekuda*, July 1994, FBIS-NES-94-165, August 25, 1994, pp. 28-29.

13. *Nekuda*, July 1994, pp. 31-35.

14. *Nekuda*, July 1994, pp. 14-15; see also, *Nekuda*, May 1995, FBIS-NES-95-115, June 15, 1995, pp. 40-42.

15. *Nekuda*, July 1994, pp. 26-29.

16. *Al Ha'mishmar*, July 22, 1994, JPRS-NEA-94-047, August 26, 1994, pp. 42-43.

17. As things turned out, the ruling coalition had to depend on the ADP and *Hadash* to defeat several non-confidence motions, as well as to compensate for the defection of some Labor parliamentarians. Inevitably, this gave credence to the opposition's argument that the Labor government has lost its support and, thus, its legitimacy. The view that "it is immoral for Arabs to determine the most fateful decisions of the Jewish people" has been increasingly popular in Israel. See *Ha'aretz*, August 10, 1995 and *The Jerusalem Post*, August 8, 1995. For the government's position see Peres' interview with *Israel Radio*, August 9, 1995, FBIS-NES-95-155, August 11, 1995, pp. 27-29.

18. *Davar*, May 23, 1995, FBIS-NES-95-099, May 23, 1995, p. 32.

19. *Israel Radio*, May 22, 1995, FBIS-NES-95-099, May 23, 1995, pp. 32-33 and *Ma'ariv*, May 23, 1995.

20. *Ma'ariv*, May 23, 1995.

21. *The Jerusalem Post*, March 7, 1995.

22. *Ha'aretz*, March 8, 1995, FBIS-NES-95-046, March 9, 1995, p. 23. See also *The Jerusalem Post*, October 22 and October 24, 1995.

23. *Israel Radio*, March 8, 1995, FBIS-NES-95-046, March 9, 1995, p. 22 and *Yediot Ahronot*, March 8, 1995.

24. The acrimony escalated to the point that, by September 1995, The Third Way was about to "sever all ties" with Labor and declare itself an independent party. Given Labor's exceedingly narrow parliamentary plurality, the defection of even one Knesset Member would have severely impacted its ability to govern. To make matters worse, the breakaway faction was led by Avigdor Qahalani, the highly acclaimed hero of the 1973 war. Qahalani's vocal opposition to and criticism of the Israeli-Palestinian peace process as a threat to Israel's security constituted a serious challenge that Labor could ill afford to ignore. *The Jerusalem Post*, September 22, 1995. Ultimately, Third Way ran as an independent faction and won 4 seats in the 1996 Knesset, clearly at Labor's expense.

25. See Kyle and Peters, pp. 133-137, for a comprehensive analysis of Likud's "march of folly" and ensuing defeat.

190   The Deadly Embrace

26. *Ha'aretz* predicted on October 19,1995 that, because "to the immigrants, the government's absorption policy is an outright failure, if the next elections depend on the Russian immigrants--and they probably will--the next prime minister will be Likud Chairman, Benjamin Netanyahu."

27. Poll quoted in FBIS-NES-94-129, July 6, 1994, pp. 43-44.

28. For a thoughtful analysis of Rabin's "hesitant leadership" in general and, specifically, his lackluster performance in the social and economic arenas, see, *Davar*, April 5, 1995, FBIS-NES-94-068, April 8, 1994, pp. 33-34. See also, *Ha'aretz*, June 14, 1994.

29. See *Ha'aretz*, June 7, 1995, FBIS-NES-95-110, June 8, 1995, p. 38, for a cogent discussion of the potential impact of further fragmentation, particularly in light of the electoral reform allowing separate ballots for the Prime Minister and the Knesset. See also, *Ma'ariv*, June 2, 1996, for a post-election analysis to the effect that: "The 1996 elections will be seen as a crossroads, in which different population groups went their separate ways....We will never be one homogeneous society, but at least four societies: The religious-traditional world, which today is producing enough energy to be an autonomous unit, independent of the secular population; the world of the round glasses, which draws its inspiration from cosmopolitan criteria; the mainstream,which aspires to combine Zionist values with a bourgeoisie life style, based on the principles of Western civilization; and the Arab public, which is trying to settle the conflict between its life experience in the democratic society the Jews have established and their belonging to the Palestinian people and the Islamic faith."

30. Gadi Wolfsfeld, *The Politics of Provocation: Participation and Protest in Israel* (Albany, NY: State University of New York Press, 1988). Ira Sharkansky goes even further, analyzing the impact of "extremism, intensity,...apocalyptic warnings [and] prophetic policy advocacy in modern Israel." See his chapter in Reich and Kieval, pp. 55-69.

31. Nadav Ha'etzni, "The Palpable Threat of Civil Disobedience," *Ma'ariv*, July 14, 1995. For an opposing view, belittling the rejectionist threat and the dangers of internal war see Gideon Levi, "Losing Points," *Ha'aretz*, July 16, 1995.

32. Attorney General Michael Ben Ya'ir's interview with *Israel Radio*, November 12, 1995, FBIS-NES-95-218, November 13, 1995, p. 44. *Ma'ariv*'s November 8, 1995 commentary, ominously titled "Watch Over Him,"goes even further to warn that: "If they harm Shimon Peres, an internecine war will break out. The same masses who obviously restrained their expressions of mourning

Analytical Assessment of Israeli Rejectionism

this week will take the law into their hands to eradicate evil. And that would be a disaster. Therefore, no security task is more crucial these days than a close watch over Peres....We must not allow anything to happen to him." Likud leaders have been also receiving "numerous threats on their lives since Rabin's assassination." Several Likud branch offices have been vandalized. *The Jerusalem Post*, November 9, 1995.

33. *The Jerusalem Post*, April 11, 1995 and *Ha'tzofe*, August 10, 1995. The approach is clearly expressed in Likud's "peace with security" campaign slogan.

34. In his first speech since election as Prime Minister, Benjamin Netanyahu issued ringing calls for unity at home and peace with the Arabs, thus seeking to assuage anxieties at home and abroad. *The New York Times*, June 3, 1996. However, his pledges of unity and continuity in the peace process contrast sharply with Likud's *Issues Platform* and campaign rhetoric. See, for example, FBIS-NES-96-101-S, May 23, 1996, pp. 4-5 and *The Jerusalem Post*, May 17, 1996. While Israeli press reported only one case of political violence--wherein alleged Likud operatives shot and wounded a Labor activist posting ads for his party in a Tel Aviv suburb--the entire campaign was conducted in the shadow of politicide. Indeed, Peres was forced to cancel his election day activities due to warnings that "Jewish elements are threatening to harm him." *Israel Radio*, May 15, 1996, FBIS-NES-96-095, May 15, 1996, p. 19, *Israel Radio*, May 29, 1996, FBIS-NES-96-104, May 29, 1996, p. 40, and *Ma'ariv*, May 28, 1996.

35. Kach's open letter to Netanyahu, *Internet Judean Voice*, June 3, 1996, FBIS-NES-96-109, June 5, 1996, pp. 27-28.

36. *Ma'ariv*, September 1, 1995.

37. *Ha'aretz*, May 17, 1996.

38. *The Christian Science Monitor*, June 1, 1995. See also, *Israel Radio*, May 30, 1995, FBIS-NES-95-104, p. 41.

39. According to a July 1995 public opinion poll, 74% of Israelis believe that there should be a national referendum before the implementation of the second stage of the Oslo Agreement. *The Jerusalem Post*, July 21, 1995.

40. Poll cited in *Ha'aretz*, August 15, 1995.

192 The Deadly Embrace

41. *The Jerusalem Post*, April 30, 1995. See also, *IDF Radio*, April 30, 1995, FBIS-NES-95-083, May 1, 1995, pp. 33-34, quoting Itamar Rabinovich, Israel's Ambassador to Washington, "expressing doubts" that the U.S. would relay such messages to Damascus. The issue resurfaced again in September 1995, when Rabin publicly accused Likud of torpedoing the peace talks with Syria by informing Damascus "that it is worth their while to wait on the peace negotiations with Israel until after the elections." Benjamin Netanyahu vehemently denied the allegations as "something so ridiculous that it belongs in the realm of fantasy." *Israel Television* and *Israel Radio*, September 6, 1995, FBIS-NES-95-173, pp. 49-54.

42. *Israel Radio*, November 17 and November 18, 1994, FBIS-NES-94-223, November 18, 1994, p. 25; See also, *The Jerusalem Post*, November 18, 1994 and "Open Letter to Senator Helms," written by one of the settlers' most militant activists, Elyaqim Ha'etzni, and published in *Yediot Ahronot*, November 17, 1994.

43. Sprinzak, p. 107.

44. *Ibid*, p. 108. Emphasis in the original.

45. *Ha'aretz*, February 8, 1985, JPRS-NEA-85-045, March 27, 1985, pp. 66-68.

46. Sprinzak, pp. 108-109.

47. The analogy between *Bnei Akiva* and the Komosomol--as well as "other movements typical of totalitarian societies"--was drawn by the left-of-center *Al Ha'mishmar*, July 22, 1994, JPRS-NEA-94-047, pp. 42-44.

48. Sprinzak, pp. 124-125.

49. Sprinzak, pp. 109-133.

50. Lustick, pp. 165-166.

51. For a detailed analysis see Lustick, pp. 42-71 and Sprinzak, pp. 107-127.

52. Sprinzak, pp. 127-128.

53. Allon Groth, "Israeli Settlements Past, Present and Future," *Middle East International (MEI)*, June 10, 1994, pp. 19-20.

Analytical Assessment of Israeli Rejectionism   193

54. *Ibid.* See also, Sprinzak, pp. 128-129.

55. Sprinzak, p. 130.

56. Meron Benvenisti, *1986 Report: Demographic, Legal, Social, and Political Developments in the West Bank* (Jerusalem: The Jerusalem Post Press, 1986), pp. 56-57.

57. Lustick, p. 10 and p. 114.

58. *Ha'aretz*, February 8, 1985, JPRS-NEA-85-045, March 27, 1985, pp. 66-70.

59. Meron Benvenisti, *1987 Report: Demographic, Legal, Social, and Political Developments in the West Bank* (Jerusalem: The Jerusalem Post Press, 1987), p. 63.

60. For a detailed description of the settlers' progressive alienation see Frankel, pp. 100-111.

61. An article under this title was published in July 1994 issue of *Nekuda*. See FBIS-NES-94-165, pp. 28-29. For earlier statements see "Rebellion in the West Bank," *Al Ha'mishmar*, November 8, 1985 and *Ha'aretz*, January 26, 1990.

62. See, for example, *Ha'aretz*, August 10, 1995 and *Israel Radio*, August 8, 1995, FBIS-NES-95-153, p. 39. Similarly, *EYAL*, implicated in the Rabin assassination, vowed to change its name and continue operations if outlawed. *Yediot Ahronot*, November 7, 1995.

63. *Ha'aretz*, January 26, 1990, JPRS-NEA-90-022, April 18, 1990, pp. 33-38.

64. *Ibid.* See also, an interview with Baruch Marzel, a *Kach* activist and a key proponent of an independent Republic of Judea, *La Republica*, October 4, 1994, FBIS-NES-94-193, October 5, 1994, p. 33.

65. *Yediot Ahronot*, November 7, 1995.

66. *Ha'tzofe*, July 11, 1995, FBIS-NES-95-135, July 14, 1995, p. 39. See also, *Ma'ariv*, July 13, 1995. According to *Yediot Ahronot* of April 4, 1994, *Aharai* has been quite active in organizing opposition to the peace process within the IDF, to include sponsoring an officers' petition against territorial compromise in general and accords with the PLO in particular. Coincidentally, the plan for joint

194   The Deadly Embrace

IDF-PNA patrols encountered difficulties, with IDF officers reportedly "refusing to participate" in the program. A scheduled training course for future patrol leaders "had to be cancelled due to a small number of attendees." While IDF spokesmen attributed the problem to young officers' career considerations, rather than insubordination, the latter appears to be at least an equally plausible explanation. Cf. *Ma'ariv*, July 14, 1995.

67. *Yediot Ahronot*, July 8, 1994, FBIS-NES-94-132.

68. *Ibid.*

69. Interview with Aharon Domb, a JAC leader and one of the first settlers in Hebron, *Yediot Ahronot*, July 8, 1994. Similarly, Internet's *Judean Voice* proclaimed that Israel's leaders "are frightened for their lives, like most dictators who refuse to allow their people to express themselves democratically." Consequently, the Security Services "must now divert funds and energy away from their campaign against *Hamas* in order to safeguard Rabin and other leftist extremist politicians who have been labeled traitors and murderers by grass roots demonstrators throughout Israel." Quoted in FBIS-NES-95-169, August 31, 1995, pp. 37-38. See also, *Yediot Ahronot*, August 30, 1995 and Benjamin Kahane's statement in a radio interview that "due to the situation created in the country, somebody might attempt to hurt state leaders." *Israel Radio*, August 30, 1995 and Israeli Television, 29, August 1995, FBIS-NES-95-168, August 30, 1995, pp. 56-57. Evidently, these and other, equally explicit warnings have not been heeded.

70. *Ha'aretz*, April 4, 1995. The establishment of *EYAL* was first reported by *Ha'aretz*, March 22, 1995.

71. Quoted in *Ha'aretz*, April 4, 1995.

72. *Ha'aretz*, August 10, 1995. See also, *Nekuda*, September 1995, FBIS-NES-95-196, October 11, 1995, p. 51.

73. *Ha'aretz*, March 22, 1995.

74. *Yediot Ahronot*, November 6, 1995.

75. *Israel TV*, September 22, 1995, FBIS-NES-95-186, September 26, 1995, pp. 40-41. According to *Jericho Voice of Palestine Radio*, *EYAL* has gone as far as "cooperation and coordination with some quarters in the Islamic Jihad Movement in order to destroy the peace process using all means." Reportedly, evidence to

Analytical Assessment of Israeli Rejectionism   195

this effect has been presented by Arafat to the PNA Council of Ministers. *Jericho Voice of Palestine Radio*, December 9, 1995, FBIS-NES-95-237, December 11, 1995, p. 11.

76. *Ma'ariv*, July 9, 1993. See also, see Allon Groth, "In Goldstein's Shadow: The Case of Kiryat Arab [sic]," *MEI*, November 4, 1994, pp. 16-18. Indeed, both *EYAL* and The Sword of David, in separate phone calls to the Israeli media, claimed responsibility for the murder of a Palestinian resident of Halhul by several assailants wearing IDF uniforms. *Israel Radio*, September 8 and 10, 1995, FBIS-NES-95-175, September 11, 1995, p. 55.

77. *The Jerusalem Post*, January 15, 1995 and *Yediot Ahronot*, January 22, 1996. The Meshulam Sect, also referred to as "the Samaria militia," is reported to be active both in Israel proper and in the West Bank, with followers "even amongst prestigious sectors of the population, such as Air Force pilots." It is apparently heavily armed and its members are seen by the Israeli police as the most violent of the country's extremist groups--"a band of staunch nationalists who will not hesitate to fight against IDF soldiers, to forcibly prevent evacuation." The Sect's actions are clearly being taken seriously by the authorities. Police Inspector General, Asaf Hefetz, briefed the Cabinet on the threat, calling for action "before it's too late." Nonetheless, the Prime Minister stated that "since the group is not registered in any formal fashion, it cannot be legally banned." Similarly, the *Yediot Ahronot* report was quickly denied by a police spokesman as "inflated and sensational." *IDF Radio*, January 22, 1996, FBIS-NES-96-014, January 22, 1996, p. 57.

78. It is important to underscore that there was plenty of public information on these groups months before the Rabin assassination. Thus, according to a detailed analysis published in the September 11, 1995 issue of *Ma'ariv*, "a new situation has emerged in the territories over the past several months, against the backdrop of the progress made in the peace process....Jewish extremists are making more threats that they would do whatever they can to frustrate these moves, warning that they will attack Arabs and, if they must, Jews too. In view of this radicalization, the Security Services have tightened their surveillance of extremist movements such as *Kahane Chai, Kach* and *EYAL*." *Ma'ariv* explicitly highlights the close links among these organizations, noting also the emergence of yet another terrorist cell called *DOV*--Hebrew acronym for *Dikuy Bogdim*, or the Suppression of Traitors. Although details remain sketchy, its targets appear to be Israeli state officials, often publicly branded as "traitors" by the rejectionists. Similarly, *Ha'aretz* of August 17, 1995 reports the appearance of yet another splinter group: *Bereshit* (Genesis). Based in Tel Aviv, Genesis issued vituperative leaflets against the government, calling for "stepping up popular resistance in

order to overthrow the traitorous [Rabin]regime."

79. According to *Ha'aretz*, August 9, 1995, "until this day, not a single serious study has been published analyzing the various shades of the settler population." Polls published after the Rabin assassination found that two fifths of self-described Orthodox and ultra-Orthodox Jews approved of illegal demonstrations against government policies and 24% supported the use of violence to that end. Extrapolating from the data gathered, the pollsters concluded that "there are at least 100,000 men and women who believe it is permissible to engage in violent protest activities." *The Washington Post*, December 3, 1995.

80. Cf. Israel Shahak, "Is Israel Heading for a Civil War?," *MEI*, June 10, 1994, pp. 17-19, particularly his quote from *Davar*, March 25, 1994; See also, *Nekuda*, May 1995, FBIS-NES-95-115, June 15, 1995, pp. 40-42. An article published in the July 1995 issue of *Nekuda* theorized that when "the interests of Israel are, sadly, in conflict with the rights of Jewish religion, religious considerations should guide our political decisions, or else we will cease being a Jewish state." The article concluded that "the government of Israel may have the right to make political decisions on territorial concessions, but it has no right to wave the rights of the Jewish religion." FBIS-NES-95-150, August 4, 1995, pp.45-46.

81. See Harkabi, pp. 147-156 for a detailed analysis. Harkabi quotes several rabbis who went as far as to advocate overtly genocide, in "fulfillment of the commandment of a divinely ordained war to destroy Amalek"--in its modern incarnation as Palestinian Arabs--as per Deuteronomy 25:17-19. For a more moderate view see Rabbi Beni Elon's statement in *Ha'aretz*, August 10, 1995.

82. See Lustick, pp. 91-152 for a detailed analysis. For more recent statements see *Yediot Ahronot*, March 18, 1994.

83. *Yediot Ahronot*, July 8, 1994, FBIS-NES-94-132, July 11, 1994, pp. 55-58 and *Ha'aretz*, July 16, 1994, JPRS-NEA-94-045, August 18, 1994, pp. 39-41. See also, *Ha'tzofe*, July 12, 1995, FBIS-NES-95-135, July 14, 1995, pp. 40-41. Former IDF commanders, now active within the secular wing of the rejectionist movement, are among the most vocal opponents of any actions liable to involve the Armed Forces in politics, or entail violation of military order and discipline.

84. According to Israeli public opinion polls, conducted after Rabin's murder, some 100,000 self-described religious citizens continue to believe that it is permissible to engage in political violence. *The Washington Post*, December 3, 1995

Analytical Assessment of Israeli Rejectionism 197

85. *Ma'ariv*, July 14, 1995. See also, *Israel Radio*, July 19, 1995, FBIS-NES-95-138, July 19, 1995, p. 40, *The New York Times*, August 13, 1995, and *Ha'aretz*, August 9, 1995.

86. *Nekuda*, June 10, 1983, p. 17, cited in Lustick, p. 117. See also, *Yediot Ahronot*, June 8, 1994, FBIS-NES-94-132, July 11, 1994, pp. 55-58.

87. Quoted in Lustick, p. 118. See also, *Ha'aretz*, January 26, 1990, *Yediot Ahronot*, March 18, 1994, *and Ha'aretz*, April 4, 1995.

88. See *Ha'aretz*, July 16, 1995 for an interesting discussion of the internal divisions and their significance.

89. For an insightful analysis of internal divisions within the NRP, accentuated by Rabin's murder, see *Ha'aretz*, December 3, 1995.

90. Lustick, pp. 91-99 and Harkabi, pp. 138-183.

91. Aronoff, pp. 82-89.

92. *Israel Radio*, June 5 and June 6, 1995, FBIS-NES-95-108, pp. 38-39. According to *Ma'ariv*, September 11, 1995, Levi's new platform attempted to stake out a centrist position, "between Likud's radical right and Labor's radical left." While his stated views on the peace process were much closer to the former, his agenda was explicitly tuned to the exoteric grievances of Israel's lower classes. In the end, Levi returned to the Likud fold and was nominated to his pre-1992 position as Minister of Foreign Affairs. For an earlier analysis of Likud power struggles and their impact on the 1992 elections see Kyle and Peters, pp. 127-131.

93. For a cogent discussion of the secular nationalists' agenda see Kyle and Peters, pp. 255-259.

94. There is a voluminous body of literature delineating the nature, evolution and determinants of U.S.-Israel relationships. Among the best are: Nadav Safran, *Israel, The Embattled Ally* (Cambridge, MA: Belknap Press, 1978), Bernard Reich, *The United States and Israel: Influence in the Special Relationship* (New York, NY: Praeger, 1984), Nimrod Novik, *The United States and Israel: Domestic Determinants of a Changing U.S. Commitment* (Boulder, CO: Westview Press, 1986), Eytan Gilboa, *American Public Opinion Toward Israel and the Arab-Israeli Conflict* (Lexington, MA: Lexington Books, 1987), and David Schoenbaum, *The United States and the State of Israel* (New York, NY:

Oxford University Press, 1993). For an insightful analysis of newly-declassified materials pertinent to the early evolution of the partnership see Douglas Little, "The Making of a Special Relationship: The United States and Israel,1957-68, *International Journal of Middle East Studies*, Volume 25, No. 4, November 1993, pp. 563-585.

95. Stuart E. Eizenstat, *Formalizing the Strategic Partnership: The Next Step in U.S.-Israel Relations* (Washington, D.C.: The Washington Institute for Near East Policy, 1988).

96. For the Israeli perspective on the issues at stake see Shamir, pp. 263-291.

97. For an enlightening discussion of the interaction between support and influence see Abraham Ben Zvi, *Alliance Politics and the Limits of Influence: The Case of the U.S. and Israel* (Tel Aviv: Tel Aviv University, The Jaffee Center for Strategic Studies, 1984).

98. Michael Beenstock, "The Determinants of U.S. Assistance to Israel," *The Jerusalem Journal of International Relations*, Volume 14, No 1, 1992, pp. 65-97. See also, Larry Q. Nowles, "Overview of U.S. Assistance to Israel" (Washington, D.C.: Congressional Research Service, The Library of Congress, February 21, 1992), pp. 1-7 and *The New York Times*, September 23, 1991.

99. *Ibid.*

100. *Israel Foreign Ministry Information Service*, 1995 (available on Internet).

101. Government Accounting Office, Report to the Chairman, Committee on Appropriations, U.S. Senate, *U.S. Loan Guarantees for Immigrant Absorption* (Washington D.C.: USGAO, 1992), pp. 1-42.

102. *The Washington Post*, July 28, 1992. See also *The Christian Science Monitor*, June 20, 1991. According to Congressional testimony cited in the June 23, 1994 *New York Review*, "Israel spent $437 million on settlement activity in the occupied territories during the last fiscal year...much to support projects started by the previous Likud government." As of this writing, Israel continues to pay the penalty for investment beyond the Green Line--"several hundreds of millions of dollars" in 1995. See, *The Jerusalem Post*, June 22, 1995, quoting Prime Minister Rabin.

103. For a thoughtful discussion see, "Win a Battle, Lose a War," *The Economist*, September 21, 1991, pp. 25-26.

104. Among the more cogent depictions of the American Jewish community's attitudes toward Israel and role in shaping the U.S.-Israel relationship are: Edward B. Glick, *The Triangle Connection: America, Israel and American Jews* (London and Boston, MA: George Allen and Unwin, 1982)and David H. Goldberg, *Foreign Policy and Ethnic Interest Groups: American and Canadian Jews Lobby for Israel* (New York, NY: Greenwood Press, 1990).

105. For an insightful analysis see Stuart E. Eizenstat, "Loving Israel - Warts and All," *Foreign Policy*, Winter 1990-1991, pp. 87-105. The essay's title neatly captures the true nature of the relationship. See also, *The Christian Science Monitor*, June 28, 1991, *The Economist*,September 21, 1991, pp. 25-26 and *The Washington Post*, November 1, 1992.

106. Eizenstat, pp. 93-94.

107. *Ibid*, p. 91.

108. For an unvarnished presentation of the Israeli perspective see Matti Golan, *With Friends Like You* (New York, NY: The Free Press, 1992). The book's original Hebrew title, *Money Instead of Blood*, captures the author's bitter assessment of Israel's relationship with the diaspora.

109. See Frankel, pp. 212-233 for a superb analysis.

110. Steven Pearlstein, "What Israel Needs Most: Independence," *The Washington Post*, March 1, 1989. See also, Frankel, pp. 222-232 and Eizenstat, pp. 94-105.

111. Frankel, p. 225.

112. *The New York Times*, February 1, 1994. It should be noted that only about 40% of the money raised by the 181 American Jewish federations is turned over to Israel. The remainder is used to support local programs in U.S. Jewish communities and to pay for the rather extensive overhead expenses associated with the elaborate fund-raising infrastructure.

113. To circumvent the legal ban in the U.S. on contributions to foreign political parties, a significant portion of the funds is channelled through fronts registered as charitable organizations. The Golda Meir Foundation, for instance, nominally an educational body, funnels money to Labor. The right wing has traditionally been served by an equally elaborate, yet less visible network of financial conduits, with much of the money coming in the form of cash raised in

synagogue and community center meetings. *The Financial Times*, October 26, 1988.

114. *The Jerusalem Post*, April 7, 1995.

115. The statement was made by Yosi Beilin, the outspoken Deputy Foreign Minister, to a January 1994 WIZO gathering. Prime Minister Rabin reacted swiftly, calling the speech "completely moronic." Clyde Haberman, "An Israeli Anxiety: Should Charity Stay at Home," *The New York Times*, February 1, 1994. More recently, Israeli economist Joel Bainerman argued that American "generosity" was actually "hurting Israel," impeding economic reform, pushing the nation further into debt and encouraging the growth of bloated bureaucracies. Joel Bainerman, "Looking the Gift Horse in the Mouth," *The Wasington Post*, October 29, 1995.

116. *The Washington Post*, July 2, 1994. These statistics put the American Jewish community well ahead of Israeli public opinion, whose support for the Oslo process stands at 52%, with 53% opposed to IDF withdrawal from the West Bank. *Ma'ariv*, July 7, 1995 and *Yediot Ahronot*, July 7, 1995, FBIS-NES-95-133, July 12, 1995, p. 48.

117. *The Jerusalem Post*, June 22, 1995. See also, A. M. Rosenthal, "The PLO Papers," *The New York Times*, June 30, 1995 and Frank Gaffney Jr., "Giving Foreign Aid a Bad Name," *The Washington Times*, July 18, 1995. Rosenthal and Gaffney allege widespread corruption and misappropriation of funds within the PLO in general and the Palestinian National Authority in particular, accusing both the Clinton and Rabin administrations of attempts to "whitewash" the fraud and abuse. Concurrently, New York Senator, Alfonse D'Amato, introduced a bill that would bar all direct aid to the PNA, channeling it, instead, through U.S. agencies and non-government organizations.

118. *The Jerusalem Post*, June 22, 1995.

119. *Ibid*. See also, *Israel Television*, June 20, 1995, FBIS-NES-95-119, June 21, 1995, p. 49 and Joel Greenberg, "Faded Icon Is Asked What's He Done Lately," *The New York Times*, June 30, 1995.

120. *The Jerusalem Post*, June 22, 1995.

121. Israeli Television, May 26, 1995, FBIS-NES-95-104, May 31, 1995, p. 42. For an earlier analysis of the widening gap between Israel and the American Jewish establishment see Akiva Eldar, "Jewish Chutzpa," *Ha'aretz*, March 21,

Analytical Assessment of Israeli Rejectionism 201

1994. Eldar characterizes AIPAC's lobbying efforts as the "cheeky actions of Jewish functionaries," and an "insolent exploitation of their political clout, in direct opposition to Israel's legitimate government." He specifically condemns AIPAC for sponsoring a congressional petition on the status of Jerusalem, portraying it as "unprecedented behavior in relations between the sovereign State of Israel and diaspora Jewry, perhaps even between any sovereign state and an ethnic minority that bears no responsibility for the consequences of its deeds and misdeeds." In October 1995, the bill was passed by a large majority, leaving both the U.S. and Israeli administrations little choice but to offer an *ex post factum* endorsement.

122. *The Jerusalem Post*, July 8, 1993. More recently, Prime Minister Rabin lashed out against "extreme rightist elements," to include "a small group of American rabbis [who] should more appropriately be called ayatollahs," whose actions "sabotage" the peace process. Although Rabin did not provide specifics, it is likely that he was referring to the mid-June, 1995 lobbying effort spearheaded by some 50 Orthodox and Conservative rabbis and aimed at convincing Congress to deny U.S. aid to the Palestinian National Authority. Interview with *Davar*, July 7, 1995, FBIS-NES-95-131, July 10, 1995, pp. 61-65. See also, *Ha'aretz*, May 23, 1994, for an assessment of the "right wing's take over" of the American Jewish establishment. In another commentary, *Ha'aretz* criticized Rabin for "wrongly assuming that 'peace speaks for itself' and abandoning the U.S. arena to the Jewish and Israeli right wing." *Ibid.*, August 30, 1995. See also Rabin's September 24, 1995 interview with *The Jerusalem Post* in which he stated that American Jews, whose sons and daughters do not serve in the IDF "have no right to patronize Israel and no right to intervene or act on issues of war and peace."

123. *The Jerusalem Post*, June 23, 1995. See also, *The Jerusalem Post*, July 20, 1994 and *The Jewish Week*, May 5, 1994.

124. *The Jerusalem Post*, July 20, 1994. See also, Robert I. Friedman, "The Brooklyn Avengers," *The New York Review*, June 23, 1994, Eleanor Shapiro, "Jewish Settlers Bring Crusade Against Peace Plan to Bay Area," *Northern California Jewish Bulletin*, November 5, 1993, and *The Jewish Week*, May 5, 1994. According to *The Jerusalem Post*'s January 1, 1995 report, a parallel Yesha Fund has been set up in Europe.

125. Friedman. See also, Mike Wallace's interview with Colette Avital, the Israeli Consul General in New York, CBS 60 Minutes, February 27, 1994 and Israeli Television interview with Shulamit Aloni, May 26, 1995. According to NRP's organ, *Ha'tzofe*, Israel's Ambassador to Washington, Itamar Rabinovich,

accused American Jewish organizations of "undercutting the legitimacy of the Israeli government and democracy" through a wide-ranging propaganda campaign, depicting Jerusalem's attempt to crackdown on Jewish rejectionists as "violations of human rights, hostility toward religion and police brutality." Rabinovich is also said to have notified the government that "right-wing Americans are attempting to garner support for their struggle among liberal circles," by applying terminology usually associated with the 1960's Civil Rights Movement to the settlers' disobedience. *Ha'tzofe*, August 31, 1995, FBIS-NES-95-170, September 1, 1995, p. 42.

126. Friedman. See also, *The Jerusalem Post*, July 20, 1994.

127. *The Jerusalem Post*, July 20, 1994. See also, *The Jerusalem Post*, December 8, 1992 and November 17, 1993. Indeed, Yehiel Leiter, executive director of *YESHA*'s foreign desk in New York, is on record stating that "if there is no *YESHA*, there's nothing to be right-wing about."

128. *The New York Review*, June 23, 1994. For an earlier expose of the often fraudulent land acquisitions see Robert I. Friedman, "The Settlers," *The New York Review*, June 15, 1989, pp. 49-56. According to *Ha'tzofe*'s August 31, 1995 report, "money from American organizations has been flowing to right-wing organizations in Israel and to the Council of Jewish Settlements in Judea, Samaria and Gaza, causing grave concern among Israeli decision-makers."

129. Quoted by Winston Pickett, "The Pipeline of Money Has Sprung a Serious Leak," *The Jerusalem Post*, June 23, 1995. See also, Herb Keinon and Marilyn Henry, "Fund-raising's Version of the Great Divide," *The Jerusalem Post*, April 7, 1995. According to *The New York Times* of December 27, 1995, the UJA's losses were significant enough to cause it to "slip to the fourth place on the Chronicle of Philanthropy's list of top charities, behind the Salvation Army, the American Red Cross and Second Harvest, a national network of food banks. In 1990, the UJA was first."

130. In a dramatic demonstration of the growing rift between the Israeli government and the American Jewish community, Conservative and Reform synagogues refused to meet with a group of senior IDF reserve officers, sent as "state emissaries" to promote the peace process. Indeed, the Israeli Foreign Office has been receiving reports from consulates "pointing to growing opposition to the peace process among American Jews....Even the American Jewish Congress, which is identified with Labor, is not concealing its displeasure with its inability to counter the growing frustration in the U.S. with regard to terror." *Ha'aretz*, September 11, 1995.

131. Robert I. Friedman, "The Brooklyn Avengers," *The New York Review*, June 23, 1994.

132. Lawrence Cohler, "Inside Kahane Chai's Money Machine," *The Jewish Week*, April 14, 1994.

133. Anti-Defamation League, Research Report, *Extremism in the Name of Religion: The Violent Legacy of Meir Kahane* (Washington, D.C.: ADL, 1994), p. 17, citing *Ma'ariv*, July 9, 1993 and *The Washington Post*, March 6, 1994. According to *Yediot Ahronot* of March 6, 1994, Kach has 8000 dues-paying members in the U.S.

134. Friedman. See also, Cohler in *The Jewish Week*. The yeshiva is located in *K'far Tapuach*--*Kach*'s only West Bank settlement. As for "American Friends of the Yishuv", the deception is reinforced by a clever play on words: "*Yishuv*" means "a settlement" in Hebrew. It is also the historic name of the entire Jewish community in pre-independence, Palestine.

135. President Clinton's message to the Congress transmitting the Omnibus Counterterrorism Act of 1995, *Public Papers of the Presidents*, February 9, 1995. See also, Joe Sexton, "Assassination of Rabin Raises Alarm Over Role of Kahane's Violent Followers in the U.S.," *The New York Times*, November 13, 1995.

136. Interview with Avi Sonenthal, Head of Baltimore's Kahane Chai Chapter, *Baltimore Jewish Times*, February 3, 1995. See also, interviews with Noam Federman, *AP Online*, January 24, 1995 and Michael Guzofsky, national director of Kahane Chai in America, *Jewish Telegraphic Agency*, January 25, 1995. All mainstream Jewish organizations--as well as the Israeli government--expressed full support for the counterterrorism act, although the Anti Defamation League voiced concern that "the Administration categorized the extreme Jewish organizations on the same plane as the Arab terrorist groups." *Jewish Telegraphic Agency*, January 25, 1995.

137. *The Jerusalem Post*, December 14, 1995.

138. *The New York Times*, December 1, 1993 and *Philadelphia Inquirer*, December 21, 1993, quoted in the Anti-Defamation League's Research Report, p. 18. Israeli media have also reported weapons' smuggling by American *Kach* activists, posing as legitimate immigrants or tourists. *See*, for example, *Ha'ir*, March 18, 1994, FBIS-NES-94-056, March 23, 1994, p. 26. Even more specifically, Michael (Mike) Guzovsky, *Kahane Chai*'s top U.S. leader, has been

reported to travel to Israel under the name Yekutiel Ben Ya'akov, with the stated objective of "setting up training camps and an armed Jewish force that would defend the settlements after IDF redeployment." *Ma'ariv*, September 11, 1995.

139. *Ma'ariv*, July 9, 1993. See also, Friedman and *Israeli Television*, August 4, 1994, FBIS-NES-94-151, August 5, 1994, p. 25.

140. *Ma'ariv*, July 9, 1993. Interestingly, according to Guzovsky, it is more difficult to operate such training camps in Israel than in the U.S. Nonetheless, as we have noted above, Guzovsky went to Israel to set up "training camps and an armed Jewish force." *Ma'ariv*, September 11, 1995.

141. See, for example, Foreign Minister Peres' interview with *Israel Radio*, February 28, 1994, FBIS-NES-94-040, March 1, 1994, p. 33, *Israeli Television*, February 28, 1994, FBIS-NES-94-040, March 1, 1994, p. 33-34, and *Israeli Television*, March 15, 1994, FBIS-NES-94-051, March 16, 1994, p. 19. The Security Services' ability to deal with Jewish terrorism was significantly expanded via an order granting the Commander in Chief, Central Command, and his counterpart in the Southern Command the authority "to define any group advocating or employing violence as a terrorist organization." Thus far, however, the charter has been applied exclusively against *Kach* offshoots. *IDF Radio*, March 13, 1994, FBIS-NES-94-049, March 14, 1994, p. 39.

142. *Ha'tzofe*, March 15, 1994, FBIS-NES-94-052, March 16, 1994, p. 20. See also, *Ha'tzofe*, March 7, 1994, FBIS-NES-94-045, March 8, 1994, pp. 48-49, *Ha'aretz*, March 7, 1994, *Ha'aretz*, March 8, 1994, and *IDF Radio*, March 6, 1994, FBIS-NES-94-046, March 9, 1994, pp. 30-31.

143. *Yediot Ahronot*, July 13, 1995 and *Israel Radio*, July 13, 1995, FBIS-NES-95-135, July 14, 1995, pp. 39-40. According to a public opinion poll conducted by the Dahaf Institute, 77% of the respondents believe that rabbis have no right to issue rulings concerning West Bank evacuation. 58% thought that legal measures should be taken against rabbis who instruct soldiers to disobey orders. 81% felt that IDF troops should disregard the ruling altogether.

144. *Yediot Ahronot*, July 13, 1995. See also, Rabin's interview with *Davar*, July 7, 1995, FBIS-NES-95-131, July 10, 1995, pp. 61-65 and *Ma'ariv*, July 14, 1995.

145. Rabin's statement to the Cabinet quoted in *Ha'aretz*, July 24, 1995.

146. *The Jerusalem Post*, August 11, 1992.

Analytical Assessment of Israeli Rejectionism 205

147. See, for example, Rabin's interview with *Israel Radio*, April 13, 1994, FBIS-NES-94-074, April 18, 1994, pp. 40-41. See also, *Ma'ariv*, March 3, 1994 and *Yediot Ahronot*, April 20, 1994. *The Jerusalem Post* of June 22, 1995 quotes Rabin as stating that "it is costing us $250,000 per family to protect the settlements, even though their contribution to security is absolutely nil."

148. *Yediot Ahronot*, March 26, 1995.

149. *The Jerusalem Post*, September 3, 1992. See also, *The Jerusalem Post*, November 14, 1994 and December 29, 1994.

150. Data provided by Ariel Sharon, Likud's Housing Minister and the chief architect of West Bank colonization, in his February 22, 1995 speech at the National Press Club. According to the May 1996 issue of *Nekuda*, Labor's overall investment in the West Bank exceeded that of the Shamir government. FBIS-NES-96-116, June 14, 1996, pp. 24-25.

151. *The Jerusalem Post*, December 29, 1994. Scarsdale is a wealthy New York suburb, with a large Jewish population. Efrat's leader, Rabbi Shlomo Riskin, formerly of the Lincoln Square Synagogue in Manhattan, has been at the forefront of the opposition to Palestinian autonomy in the West Bank. A veteran of the American civil-rights movement, Rabbi Riskin and his U.S.-born followers claim to have brought Vietnam-era style of protest to Israel. Whether their actions indeed constitute legitimate civil disobedience--as opposed to sedition,--is, at best, debatable. Serge Schmemann, "Rabbi Takes U.S.-Style Protest to Israel," *The New York Times*, August 7, 1995 and Joel Greenberg, "Israel Faces the Limits of Dissent," *The New York Times*, August 13, 1995.

152. *Israel Radio* interview with Rabin, July 12, 1995, FBIS-NES-95-134, July 13, 1995, p. 50. See also, *The Jerusalem Post*, July 10 and July 18, 1995.

153. See, for example, *The Washington Post*, June 26, 1995; *The New York Times*, June 15, 1995; *Davar*, June 22, 1995; *Israel Radio*, June 17, 1995, FBIS-NES--95-117, June 19, 1995, pp. 29-30; *Israel Radio*, June 19, 1995, FBIS-NES-95-118, June 20, 1995, p. 40. Clear orders to stop settlers from blocking roads and "not to tolerate any further disruption of daily life" were not issued until July 23, following a series of skirmishes between the IDF and the settlers. *Ha'aretz*, July 23, 1995.

154. *The New York Times*, August 4, 1995, *Ma'ariv*, August 7, 1995, *Ha'aretz*, August 4, 1995. According to an unusually candid statement by Elik Ron, commander of the Judea and Samaria Police, "the settlers could see that the

paratroopers were ineffective when it came to dispersing a mob. They are kids who have not been trained for this job, and they did not know what to do. I believe that we should refrain from using soldiers to disperse such demonstrations to the extent possible....The possibility of using the army exists. The IDF is a legitimate tool when what needs to be upheld is not just the law but also democracy; however, this is a tool that should be saved for situations in which there is no alternative. Policemen are both better trained for the job and older. They willingly chose their profession and they are aware of the fact that they may be called upon to handle such difficult situations." *Yediot Ahronot*, August 3, 1995.

155. Indeed, within a few days of its decision to minimize reliance on the IDF, several companies from the Army's officers' school were dispatched to the West Bank to contend with rioting settlers. A senior Central Command spokesman explained the reversal as "involving only experienced soldiers." *The Jerusalem Post*, August 10, 1995. Given that IDF officer-candidates average 6-18 months of prior enlisted service, they can be considered "experienced" only in the most relative of terms.

156. Militant settler leaders readily acknowledged that the military was the main target of their campaign, precisely because "it is the people's army." Thus, their "message to Rabin and the military command was that they don't have the troops for this." The extremists further expected that, when faced with tens of thousands of resisting settlers and supporters, the IDF will be simply "paralyzed." *The New York Times*, August 13, 1995. Indeed, according to a public opinion poll published in *Ma'ariv*, August 3, 1995, 80% of the respondents believe that violence is unavoidable, since the settlers would use force to resist any further extension of Palestinian rule.

157. Jonathan Ferziger, "Israel Struggles with Settler Violence," *United Press International*, November 13, 1993.

158. In the wake of the Hebron massacre, Foreign Minister Peres condemned "right wing extremists" as "enemies of the people, who must be treated as enemies." *Israel Radio*, February 28, 1994, FBIS-NES-94-040, March 1, 1994, p. 33. See also Rabin's interview with *Davar*, July 7, 1995 and *IDF Radio* interview with Peres, July 11, 1995, FBIS-NES-95-132, July 11, 1995, p. 56.

159. *IDF Radio*, July 16, 1995, FBIS-NES-95-137, July 18, 1995, p. 53. In any event, charges against settlers engaging in anti-Palestinian violence are usually dropped "for lack of evidence." *Davar*, March 9, 1994, FBIS-NES-94-047, March 10, 1994, p. 21.

Analytical Assessment of Israeli Rejectionism 207

160. *Yediot Ahronot*, June 23, 1995. Reportedly, the Attorney General was well aware of the IDF's opposition to his plan to try settlers in military courts and has, therefore, abstained from executing his authority, while holding open the prospect of court martialling the settlers should "the situation become more acute."

161. *Ibid*. See also, *Israel Radio*, March 11 and March 13, 1994, FBIS-NES-94-049, March 14, 1994, p. 44, and *Ha'aretz*, March 15, 1994. According to *Ha'aretz*, in December 1993 the General Staff's Operations Directorate published a pamphlet delineating "expected" disturbances and attacks by the settlers. Specifically, three categories of anticipated activities were noted, ranging from "public disturbances, protests and demonstrations," through "riots in populated areas," to "violent actions that might endanger lives by stone throwing, burning property, use of cold-steel weapons, or shooting." Nonetheless, the manual stressed, in an underlined passage, that "a soldier shall not use arms against an Israeli." The pamphlet also specifically mentioned the locations in which such actions were to be expected, singling out Hebron as a hotbed of trouble. Yet, when Baruch Goldstein actually went on his killing spree two months after the manual was published, the reaction was one of "total surprise" and outright bewilderment. See also, *IDF Radio*, March 13, 1994, FBIS-NES-94-049, March 14, 1994, p. 39.

162. Lieutenant General Ehud Barak, Chief of the General Staff, *Israel Radio*, March 29, 1994, FBIS-NES-94-061, March 30, 1994, p. 31. See also the Cabinet's statement of "determination to enforce the law on an egalitarian basis, against anyone who conspires to commit murder, meaning, regardless of whether the offender is an Arab or a Jew. The government will not tolerate terrorism from any quarter whatsoever." *Israel Radio*, September 18, 1994, FBIS-NES-94-181, September 19, 1994, p. 44.

163. For a superb insight into the IDF's predicament during the *Intifada* see Frankel, pp. 67-90. The chapter's title, "Buried Alive in the West Bank" captures the difficulties involved in employing an armed force trained and equipped for fast maneuver warfare against a civil uprising.

164. Attorney General Michael Ben Ya'ir, quoted in *Ma'ariv*, June 23, 1995.

165. *The Washington Post*, February 5, 1984. More recent assessments indicate that little has changed in this regard. See, for example, *Ma'ariv*, February 13, 1995. According to Attorney General Ben Ya'ir, "over the years the police and IDF troops in the territories developed a deep affinity for the settlers. The main reason is that most Jewish policeman also work in a hostile environment, suffer

the same attacks as the settlers do and, more importantly, feed on the Israeli government's message with regard to the territories: Jewish citizens control the area and live under the Arab threat, while the Arabs are the controlled party." *Ma'ariv*, June 23, 1994.

166. *Ma'ariv*, July 1, 1994 and September 9, 1994. For an earlier assessment see also, *Ha'aretz*, January 26, 1990, FBIS-NEA-90-022, April 18, 1990, pp. 33-38.

167. *Ma'ariv*, February 13, 1995. See also, *Ma'ariv*, July 1, 1994.

168. *Ibid.* See also, *Yediot Ahronot*, June 23, 1995.

169. See, for example, *Ma'ariv*, February 13, 1995, *Ma'ariv*, July 1, 1994, and *Yediot Ahronot*, June 23, 1995.

170. *Ha'aretz*, November 14, 1995.

171. Sprinzak, p. 50, Lustick, pp. 55-56, and Israel Shahak, "Is Israel Heading for a Civil War?," MEI, June 10, 1993, pp. 17-19.

172. Lustick, p. 156 and 166. In an informal interview with one of the present authors, a senior IDF officer suggested that religious soldiers accounted for almost 50% of the casualties suffered during the incursion into Lebanon.

173. *Israel Radio*, December 4, 1995, FBIS-NES-95-233, December 5, 1995, pp. 29-30. The rabbinical edict that effectively sanctioned politicide by declaring Rabin a *rodef* and *moser*--i.e., a person who is condemned to death because he imperils the life of Jews or turns Jewish property to Gentiles--was also reported to have originated with *Yeshivoth Hesder* rabbis. *Ha'aretz*, November 27, 1995.

174. According to *Ma'ariv*'s July 14, 1995 interview with several of the 15 rabbis who authored the ruling, the initiative for the injunction did not come from the rabbis themselves but from the ranks: Religious soldiers serving in the IDF "inundated their mentors with calls for clear guidance." As promulgated, the ruling is all too clear. It states that: "Since the Torah commands not to hand over territories or evacuate settlements, decisions of a legitimate secular government cannot bind a Jew when they contravene religious law. Thus, there is a Torah ban on uprooting IDF camps and transferring the sites to the Gentiles, since this contravenes a positive commandment and also endangers life and the existence of the state."

Analytical Assessment of Israeli Rejectionism 209

175. Unity of command and unity of effort are universal military principles. Even in Lenin's and Stalin's heyday, when orders had to be co-signed by the political commissar, the principles were upheld, if not always followed in practice.

176. *Ma'ariv*, September 19, 1994, FBIS-NES-94-181, September 19, 1994, p. 44.

177. *Israel Radio*, September 19, 1994, FBIS-NES-94-181, September 19, 1994, p. 45. The IDF Spokesman confirmed that the Central Command had set up a Military Police company whose personnel are trained to prevent rioting by both Arabs and Jews and "stop any violations of the law."

178. *Ibid*. See also, Sprinzak, p. 136.

179. Davar, August 15, 1998. See also, *Ha'aretz*, April 5, 1994, Allon Groth, MEI, November 4, 1994 and Israel Shahak, MEI, June 10, 1994.

180. *Ha'aretz*, January 26, 1990, *The Jerusalem Post*, September 16, 1994, *Yediot Ahronot*, June 23, 1995, and *Ha'aretz*, June 28, 1995. For earlier assessment see, *The Washington Post*, February 5, 1984.

181. Sprinzak, p. 91.

182. These units were being set up as part of the IDF's redeployment plan. According to *Ha'aretz* of June 28, 1995, a separate unit will be responsible for each settlement's security, with its size to be determined by the number of resident families.

183. *Ha'aretz*, March 25, 1995.

184. *Israel Radio*, July 19, 1995, FBIS-NES-95-138, July 19, 1995, p. 40. See also *Israel Radio*, October 10, 1995, FBIS-NES-95-195, October 10, 1995, p. 64, reporting that "a group of 10 reserve soldiers, most of them officers, decided to refuse reserve duty because of the peace agreement signed by the government with the PLO."

185. *Israel Radio*, August 16, 1995, FBIS-NES-95-158, August 16, 1995, p. 42.

186. See, for example, *Israel Radio*, June 19, 1995, FBIS-NES-95-117, June 19, 1995, p. 28 and *Davar*, July 7, 1995.

187. Indeed, Yosi Beilin, Peres' close associate and chief negotiator with both the Palestinians and the NRP, declared that "we can attain a permanent arrangement in which most of the settlers would remain in their settlements and the areas they live in would be annexed to Israel and become part of sovereign Israel." *Ha'aretz*, November 28, 1995.

188. Surprisingly, the effort to engage the opposition gathered momentum in the wake of Rabin's assassination, with Peres apparently ready to endanger his partnership with the left-wing *Meretz* in order to woo the NRP and *Agudat Israel* into the coalition. *Jerusalem Government Press Office*, November 28, 1995, FBIS-NES-95-230, November 30, 1995, pp. 39-40. Moreover, Peres made several election-eve promises to expand construction in existing settlements. *Ma'ariv*, May 28, 1996.

189. *IDF Radio*, November 19, 1995, FBIS-NES-95-223, November 20, 1995, pp. 49-50.

190. *Ibid.*

191. *IDF Radio*, December 4, 1995, FBIS-NES-95-232, December 4, 1995, p. 45 and *Israel Radio*, November 23, 1995, FBIS-NES-95-226, November 24, 1995, p. 37.

CHAPTER FOUR

THE CONTEXT OF PALESTINIAN REJECTIONISM

CHAPTER IV

THE CONTEXT OF PALESTINIAN REJECTIONISM

Fight the unbelievers who gird about you and let them find firmness in you and know that Allah is with those who fear him.

Koran 9:123

Israel can beat all Arab armies. However, it can do nothing against a youth with a knife or an explosive charge on his body.

Imad al-Faluji, *Hamas* Leader in the West Bank and Gaza in *Frankfurter Rundschau*, May 3, 1995

Cursed be those who show fear and sell out. Cursed be those who are insensitive to the taste of humiliation and disgrace. It is a revolution until the liberation of land and man.

Al-Quds Palestinian Arab Radio, April 25, 1996

Historical Overview

Palestinian rejectionism is as old as the Zionist movement. Its essence is not just the refusal to accept particular tacit or formal agreements with Israel, but a denial of the very idea of a Jewish state. From the very beginning of Jewish migration to Palestine early in this century, there was periodic violence between the indigenous Arab population and the ever-growing Jewish settlement.[1] The creation of the State of Israel in 1948 and the subsequent Israeli victory in the War of Independence did little to change this. If anything, the shattering impact of the war intensified the Arab refusal to accept Israel's existence.

The Impact of 1948 - Defeat, Dispersal and Dejection: Three specific outcomes of the 1948 war were particularly significant for the Palestinians: the flight of the refugees, the expansion of Israel, and the extension of Egyptian and Jordanian control to the Gaza Strip and West Bank, respectively.

The large exodus of refugees from Israeli-controlled areas was due to several factors. Many fled because of systematic and deliberate coercion by the Zionists, while others simply followed the example of their own leaders who had departed for safer grounds. There were also cases of Palestinian notables encouraging people to flee, in the mistaken belief that Arab victory was a foregone conclusion and the exile would be short-lived. Lastly, there were those who always seek refuge from the ravages of war. Whatever the reason, the important fact for this study is that hundreds of thousands were displaced or dispossessed. For over three decades, most would languish in refugee camps, located in close proximity to Israel's borders, while the remainder would disperse throughout the Middle East and other parts of the world.

Although the Palestinian diaspora was physically separated from the homeland, the Palestinians--like their Jewish counterparts --did not forget it. Yet, while the attachment to Palestine was kept alive, strengthened and, at times, idealized in art, literature and poetry, reconquest was left to the Arab states. Thus, for the better part of twenty years, the Palestinians waited in vain for the Arab armies to transform their yearning to return into a reality.

The inability of the Arab states to effect this transformation was due to another outcome of the 1948 war, namely, the expansion of Israel to a size that was more defensible than it had been under the 1947 United Nations' partition plan. Exploiting breakdowns in cease-fire arrangements that punctuated the 1948 fighting--and capitalizing on its growing military prowess--Israel seized the Negev desert in the south and Upper Galilee in the north, both of which were considered vital for its security.

After the final armistice, Egyptian administrative control was extended to the Gaza Strip. Soon thereafter, in 1949, Jordan annexed the West Bank. This third outcome of the War of

The Context of Palestinian Rejectionism

Independence meant that the Palestinians were not only denied any form of statehood, but they also became the political pawns of the Arab regimes.

Though a younger generation of Palestinian leaders came to the fore in the 1950's, their dispersal subjected them to the various currents of secular ideology and nationalism in the area, such as Syrian and Iraqi Ba'thism, Egyptian Nasserism, and Marxism. This situation could not but further fragment the Palestinian community.

Emergence and Submergence of Organized Resistance: During the 1960's, two major organizations emerged to rectify this desultory state of affairs: the Palestine Liberation Organization (PLO) and *Al-Fatah*. (*Fatah* means "conquest" and is an acronym that reverses the order of letters in the Arabic name of the Palestine National Liberation Movement--*Harakat at-Tahir al-Watani al-Filistini*).

The PLO was established in 1964, at an Arab summit meeting, as the official voice of the Palestinian people. Shortly thereafter, it proceeded to set up a military wing, the Palestine Liberation Army (PLA). Despite claims to autonomy, the PLO was heavily influenced by Egypt. Since the PLA's main base of operations was in the Gaza Strip, Cairo was able to keep it on a short leash, lest it create problems with Israel at inopportune moments. The PLA's linkage with Egypt and its conventional force structure resulted in a low level of insurgent activity. This, in turn, led a number of Palestinian organizations to criticize the PLO for lack of revolutionary fervor.[2]

It was not long after the creation of the PLO that *Fatah* made its presence felt. *Fatah* was an ardent proponent of irregular--rather than conventional--warfare, as the best way to liberate Palestine, regardless of the strategy and views of Arab leaders. Consequently, it spent the years following its formation in the late 1950's planning guerrilla raids against Israel.[3] It carried out its first attacks in 1965, under the name *Al-Assifa* (the Storm).

With the exception of Syria, the Arab governments were either opposed or indifferent to *Fatah,* and many of its young recruits ended up in Arab jails. Moreover, there were a number of violent clashes with Jordanian and Lebanese forces, seeking to prevent guerrilla raids from originating in their territories for fear of Israeli reprisals.

The restrictions placed on PLO and *Fatah* activities meant that, until the late 1960's, the leadership of Arab rejectionism remained in the hands of the Arab states. While a number of specific attacks against Israelis in border areas, especially near the Gaza Strip, were carried out by Palestinians, the fighters were ultimately under the controlling influence of Arab governments, principally Egypt and Syria. The fact of the matter was that these regimes had little or no interest in seeing their claims and aspirations to leadership challenged by upstart Palestinians, bent on enhancing their own nationalist credentials. Thus, it was the policies of the Arab states --combined with the relative disorganization, lack of leadership and historical social factiousness of the Palestinian community--that made the PLO's and *Fatah*'s political clout negligible at best.

In spite of their asymmetrical political relationship, the PLO and the Egyptian leaders were united in their goal of eliminating the State of Israel. What they disagreed on was the strategy for achieving the common objective. For a number of Palestinian leaders, especially those inspired by the Chinese, Vietnamese, Algerian, and Cuban successes, the answer was clear: protracted people's war, relying on mass support and guerrilla attacks to weaken the enemy.[4] For Gamal Abdel Nasser, Egypt's charismatic leader, this was a ludicrous notion, given the size, topographical features and demography of Palestine. As he saw it, Israel's small size, its open, flat terrain and its majority Jewish population were hardly conducive to the kind of popular armed struggles which had succeeded in the jungles and mountains of Asia. Such thinking was, of course, entirely compatible with Nasser's belief that only Arab military forces, led by Egypt, could defeat the Israelis. The crushing rout of the Arab military forces in the 1967 Six Day War would soon modify this perception.

The Perils of Autonomy: Israel's lightning victory and conquest of the Sinai, Golan Heights and, especially, the Gaza Strip and West Bank, significantly expanded the physical territory and

The Context of Palestinian Rejectionism 217

population under Israel's control. Accordingly, some Palestinian leaders came to believe that the key arguments against their strategy of protracted armed struggle had been negated. Now there was expanded space and a population to sustain the insurgents. To borrow Mao's famous aphorism, there was water within which the fish could swim.

Buoyed by the August 29-September 1, 1967 Arab summit conference in Khartoum that flatly rejected any settlement, negotiations or recognition *vis-a-vis* Israel, the Palestinians began to carry out both guerrilla and terrorist attacks from adjacent Arab states, specifically Jordan and Lebanon. What distinguished these operations from incursions undertaken in the prewar period was that, for the most part, they were independent of Arab state control. Given the disgraceful defeat suffered by the Arab armed forces, the ensuing need to redeem wounded honor, and the concomitantly rising popularity of the Palestinian *fedayeen**, the establishment of bases and the conduct of cross-border operations could now proceed with far less obstruction by Arab governments.

As *fedayeen* guerrilla attacks and terrorism intensified during 1968, the Israelis began to strike back, often attacking across the borders with commando raids, aircraft and, at times, sizeable search and destroy missions. While not always fully successful--as demonstrated by the March 21, 1968 Karamah operation, in which the Israelis encountered stiff Palestinian and Jordanian resistance-- the punitive raids did raise the costs of acquiescing in *fedayeen* attacks and, thereby, brought renewed pressure to bear on Jordan and Lebanon to curtail, if not end, such activity. This, in turn, contributed to periodic clashes between Palestinian groups and local security agencies and armies. In Jordan, the situation reached the boiling point by late Summer, 1970, as a result of attempts by two Marxist groups--the Popular Front for the Liberation of Palestine (PFLP) and the Democratic Front for the Liberation of Palestine (DFLP)--to overthrow the Hashemite regime though

---

* *Fedayeen* means "men of sacrifice." The term is commonly used in reference to all Palestinian insurgents, regardless of organizational affiliation.

sabotage and political prosyletization. This sparked a brutal civil war that led to the seizure of Palestinian arsenals, the decimation of Palestinian fighting forces and their expulsion from Jordan.[5] Consequently, for the next few years, *fedayeen* militancy was limited mostly to terrorism both inside and outside the Middle East.

The Pragmatist-Rejectionist Split: While the terrorist attacks were often spectacular--and always painful and well-publicized--their strategic impact was minimal. In fact, they reflected a diminution of *fedayeen* capability, a trend which was reinforced by the growing credibility of Egyptian and Syrian conventional forces, regained through their partial successes in the October 1973 war.

Reduced to terrorism and severely limited when it came to guerrilla attacks, PLO Chairman Yasir Arafat began to reassess the overarching goal of destroying Israel, emphasizing, instead, the creation of a Palestinian authority in the West Bank and Gaza. Not surprisingly, this was strenuously opposed by Palestinian hard-liners. Arafat was condemned as a traitor by the PFLP, the renegade Abu Nidal Organization (ANO) and several smaller radical groups. Attempts by Palestinian spokesman--such as Arafat's deputy, Salah Khalaf (aka Abu Iyad)--to assuage critics with promises that a Palestinian authority would be only the first step in a phased approach to the liberation of Palestine, were perceived as little more than unconvincing equivocation. Palestinian rejectionists argued that accepting such an embryonic state would ensnare its cadres in the day-to-day business of governing and, thereby, sap their revolutionary fervor and doom the resistance.[6] The Israelis, of course, saw the phased solution as nothing more than incremental politicide (murder of a state).

Distrusted by adversaries and erstwhile allies alike, Arafat persisted in the search for a political breakthrough, while supporting continued terrorist and guerrilla attacks against Israel. As a consequence, he and his followers became the targets of both Arab and Israeli agents. To prevent any progress toward accommodation--however fragile and wistful it might have been-- Palestinian rejectionists pursued two courses of action. First, they

The Context of Palestinian Rejectionism 219

targeted Israeli civilians in the hope of provoking violent over-reaction. Second, they carried out assassinations against PLO pragmatists to dissuade others from dealing with Israel. Syria, fearful that the PLO might reach an accord with Israel--probably in conjunction with Jordan, thereby leaving Damascus without allies in its quest to compel Israel to return the Golan Heights--facilitated these actions.

In spite of considerable international pressure to terminate the presence of particularly notorious terrorist groups, like the PFLP-GC, in Syria, Damascus continued to support the rejectionists throughout the 1980's, both inside its own borders, as well as in Lebanon and Jordan. In the case of Jordan, the Syrian regime sponsored hit teams which targeted so-called "capitulationist" officials of the Hashemite government--a situation that, at the time, led high-level Jordanian military officers to refer to Israel as "the enemy," but to Syria as "the threat," in off-the-record conversations with one of the authors.[7] Understandably, King Hussein refrained from taking any bold steps without the political cover of PLO concurrence. Meanwhile, Egypt--clearly unfettered by such concerns--pursued its own strategic objectives, successfully concluding the first ever Israeli-Arab peace agreement. With the exception of Sudan and Oman, the U.S.-sponsored Camp David Accords received no support from either the Arab states or Palestinian organizations. Egypt was thrown out of the Arab League, with both the rejectionists and the pragmatists unequivocally blasting the agreement as a sellout of the Palestinian people. Even though Sadat had pledged himself repeatedly to pursue the "restoration of legitimate Palestinian rights," the accord left any serious pursuit of that somewhat ambiguous endeavor to the future. Simply put, the Camp David agreement was a land-for-peace deal between Israel and Egypt. It entailed the return of the Sinai in exchange for a long-standing Israeli national security objective: namely, recognition by and non-belligerence with its most powerful Arab neighbor. There was nothing in the Camp David Accords to entice even the pragmatist wing of the PLO. Consequently, the latter joined the hard core rejectionists in a loose alliance known as the Front of Steadfastness and Confrontation.

While verbally symbolizing the opposition to Camp David, the alliance, like many other past and future compacts, had neither organizational nor operational punch. It simply masked the enduring personal, ideological, teleological, and strategic differences that continued to divide the Palestinians. Ironically, the Front of Steadfastness and Confrontation played directly into Israel's hands, reinforcing its position that it was foolhardy and dangerous to differentiate among Palestinian groups.

In 1982, a floundering PLO was dealt another devastating blow when Israel's invasion of Lebanon led to the expulsion of most of its fighters to the far corners of the Arab world. Israel's principal war aims were shaped by Defense Minister Ariel Sharon and approved by Prime Minister Begin. In essence, they involved: removing an immediate threat to northern Israel, posed by the growing stockpile of conventional weaponry in the hands of the PLO; eliminating the Syrian presence in and influence over Lebanon; installing a friendly Maronite government, led by Bashir Gemayel; and, last but not least, consolidating Israeli control over the West Bank, by marginalizing popular support for the PLO through its ignominious military defeat.

The invasion--condemned by many Israelis as an ill-fated, unjust,and excessively costly enterprise--achieved, at best, only its first objective. Nonetheless, the dispersal of Arafat's followers eviscerated what little military capability the PLO had. Thus, by mid 1980's, the organization found itself all but ignored by Arab states that were increasingly preoccupied with the Iran-Iraq war. And, as if to add insult to injury, its remaining members in refugee camps in Lebanon were besieged at various times by both *Amal* (Hope), a militant Lebanese Shiite organization, and Syrian-backed Palestinian rejectionists.

The *Intifada*: In December 1987, a Palestinian uprising--the *Intifada* or "shaking off"--erupted in the Gaza Strip, spreading quickly to engulf the entire West Bank. For the next three years, the mixture of civil disobedience and low-level violence that characterized the uprising was met with a heavy-handed--and

The Context of Palestinian Rejectionism

largely ineffectual--Israeli response, magnified still further by the obvious disparities between the two combatants.[8] Although the *Intifada* began spontaneously, the PLO moved quickly to gain as much control over events as it could. While not entirely successful, it was nevertheless able to reap substantial political benefits from both the uprising and the extensive international media exposure which accompanied it. This allowed the PLO to recoup the momentum and restore some of the prestige it had lost in the early eighties. Unhappily for the PLO, the turnabout in its fortunes was soon aborted by the dramatic shift in world attention to the Iraqi invasion of Kuwait in 1990 and Arafat's ill-fated decision to back Baghdad.

The *Intifada* did not end the pragmatist-rejectionist cleavage in Palestinian ranks, nor, for that matter, within the Arab world at large. For the rejectionists, the *Intifada* was the *cause celebre* around which to rally support against "the violent repression of the Zionists." For Arafat, in contrast, the uprising provided an opportunity to bring international pressure to bear on an intransigent, right wing government in Israel that was rejecting his overtures. Yet, at no time during the *Intifada*, or the Gulf War, did Arafat back away publicly from his pragmatic stance on the Israeli question. In November 1988 he succeeded in getting the PLO's parliament in exile, the Palestine National Council (PNC), to endorse UN Security Council Resolutions 242 and 338, thereby implicitly recognizing Israel's existence. He took the next major step toward peace on May 3, 1989, declaring the Palestine National Charter's calls for Israel's destruction to be null and void.[9]

In the wake of these developments, Arafat was severely castigated by the rejectionists and largely ignored by Israel's Likud government. As noted, he hardly helped matters with his ill-advised support for Saddam Hussein, which left him weaker and more isolated than ever following the war. Nonetheless, as he had done so often in the past, Arafat rose like a phoenix from the ashes to become a key player in the negotiations between Israel and the Arabs--a participation made possible first by Washington's decision to support an indirect PLO role as part of a combined delegation with Jordan and, subsequently, by a change of administration in Jerusalem.

The new Israeli government, led by the Labor Party, was committed to a territorial compromise with the Arab states, but not the PLO. When Israel indicated that it preferred to deal with independent Palestinians from the territories and Jordan, it met stiff resistance from the Arabs. Stonewalling such resistance might have been feasible, were it not for a growing problem that was, in part, of Israel's own making: the emergence of a particularly virulent form of rejectionism, namely, militant Islamic fundamentalism.

Islamic Rejectionism: A New Factor in the Equation: Israel's rationale for tolerating, if not effectively fostering, the growth of Islamic activist groups in the territories was to establish a counterbalance to the PLO.[10] Much to Israel's dismay, however, the stratagem backfired when these groups categorically rejected Israel's right to exist, calling, instead, for an Islamic state in all of Palestine. In the words of Musa Abu-Marzuq, putative head of the Political Bureau of *Hamas*, the largest and most important of the Islamic militant groups: "Palestine, from the [Mediterranean] Sea to the [Jordan] River is Palestinian land that must be liberated. Responsibility for its liberation belongs to the Islamic community, especially the people of Palestine."[11]

Hamas ("zeal") is the acronym for *Harakat al-Muqawama al-Islamiyya*, or Islamic Resistance Movement. As we shall discuss in more detail in the next chapter, it evolved from the Palestinian branch of the international Muslim Brotherhood as an initially non-violent, political-religious organization, dedicated to the credo of a general Islamic renaissance in the Middle East that would usher in the liberation of Palestine. Since the Palestinian Muslims themselves would be the key instrument of this liberation, the members of *Hamas* busily concentrated on winning support through a combination of religious appeals, organizational efforts--especially on university campuses--and the provision of social services. In contrast, the smaller Islamic Jihad Movement in Palestine (IJM) proclaimed that liberation was possible without waiting for the antecedent Islamization of society. Seeing violence

The Context of Palestinian Rejectionism 223

as both a necessary and effective means to its ends, the IJM bolted from the Muslim Brotherhood in 1980 and established its own organizational structure. As things turned out, many of the differences between the two groups dissipated during the *Intifada*, when *Hamas*, under pressure to act more forcefully, reluctantly opted to engage in violence.

In the late 1980's, with *Hamas* and the IJM gaining support in the territories and becoming increasingly violent, the pragmatic--if still distrusted--PLO emerged as Israel's only viable alternative to rising Islamic militancy. More than anything, it was this ironic twist of fate that led the Labor government to gradually--and grudgingly--engage the PLO, first in the context of a joint PLO-Jordanian delegation, then directly. Alarmed by this Israeli about-face with respect to the PLO and the Islamists, the rejectionists sought to undo the damage by closing ranks and creating a coalition of ten militant groups. Headquartered in Damascus, the so-called Group of Ten joined the PFLP, the PFLP-GC, the DFLP, the Palestine Struggle Front, the Palestine Liberation Front, the Revolutionary Communist Party, the Palestinian National Resistance Movement, *Fatah* (also called *Fatah*-the Uprising and led by the Syrian-backed dissident Abu Musa), *S'aiqa, Hamas* and the IJM. On January 6, 1994, the members formalized their alliance--henceforth known as the Alliance of Palestinian Forces (APF)--with a detailed statement of goals, to include full national independence, as well as a call to step up the armed struggle and the *Intifada* as "the main arena of conflict with the Zionist enemy." Despite this proclamation and an associated commitment to create a Central Command to formulate decisions, policies and objectives to support its program, there was little coordination among the member-groups in the ensuing months.[12]

The main impetus for forming the APF had been provided in September 1993, when years of determined effort--and U.S. pressure--culminated in one dramatic moment, as heretofore bitter enemies shook hands on the White House lawn. As rejectionists on both sides watched in stunned disbelief, the mutual recognition between Israel and the PLO was followed, within a year, by turnover of territory, to include most of the Gaza Strip and the West Bank town of Jericho. All this, according to the APF, was tantamount to "national treason."[13]

Upon assuming control in Jericho and the Gaza Strip, Arafat confronted a host of long-festering social and economic problems. Adding to the already considerable burden placed on the fledgling Palestinian National Authority were implicit and explicit security requirements. While the IDF retained overall responsibility for safeguarding the territories and defending Jewish settlements, the PNA was held responsible for curbing internal violence and preventing terrorist attacks. Yet, despite pressure from the United States and Israel to crack down on *Hamas*, Arafat lacked both the resources and the will for an all-out confrontation.

There were several reasons for Arafat's initially lackluster performance. For one--like his Israeli counterparts--he was wary of precipitating a clash that could lead to fratricide in the Palestinian community. For another, given the meager territorial and economic gains he had achieved in the peace process, there was little incentive to take inordinate risks. The flaw inherent in this posture was that it communicated weakness, thus emboldening the rejectionists while exposing the PNA to further U.S. and Israeli pressure. Insofar as security was perceived as a test of Palestinian sincerity and, thus, a condition for further Israeli concessions in the West Bank, Arafat's initial vacillation trapped him in a classic Catch-22 situation. To make matters worse, the PNA's inability to prevent the Gaza Strip from becoming a springboard for terrorism strengthened the hand of Israeli rejectionists, lending credence to their argument that any dealings with the PLO spelled a mortal danger to their nation.

The rejectionists' admonitions notwithstanding, Palestinian and Israeli negotiators pressed ahead and, after gruelling talks, concluded a major agreement in the Egyptian town of Taba. The September 1995 accord provided for the transfer of much of the West Bank to the PNA. Although implementation involved convoluted, phased arrangements and postponed the resolution of such core issues as refugees, Jerusalem and water rights, it was

The Context of Palestinian Rejectionism

greeted as a positive step by most Palestinians, with the notable--and expected--exception of the APF and its supporters.

The Taba Accord (also called Oslo 2) clearly boosted the peace process. For the time being, rejectionists on both sides were thrown off balance by the international, regional and local support for the agreement. Although much of this backing was guarded, if not conditional, it symbolized progress and continued momentum for peace. Consequently, PNA efforts against rejectionist terrorism grew more robust, and there were increasing reports of a widening split within *Hamas* over whether or not the armed struggle should be suspended. Yet, while the successful Palestinian elections of January 1996 further reinforced the hopes for progress, the optimism was short-lived. Within the span of several weeks, an outbreak of *Hamas*-sponsored suicide bombings, followed by Likud's return to power, cast a pall of uncertainty over the future.

Goals and Strategies

At first glance, all Palestinian rejectionist groups appear to aim at shared goals. However, this impression, created by their virulent anti-Israeli rhetoric, breaks down under closer scrutiny. In reality, Palestinian rejectionism is quite differentiated in terms of the ends, ways and means comprising its strategies. There are also critical distinctions as to the desired end-state, that is, the ultimate political order to be established in Palestine, as well as the feasibility of cutting a deal with Israel. In this sense, Palestinian rejectionism is as nuanced and diverse as its Israeli counterpart.

The Different Faces of Rejectionism: At one extreme are the total rejectionists--both secular and religious--who dismiss the very notion of a Jewish state in Palestine. The most prominent secular groups here are: The Abu Nidal Organization and the Popular Front for the Liberation of Palestine-General Command (PFLP-GC), led by Ahmed Jibril, who has longstanding ties to Damascus. George Habash's PFLP remains close to the total rejectionists, even though, over the past few years, it has equivocated somewhat with respect to several of Arafat's policies, particularly those related to deals with Jerusalem that could lead to a Palestinian state side-by-side with Israel. Like the PFLP-GC and the more pragmatic DFLP, led by Naif Hawatmah, the PFLP is an egalitarian insurgent organization which ostensibly strives for a Marxist-Leninist political system in the new Palestine. The ultra-nationalist ANO, by contrast, pays little attention to prescribing the values, norms, structures, and institutions of a future Palestinian Arab polity.[14]

The Islamic groups, *Hamas* and the IJM, are made up of total rejectionists who unequivocally deny Israel's right to exist because Islamic jurisprudence expressly forbids usurpation of Muslim land and/or the imposition of infidels' authority over Muslims. Both are viewed as the cardinal sins the Zionists have committed when they seized Palestinian areas.

The Islamists see little or no value in either the nationalist, or the leftist ideological beliefs of the secular rejectionists, whom they have long distrusted--if not detested--as rivals in the Palestinian arena. *Hamas* and the IJM are, in our lexicon, reactionary-traditionalists who, as Ziyad Abu-Amr points out, are seeking to transform contemporary societies into communities "modeled after the first Islamic society."[15] Essentially, "the different types of Islamic groups believe in the need to establish an Islamic state, apply Islamic principles, and consider the Koran and the *Sunnah* [sayings and doings of the Prophet, established as legally binding precedents] as the basis for all facets of life...."[16] Thus, these groups' desired end-state is an Islamic political system in the new Palestine that will ultimately become a part of the universal Islamic community (the *umma*).

In fact, the struggle in Palestine is itself viewed as a propitious development, because of the redemptive role it can play in returning Muslims to "the true path." In the words of Abu Mus'ab, the Palestinian endeavor "...is an ordeal, because it is the dirtiest and vilest sort of human, the Jews, who are polluting the cleanest, noblest place on earth, the cradle of revelation, the point of the Prophet's ascension....It is a blessing because it came when the Islamic world was in the twilight of need, in order to lift the veils

The Context of Palestinian Rejectionism

of disgrace, and lay bare the surrender of Islamic souls, and to guide the people to death's rapture, beauty, splendor, and gain."[17] The similarities, in both tone and content, between these views and the positions espoused by the Israeli zealots are striking.

That such thinking is ultimately incompatible with the existence of a Jewish state in Palestine is clear from the following comments by the late IJM Secretary General, Fathi al-Shaqaqi:

> Palestine is a small country and consequently it cannot accommodate more than one state. This is something the Israelis understand and insist upon in their own particular way. This is too what we should understand and insist upon and struggle for through the Arabism and Islamism of Palestine. There can be no stability in the region without this. Besides, the establishment of a truly independent Palestinian state with the existence of Israel is not possible. This is because the nature of Israel as a state and as a function does not permit such a thing. I have already said that we understand this attitude toward Palestine as being the nucleus for our revival plan. Hence, the acceptance of a Palestinian state alongside Israel, besides being not possible, constitutes a dwarfing of the Palestinian question and conflicts with our revival plan.[18]

Less dogmatic and more opportunistic than the Islamists are the partial rejectionists, who oppose Arafat's compromises as give-aways for which the Palestinians have received little in return. They demand major Israeli concessions on issues like Jerusalem, the dismantling of Jewish settlements, the return of refugees, and so forth--before even considering a deal with Israel. They also denounce what they see as Arafat's overly authoritarian decision-making style. Included in these ranks are the DFLP, a Syrian-sponsored group called *S'aiqa* (the Thunderbolt), an Iraqi-backed organization, the Arab Liberation Front (ALF), and *Fatah*-the Uprising.

Despite its recent hard-line stance on the substance of Arafat's negotiating policies, the DFLP has never sided with the total rejectionists. In fact, it aligned with him against the total rejectionists in the 1970's and, as recently as 1994, its secretary general called for "an independent Palestinian state by the side of the state of Israel."[19] *S'aiqa* and the ALF, in contrast, follow instructions from their patrons in Damascus and Baghdad. In practical terms, this means they will oppose the peace process as long as that is in the interest of their sponsors, and come to terms with Israel if and when Syria and Iraq decide to do so.

Hezbollah (the Party of God), the radical Shiite group which surfaced in Lebanon in the early 1980's, is another rejectionist organization that clearly deserves attention. Although an outsider that has no ambition to supplant *Hamas* or the IJM, *Hezbollah* continues to be the most effective practitioner of guerrilla warfare against Israel. Unlike its more moderate Shiite rival in Lebanon, *Amal*, which strives for Israeli withdrawal from the so-called Security Zone in southern Lebanon, *Hezbollah* wants Israel, which it refers to as "Northern Palestine," expunged from the map of the Middle East. It also indulges in racist tantrums about the corrupting, criminal and treacherous nature of Jews. As Sheik Subhi al-Tufayli, *Hezbollah's* former Secretary-General and, subsequently, its representative in the al-Biqa Valley, bluntly put it: "Our goal is to destroy the Zionist entity, and in the near future there won't be a single Jew or Zionist left in Palestine." To accomplish this aim, he has vowed that, even if Israel withdraws from Lebanon, the resistance will go on.[20] Since most *Hezbollah* attacks are justified as legitimate acts of Lebanese national liberation, the question for the future is whether an Israeli decision to withdraw from its Security Zone would, in fact, alter the goal of destroying Israel or merely relegate it to the rhetorical sphere.

Strategic Incoherence

In terms of strategy--that is, the orchestrated use of resources to achieve political aims--there is significant incoherence among the Palestinian rejectionists. As a general matter, groups that surfaced in the late 1960's and early 1970's shared a commitment to a protracted armed struggle, based on mass support, strong organization and guerrilla attacks as the way to defeat Israel. The

The Context of Palestinian Rejectionism

operationalization of this protracted popular war strategy, however, left much to be desired.[21] Some groups, most notably the DFLP and, to a somewhat lesser degree, the PFLP, stressed the need to engage in extensive political organization and mobilization, especially in the refugee camps, prior to escalating violence. Others, like the PFLP-GC and the ANO, impatient with the time and effort that needed to be expended on political work, opted instead to emphasize violent activity. In so doing, they departed from the protracted popular war strategy and, in effect, adopted a military focus strategy of the kind popularized by Che Guevara in Cuba and discussed in Chapter I.[22] Somewhere in between, but inclined to the military focus strategy, was *Fatah*. *S'aiqa* and the ALF, by contrast, evinced little in the way of strategic thinking, which was hardly surprising since they were merely doing Syria's and Iraq's bidding.

Further complicating the Palestinians' strategic calculus was a basic assumption by the PFLP, the DFLP and some other Marxist groups that the liberation of Palestine was contingent on the prior overthrow of such "reactionary" Arab regimes as those in Jordan and Saudi Arabia. This line of reasoning was rejected by *Fatah* and the other pragmatists, who feared that it could undermine desperately needed external support from the Arab states. Their argument proved to be prophetic when a civil war--precipitated by PFLP and DFLP attempts to sabotage the Hashemite regime in 1970--led to the PLO's disastrous defeat at the hands of the Jordanian Armed Forces.

The problem of strategic dissensus did not resolve itself after the 1974 pragmatist-rejectionist split. Basically, the groups continued down their vague pathways, with their actions taking on an increasingly *ad hoc* character. While the rhetoric of armed struggle continued to fill the airways of the Middle East, guerrilla operations and terrorism became increasingly episodic.

Concurrently, there was an escalation in internecine violence between the pragmatists and their rejectionist opponents. The conflict between Arafat's supporters and those of Abu Nidal became especially deadly, as the latter lashed out at PLO moderates, officials from Arab states, Israelis, and innocent citizens from various non-Middle Eastern countries. The violence continued into the 1990's, with activists on both sides battling each other on and off in southern Lebanon and elsewhere. Among the many casualties of these bloody clashes was Arafat's main lieutenant, Abu Iyad, assassinated by an Abu Nidal gunman in Tunis.[23]

The secular rejectionists' strategic ineffectiveness has never been rectified, in large measure because of their endemic fragmentation. Poorly defined merger schemes, such as the one announced by the PFLP and the DFLP in the fall of 1994, were reminiscent of similarly stillborn PLO plans conceived in the 1970's. What was missing from the lofty rhetoric that accompanied these attempts at unity was any indication of a clear, detailed, systematic strategy that would go beyond shopworn calls for mass support and struggle.

Whether the IJM and *Hamas* have comprehensive strategies is also open to debate, since they are yet to produce anything even remotely comparable to the previously discussed, systematic blueprints of past insurgent leaders, like Mao, Che, Ho Chi Minh and their disciples. Instead, confusion and contradictions reign. Thus, for example, comments by the IJM's al-Shaqaqi about the need to mobilize the Palestinian and Arab masses for a total struggle--which will reverse what he characterizes as an "unfavorable balance of power"--leave the impression that the IJM organization is guided by the protracted popular war strategy. However, the actions and statements of other members are more akin to a military focus strategy.[24] Indeed, just like Ahmed Jibril of the PFLP-GC on the secular side, the IJM's words extol mass support, while its deeds center more on violence than on the painstaking and extensive organizational tasks necessary to actualize such support. Armed *Jihad*, according to al-Shaqaqi, is the movement's *raison d'etre*.[25] What is missing from the rhetoric is any compelling discussion of just how--and in what sequence-- these general concepts are to be operationalized and translated into political outcomes.

The Context of Palestinian Rejectionism

As for the larger and more important *Hamas*, there are, to be sure, elements of a comprehensive strategic design in both its efforts to build a following through the provision of community services at the grass roots level, as well as in its violence against Israelis and Palestinian collaborators. What one cannot find, however, is a carefully thought out, programmatic plan for pulling it all together.[26] In fact, one close observer of *Hamas* goes so far as to say that it does not even have a specific political program or position *vis-a-vis* the Gaza Strip and the West Bank, because of its fixation on the regional status of Islam.[27]

Furthermore, given the tactical shifts of both *Hamas* and the IJM in regard to terrorism, it is difficult to avoid the impression that the violence they espouse is more an impulsive proclivity than a means perceived to be necessary to attain a specific strategic end.

To wit, the Islamists' assertions that terrorist attacks on Israeli civilians are launched only in response to Israeli violence against Palestinians are often contradicted by equally emphatic statements that attacks on civilians will end when Israel withdraws from Gaza, the West Bank and Jerusalem. And, as if to dispel any moral qualms, there is, at times, the accompanying casuistic reasoning that, since all Israeli civilians are soldiers, be it active duty or reserve, they are always a legitimate target.[28]

While such rhetoric might serve as justification for tactical operations, it fails to provide a strategic vision, or specify the role terrorism is to play in accomplishing mid- and long-term goals. Absent also is a clear notion of its explicit relationship to--and synergy with--the various political ploys that are being used along the way. Indeed, if *Hamas* official Imad al-Faluji is to be believed, there might even be a 10-year or 100-year truce with Israel.[29] To muddle matters still further, there are periodic suggestions that the struggle must be construed in terms of centuries (like the crusades), rather than decades.[30] Just how such time-lines might fit in the larger scheme of things is never specified. In short, the conceptual--and practical--distinction between strategic objectives and the instruments employed to attain those objectives is blurred, if not lacking altogether.[31]

Perhaps this void in strategic thinking is to be expected, given *Hamas'* reluctance to engage in violence in the first place, in part out of a belief that the replacement of apostate Arab regimes by Islamic structures--and the subsequent active involvement of the Muslim masses throughout the region--are necessary preconditions for defeating the Zionists.[32] For such an approach submerges the Palestinian question in the regional Islamic milieu. Thus, it obviates the need to come to grips with the myriad bedeviling details of a coherent approach that would assure the Islamization and liberation of Palestine. It is also instructive to note that the notion of toppling "corrupt, reactionary" regimes in the Arab arena outside Palestine is similar to the thinking of the PFLP and DFLP in the late 1960's regarding class enemies, which we noted above. Now, as then, it is a sure-fire way to make new adversaries and re-energize old ones.

Given the obvious flaws in the strategic thinking of the various Palestinian resistance organizations, it should come as no surprise that the Alliance of Palestinian Forces could not arrive at a common approach beyond a general--and vehement--opposition to the peace process. Although George Habash claims that the APF's main intermediate objective is to revitalize the *Intifada*--restoring it to the 1988-89 zenith, to undermine the Israeli economy--there is no way to ascertain whether he expects civil disobedience and low-level violence to suffice or whether, as he later suggests, armed struggle is also necessary.[33] Of course, if and when Habash provides a clearer definition of APF's strategy, there will still be a need for the other organizations to follow suit. Given the rejectionists' past track record with respect to integrated thinking, policies and behavior, this is likely to be easier said than done.

For now, absent an overarching strategic consensus, each member group is essentially left to its own devices in designing the ways and means by which to accomplish the aim of torpedoing the peace process. As a leading Palestinian figure told the London Arabic newspaper *Al-Hayah*: "Every faction [in the APF] differs with the other on fundamental matters related to their strategic or tactical concepts of the Palestinian situation."[34] It would not be an

The Context of Palestinian Rejectionism

overstatement to suggest that this kind of discord constitutes a grave deficiency for any political movement--particularly one which acknowledges that the current balance of power favors the adversary.

The Price of Strategic Incoherence: As any serious student of warfare knows, a clearly articulated and comprehensive strategy is a crucial ingredient of military and, ultimately, political success. This enduring truth is often obscured by the popular images of war as a series of discrete tactical engagements, the outcomes of which are determined by passion, valor, or a morally compelling cause. The inescapable reality is that attributes such as these lose their value in the context of flawed strategic thinking. For it is grand strategy that specifies, clarifies and integrates political and military goals with the means to achieve them. It also provides a common sense of purpose, parameters for action, and the imperative for coordinating and orchestrating the myriad specific tasks--such as financing, propaganda, training, intelligence gathering and dissemination, operational planning, logistics, and so on--which ultimately assure victory. Where these things are done differently by disparate groups, contradictions, neglect, non-performance, wasted effort, and, in the end, failure are literally a foregone conclusion.

As we emphasized in Chapter I, nowhere is the need for a sound, well-conceived strategy more vital than in internal wars, where governments usually have a preponderance of strength at the outset. It is hardly coincidental, therefore, that successful insurgent leaders have consistently emphasized sound strategic thought as a necessary prerequisite for victory. Understanding this essential point throws the Palestinian situation into bold relief. Since the rejectionist organizations face not only the old Israeli foe, with its preponderant power, but also the PNA, a newly emerging opponent, their failure to craft and agree upon a comprehensive grand strategy is nothing less than a recipe for defeat.

Forms of Warfare

Clearly, terrorism and guerrilla warfare are the Palestinian rejectionists' preferred forms of warfare. No attention is paid to conventional engagements, since they are well beyond these organizations' current capability. When the Palestine National Charter established commando actions as the central mode of operations in the late 1960's, guerrilla attacks against Israeli military, paramilitary and police forces--as well as civilian targets--escalated in terms of both frequency and scope.[35]

Israel's initially lackadaisical reaction was quickly replaced by an effective counter-guerrilla program that reduced the number and effectiveness of guerrilla actions. Combined with the devastating impact of the civil war in Jordan, the strategy fashioned by Israel severely curtailed the Palestinian ability to sustain this demanding form of warfare. Consequently, the Palestinians turned increasingly to terrorism--i.e., attacks against noncombatants, especially innocent civilians--inside Israel, in the occupied territories and elsewhere in the world. Although many such attacks were carried out by Black September, a clandestine group created by *Fatah's* intelligence apparatus, the PFLP and the PFLP-GC were also heavily engaged. Terrorism was not new to either of these organizations, since both had been involved in notorious incidents before.[36]

The short-term objectives of terrorist acts varied by group and situation, and the same kinds of actions often had very different purposes. Two hostage and barricade situations in the Spring of 1974 in northern Israel--one at Ma'alot, the other at Qiryat Sh'mone--are illustrative. In the former case, the DFLP held children hostage and demanded the release of prisoners from all groups, in order to enhance its stature as a serious player in any forthcoming peace talks. In the latter case, the PFLP-GC's seizure of residents in an apartment building was designed to torpedo the very possibility of peace talks.

Situations such as these help explain why it is so difficult to generalize even about the short-term aims of terrorist actions--beyond the usual common denominator of gaining publicity and

The Context of Palestinian Rejectionism 235

credibility. As for the longer term, it has never been clear how the cumulative impact of acts with diverse and, sometimes, contradictory objectives was to contribute to the achievement of strategic goals. Much the same could be said about terrorist attacks executed outside the Middle East.

The well-publicized transnational terrorist attacks on airliners, airline terminals, Olympic athletes, cruise ships, and so forth during the early 1970's were eventually criticized by a number of Arab states, which themselves, at times, fell victim to such behavior (e.g., Saudi Arabia). As a result, the outrages subsided, only to be resurrected in reaction to Sadat's political success in the 1973 war and his ensuing willingness to negotiate directly with Israel. Then, when the PLO split apart a year later, terrorism came to be associated mostly, but not exclusively, with the newly emergent rejectionist constellation. In fact, with few exceptions, the PFLP, PFLP-GC, ANO, and Abu Abbas' Palestine Liberation Front targeted civilians in the hope of provoking Israeli over-reaction that would undermine any and all peace efforts. Moderate Arab political figures, including members of the PLO, were also among the victims. Ironically, Abu Nidal's outrages were said to have been inspired by Vladimir Ze'ev Jabotinsky's thinking and the example set by Jewish terrorist groups during the British Mandate.[37] To justify their violent acts, these groups--like their counterparts worldwide--invariably claimed the freedom fighter's mantle, thus further confusing ends and means.

The appearance of Islamic *Jihad* and *Hamas* simply added more incidents to the terrorist ledger. With few exceptions, the attacks carried out by these groups in the late 1980's and 1990's were targeted against civilians in the territories and in Israel proper and involved a good deal of indiscriminate killing. As of this writing, there have been no transnational terrorist attacks by either *Hamas* or the IJM, although the former warned that if Israel attacked its operatives abroad--presumably with hit teams--*Hamas* would carry the battle outside the region.[38]

Be that as it may, the short-term aims of the Islamists' terrorist attacks have been, thus far, similar to those pursued by the secular rejectionist groups. Abu-Amr, for example, notes that violent acts by *Hamas* are designed to embarrass the negotiating groups and bolster its own status as a force to be reckoned with--a force without which no peace accord could be reached.[39]

Hezbollah's operations in southern Lebanon contrast sharply with *Hamas* and IJM terrorism. The Iranian-sponsored Party of God succeeded in enmeshing the IDF and Israeli security forces in a costly guerrilla war, which began in the early 1980's and became very effective and sophisticated by the 1990's.[40] Indeed, we would posit that the April 1996 outbreak of full-scale hostilities, which involved, once again, Israeli air strikes, naval bombardments and artillery barrages--as well as high-level U.S. diplomacy--as against *Hezbollah*'s *Katyusha* rocket attacks, was an outgrowth of Israel's abject failure to deal effectively with the "nasty little war" in southern Lebanon. A comparable capability to conduct systematic, sustained guerrilla attacks has, so far, eluded *Hezbollah's* Palestinian rejectionist counterparts.

Thus, looking back over twenty years of Palestinian rejectionist activity--of whatever political coloration--it is quite clear that, all sophistry to the contrary aside, terrorism has been and remains their principal form of warfare. While particular terrorist acts may have achieved some short-term benefits--e.g., publicity, demonstration of potency, suspension of negotiations, or Israeli over-reaction--their contribution to the rejectionists' ultimate aims has been far from evident. The absence of a well-conceived, coherent strategy--as discussed in the previous sections--is a key reason for this sorry state of affairs. Other impeding factors will become evident in the analytical assessment, to which we now turn.

Notes

1. There is voluminous literature on the creation of Israel and the associated violence between Arabs and Jews. The following are particularly useful: Walid Khalidi, ed. *From Haven to Conquest, Readings in Zionism and the Palestine Problem Until 1948* (Beirut: The Institute for Palestine Studies, 1971), especially the introductory section; J. C. Hurewitz, *The Struggle for Palestine* (New York,

The Context of Palestinian Rejectionism

NY: Norton, 1950); Christopher Sykes, *Crossroads to Israel* (New York: World Publishers, 1965). For an excellent and succinct comparison of the Arab violence in the thirties with the recent *Intifada* see Kenneth W. Stein, "The *Intifada* and the Uprising of 1936-1939: A Comparison of the Palestinian Arab Communities," *The Intifada*, Robert O. Freedman, ed. (Miami, FL: Florida International University Press, 1991).

2. Rashid Hamid, "What Is the PLO?" *Journal of Palestine Studies*, Summer 1975, pp. 94-95. There are numerous books and a veritable avalanche of articles and monographs on the Palestinian resistance that can be easily accessed. A good overall treatment of the PLO is John W. Amos, *Palestinian Resistance: Organization of a Nationalist Movement* (New York, NY: Pergamon Press, 1981).

3. Michael Hudson, "The Palestinian Resistance Movement: Its Significance in the Middle East Crisis, *The Middle East Journal*, Summer 1969, p. 299 and Walter Laqueur, *The Road to War* (Baltimore: Penguin Books, 1968), p. 68 place the origin of Fatah in 1956, while Abdullah Schleiffer, "The Emergence of Fatah," *The Arab World*, May 1969, p. 16 traces Fatah to a 1957 summer meeting of a dozen or so Palestinians on a Kuwaiti beach.

4. The ultimate goal of destroying Israel (the "Zionist entity" in polemical terms) was formally and clearly set forth in the Palestinian National Charter. See articles 1, 8, 14, 15, 19 and 20-23 in Leila S. Kadi, comp. and trans., *Basic Political Documents of the Armed Palestinian Resistance Movement* (Beirut: Palestine Liberation Organization Research Center, 1968), pp. 137-142. These and other passages offensive to Israel were nullified by the Palestinian National Congress in April 1996. See the text of the political statement issued by the 21st session of the Palestine National Council in Gaza, Jericho Voice of Palestine, April 26, 1996 in FBIS-NES-96-083, April 29, 1996, pp. 2-5.

The idea of a popular armed struggle was prominent in some Palestinian circles prior to the 1967 war and became even more popular after that event. As a weapon of the weak against the strong, it was very much in vogue in the Third World during the 1950's and 1960's, particularly in light of the successes in China, Vietnam (against France) and Algeria. Its influence on Palestinian thinking can be seen in a two-part series of pamphlets entitled *Revolutionary Studies and Experiences* (Beirut and Amman: Fatah, 1967-1970). More accessible commentaries may be found in Y. Harkabi, *Fedayeen Action and Arab Strategy,* Adelphi Papers, No. 53 (London: The International Institute for strategic Studies, 1968), pp. 7-8 and 13-17; Tom Little, *The New Arab Extremists*, Conflict Studies No. 4 (London: Current Affairs Research Center, 1970, pp. 11-12; the interview of George Habash cited in *Arab Report and*

Record, March 1-15, 1969, p. 12; the interview of K. Kudsi (Fatah) in *Free Palestine*, August 1969, p. 6 and September 1969, p. 6.

5. The Palestinian-Jordanian relationship has been a rocky and frequently violent one. While many factors have accounted for the strife and distrust, the basic problem is the division between the Hashemites, who originated in Saudi Arabia and rule Jordan in conjunction with indigenous Bedouin tribal allies, and the larger Palestinian community, which perceives itself to be the real natives. See Bard E. O'Neill, *Armed Struggle in Palestine* (Boulder, CO: Westview Press, 1978), pp. 164-169.

6. *Ibid.*, pp. 214-217; Muhammad Y. Muslih, "Moderates and Rejectionists Within the Palestine Liberation Organization," *The Middle East Journal*, Spring 1976, pp. 127-140. An excellent account of the emergence of the rejectionist front may be found in Patrick Seale, *Abu Nidal: Gun for Hire* (New York, NY: Random House, 1992), pp. 93-100.

7. King Hussein showed that he could play the same game as his antagonists in Damascus by supporting Muslim Botherhood groups carrying out acts of violence against Assad's Alawite-based regime. The nasty relations between Jordan and Syria are rooted in Syrian nationalist and ideological views that depict Jordan as part of southern Syria and its monarchy as anachronistic. There is also bitterness and distrust as a result of Syria's support for the Palestinians in the 1970 civil war. That things had not improved in 1995 could be seen in the comments of a senior Jordanian official who stated: "We read reports daily showing that some senior party and state officials in Syria still regard Jordan as southern Syria. If I told you that we trust the Syrian leadership, we would be deceiving ourselves and you as well." See *Al-Bilad* (Amman), October 4, 1995 in FBIS-NES-95-192, October 3, 1995, p. 58. A strong case can be made that Syria's support for the rejectionists has always been tactical rather than strategic. Thus, Damascus has not supported efforts by the PLO to create an independent Palestinian state because, *inter alia*, Syria perceives Palestine as part of southern Syria and believes the notion of particularistic Palestinian nationalism to be at odds with the Ba'thist ideological stress on integral Arab unity. None of this has prevented Assad from using various rejectionist groups like the PFLP-GC, the Abu Nidal Organization, the PFLP, the Abu Musa Organization and so on to attack Israelis and thus exert pressure on the latter to makes concessions on the most immediate Syrian concern, the liberation of the Golan Heights. Denials that groups engaged in terrorism (attacks on civilians) are not assisted by Syria are not to be taken seriously, given the presence of these groups in Syria proper and Syrian-controlled areas of Lebanon. Indeed, this is but another manifestation of Syria's penchant for supporting insurgent organizations opposed to neighboring regimes,

The Context of Palestinian Rejectionism

in order to achieve national goals *vis-a vis* those regimes (e.g., support for the Kurdish Worker's Party, *Dev Sol* and Armenian terrorists in Turkey). During two separate visists to Damascus by one of the authors (O'Neill), Syrian officials, including Foreign Minister Farouk Al-Shar'a and Chief of Staff Hikmat Shihabi echoed the familiar argument that, if proof of terrorism by Damascus-based groups were found, Syria would take corrective action. The problem with this, of course, is that proof consisted of a so-called smoking gun.

8. Not surprisingly, the *Intifada* has spawned voluminous literature. Among the most useful volumes is previously cited *The Intifada,* Robert O. Freedman, ed. The idea that the *Intifada* was a creation of Islamic militants is a gross misunderstanding of its multiple causes. On this point see John L. Esposito, *The Islamic Threat* (New York, NY: Oxford University Press, 1992), pp. 182-183.

9. Congressional Quarterly, *The Middle East,* 7th ed. (Washington, D.C.: Congressional Quarterly, Inc., 1991), pp. 295-296.

10. It is common knowledge that, prior to the *Intifada,* Israel consciously tolerated the emergence and stregthening of Palestinian Islamic groups, notably Hamas' precursor, the Moslem Brotherhood, as a way to sow dissention in the Palestinian community and to contain the immediate violent threat posed by the secular nationalist organizations. David Shipler, *Arab and Jew: Wounded Spirits in the Promised Land* (New York, NY: Penguin Books, 1986), p. 177 quotes the Israeli military governor of the Gaza Strip as saying he was given a budget by the government which he in turn dispensed to the mosques. For more on Israeli support for the Islamists see Interview of Sheik Ahmad Yasin *[Hamas* leader] by Oded Granot, *Ma'ariv, Shabat* supplement, (Tel Aviv), January 2, 1995 in FBIS-NES-95-106, June 2, 1995, p. 9; Alan Cowell, "Militants, Once Seen as Useful to Israel, Are Now Its Main Foe," *The New York Times* (hereafter *NYT*), October 30, 1994; and, Ziyad Abu-Amr, *The Islamic Movement in the West Bank and Gaza Strip* (Jerusalem and Akko: al-Aswar House, 1989), trans. in *Joint Publications Research Service, Near East and South Asia* (hereafter JPRS)-NEA-90-011-L, June 14, 1990, pp. 2-3 and 20-21. [Abu-Amr's last name actually appears as Abu-Amru in this publication. However, since it appears as Abu-Amr in his other works, we shall use the latter version to avoid unnecessary confusion.] A longer term perspective on Israel's role in undermining secular nationalists and contributing to the rise of militant Islamism may be found in Michael Dumpter, *Islam and Israel: Muslim Religious Endowments and the Jewish State* (London: I. B. Tauris, 1994). The importance of the PLO's weaknesses in the rise of *Hamas* is treated in Hisham Ahmed, *Hamas: From Religious Salvation to Religious Transformation* (Jerusalem: The Palestinian Academic Society for the Study of International Affairs, 1994).

11. Interview of Dr. Musa Abu-Marzuq, *Filastin al-Muslimah* (London), June 1994 in JPRS-NEA-94-041, August 5, 1994, p. 1.

12. The APF statement may be found in *Al-Quds* Palestinian Arab Radio, January 6, 1994 in FBIS-NES-94-005, January 7, 1994, pp. 6-7.

13. *Ibid.*, p. 6.

14. On the Abu Nidal organization see Seale, *op. cit.* and Matti Steinberg, "The Radical Worldview of the Abu-Nidal Faction," *Jerusalem Quarterly*, Fall 1988. The PFLP refusal to recognize and negotiate with Israel is longstanding. Although it accepts the aim of creating a Palestinian state, its leader, George Habash, has made it trenchantly clear that such a state does not and should not mean recognition of Israel (the enemy entity). See *Paris Monte Carlo Radio*, August 15, 1988 in FBIS-NES-88-159, August 17, 1988, p. 4. In 1996, Habash was emphatic that the ultimate strategic goal of his organization was a Palestinian state over the entire territory of Palestine. Since the international balance of forces and public opinion made that impractical in the interim, he indicated that an independent Palestinian state, with Jerusalem as its capital, was acceptable. See his comments in *Yediot Ahronot* (Tel Aviv), February 16, 1996, in FBIS-NES-96-033, February 16, 1996, p. 3. The PFLP-GC's totalistic goal has been consistent down through the years and was recently restated in a cable from Jibril congratulating *Hamas* for its terrorist attacks in Israel in February and March 1996. He applauded the "martyrs" because they proved the children of Palestine would not cede one inch of their homeland, Palestine, from the sea to the river. See *Al-Quds* Palestinian Arab Radio, February 26, 1996 in FBIS-NES-96-030, February 27, 1996, pp. 2-3.

15. Abu-Amr, *The Islamic Movement in the West Bank and Gaza Strip*, p. 2. The reactionary-traditionalist aspect, which involves the image of a golden age of the past, has been exploited by the recently established Palestine National Authority which refers to the Islamist movement as an ancestral one that futilely seeks to restore a previous historical model. See *Al-Sabil* (Amman), February 7-13, 1995 in FBIS-NES-95-032, February 16, 1995, p. 12. For a clear exposition of the rejectionist interpretation of the Islamic position on usurpation and infidel rule over Muslims and its application to the Palestinian situation, see the interview of *Hezbollah's* Shi'ite cleric, Muhamad Husayn Fadallah, in *Filastin Al-Muslimah* (London), September 1995 in FBIS-NES-95-177, September 13, 1995, pp. 1-2.

16. Ziyad Abu-Amr, "Hamas: A Historical and Political Background," *Journal of Palestine Studies*, Summer 1993, p. 2. The quotes from the charter of *Hamas*

The Context of Palestinian Rejectionism 241

may be found in a translated and annotated version of the covenant of *Hamas* entitled, "The Charter of Allah: the Platform of the Islamic Resistance Movement (*Hamas*)," *Israeli Affairs*, Vol. 2, No. 1, 1995, pp. 275-276.

17. Abu Mus'ab, "Palestine in the Thought of Martyred Imam Hasan al-Bana," *Liwa Al-Islam*, February 1989, p. 17 as quoted in Abu-Amr, *The Islamic Movement in the West Bank and Gaza Strip*, p. 17.

18. Interview with Fathi al-Shaqaqi *Al-Sharq al-Awsat* (London), March 17, 1995 in FBIS-NES-95-056, March 23, 1995, p. 13. The notion of creating an Islamic state in Palestine, *ipso facto*, means the elimination of Israel. Although few, if any, analysts would deny that the ultimate aim of *Hamas* and the IJM is to replace Israel with an Islamic state, *Hamas* has occasionally cast its objectives in terms of the occupied territories and thus led some to believe that it might settle for half a loaf. See *Al-Diyar* (Beirut), May 5, 1995 in FBIS-NEA-95-090, May 10, 1995, pp. 10-11. The new IJM Secretary-General, Ramadan Abdallah Shalah, has categorically rejected the idea of a truce with Israel. On this and his reaffirmation of the totalistic goal of the IJM see his interview by Ibrahim Humaydi in *Al-Wasat* (London), April 1-7, 1996 in FBIS-NES-96-066, April 4, 1996, pp. 5 and 8.

19. Muslih, "Moderates and Rejectionists...," pp. 127-131. Unlike *S'aiqa* and the ALF, the DFLP is an independent organization. An excellent example of its assessment and rejection of the Oslo accords--which specifies their negative failings with respect to sovereignty, water, security, settlements, Jerusalem and refugees--may be found in the interview of Nayif Hawatmah by Sami Amarah in *Al-Sharq Al-Awsat* (London), October 3, 1995, FBIS-NES-95-192, October 4, 1995, pp. 10-12. The Hawatmah quote may be found in *Paris Radio Monte Carlo*, October 6, 1994 in FBIS-NES-94-195, October 7, 1994, p. 4.

20. Interview of Sheik Subhi al-Tufali, *Agence France Press*, December 9, 1994 in FBIS-NES-94-237, December 9, 1994, p. 34. An example of the bigoted and inflammatory rhetoric of *Hezbollah* may be found in the remarks of its Secretary General, Hasan Nasrallah, in *Ba'labakk* Voice of the Oppressed, June 12, 1995, FBIS-NES-95-112, June 12, 1995, p. 49. In April 1996, Nasrallah registered his qualms about a cease-fire accord as follows: "We object to certain terms in this accord, including the wording 'northern Israel,' because in the view of the Islamic resistance 'northern Israel' is in reality northern Palestine." See Tehran IRNA, April 26, 1996 in FBIS-NES-96-083, April 26, 1996, p. 73. One writer who asked another *Hezbollah* official whether the basic motivational factor for the organization was to liberate south Lebanon, to destroy Israel, or to emulate Imam Hussein and reach paradise, was given the answer: "all three." See

Trendle, *"Hizbullah's* Guerrilla War...," p. 19. For a comparison of *Hezbollah* and *Amal* see Marius Deeb, Shia Movements in Lebanon: Their Formation, Ideology, Social Basis, and Links with Iran," *Third World Quarterly*, April 1988, pp. 683-698. On informational warfare see *Al-Ahd* (Beirut), April 11, 1996 in FBIS-NES-96-071, April 11, 1996, pp. 45-46.

21. On the dismal record when it came to operationalization of the protracted popular war strategy see O'Neill, pp. 63-223.

22. On strategic differences see *Ibid.*, pp. 210-213.

23. A succinct accounting of the violent differences between *Fatah* and the ANO, which includes a chronological summary of ANO attacks against *Fatah* members, citizens from Arab states and others, may be found in *Terrorist Group Profiles* (Washington: U.S. Government Printing Office, 1989), pp. 5-8.

24. Interview with Fathi al-Shaqaqi, *Al-Sharq Al-Awsat* (London) March 17, 1995 in FBIS-NES-95-056, March 23, 1995, pp. 12-14.

25. Interview with Fathi al-Shaqaqi, *Al-Majd* (Amman), October 24, 1994 in FBIS-NES-94-209, October 24, 1994, p. 7.

26. Abu-Amr's discussion of the strategy of *Hamas* in, *The Islamic Movement in the West Bank and Gaza Strip*, p. 39, is a a good reflection of the reality of "soft" strategic thinking in that it concentrates on general perceptions of where Palestine fits in the Arab context, despair with peaceful solutions, the primacy of *jihad*, and cooperation and differences with the PLO, rather than the exposition of an integrated scheme for using available resources to achieve its short-, medium- and long-term aims.

27. *Ibid.*, p. 18. Another reflection of the sloppy strategic thinking of *Hamas* may be found on p. 38, where its leaflets during the *Intifada* were faulted because they were devoid of an integrated plan of action for a specific time frame. Perhaps it would have been wishful thinking to expect much in the way of solid operational strategy in the absence of a coherent grand strategy. The strategy portion of the *Hamas* covenant may be found in, "The Charter of Allah...," *op cit.*, pp. 278-285.

28. Carrying out terrorist attacks to provide gratification for those seeking vengeance collides with *Hamas'* uneasiness with suicide attacks and its long-term preference to rely on patience. The result is strategic confusion and contradictions. See Nir, "Forbearance and Several Interim Gratifications," *op cit.*,

The Context of Palestinian Rejectionism 243

pp. 22-23.

29. Interview with Abd-al-Majid Dhunaybat, *Teheran Voice of the Islamic Republic of Iran*, April 1, 1996 in FBIS-NES-96-064, April 2, 1996, p. 55. The reactive aspect of the Islamic groups is typified by the remarks of the secretary general of the IJM in the aftermath of the assassination of Mahmud al-Khawajah to *Al-Hayah* (London), June 23, 1995 in FBIS-NES-95-122, June 26, 1995, p. 10. The tit for tat approach to attacks on civilians in *Hamas* is exemplfied in the comments of its spokesman, Ibrahim Ghawshaw, in *NRC Handelsblad* (Rotterdam), November 21, 1994 in FBIS-NES-94-226, November 23, 1994, p. 8. The linkage between withdrawal from Gaza, the West Bank and Jerusalem and an end to attacks on civilians is made by Mustafa al-Liddawi, *Hamas* representative in Lebanon, in *Al-Shira* (Beirut), October 31, 1994 in FBIS-NES-94-213, November 3, 1994, p. 8. Similar comments by *Hamas* leader, Sheik Ahmad Yasin, may be found in *Ma'ariv* (Shabat supplement), June 2, 1995 in FBIS-NES-95-106, June 2, 1995, p. 10. Besides the familiar casuistic reasoning cited in the text, another variation is that Israeli occupation is sheltered by civilians who are used to tighten domination of Palestine. Hence, according to the Deputy Secretary General of *Hezbollah*, "We do not consider that we are killing civilians; rather, Israel is killing them by its occupation of the land and its practices." See telephone interview with *Hezbollah* Deputy Secretary General, Shaykh Na'im Qasim, *Teheran Voice of the Islamic Republic of Iran*, March 31, 1996 in FBIS-NES- 96-063, April 1, 1996, p. 52.

30. See interview with *Hamas* leader, Imad al-Faluji, by Malik Abu-Zayd, *Al-Muharrir* (Paris), November 28, 1994 in FBIS-NES-94-228, November 28, 1994, p. 9.

31. Interview with *Hamas* official spokesman, Ibrahim Ghawshaw, in *Al-Ahram Weekly*, December 7-13, 1995 in FBIS-NES-95-240, December 14, 1995, p. 11. The term *sabr* and its impact on *Hamas*' strategic thinking is discussed by Ori Nir, "Forbearance and Several Interim Gratifications," *Ha'aretz* (Tel Aviv), January 5, 1995 in JPRS-TOT-95-001-L, January 19, 1995, pp. 22-23. The importance of the analogy with the Crusades is clearly established by article 35 of the *Hamas* covenant. See "The Charter of Allah....," *op cit.*, p. 292.

32. The point that *Hamas* lacks an agreed-upon strategy seems evident in a discussion of three options--political action; resistance by *jihad*; and resistance and political action--by Dr. Ahmad Yusuf in *Filastin Al Muslimah* (London), June 1994 in JPRS-NEA-94-041, August 5, 1994, pp. 4-5. All three are described as possible *future* courses of action. The implication, of course, is that none has been clearly chosen. In effect, number three has been followed.

33. Abu-Amr, *The Islamic Movement in the West Bank and Gaza Strip*, pp. 17-18.

34. On the Habash version of the APF's aims and strategy see *Jordan Times* (Amman), February 15, 1994. Habash's penchant for generalities and slogans when it comes to current strategy can be seen in an interview he gave to *Al-Bayadir Al-Siyasi* (Jerusalem), August 27, 1994. He says the clear option is "...struggle, and more struggle, and more struggle, in order to win [the Palestinian people's] complete and undiminished freedom and independence." Later in the same interview he depicts the alternative to bargaining with Israel as "...resistance and rejection of the Zionist plan, and opposition to it, building the conditions for resistance to it, in nationalist and pan-Arab terms, unifying the efforts of our patriotic forces in their various factions, in one unified front." A student of strategy who looks for a substantive elaboration of such statements in the lengthy interview will do so in vain. See FBIS-NES-94-054, October 20, 1994, pp. 1-7; quotes, p. 2.

35. *Al-Hayah* (London), October 6, 1994 in FBIS-NES-94-195, October 7, 1994, p. 4.

36. The centrality of commando action was established in the National Charter of the PLO. See Kadi, p. 138.

37. O'Neill, pp. 74-89.

38. The impact of right-wing Jewish terrorism, particularly the *Irgun* and the Stern Gang, on Abu Nidal's thinking is discussed by Seale, pp. 71-72.

39. Interview with Mustafa al-Liddawi, *Hamas* representative in Lebanon, in *Al-Shira* (Beirut), October 31, 1994 in FBIS-NES-94-213, November 3, 1994, p. 8.

40. Abu-Amr, "Hamas: A Historical and Political Background," p. 15.

41. *Davar Rishon* (Tel Aviv), May 13, 1996 in FBIS-NES-96-094, May 14, 1996, p. 7.

42. Hezbollah's military activities have improved to the point where the organization is probably the most formidable guerrilla threat Israel has faced thus far. See Emanuel Rozen, "The Security Zone: The Price Is Too High," *Ma'ariv* (Tel Aviv), August 27, 1993 in JPRS-NEA-93-017L, September 21, 1993, pp. 4-6 and Ron Ben-Yishay, "Why Is Israel Holding Back?," *Yediot Ahronot*,

The Context of Palestinian Rejectionism 245

Leshabat supplement, August 12, 1994 in FBIS-NES-94-164, August 24, 1994, pp. 37-39. Parenthetically, we should note that, while there is no clear proof, *Hezbollah* is a major suspect in two bombings against Israelis and local Jews in Argentina, the putative motive being revenge for Israeli attacks on *Hezbollah* officials inside Lebanon. During the March-April 1996 Israeli-Hezbollah hostilities, Nasrallah threatened to resist Israel everywhere. On the latter point see *Beirut Radio Lebanon*, March 11, 1996 in FBIS-NES-96-049, March 12, 1996, p. 68.

CHAPTER FIVE

ANALYTICAL ASSESSMENT OF PALESTINIAN REJECTIONISM

CHAPTER V

AN ASSESSMENT OF PALESTINIAN REJECTIONISM

> *The enemies of yesterday [Israel and the PLO] share a common enemy today: the terrorism that sows death in our homes and on the buses that ply the streets. The sounds of celebration here cannot drown out the cries of innocent citizens who travelled those buses to their deaths. And your eyes shining here cannot erase for a single moment the sight of lifeless eyes of the students who were going to their classes and the housewives who were on their way to market when hatred struck them down. We are pained by their deaths, and remember them with love.*
>
> Yitzhak Rabin, September 28, 1995

> *One could talk about an agreement for a limited period, say 15 years, not about a peace agreement forever.*
>
> Sheik Ahmad Yassin, *Hamas* Leader,
> June 2, 1995

Having set the Palestinian rejectionists' goals, strategies and forms of warfare in their proper context, we can proceed with a more systematic analysis of the movement. Our objective is threefold: to evaluate the Palestinian rejectionists' strengths, weaknesses and longer-term prospects; to draw further comparisons between Palestinian rejectionism and its Israeli counterpart; and to highlight the points at which the two movements intersect. We will then proceed with our final assessment of their interaction and explore the ways through which the deadly embrace locking the Israelis and the Palestinians could be broken--in the interest of peace and regional stability.

Environment

The physical environment is, of course, the same for all Palestinian insurgents, regardless of affiliation, as it is for the Israeli rejectionists. Since all factions operate on home turf, there is no discernible strategic advantage derived from the terrain itself or familiarity with its peculiar features.[1] The main area of operations is small and relatively open. Thus, it is not conducive to a strategy predicated on concealment and protected bases for guerrilla forces. Moreover, the road and transportation system, as well as the communications network, are quite modern and extensive, facilitating the mobility of government forces. The notion of marshalling sizeable guerrilla units for swift hit-and-run attacks is, therefore, highly impracticable. The one notable exception is the rocky, mountainous, wooded terrain of southern Lebanon, where, as mentioned previously, *Hezbollah* has operated with impressive effectiveness, engaging Israeli forces in a tenacious guerrilla and terrorism campaign. In the words of Giles Trendle: "The hills and wadis, the rugged and steep inclines, with large boulders and bush thickets which can provide adequate cover for guerrillas, [are] well suited to *Hezbollah's* kind of warfare."[2]

The limitations posed by the physical environment have always bedeviled the Palestinian militants, rendering their exhortations about protracted armed struggle against Israel more a matter of lofty rhetoric than actual strategy. This is one reason why Palestinian guerrilla warfare pales into insignificance, especially in comparison with insurgencies in places like China, Vietnam, Algeria and Afghanistan.

The implications for today's rejectionists are obvious. Because any significant concentration of fighters is easy to detect, the only viable option is a mixture of small-scale, high-impact guerrilla and terrorist attacks, carried out by cellular groups based in the West Bank and the Gaza Strip. While many of these attacks--like the recent series of suicide bus bombings in Tel Aviv and Jerusalem--garner headlines and inflame passions, they are hardly a substitute for a systematic, escalating guerrilla campaign.

Despite the bleak prospects for ultimate strategic success--minimally defined as the replacement of Israel by a Palestinian state--inherent in small-scale, episodic violence, such operations could influence Israel's calculus as to the eventual disposition of the rest of the West Bank. Indeed, there is every reason to believe that the costs of sustaining the *status quo* could, eventually, contribute to an Israeli decision to carry out further withdrawals from Judea and Samaria--as was the case with the Gaza Strip and Lebanon. But, such a turn of events would benefit the Palestinian pragmatists, rather than boost the rejectionist cause. On the other hand, the daily grind of low-level violence--interspersed, as it has been, by spectacular terrorist attacks--plays directly into the hands of Israeli rejectionists, solidifying their opposition to territorial compromise. Thus, in the final analysis, while any violence fuels the insidious interaction among the enemies of peace on all sides, its strategic impact is severely limited by the topography and size of the contested area.

The human environment--i.e., social groups and their relationships, community values and structures, economic trends, and the political system--presents both advantages and disadvantages for the rejectionists. Without a doubt, the Arab-Jewish cleavage is at the root of the conflict. With the partial exception of some Arabic-speaking Sephardi Jews, the two societies differ in their language, culture and religion. These inherent divisions have hardened over the years, becoming suffused with distrust and hatred born of struggle over the same ancestral land. Accordingly, the conflict is not just over concrete issues, but also over such critical intangibles as group honor, identity and solidarity. Since compromise does not come easily under such circumstances, rejectionists can always find supporters who believe that trading land for peace is tantamount to selling one's eternal soul. As we have demonstrated in preceding chapters, such sentiments are at play on the Israeli side as well, exacerbating the existential nature of the conflict and aggravating the difficulties involved in its peaceful resolution.

Thus far, the Muslim-Christian division within the Palestinian

Arab community has not undercut the rejectionists in any significant way. In fact, the Christian minority has been an integral part of the resistance to Israel, with several of its members--like George Habash, head of the PFLP--rising to leadership positions among the secular rejectionists. What the future holds is less certain, given the growth of militant Islamic groups and their stated goal of establishing an Islamic state in which Christians would be, at best, second-class citizens and, at worst, might be subjected to violent repression. That the worst-case scenario is not to be dismissed out of hand is clearly evident from slogans advanced by *Hamas* activists during the *Intifada*, stating that the land of Palestine is an Islamic trust (*waqf*), the annihilation of Israel is foreordained by the Koran, and that "after Saturday would come Sunday," i.e., that after destroying the Jews, the Christians would be dealt with in a similar manner. Such grim prospects, in turn, could compel some rejectionist Christians, at a future point, to cooperate with secular pragmatists on the basis of common opposition to the idea of an Islamic state.[3]

Whatever the eventual outcome of the Christian-Muslim cleavage, the fact remains that the Arab-Jewish division has been and remains the principal catalyst of armed struggle. Its sustainment over the long term, however, has been hindered by the social values and structures characteristic of the Palestinian community. As far as values are concerned, the Palestinians, like most Arabs, place great emphasis on personal ties, centrality of the family, respect for age, courage, honor, and dignity. Unlike some of their Arab brothers, however, the Palestinians also have a strong secular tradition, resulting from and reinforced by their impressive educational achievements. Over the long term, this imbedded secularism--akin to the majority culture in Israel--could become a force for mitigating the impact of militant fundamentalism.[4]

The fractious nature of Palestinian society, with its segmentary structure of competing families and clans led by senior males, admixed with residual loyalties of some local elites to the Hashemite regime in Jordan, which are rooted in ongoing patron-client relationships, has always impeded insurgent efforts to

Analytical Assessment of Palestinian Rejectionism   253

mobilize and rally the people to their cause. Even the newly emergent professional middle class--physicians, lawyers, teachers, civil servants, etc.--has not proven to be a unifying force, despite its general support for the PLO. Among the reasons underlying this reality are: the professionals' ties to the traditional order and the patronage that continue to sustain their station in life; their affiliations with different groups within the PLO; and their aversion to violent activity that could threaten their social and economic well-being. Thus, the chronic disunity of the Palestinian resistance stems, in large measure, from the divergent interests and societal fragmentation of the larger community within which it operates.

Whether current rejectionists will do any better than their predecessors in providing at least a modicum of political cohesion-- despite the centrifugal tendencies of the social order--is open to question. To a degree, the outcome might be shaped by the extent and pervasiveness of the defiance of parents and other senior authority figures, demonstrated, during the *Intifada*, by young activists who had become disillusioned with the weakness and passivity of their fathers. Seeking to explain this behavior, some observers went so far as to argue that, in place of the patriarchal order, a tri-level leadership had emerged during the *Intifada*: (1) "Drawing room leaders," or "coffee house intellectuals"--e.g., Hanna Sinyorah, Sari Nuseiybah, Raja Shihadah and Faysal al-Huseini--whose influence derives from PLO and foreign connections; (2) members of the Unified National Command of the Uprising, who published leaflets during the *Intifada* and provided a link between the masses and the "drawing room leaders"; and (3) the "street leaders", who actually led neighborhood youths in various acts of defiance.

Undoubtedly, the Palestinian social system has been altered by the *Intifada*. However, we see no convincing evidence that the patriarchal order has been displaced. Rather, as is often the case during periods of social change, there is a clash between the old and the new, with the outcome still uncertain. The real question is which order will emerge ascendant. Clearly, a resurgence of conformist patriarchy would tend to work in favor of the pragmatists and the Israelis. A further erosion of traditional patterns, in contrast, could foster rejectionism, particularly given the relative youth of the Palestinian population (close to 50% are under age 15) and the seemingly natural inclination of young people toward more extremist solutions than those generally favored by their elders.[5]

Another critical facet of Palestinian society is the geographic separation of its constituent elements and the divergent sociopolitical experiences derived therefrom. Without a doubt, the most militant Palestinians have been those living in the near-diaspora, especially in the squalor of refugee camps in the occupied territories, as well as in Jordan, Lebanon and Syria. Subsisting on the margins of society, divorced from their original habitats and distrusted--if not despised--by host Arab governments, they have had little stake in stability. Rootless, poor, frustrated, and angry, many became the cadre and foot soldiers of the various commando organizations. In contrast, Palestinians who had settled--be it permanently or for employment purposes--in the Persian Gulf and farther afield, have been less involved with the resistance. For the most part, they made do with sending money and proffering moral and political support. Similarly, those in refugee camps in the occupied territories tended to be more militant, while those with homes and a livelihood often shied away from active support for the resistance. To wit, the West Bank, with its larger proportion of settled Palestinians and fewer refugees, was less violent and less supportive of the *fedayeen* than the turbulent Gaza Strip.

The proclivity of the refugee population to support armed resistance should not be taken to mean that its attitudes toward the peace process cannot change, given the right political developments. While a poll conducted by the Jerusalem Media and Communications Center in 1995 found that 60.8% of the Palestinians interviewed refused to forgo the "right of return" (to their former homes within the Green Line), a surprising difference emerged between the West Bank and Gaza Strip respondents. Although Gaza has far more refugees who hail from Israel proper, Gazans were more willing to forgo the right of return in exchange

Analytical Assessment of Palestinian Rejectionism 255

for a Palestinian state, felt more secure, and were more optimistic about the peace process than their West Bank counterparts.[6] No doubt, the self-rule status accorded to the Gaza Strip, compared to the continued Israeli occupation of the West Bank, accounts for the difference in positions. Since attitudes clearly can be shaped by significant political changes, it is possible that another major breakthrough in the West Bank will help shift the range of opinion on this and other core issues.

Palestinians living in Israel proper have been least supportive of rejectionism. In spite of their self-perception as second-class citizens in a system that discriminates in favor of the majority Jewish population, their standard of living and political circumstances have always been significantly better than those typical of the Palestinian diaspora. This reality explains the Israeli Palestinians' relative passivity and preference for non-nonviolent approaches, accounting, *inter alia*, for their minimal involvement in the *Intifada*, as well as for their quiescence during five Arab-Israeli wars.

How these factors might evolve over the longer term is, of course, a different matter altogether. For example, progress in Israeli-Palestinian negotiations that results in significant political gains for the Palestinian National Authority could increase the restiveness of the Arab community inside the Green Line, potentially leading to a "mini *Intifada*," that is, an uprising designed to improve the Palestinians' social, economic, and political lot. The extent of the socio-economic misery is significant: according to Amin Faris of the Institute for Israeli Arab Studies, 50% of Arab families, including 70% of the children, live below the poverty line. Should the deprivation continue and lead to more assertiveness, the Islamic groups would be the main beneficiaries of the radical backlash. The Islamic Movement, which is linked to the Muslim Brotherhood but accepts Israel's existence, already commands the support of one-quarter to one-third of Israel's Arabs, due, in large measure, to its extensive--and growing--organizational efforts.[7]

While the Palestinian community's fragmentation and diversity have combined to limit the effectiveness of the Palestinian insurrection over the years, the political system and economic trends have had an opposite effect. From the Palestinian perspective, the Israeli occupation of the Gaza Strip and the West Bank was nothing less than an imperialist arrangement. Moreover, when the settlements began to spread, especially under the Likud government, a classical colonialist order took hold, in which local inhabitants were discriminated against with respect to economic affairs, land, access to water, civil rights, and due process. The economic regression of the 1980's--following a decade of improvement in the standard of living in the territories under Labor's rule--played a significant role in eroding the Palestinians' grudging tolerance of existing political arrangements. Likud's unwavering commitment to territorial maximalism--and its concomitant opposition to any compromise that would yield authority or land--effectively foreclosed whatever opportunities there might have been for diverting attention from economic troubles, thereby relieving festering tensions by responding to Palestinian grievances.

In any event, economic recession and political unresponsiveness in the territories combined with the PLO's demonstrable internal and international weakness to spark--and sustain--a spontaneous uprising by an increasingly frustrated population. It was during this time that the Islamic rejectionists saw their fortunes ascend. The establishment of Palestinian authority in Jericho, the Gaza Strip and major West Bank Arab population centers in 1994-95, under the control of Arafat and his pragmatic PLO colleagues, has done little to change things: The economy is still in shambles, administration is rudimentary, corruption is prevalent, and the opportunity for meaningful political participation and influence for those outside Arafat's immediate circle is severely circumscribed.

In fact, despite the presidential and national council elections of January 1996, it will no doubt take a long time for Arafat to divorce himself from the patrimonial style of highly personalized, authoritarian, divide-and-rule politics he has been practicing throughout his political career. As a respected psychiatrist from

Gaza put it: "People are intimidated. There is an overwhelming sense of fear. The regime is corrupt, dictatorial, oppressive."[8] Until these tends are reversed--in the context of an overall acceleration of the peace process--rejectionism, fuelled by Islamic fundamentalism, will continue to thrive.

Popular Support

Historically, popular support for rejectionist organizations has been moderate to low among the Palestinians. In the absence of polls, or reliable survey data in the late 1960's and 1970's, there is no way to assess with any degree of precision how many active and passive supporters rallied to groups like the Popular Front for the Liberation of Palestine, the Democratic Front for the Liberation of Palestine, the Popular Front for the Liberation of Palestine-General Command, and the Abu Nidal Organization. Nonetheless, reports by informed observers and estimates of direct membership in such groups have always suggested a distinct minority status within the overall resistance movement. For instance, typical assessments put the membership of the PFLP near 3,000; the DFLP near 350; the PFLP-GC about 500; and the ANO around 500. By contrast, *Fatah* was usually said to have over 10,000 adherents.[9]

Thus, even if the numbers for each faction were arbitrarily increased by a few thousand, they would still be relatively small organizations. Membership estimates aside, there is no reason to believe that popular support for the leftist groups has been any greater than indicated above. Although the lack of reliable data again precludes certainty, their continued limited appeal was confirmed to one of the present authors on several occasions in the past fifteen years, most notably during discussions with knowledgeable UNESCO officials at the large Bekka refugee camp in Jordan.

Over the past few years, polling has improved sufficiently to provide a more reliable gauge of popular sentiments. Surveys conducted by the Center for Palestine Research (CPR) consistently reveal minuscule support for the leftist groups. A typical example was a May 1994 CPR poll which put the number of those who back the PFLP at 6.6%. A few months later, the same organization reported that, if elections were held, only 2% of the respondents would vote for the DFLP and 2.3% would cast a ballot for the PFLP. In 1995, the Jerusalem Media and Communications Research Center reported the PFLP support figure at an improved, but still unimpressive 4%. None of this is to suggest that the impact of the leftist groups has been negligible. To the contrary, despite their consistently poor showing in surveys, their political clout and violent actions have been substantial enough over the years to deter the largest group, *Fatah*, from instigating a showdown.[10]

The limited appeal of the "popular fronts" stems, in large measure, from their esoteric appeals, which are based on Marxist-Leninist ideological concepts that are outside the Arab cultural, religious and political mainstream. The ANO's meager following, by contrast, results not from espousal of an alien ideology but from its small-scale organization and excessive secretiveness, which effectively preclude broad-based mobilization of support. As of this writing, the situation remains unchanged. If anything, the attraction of the left-wing groups has diminished as a result of the collapse of the Soviet Union and the general discrediting of Marxism as a viable political philosophy. Their future is equally bleak: While they may carry out terrorist attacks from time to time, none of these groups is likely to shed its minority status, or galvanize significant popular support.[11] The same cannot be said of the Islamic rejectionists.

Both anecdotal and polling evidence makes it abundantly clear that the Islamic militants receive the lion's share of popular support among the rejectionists. The May 1994 poll noted above put support for *Hamas* at 12.3%, while an August 1994 CPR poll showed a rise to 13.9% (the IJM got a mere 3%). A Spring 1995 poll by the Jerusalem Media and Communications Center showed *Hamas* at 18% and the IJM's at 4%. Western observers report support for *Hamas* at a 15-25% range, a trend confirmed in March 1995 by a senior Israeli intelligence officer, who put the potential

Analytical Assessment of Palestinian Rejectionism 259

support for *Hamas* as high as 400,000-600,000 people.[12]
What is less clear is how much of this commitment is active--that is, involving a readiness to sacrifice life and limb, or risk incarceration, to aid the insurgents--and how much is merely passive support. That a good deal of the support may well be passive, or "soft," is strongly suggested by the outcome of the Palestinian elections in January 1996. Not only did Arafat win 88% of the vote but, more importantly, the largest turn-out of voters--85%--was in Gaza, where *Hamas*, which called for a boycott, is strongest. Be that as it may, the general lack of clarity as to passive versus active support is due, in large measure, to the different motives that have led many Palestinians to embrace the Islamic militants.[13]

While the lack of systematic survey data precludes a comprehensive analysis of the reasons underlying the militant Islamists' popular appeal, what we do know from polls and reputable observers enables us to develop several reasonable propositions. These will be formulated in terms of the techniques-- discussed in some detail in Chapter I--that insurgents use to garner popular support. Three of these methods are key in the Islamists' case: esoteric appeals, exoteric appeals and demonstrations of potency.

Esoteric appeals are most resonant among a zealous core of Palestinians with higher-than-average education, who have been largely disillusioned with *Fatah*'s nationalist orientation. For this group, Islam provides authenticity and a holistic system of ideas and beliefs. That system renews meaning and worth, provides hope for the future and defines a target for the frustrations spawned by all that is wrong, namely, the "cruel," "devious," "cunning," " harsh," and "faithless" Jews, who have "usurped the Palestinian land."

It is important to note that, in the eyes of the true believers--on both the Palestinian and Jewish sides--there is a strict taboo on making peace between Arabs and Israelis. On the Islamic side, such an act would legitimatize the stealing of property. Moreover, it would entail the sacrilege of placing things that are hallowed--in this case, the land--in the custody of infidels. To die in the defense of property and honor, in contrast, would make one worthy of being a martyr, whose place in paradise is assured.[14]

While the esoteric appeals directed at intellectuals find their theoretical wellsprings in the past and present writings of militant Islamists, especially *The Neglected Duty* (*Al-Farida al-Gha'ibah*) by Muhammad Abdel Salam al-Faraj and *Signposts Along the Way* (*Ma'alim fi al-tariq*) by Sayid al-Qutb (both Egyptians), a far less sophisticated esoteric appeal--blending Islamic slogans and cliches with unexamined quotations from the Koran--is directed at the people at large. One astute observer notes that the success demonstrated by Arab demagogues in unifying their followers is due, in no small measure, to their shrewd use of the idioms of the street. These slogans, dismissed by the intellectual elite as babble, strike a resonant chord with the uneducated poor, who cannot comprehend the linguistic discourse of the educated classes. As the Director of the Arabic Language Institute at the American University of Cairo put it: "The slogans satisfy a real need. Because the poor lack the educational tools to dissect a cliche, or a slogan, they accept it whole and do not question it."[15]

It would be misleading, however, to ascribe the growing support accorded to the Islamic rejectionists exclusively to their esoteric appeals. The repressive measures implemented by the Israeli government in general and the settlers' provocative behavior in particular, as well as an array of complaints against the fledgling PNA, provide ample exoteric grievances for the Islamists to exploit, thus gaining additional backing from the Palestinian rank and file.

Indeed, Arafat himself has become the target of considerable verbal battering for his narrowly-based, authoritarian decision-making style, administrative ineptitude, failure to move the economy forward, and perceived tolerance of corruption among his own family and political cronies. By contrast, *Hamas* has been able to alleviate the social and economic misery suffered by many Palestinians, through the provision of critically important material assistance. Concurrently, it has sought to relieve the despair of

Analytical Assessment of Palestinian Rejectionism 261

unemployment and poverty via the organization of social, vocational, cultural, and educational activities. Thus, it is hardly surprising that a senior Israeli military officer who follows *Hamas* closely estimated that 95% of the money *Hamas* raises goes to civilian activities, with only 5% allocated to military undertakings.[16] Its success is most apparent in the educational sector, where *Hamas*, believing that "today's toddlers are tomorrow's soldiers," is said to operate two thirds of the kindergartens in the West Bank.[17] Meanwhile, its counterpart, the Islamic Movement, has gained a considerable hold on the education of Arabs at all levels inside Israel.[18]

In a word, *Hamas* has been able to demonstrate its own potency by going beyond mere censure of Israel's--and the PNA's--sins of omission and commission. Its ability to provide tangible benefits has been particularly crucial, responding directly to the people's core concerns. To wit, polls reveal that Palestinians see economic regression and unemployment as their two biggest problems.[19] The true meaning and implications of these frustrations are encapsulated in the words of a high-school student in the Gaza Strip: "I am not living like a human being. This is not a dignified life. Either an honorable life or martyrdom."[20]

In the eyes of many, martyrdom is the ultimate form of popular support. It brings together the miseries of the socio-economic context; the salvation promised the *shahid* (a holy victim in the struggle for Islam); the psychological dysfunctionalism of individuals who are, by and large, young, unemployed, troubled, or ill-tempered bachelors; and, occasionally, the desire to avenge a death of a friend or relative at the hands of the Israelis.

Usually middle children with no responsibility to support the family, the would-be martyrs fantasize about death being a preferable alternative to the wretchedness of life. The result is altruistic suicide, an act that is almost impossible to prevent. In the view of one close and professionally knowledgeable observer, Eyad Sarraj of the Gaza Community Mental Health Center, there is no single explanation for suicide operations. Rather, it is to be found in a combination of factors: desperate economic conditions, the hopelessness of youth, the selective use of Islamic teachings by the clerics, and the weakness of the father-figure during adolescent years.[21] The last-mentioned factor is especially noteworthy, because it provides *Hamas* and the IJM with an opportunity, which they gratefully seize, to mentally isolate recruits from their families and replace weak fathers with a strong group identity. Additionally, there is a promise of *istishhad* (the death of a hero) and paradise--an afterlife with, *inter alia*, golden palaces, delicious food and even-tempered, exquisite women--in place of the hell on earth. As Sarraj puts it, for the suicide bomber, "the final act is the act of defiance, defiance against defeat. These people go to death with a smile. They believe it is the shortest way to heaven."[22]

While suicidal acts of martyrdom have been useful in garnering some popular support, they have not heretofore been a widespread method of warfare. In fact, Matti Steinberg of the Hebrew University has pointed out that while volunteers for suicide operations receive the organization's blessing, *Hamas*, as a movement, has not officially promoted suicide attacks.[23] Nevertheless, since April 1994, there have been at least eleven significant incidents, the most notable being the cluster of attacks in February and March 1996. Whether these attacks will prove to be a harbinger of more and worse things to come remains to be seen, especially in light of reports that many are waiting in line for the one-way, express ticket to Paradise.

The reliance of *Hamas* and the IJM on suicide operations and other forms of terrorism to demonstrate potency and provide an outlet for the desire to take revenge on Israel has become a double-edged sword, due to the economic costs inflicted on the Palestinians in the territories by Israeli border closings. While at first such hardships were blamed on Israel, the mayor of Gaza indicated in late 1995 that popular anger had been redirected toward *Hamas* and a direct linkage established between violent actions and closures, which cost 100,000 jobs and 120 lost work days a year.[24]

Looking ahead, it is altogether possible that support for *Hamas* and the other Islamists will experience another period of growth.

Analytical Assessment of Palestinian Rejectionism 263

By the same token, Arafat's residual popularity--which received a considerable boost from the 1995 accord with Israel, the subsequent elections and withdrawals from major Arab towns in the West Bank--could well suffer a major setback if the PNA escalates repression and human rights violations, if economic problems remain unaddressed, and/or if Israel, pressured by its own rejectionists, backslides on the expansion of Palestinian autonomy.[25]

The prospect that, over time, the highly secularized nature of Palestinian culture will mitigate the impact of extreme Islamism is hardly reassuring given that, in the short- to-mid term, a surge of active support might generate enough critical mass to intensify and sustain violence, thus effectively undermining the peace process. Should that transpire, newly energized rejectionist activity in the territories could, conceivably, be synchronized with a recrudescence of violence by 1948 refugees in Jordan and Lebanon, who feel they have been left out of Arafat's plans.[26] Whether such an ominous scenario occurs will be, in part, a function of external support, particularly that provided by Syria, a subject to which we will return later.

Organization

The varying levels of popular support accorded to the Palestinian rejectionists are closely related to their organizational characteristics. Since, as we pointed out previously, the Alliance of Palestinian Forces is little more than a public-relations facade, devoid of any serious organizational substance, an analysis of this linkage must perforce focus on the individual rejectionist groups themselves.

Over the years, both the PFLP and the DFLP have stressed the importance of building a solid, Leninist-style organization, complete with a Politburo, a central committee, a secretary general, etc. Like Mao, however, their idea has been to transcend the limitations imposed by Leninist-style conspiratorial thinking and use this vanguard as the central core of an expanding organization, designed to mobilize mass support. Despite such strategic aspirations, the stark reality is that their organizational structures have remained quite limited. Similarly, although they have virtually ruled entire sectors of refugee camps in Jordan and Lebanon in the late 1960's and 1970's, the leftist groups never had much success in extending that control, especially to the occupied territories. Moreover, as events during the Jordanian and Lebanese civil wars and their carefully controlled presence in Syria have demonstrated, the PFLP and the DFLP were rarely welcomed guests.

The ANO and the PFLP-GC, which also recognize the importance of popular support, albeit within the framework of military focus strategies, have even smaller organizational structures than the PFLP and the DFLP. These are comprised of tightly organized cells, operating independently of one another. To understand just how deficient such meager organization is for those whose strategy calls for popular support, one has only to compare it to insurgencies that have enjoyed significant backing within the context of both the military focus and, especially, the protracted popular war strategies. The remarkable achievements of the out-gunned and out-manned Confederacy in the American Civil War and the Viet Cong, respectively, come readily to mind. In both cases, extensive organization, however imperfect, played a key role in marshalling the people to provide soldiers and resources.

In contrast, even if one credits the four Palestinian groups just noted with skillfully organizing their active followers into a tightly-knit vanguard, the reach of the committed core has never been great.[27] While this might suffice for factions espousing either an urban warfare or a conspiratorial strategy, such is not the case for those who embrace a protracted popular war or military focus strategy. The yawning gap--if not total disconnect--between the professed need for mass support and the organizational tools fashioned for its acquisition could not but undercut these groups' credibility, effectively dooming them to the margins of the Palestinian struggle.

On the Islamic side, the IJM is similar to the small leftist groups in terms of the incongruity between calls for mass support and the

Analytical Assessment of Palestinian Rejectionism 265

organizational mechanisms for actualizing it. If anything, its organizational efforts are, in fact, even less impressive. The experience of *Hamas* is quite different from that of both the IJM and the secular rejectionists. As we saw in the preceding chapter, its origins and, hence, support base, lie in the regional Muslim Brotherhood, rather than in the Palestinian community alone. The Brotherhood, established in Egypt by Hasan al-Bana in 1928, has branches throughout the Arab world and is dedicated to replicating the early Muslim community through the establishment of states (and, eventually, a universal community--the *umma*), based on the *shariah* (Islamic law). By the 1940's, it had set up several branches (*shuba*) in Palestinian towns, with a membership of over 12,000 that was subject to the Brotherhood in Cairo.[28] Until the 1970's, its activities in Palestine were largely social and economic, rather than political. Thus, the Brotherhood played no role in the early stages of the Palestinian armed resistance.[29]

In 1973, a preacher named Sheik Ahmed Yasin created the Islamic Center, an organization that pulled together almost all the religious institutions associated with Brotherhood. This was soon followed by a merger of the Brotherhood groups in the Gaza Strip, West Bank and Jordan. The members then spent several years countering secular ideas in general and the PLO in particular, while paying only secondary attention to the Israeli occupation. These priorities reflected their belief that the transformation of society must precede armed struggle. The *Intifada* would radically change this approach.[30]

As the popular support for the uprising spread, the Brotherhood came under intense pressure to act more decisively. Fearing it would lose out to its secular rivals, it established *Hamas*--an ostensibly separate group that would engage in active opposition to the occupation, while the Brotherhood would cling to its traditional reformist agenda.[31] As events unfolded, the two organizations quickly became intermeshed.

Although *Hamas* lacks the PLO's complicated bureaucracy, it is, nevertheless, reasonably well-organized and, in the opinion of a former deputy head of Israel's internal security service, very disciplined.[32] Unlike the PLO apparatus, which has always been more effective in fostering relations with the global community, while providing services and exercising political control outside the occupied territories, *Hamas* has been more successful on the inside. This is directly attributable to its organizational presence at the grass roots level, i.e., in the mosques (most of which it controls), hospitals, schools, and universities, where it dispenses an annual budget estimated at $70 million. Commenting on the extent of *Hamas'* penetration of the socio-economic structures in the occupied territories, a senior IDF officer observed that, when a resident needs help, "instead of seeking it from the official authorities, there is a good chance he will find his way to *Hamas*."[33]

Overall leadership of *Hamas* is in the hands of Musa Abu Marzuq, who was arrested in the United States in 1995, and a Consultative Council. There are four regional sectors, each with its own command: one in Gaza and three in the West Bank. The shock troops in each sector are lay people, organized into groups referred to as *dawa* (the Call). While *dawa* groups carry out socio-economic activities, the Islamic Youth Organization, set up in 1988, has been responsible for civil disobedience, including the staging of demonstrations, writing slogans on walls, passing out leaflets, and clashing with Israeli troops. In addition, there is the Medical and Scientific Association, which operates hospitals; the Islamic Cultural Center for Women; the Science and Cultural Association, which runs schools; and the Council of Religious Sages, a group of 164 clerics who coordinate political sermons in mosques.[34]

There are three levels of membership in the Muslim Brotherhood. The first consists of a highly committed core of believers, who give full faith and obedience to the leadership. The second level is composed of participating members, who seek to become full members by showing their worthiness through various forms of involvement. Finally, there are the supporting members, who render financial backing and engage in various activities, but do not seek formal membership. Since this three-tiered approach allows

Analytical Assessment of Palestinian Rejectionism 267

the Brotherhood to carefully observe and assess the suitability of potential members, it enhances discipline and minimizes divisiveness in its ranks.[35]

Besides the formal organizational activities, *Hamas* engages in a range of informal undertakings. To gain acceptance and credibility, it maintains a network of close connections with important people in the community, including independent religious leaders, traditional elites and wealthy businessmen. In return for support from this network, *Hamas* stands ready to defend its allies against charges of unpatriotic behavior by secular nationalists. Funding for the movement during the 1970's and 1980's, according to the estimate of Mohammed K. Shadid, came from local *zakat* (tithes) committees, wealthy *zakat* committees in the Persian Gulf states, as well as the government of Saudi Arabia.[36]

The *Izz al-Din al-Qassam* Brigades, also created in 1988, serve as *Hamas'* critically important violent arm. Named after a Syrian "martyred" by the British in 1935 and revered as the first leader and father of armed Palestinian resistance, the *al-Qassam* Brigades are commonly thought to have a total membership of some 100 men, organized into small, compartmentalized cells. Since the cells are separate from one another and directed from outside the territories, they are exceedingly difficult to penetrate--particularly since there is no centralized leadership in the West Bank or Gaza.[37] Nonetheless, in 1996, many of their members were incarcerated by the PNA, a development that led to reports that a new, secret wing of the *al-Qassam* brigades, called *Jihaz al-Siri* (The Secret Apparatus), has been created.[38]

The compartmentalization of the political and military wings of *Hamas* is reminiscent of the Sein Fein relationship to the military arm of the Irish Republican Army. As one senior *Hamas* leader put it: "The political leadership of *Hamas*, which I represent, has nothing to do with terrorism. The *Izz al-Din al-Qassam* Brigade is a separate armed military wing, which has its own leaders who do not take their orders from us and do not tell us of their plans in advance."[39] As with the IRA, Basque Homeland and Liberty, and other insurgent groups which maintain such a fictional decoupling of the political and military arms, the inherent advantage is the absolution of political leaders from responsibility for terrorism and their ensuing immunity from detention. Beyond that, such plausible deniability makes them eligible interlocutors for peace negotiations, if and when they are deemed useful for bringing the violence to an end, as was the case with Sein Fein's Jerry Adams.

Over the past few years, *Hamas* has also struggled with a proposed change to its political structure. The issue was whether to form a political party that would be affiliated with it but, like the *al-Qassam* Brigades, maintain a semblance of autonomy through organizational compartmentalization. Such a party would give *Hamas* the political cover needed to participate in PNA elections and administrative agencies, while steadfastly maintaining its opposition to agreements with Israel. The obvious disadvantage would be the transparency of the party's connection with *Hamas*, thus psychologically undermining its total rejectionism and unwavering commitment to armed struggle. In addition, by participating in the political process, such a party would run the risk of lending legitimacy to the secular PNA, if not its policies.

Apparently unwilling to await the uncertain outcome, Arafat was reported to be crafting a plan of his own to form a new Islamic party. Before he could do so, however, events of early 1996 forced the issue for *Hamas*. Threatened by a combined Israeli-PNA crackdown, it moved to establish the Islamic National Salvation Party (INSP)--reportedly with Arafat's backing. To no one's surprise, the INSP committed itself to achieving a geographically complete Palestinian state, albeit through legal, rather than violent means.[40]

What all this adds up to is a complex organization that is functionally differentiated, secure, and fully capable of carrying out a wide range of social and political activities, alongside small scale--but deadly--guerrilla and terrorist attacks. What it does not add up to is an extensive and expanding military structure, capable of sustained, intensive operations. This assessment, in turn, suggests that *Hamas*' military activity could be contained through coordinated intelligence gathering, police work and judicial activity,

Analytical Assessment of Palestinian Rejectionism 269

involving the PNA and the Israelis. The rub, of course, is that such cooperation remains, as of this writing, in its embryonic stage, mired in mutual suspicions and, thus, hardly as efficient or effective as it needs to be. Consequently, barring a fundamental change of attitudes in Jerusalem and Gaza that goes beyond short-term responses to crises like the multiple bombings of February and March 1996, terrorism is likely to continue to stoke the fires of rejectionism. Worse, in the absence of significant social and economic steps to alleviate the Palestinians' plight, it could fan these flames into a conflagration which would destroy the peace process.

Cohesion

To the extent that Palestinian rejectionism threatens the peace process, this effect results primarily from *Hamas'* activity. The small size of the other groups, both secular and religious, limits their impact. Moreover, their potential to mobilize and systematically use their resources within the framework of the Alliance of Palestinian Forces has never been actualized because of personal, ideological and strategic discord. The rivalries and petty jealousies among the most important left wing secularists, such as the PFLP's George Habash and the DFLP's Nayif Hawatmah--which go back to a 1968 attempt by the latter to take over the PFLP while its leader was incarcerated in Syria--are well known. They reflect, at least in part, the general factiousness of the Palestinian political culture and the egocentricity of the individuals involved. Much the same could be said of the Palestinian Revolutionary Party, led by Arabi Awwad, and the Palestinian Popular Struggle Front, led by Khalid Abd-al-Majid. Neither merits further attention because of their relative insignificance.

The ideological and strategic differences dividing the Marxists only exacerbate the personal animosities. Ideologically, as we have pointed out, the DFLP leans towards a Maoist emphasis on political mobilization, whereas the PFLP has paid less attention to mobilizing mass support and more to violent action. Furthermore, while in the past both groups agreed on the need to overthrow reactionary Arab regimes, the DFLP argued that "all relations of subservience" should be attacked, whereas the PFLP exempted "progressive" governments.[41] Beyond that, the DFLP repudiated the transnational terrorist operations undertaken by PFLP and indicated that it was at least ready to entertain the idea of an eventual settlement with Israel--a notion hitherto unequivocally rejected by the PFLP. Ironically, the DFLP itself split in 1990, when Hawatmah's deputy, Yasir Abd Rabu, and his followers claimed to be the real DFLP and called for a more aggressive pursuit of peace, involving a willingness to be more forthcoming toward Israel.[42]

An even deeper fault line within the Marxist camp separates the PFLP-GC from both the PFLP and the DFLP. The General Command categorically opposes the very idea of a peace process. Instead, it advocates more violent action--and even less attention to politics, propaganda, and mobilization of support than the PFLP--as the formula for eliminating the Jewish state.[43]

On the religious right, meanwhile, there is acrimony between *Hamas* and the smaller IJM. Divisions abound within the two organizations as well (e.g., differences within both the political and military echelons of *Hamas* and a three-way split in the IJM). Aside from the ever-present rivalries among individuals vying for political power, there are abiding differences over strategic priorities and linkages with outsiders, as well as apparent discord within *Hamas* over the prudence and timing of terrorist attacks against civilians.

As we have seen, *Hamas* considers the Palestinian issue an integral element of the larger Islamic quest to reform Arab societies. The liberation of Palestine and the establishment of an Islamic political order are expected to follow the societal change. The IJM, in contrast, insists on engaging in an armed struggle to achieve these very aims, without waiting for success in the reformist transformation. In addition, *Hamas* is not enamored with the IJM's close ties with Shiite Iran. For all practical purposes, the

Analytical Assessment of Palestinian Rejectionism 271

ideological distinctions have been blurred by the establishment of *Hamas' al-Qassam* Brigades during the *Intifada* and the subsequent espousal of violence as a legitimate means to an end. However, this by no means signifies an impending merger of the groups, or even any meaningful cooperation.[44]

The rifts that separate the secular leftists from the religious groups are even deeper than those causing internal disunity within each camp. Indeed, there has never been a meeting of the minds between secular Palestinians, who subscribe to a Marxist philosophy, and the Islamists, who anathematize it as diabolical atheism. The two sides' fundamentally disparate visions of man's place in the universe and the nature of the desired political order are simply irreconcilable.

The debilitating effects of schism and friction within the rejectionist camp have been recognized by the movement's leaders. Nevertheless, efforts to coordinate rejectionist activity have been largely ineffectual. The track record of the Alliance of Palestinian Forces in addressing the question of coordination is hardly impressive. The members have been simply unable to overcome their bitter rivalries and deep divisions. Consequently, they have failed to resolve such basic issues as the distribution of political power and leadership positions. Most notably, the leftists emphatically refuse to accept *Hamas'* persistent demands, based on public opinion polls, for a 40% representation on all joint committees, thus effectively dooming the organization to systemic paralysis.

The present scramble for at least a semblance of cohesion is reminiscent of the PLO's abortive efforts to unite its ranks in the 1970's. At that time, an entire series of supra-structures was created--for example, the Palestine Armed Struggle Command, the Unified Command of the Palestinian Resistance, the Central Committee of the Palestinian Resistance, and the PLO Executive Committee--all designed to coordinate the efforts of the various groups.[45] With the partial exception of the Executive Committee, the experiments ended in abysmal failure.

By the same token, the Alliance of Palestinian Forces has been unable to evolve a common strategy or the structures--like a national council, or popular conferences--necessary to promote systematic political and operational cooperation among its members. In the words of one frustrated Islamic rejectionist: "The opposition's failure to agree on a strategy is paralyzing it, preventing the unification move from reaching the masses."[46]

Overall, the Alliance of Palestinian Forces has failed to fulfill its aim of becoming a viable counterweight to the PLO. Joint planning and execution of the myriad political and military tasks associated with a viable insurrection are yet to materialize, in part because the Alliance remains mired in squabbles over the composition and functions of the very organizational structures it needs to support its operations. Indeed, its accomplishments to date boil down to periodic meetings where leaders vent their anger, take advantage of photo opportunities, and promulgate fiery communiques denouncing the peace process in general and the various agreements that have been reached between its participants in particular.[47]

What is lost in the swirl of passionate rhetoric and public hype is a serious, sustained, coordinated, action-based strategy. It would be as if Mao, Chou En-lai and Chu Te never went much beyond meetings and press conferences in the mountains of Yenan, or Ho Chi Minh and Vo Nguyen Giap contented themselves with verbal denunciations of the French and Americans, followed by some episodic terrorist and guerrilla raids. Needless to say, if the Chinese and Vietnamese leaders had used a Palestinian rejectionist play-book, history would have passed them by with little more than a nod of bemused recognition, if that.

The devastating effects of this situation have been candidly summarized by one of the DFLP's leaders, Muhammad Jadallah. In explaining the reasons for a major loss of popular support for both the left and right wing rejectionist organizations in 1995, he singled out disorganization as the main culprit. Concurring with this assessment, Riyad al-Maliki of the PFLP stated pointedly: "The opposition has failed because it did not practice what it preached. Ideas cannot be implemented on the ground without an appropriate mechanism and a timetable."[48]

In a revealing interview published in September 1994, the IJM's Secretary General elaborated on the sorry state of affairs in the rejectionist alliance, censoring all factions for "internal flabbiness," caused by years of bureaucracy, militarism, despotism and something he called "pseudo-genius" [presumably, pretensions to omniscience]. Rejuvenation, he argued, would necessarily involve a serious effort, with success predicated on the rejectionists' ability to: overcome the debilitating crisis of confidence; deal with mutual distrust and lingering doubts about the seriousness of some factions; place the common interest above the parochial concerns of individual groups; and, finally, develop--and sustain--a viable action program.[49]

It is difficult to quarrel with this diagnosis--or with the courses of action suggested as potential solutions. Yet, since disunity is both endemic and deeply rooted, we would assess the probability of success as fairly low. Like their Israeli counterparts, the secular and religious branches of Palestinian rejectionism are split as to the desired end-state, as well as the ways and means necessary to bring it about. Worse, in the Palestinian case, the contradictory aims espoused by the secularists and the Islamists have resulted in fierce competition for dominant, if not exclusive control over the entire rejectionist effort, thus effectively dooming the long-term survival of any tactical compromise. To complicate matters still further, the internal causes of discord combine with the fragmented patterns of external support to render the story of Palestinian resistance a long and tormented tale of deep--and deepening--schisms.[50]

External Support

Hortatory rhetoric about the exigencies of armed struggle notwithstanding, external support for the Palestinian resistance has rarely been unconditional. In most cases, actual or prospective backing reflected the donors' ulterior motives. Of course, just about everyone in the Arab world and the former Soviet Bloc has, at one time or another, heaped verbal accolades on the various resistance groups and their "brave fighters." But, when it came to something more tangible than moral support, the picture immediately became more complex, since forthright alignment with the ultimate political goals of the Palestinians was often tantamount to undercutting the political aims of potential benefactors.

Consider, for example, the goal of creating a so-called secular, democratic Palestinian state to replace Israel--a declared objective on which, until 1974, there was universal agreement among the Palestinian groups. For those who aspired to lead the Arab world-- like Gamal Abdel Nasser and, later, Hafiz al-Assad and Saddam Hussein--there was little to be gained from sponsoring Palestinian parochialism. Not only did the endeavor conflict with the Pan Arab ideas then in vogue, but it was articulated by such obscure upstarts as Arafat. For other, less ideologically motivated leaders, like Jordan's King Hussein, the notion of an independent Palestinian state was hardly an appealing prospect for a number of reasons, not the least of which was the possibility that it could become a base of irredentism, supporting operations against the Hashemite throne in collaboration with dissidents from Jordan's Palestinian majority.

Such considerations produced a carefully calibrated aid program, more often serving the benefactors' aims than the recipients' actual needs. Thus, if and when material assistance to, or physical presence of, the Palestinians was perceived as a threat to the host regime, *raisons d'etat* always took precedence. To wit, in the late 1960's and early 1970's, Jordan and, to a lesser extent, Lebanon severely--and brutally-- circumscribed Palestinian activities in and from their countries, effectively engaging the PLO in open warfare. Likewise, Syria has been quite reluctant to permit the use of its territory as a staging base for attacks against Israel-- lest it invite massive retaliation.

In part, these attitudes reflected the basic distrust towards the Palestinians harbored by Arab presidents, kings and sheiks. Many of these leaders were, with very good reason, particularly wary of the Marxist organizations' stated goal of overthrowing the traditional Arab rulers as an ideological prerequisite for the

Analytical Assessment of Palestinian Rejectionism 275

eventual victory over Israel. The actual response varied by regime. While the Syrians tended to deal with the political threat posed by these groups through repression, incarceration and encapsulation in refugee camps, others, like the Saudis, chose to buy protection, effectively paying ransom to safeguard their kingdom.

Given the historical pattern, the fact that Damascus, Beirut, or Amman currently tolerates the presence of these groups on its territory should not be taken as an indicator of what the future might hold. Indeed, with little more than the snap of a finger, the accommodation might fall victim to domestic pressures, to the whims of the incumbent leader, or to the imperatives of politics. Moreover, if past behavior is a guide, the Palestinian rejectionists would be quickly isolated and carefully monitored, as has been the case in Jordan following its treaty with Israel. They could also be sacrificed outright on the altar of a peace accord that would serve the higher interests of Arab leaders. Even such groups as the PFLP-GC, which have enjoyed particularly close ties with Damascus, fully expect to be sold out by Syria in the context of a comprehensive peace.[51] Given the low tolerance of the Syrian authorities for dissent, any indication of rejectionist discord could easily lead to jail or exile.

Thus, the relationship between the secular rejectionists and their Arab sponsors, principally Syria, is quite tenuous. It is based on short-term calculations of convenience, interest and expedience-- related to what they can do for each other here and now--rather than being anchored in shared, enduring strategic aims, or ideological affinities. The situation is even more precarious for the Islamic militants--unless, of course, the governments in Damascus, Beirut, and elsewhere were to fall under fundamentalist control.

While there is plenty of moral support for *Hamas* and the IJM throughout the Arab world, as well as in Iran, there is also serious equivocation when it comes to political backing for the Islamists' ultimate goals. The reality is that, despite resounding verbal applause for rejectionist actions against "Zionist oppression," none of the states surrounding Israel looks forward to the creation of an Islamic state in Palestine, since all have had serious problems with their own militant fundamentalists. While these attitudes do not preclude the movement of people and money--as well as quiet acquiescence in arms smuggling across borders--the deep-seated mistrust accounts for the strictly monitored and carefully delimited assistance rendered to such groups. Even the presence of *Hamas* and IJM operatives and leaders in Damascus is deceptive, for it by no means signals Syrian support for an Islamic state in Palestine. Not only would such a development clash with the secular ideology of the *Ba'th* party and Syria's ambition to exercise dominant influence in Palestine (which it considers as "southern Syria"), but it would bring to power members of the Muslim Brotherhood who have, quite recently, enthusiastically supported Assad's most bitter internal enemies and declared that killing Assad was the duty of every Muslim. None of this is lost on the Syrian leader, who has a well-deserved reputation for remembering and punishing his enemies.[52]

Truth be known, Assad's moral support, permission to broadcast rejectionist messages on *Al-Quds* (the PFLP-GC mouthpiece) and other radios, and provision of a safe sanctuary for leaders of both partial and total rejectionist Palestinian groups--some of which, e.g., *Sa'iqa*, *Fatah*-the Uprising and, to a lesser extent, the PFLP-GC, owe their very existence to him--have always been based on *realpolitik*. Simply put, the various rejectionist organizations are very useful as leverage against Israel in the quest to regain the Golan Heights. Thereby, they serve Assad's core interest of securing the rule of his minority-based *Alawite* regime. If and when a peace agreement with Israel is perceived to be in Syria's vital interest, Assad can be expected to conclude it, even if it constitutes a mortal blow to the rejectionists. Although Syrian Chief of Staff, Hikmat al-Shihabi, has reportedly assured the Palestinian rejectionist organizations that their activities will not be curtailed as a result of an accord with Israel, it is inconceivable that Jerusalem would accept such a situation.[53]

Despite the fact that political support for the rejectionists leaves much to be desired, limited sanctuary for leaders, spokesmen, fund raisers, and the like are permitted in Syria, Lebanon and Jordan.

However, major sanctuaries--of the kind that Algeria provided for the Polisario at Tindouf--are out of the question, for fear that they would pose as much of a threat to the host country as to the PNA or Israel. In this sense, Jordan's sad experience with the PLO in 1970 remains a valuable lesson-learned. Consequently, one would fully anticipate a crackdown on *Hamas* and Islamic *Jihad* the moment an Arab regime sees continued Islamist activity as inimical to its larger interests.[54] This, in turn, would severely hamper both the quantity and quality--and, thus, the overall effectiveness--of support provided by more distant donors such as Iran.

For the time being, Iran is the major supporter of the IJM and, to a lesser extent, *Hamas*. Statements of both moral and political backing for the agendas of both are clear, continuous and categorical. Iranian officials and the state-controlled media constantly applaud the activities and policies of the rejectionist groups, echoing their call for the destruction of Israel. The *Velayat-e Faqi* (Supreme Jurisconsult, or religious leader), Ayatollah Ali Khamene'i, for example, has referred to Israel as "a cancerous tumor formed within the Islamic body," a "forged government and a false nation" that "should be eliminated." Similar sentiments have been expressed by President Ali Akhbar Hashemi Rafsanjani and other officials. For example, Hussein Sheikoleslam told the Iranian Republic News Agency after a March 1996 meeting in Damascus with *Hamas* and IJM leaders that: "There is no peaceful solution. The Israelis must return to the countries they came from."

To underscore their support, the Iranians have held major conferences with both secular and religious rejectionist organizations and provided financial aid, training, weapons, and equipment either directly or through such front organizations as the Martyrs' Foundation, the 5th of June Organization, the Imam's Relief Committee, and the Revolutionary Guards. Moral, political and limited material support also comes from Sudan, from private individuals, like the expatriate Saudi billionaire Usamah bin Ladin, and from various militant Islamic groups in the area, as well as from sympathizers in the United States (e.g., the Holy Land

Foundation for Relief and Development in Dallas, Texas). Nonetheless, there is no doubt that, along with Syria, Iran is one of two centers of gravity anchoring external support for the rejectionists. Thus, the removal of Teheran from the equation would be a devastating blow.[55]

Iran's role raises a further point that we would be remiss to ignore, namely, the part played by *Hezbollah*, its follower--if not outright client--in Southern Lebanon.[56] Essentially, *Hezbollah* provides moral and political support, as well as tacit military backing to the Palestinian religious rejectionists. Concurrently, as noted in earlier contexts, *Hezbollah* has carried out an increasingly successful guerrilla campaign against the Israelis--independent of *Hamas* and the IJM--effectively engaging the IDF in an outright war.

Hezbollah remains committed to the destruction of Israel. Its actions and those of the Palestinian Islamists are mutually supportive, in the sense that they are aimed at a shared strategic objective. Direct cooperation and coordination, however, are rather unlikely, due to historic animosities between the Shiites and the Palestinians, rooted in resentment of the PLO's overbearing and exploitative control of southern Lebanon (so-called "Fatahland") in the 1970's and early 1980's, as well as the ever-present Sunni-Shiite cleavage.[57] It also bears noting that while *Hezbollah* is a home-grown organization, motivated primarily by events in Lebanon, there are few, if any, serious observers who would deny that a withdrawal of Iranian material support would cripple its military abilities--unless, of course, Syria decided to risk international opprobrium and a confrontation with Israel by stepping into the breech and supplying *Hezbollah*.

For the present, Syria has limited itself to providing moral support and facilitating the flow of arms and personnel from Iran to *Hezbollah*. Moreover, *Hezbollah* operates in and out of Lebanon at the sufferance of Damascus. In the words of its deputy leader, Sheik Na'im Qasim, "...Damascus facilitates our activity on the ground in the regions where its troops are deployed."[58] Clearly, then, Syria has the capability to squash the resistance by severing

Analytical Assessment of Palestinian Rejectionism 279

its material support linkage with Iran. Whether it would muster the political will to do so--thus serving both its own national interest and promoting regional peace--is, of course, a different matter altogether.[59]

Returning to our main concern, it is fair to say that, in the final analysis, moral support for the most important groups, *Hamas* and the IJM, is considerable; political support is weak; material aid is limited; and sanctuary is circumscribed. Moreover, the support base lacks the depth and redundancy to either permit significant expansion or to provide ready replacement, should one of the extant sources of assistance collapse. The rejectionists are thus quite vulnerable to a cut-off and are dependent on the good-will-- and longevity--of essentially unstable regimes. These obvious weaknesses notwithstanding, we assess the external support as sufficient to sustain the Palestinian rejectionists' social, political and military activities at their present levels. Growth potential, in contrast, is severely constrained by the already thinly stretched human and material resources, as well as by the inherent fragility of the support base. Moreover, the potential could evaporate overnight if there are major breakthroughs in the peace process, especially with respect to Syria.

Government Response

The government response to the Palestinian rejectionist problem falls into two distinct, if related, phases: The 45 years during which Israel faced Palestinian extremism alone and the new, still embryonic era of joint Israel-PNA operations. With regard to the former, our focus is on the post-1948 time-frame, although we recognize the early actions against Arab rejectionists undertaken by Jewish underground organizations--from the mainstream *Haganah* to the extremist *Irgun* and *LEHI* (aka the Stern Gang).

Following Israel's War of Independence, the principal rejectionist threat emanated from the Arab states. It was manifested in implacably hostile propaganda, non-recognition, a full-scale boycott, and a spiraling arms-race. The Israeli response spanned the gamut from determined diplomatic and informational efforts, to conventional military measures. The concomitant threat posed by guerrilla raids and terrorist attacks was dealt with through both active defense--e.g., patrols and ambushes--and retaliatory strikes against sanctuaries. Israel's actions were predicated on the assumption that the cross-border operations were staged with at least the tacit approval of the Arab governments from whose territories they originated. Since Jerusalem sought both to punish past transgressions and deter future attacks, its doctrine of "striking at the source" had the added rationale of extracting a heavy price from its Arab neighbors for their continued support of Palestinian resistance.

The post-1967 emergence of independent *fedayeen* groups, committed to Israel's destruction, compelled a change of strategy. Although Israel continued to hold the Arab states accountable, it soon came to realize that it was facing a qualitatively different threat, which could not be blithely dismissed. As a number of Palestinian organizations took on a life of their own, the costs and incidence of guerrilla and terrorist attacks in Israel and the occupied territories gradually escalated in 1968 and 1969. Accordingly, the Labor government crafted a reasonably effective counterinsurgency strategy.

Air strikes and combined-arms cross-border operations continued unabated, with the enduring objective of raising the cost of harboring the *fedayeen*. Concurrently, the search-and-destroy conventional operations against adjacent Arab states were augmented by an extensive campaign of often-daring, long-range commando raids, executed by the IDF's elite units: paratroops, rangers/pathfinders (known as *Sayarot*, or scout units), and naval commandos (equivalent to the U.S. SEALS). In addition, passive defenses--such as sophisticated barriers, fences and detection systems constructed along the borders--made infiltration of men and material both riskier and more difficult. As a result, by the eve of the 1970 civil war in Jordan, there was a significant decline in the frequency and effectiveness of guerrilla attacks.[60] Likewise,

Analytical Assessment of Palestinian Rejectionism 281

the terrorist problem--both inside and outside the Green Line--was addressed through a combination of political, economic and security measures. Aware that small terrorist cells were better handled by the police, courts and intelligence agencies than by regular IDF forces, Israel sought to penetrate the terrorist structures by establishing a network of informants, if not outright collaborators, among the Palestinians. Moreover, it attempted to discourage potential supporters--and would be recruits--by raising the standard of living of the settled Arab population and maintaining open borders with Jordan, albeit under tight security scrutiny.

Israel's key objective was to reduce friction between the Palestinian population in the territories and the military government. To this end, it sought to give the people a stake in stability.[61] Operating under the premise--or the self-delusion--that the occupation was temporary, Jerusalem could not, realistically, expect that the Palestinians would ultimately accept the legitimacy of Israeli rule. The best that could be achieved in the first decade after the 1967 war was a grudging acceptance of the occupation and manageable, steadily decreasing levels of violence. Given the shortcomings of Israel's strategies, this was probably also the best that could be hoped for.

Israel's tough anti-terrorism policies included detention without trial, deportations, restrictions on movement, and collective punishment, with the latter often entailing the destruction of the homes of known *fedayeen*. Dwellings belonging to real or imagined PLO supporters were also targeted, usually with little legal recourse. While such measures were understandable against clearly identified perpetrators, they also victimized innocent people. This was particularly true with respect to collective punishment, inflicted on those who knew of impending incidents and failed to report them for fear of retribution from the terrorists. Complicating matters still further--and adding to the mounting ill-will--was the daily friction with Israeli settlers and the tendency of some irate Jewish civilians to lash out against innocent Palestinians in the wake of terrorist incidents.

Fortunately, the Labor government took active steps to reign in collective punishment. New, more stringent criteria reduced its frequency. In addition, indiscriminate attacks on Arabs were publicly condemned, Israeli leaders quickly visited the scene of such incidents to underscore their chagrin by apologizing to the victims and, in cases where IDF personnel were involved, court martial proceedings and reprimands were used. Likewise, an energetic public information campaign helped bring spontaneous outbreaks of Jewish civilian violence under control.[62]

Thus, despite the distrust and hatred of the Israeli occupation authorities, the security situation in the territories was relatively stable by the early 1970's. This, in turn, meant that the prospects for a rejectionist success in a protracted armed struggle were bleaker than ever. Recognizing this, the PLO undertook a thorough reappraisal of its strategy. As noted in the previous chapter, by 1974, the movement split into pragmatists and rejectionists--a bifurcation that, at the time, went largely unnoticed by the Israelis.

While Jerusalem continued to dismiss the pragmatist-rejectionist schism as little more than a smoke screen, in the short term the internecine strife inside the PLO could be seen as a success of Israel's counter-insurgency policy. Beneath the surface, however, longer-term problems--such as the political future of the territories and the status of the Palestinian refugees--remained unresolved, causing the resentment toward Israel to build and fester. This, in turn, redounded in the rejectionists' favor. The situation was further exacerbated by the regressive counter-insurgency policies that gathered momentum after the Likud government assumed power in 1977.

Espousing a maximalist territorial approach that laid claim to the entire West Bank and Gaza Strip, and consistently discriminating against the Arab population, Likud emerged as the best ally the Palestinian rejectionists could have dreamed of. Likud's behavior effectively validated the rejectionists' argument that the pragmatic wing of the PLO had no chance of success in the face of a government that had made it all too clear that there would be no trading of land for peace.[63] With Palestinian frustrations mounting

Analytical Assessment of Palestinian Rejectionism

against the backdrop of the government's massive effort to expand and "thicken" Jewish settlements in the territories, the situation was ripe for an explosion.

When the *Intifada* erupted in 1987 as a mixture of low-level violence and widespread civil protest, Israel's initial response was, to put it mildly, counterproductive. The myopic and misguided policy undertaken by Israel's fragile coalition government was only aggravated by its almost exclusive reliance on coercion. Employing military units largely untrained for riot duty, Israel suddenly found its David-against-Goliath image reversed, as worldwide television audiences watched the beatings and shootings of unarmed Palestinians on a daily basis. With the Palestinians now cast in the underdog's role, Israeli spokesmen candidly admitted hat they were losing the all important public relations battle on the international stage.

The *Intifada*'s domestic toll was even heavier. As we have noted in preceding chapters, during the 1980's, Israel's national consensus has been severely stressed by divergent attitudes towards the Palestinians in general and the disposition of the occupied territories in particular. As the military's inability to stamp out the *Intifada* grew increasingly apparent, IDF officers began to express serious concerns with the corrosion of morale, combat readiness, and discipline. An angry confrontation between reserve paratroopers and Prime Minister Yitzhak Shamir in Nablus in January 1989 was symptomatic of the onerous strain generated by daily clashes between a military--trained to carry the war to the enemy--and stone-throwing civilians.[64]

Fortuitously for the Israelis, Iraq's August 1990 invasion of Kuwait and Arafat's ill-advised--and well-publicized--support of Saddam Hussein's aggression diverted attention from the turmoil in the Gaza Strip and West Bank. Subsequently, as Iraqi SCUD missiles rained destruction on its population centers, Israel's suffering and forbearance went a long way towards redeeming its tarnished international image. Yet, while Desert Storm overshadowed the *Intifada*, it did not end the uprising nor eliminate the resentment that fuelled the daily clashes.

Israel's failure to quell the *Intifada* aside, other facets of its counter-insurgency program met with mixed success. On the plus side, the *Shin Bet* (*Sherut Bitachon Klali*, or internal security service) and IDF special forces, often acting on information provided by collaborators, were able to contain anti-Israeli violence by forestalling some planned attacks and eliminating, imprisoning, or deporting captured terrorists. On the negative side, Israel's longer-term stratagem of nurturing Islamic fundamentalists as a check and balance against the hated PLO, probably contributed to both the rise of *Hamas* and the concomitant growth of Palestinian rejectionism. This, in turn, would bedevil the Labor coalition that took power following Likud's 1992 electoral defeat.

Buoyed by what initially appeared as a clear mandate to end a century of Jewish-Arab violence by trading land for peace, the new government moved quickly to recognize the PLO as a viable--but indirect--negotiating partner. Following the peace accord with Jordan and the establishment of a Palestinian National Authority in Gaza and Jericho, the response to insurgent violence entered a new era. Henceforth, the focus would be on the rejectionist threat, with cooperation between two erstwhile enemies--Israel and the PLO--the *sine qua non* for success.

The importance of such cooperation was underscored by a series of bloody terrorist and quasi-guerrilla attacks, carried out by the IJM and *Hamas*' *al-Qassam* Brigades. In response, Israel undertook a number of unilateral, bilateral and multilateral steps, all designed to stem the violence.

First, on the unilateral level, Jerusalem conceded that while it could not hope to hermetically seal the borders between Israel proper and the territories, it could reduce the threat by temporarily halting and, then, carefully monitoring the flow of Palestinian laborers from the West Bank and Gaza into Israel. In the near term, borders were closed in the wake of terrorist attacks, while in the long term the number of employees from the territories was reduced. Yet, the closures and replacement of Arab workers by Asians and other outsiders had the paradoxical effect of aggravating the socio-economic misery that contributes to terrorism.

Analytical Assessment of Palestinian Rejectionism   285

As for dealing directly with terrorism, the police, courts and intelligence services occupied center stage. The policy of destroying the homes of terrorists was reinstated, albeit not without criticism from those who challenged both its effectiveness as a deterrent and its fairness, since the homes of Israeli terrorists have never been destroyed.[65] In addition, Israeli Security Services were authorized to use "physical pressure", i.e., torture, during interrogations of terrorist suspects, as well as to tighten overall operational security. The use of physical pressure was justified by the so-called "ticking bomb" criteria, established by the Landau Commission during its investigation of the past use of torture. The "ticking bomb" refers to a case where interrogators have knowledge of an impending attack and believe the individual they are detaining has vital information that can prevent it. Although the issue was bound to be controversial in a democracy such as Israel's and the decision was, in fact, criticized by Israeli human rights groups, there was little popular indignation. The common belief that the approach quite literally saved lives was underscored in 1995, when the Security Service claimed that more than 50 planned terrorist attacks had been prevented as a result of physical interrogation.[66]

Another step taken to deal with increasingly costly terrorist acts, especially by the IJM, was the reported reactivation of "hit teams"-- witness the assassination of the IJM's leader, Fathi al-Shaqaqi in Malta in November 1995 and the death of the notorious *Hamas* terrorist bomber, Yahya Ayyash (aka "the Engineer") in January 1996.[67] While the latter took place in the Gaza Strip, the former demonstrated that such activity would not be limited to Israel and the territories. Like attacks by special units against terrorist leaders inside the occupied territories over the years, the purpose of the hit teams was not only to eliminate particularly dangerous individuals, but also to send a message to their colleagues that they too could pay the price for carrying out or supporting acts of terror. In so doing, the Israeli high command hoped to replicate the success of a previous campaign against Palestinian operatives in Europe during the early 1970's.[68]

Second, on the bilateral level, Israel demanded greater efforts from the Palestinian National Authority in general and from Arafat in particular to curb the rejectionist organizations. Specifically, Israel expected full cooperation in the gathering and sharing of intelligence, as well as joint actions to prevent attacks through the incarceration of known and suspected terrorists. While rather obvious and logical, these steps were exceedingly difficult to implement. Initially, Arafat's hold on power was simply insufficient to allow vigorous moves against the rejectionists. With the peace process barely inching forward and economic conditions in the territories deteriorating--due, at least in part, to the vicious circle of escalating terrorism--Arafat's already waning legitimacy was bound to take a precipitous dive were he to be perceived as an "Israeli puppet." Absent a sea-change in attitudes, collaboration with Israel--meaning, among other things, readiness to hunt down and throw Palestinian "brothers" in jail--was unlikely to become the preferred way of gaining popular support any time soon.[69] Worse, since the PNA apparatus was still in the throes of a difficult transition from insurgency to counter-insurgency, it was hardly primed to undertake its new mission with the requisite resolve, enthusiasm and energy.

To help overcome this deficiency and provide the impetus to structured cooperation, Israel and the PNA set up a security liaison and coordination network for all of the territories. Supervised by a Joint Security Liaison Committee, the system is composed of District Liaison and Coordination offices (DCOs) in several parts of the West Bank and two in the Gaza Strip. The DCOs, in turn, monitor the activities of joint patrols operating around the clock. While quite obviously a good start, the effective functioning of the organizational apparatus is contingent on the evolution of trust among the participants on both sides--until very recently, bitter foes.[70] It was not surprising, therefore, that initial cooperative efforts between the IDF and Palestinian policemen in 1994-95 left much to be desired. For example, a document drafted by the DCO in Hebron was sharply critical of what it depicted as favoritism, lack of discipline and professional incompetence on the part of the

Palestinian police.[71]

Yet, despite these political and psychological impediments, by the end of 1995, Arafat was able to step up his security efforts. To wit, both the IDF Intelligence Branch and Major General Gabi Ofir, the Israeli commander in the West Bank, were reporting significant improvement in Palestinian police attitudes and efforts in the field.[72] Shortly thereafter, the outgoing head of the *Shin Bet* revealed that the Palestinian security services had helped prevent some 80 planned attacks. The IDF commander of the Israeli-Palestinian joint patrol office near Gush Katif in the Gaza Strip reported that the two sides were even carrying out joint ambushes.[73]

While some thought was apparently given to the liquidation of *al-Qassam* Brigade's top leaders, the notion was discarded because of its anticipated counterproductive effects.[74] Nonetheless, the generally propitious trend in PNA security efforts was further underscored by Arafat's unequivocal condemnation of terrorism-- specifically the bombings in Tel Aviv, Ashqelon and Jerusalem-- during his address to the first session of the Palestine Legislative Council on March 7, 1996; by the PNA's banning of all paramilitary organizations in the wake of the Jerusalem attack; and by the April 1996 decision to revoke passages in the Palestine National Charter calling for armed struggle and Israel's destruction.[75]

The progress was not without serious, if hidden dangers, however. An extensive Palestinian police effort was required to sustain Arafat's rule against opponents and to counter the *al-Qassam* Brigades. This engendered several separate organizations, including the General Intelligence Service, the Preventive Security Service, the Presidential Guard, Force 17, and the Special Security Force. That such groups were quickly charged by knowledgeable observers with significant human rights violations and repression of the media and political opponents came as no surprise to seasoned Middle East analysts.[76] The problem was, of course, that indiscriminate repression would, as in other insurrections, simply sow the seeds of future violence.

In addition to the steps just noted, there are indications that the

PNA had developed a fairly detailed counter-insurgency plan targeted at *Hamas*. According to PNA documents reportedly leaked to the Jordanian publication *Al-Sabil*, the blueprint wisely eschewed a narrow military approach in favor of a blend of socio-political, economic and security measures, to include a concerted effort to neutralize *Hamas*' religious appeal. In this vein, the purported plan recommended preemptive proselytizing, that would stress the contradictions in the fundamentalists' political approach, condemn their espousal of wanton violence, and expose their abuse and distortion of religion for self-serving purposes.

As noted earlier, there were also indications that the PNA intended to establish a new "Palestinian Islamic Party," with a platform proclaiming all of Palestine to be sacred Muslim land, yet supportive of the truce with the Israeli "enemy" as an alternative to what it called "chasing political mirages." Such a party was to compete with *Hamas* on its own ground, potentially fragmenting the fundamentalists' base of popular support. This plan, which represented a sensible, pragmatic departure from the emotionalism, bombast and rhetorical wheel-spinning that so often characterized PLO policy statements and schemes in the past, was finally actualized in March 1996 when, as we pointed out, the PNA backed the creation of the INSP by *Hamas*.[77]

Previously, *Hamas* had excoriated the idea of such a party as a Zionist plot adopted by the PNA. Recognizing it as a serious challenge, designed to dry up its economic, social and political resources, *Hamas* was particularly sensitive to the threat posed to its popular charity committees and institutions, which, it claimed, "had won the confidence of our people through the long, bitter years of occupation."[78] The extent of such concerns about successful PNA inroads has been reflected in the INSP's somewhat surprising declaration of May 1996 that its members would participate in the Palestinian government, albeit only in portfolios offering services to the population.[79]

Whether or not *Hamas*' worst fears will materialize hinges on three things: its own ability to maintain control of the INSP; the PNA's will to follow through and build on the security measures

Analytical Assessment of Palestinian Rejectionism 289

taken in response to the 1996 spate of suicide bombings (i.e., the closure of over 40 *Hamas* institutions, arrests of several hundred suspected terrorists and harsh, public condemnation of the bombings by some 30 Palestinian leaders); and Arafat's ability to avoid igniting a Palestinian civil war.[80] This, in turn, is contingent on a more forthcoming Israeli position at the negotiating table, as well as on reduced external support for the rejectionist cause and increased economic backing for the PNA.

Thus far, economic assistance has been wanting. According to Nabil Sha'th, Palestinian Minister for International Cooperation, as of late April 1996, only 27 million of the 886 million dollars pledged by donors in 1996 and the 500 million still owed from 1995 have been paid to the PNA.[81] Yet, such outside support is crucial, if the PNA is to meet basic socio-economic needs. Furthermore, any serious effort to reduce or eliminate the services offered by *Hamas*, without providing an effective substitute, will surely backfire in the longer term.[82]

Lastly, on the multilateral level, Israel's response to rejectionist violence involved bringing pressure to bear on Egypt and Jordan to curtail the smuggling of money, weapons and equipment across their borders. In the case of Jordan, Israel also sought to mute the rejectionist propaganda emanating from Amman, arguing that tolerance of *Hamas* and the IJM was hardly compatible with the formal treaty normalizing relations between the two nations. During the Spring of 1996, Israel's criticism of Amman was amplified by various PNA officials, who argued repeatedly that *Hamas* leaders in Jordan were playing a much more significant role than generally acknowledged.[83] In response, Jordanian authorities carried out a partial crack-down on the Palestinian Islamists, effectively exploiting the opportunity to quell internal opposition to the peace process.

Elsewhere in the Middle East, Israel complained about support for terrorism from Syria and Iran, as well as private financing from Saudi Arabia. Aware of its own limited leverage, Israel enlisted American support in the hope of persuading Riyadh and other Arabs capitals to exert more control over their residents.

Moreover, the Israelis prevailed on the United States to better monitor and curtail material aid provided by American citizens of Middle-Eastern origin to militant Islamic organizations. The policy received a favorable and concrete response from the Clinton Administration in early 1995, in the form of the Omnibus Counterterrorism Act.[84]

In the context of its diplomatic and informational campaign, Israel also focused on Iran's support for various militant fundamentalist groups, both inside and outside the Middle East. In so doing, it was successful in obtaining U.S. support for political and economic steps designed to further isolate Teheran. By the Spring of 1996, it was reportedly making some headway in persuading the European Union to toughen its policy toward Iran because of the latter's support for rejectionist violence. Israel's efforts to deal with the Iranian problem raised the question of transnational terrorist acts, such as attacks against Jewish citizens of Argentina, Britain and France. It also directed attention to *Hezbollah*'s guerrilla attacks and terrorist activities.

As noted before, *Hezbollah* is a militant Lebanese Shiite group that shares the rejectionist aims of its Palestinian counterparts. Composed of an estimated 3,000 fighters, its activities have attracted continuous attention from the IDF since the early 1980's, when Israel's invasion of Lebanon and subsequent harsh treatment of the Shiites contributed to its rise. The main battleground is the South Lebanon security zone, which was originally established to deal with the PLO. This enclave, manned primarily by Lebanese Christians and a smattering of Shiites and others, buttressed by IDF units, has been a special target of *Hezbollah* guerrilla attacks and occasional terrorism. From time to time, the fighting has involved Hezbollah rocket attacks against settlements and towns in northern Israel and IDF attacks against Arab villages outside the zone. Since *Hezbollah* has never disavowed its long-term aim of eradicating Israel--despite the doubts expressed by some of its members, such as its spiritual leader, Muhammad Husayn Fadallah --Jerusalem sees it as a serious threat, rather than a passing nuisance.[85]

Accordingly, Israel has reinforced its presence and conducted daily operations against the Shiite militants, to include: extensive small unit patrolling; air raids and artillery attacks against *Hezbollah* units and, at times, civilian villages; and a naval blockade along Lebanon's coast to raise the price of tolerating *Hezbollah*. Until recently, the most notable episode was Operation Accountability of July 1993, during which Israeli artillery fired 25,000 rounds across the border, driving 250,000 people from their homes.[86] Although the clash ended with an unwritten agreement--brokered by the United States and Syria--calling on both sides to refrain from attacking civilians, it did not arrest *Hezbollah's* increasingly effective guerrilla attacks inside the security zone.

Those attacks were directed at both the IDF and the South Lebanese Army which, in keeping with sound counterinsurgency practice, was created in order to reduce Israeli casualties and manpower demands. Unfortunately for the IDF, as the spring of 1996 approached, *Hezbollah* attacks were exacting a painful price and Israel, out of frustration, was threatening to attack targets outside the security zone. Such a response to intra-zonal attacks, as Israel's highly respected military columnist, Ze'ev Shiff, warned, would constitute an Israeli violation of the agreement not to attack each other's civilians outside the zone.[87]

Undaunted--and convinced that civilian villages sustained *Hezbollah* attacks--Israel launched Operation Grapes of Wrath on April 11, 1996. The assault featured massive artillery barrages along the entire border, as well as air and naval attacks against populated areas elsewhere. Ensuing events followed a familiar pattern: a large exodus of refugees, media images of massive carnage and devastation wrought by Israeli attacks, energetic American diplomacy, and an eventual agreement to refrain from further attacks on civilians.

While the new agreement is in writing--and includes a multinational monitoring committee--it is as flawed as its predecessor, because it fails to curb the costly guerrilla attacks against the IDF inside the security zone. Since Operation Grapes of Wrath did little damage to the guerrilla fighters themselves, renewed raids are to be expected. Indeed, *Hezbollah* has pledged to continue its struggle.[88]

Unless something is done to effectively address both the reported penetration of the South Lebanese Army by *Hezbollah's* agents, as well as the surprising laxity that has reportedly characterized the execution of Israeli ambushes and patrolling operations, the pain quotient is bound to increase, opening the door to yet another round of cross-border violence.[89]

Despite *Hezbollah's* tactical gains, it is our conclusion that, thus far, Israel's **overall** containment of militant rejectionism has been successful, in the sense that none of the rejectionist groups poses a mortal threat to the state. The main reasons for this are: the limitations imposed by the physical environment; a narrow base of active popular support; lack of effectively functioning supra-organizational mechanisms; chronic disunity and tenuous external support; and a reasonably efficacious and improving counterinsurgency program involving Israel and the PNA.

At the same time, however, the level of pain generated by terrorism has risen steadily, fostering more hawkish attitudes toward territorial compromise. This creates a vicious circle and a seemingly unsolvable dilemma, since progress in the larger peace process is the only viable way to reduce and, eventually, eliminate rejectionism--on both sides. Yet, as terrorism continues, the momentum toward peace is thwarted by the growing misgivings of the Israeli public and the outright hostility of Israel's own rejectionists. Indeed, many observers believe that the perceived lack of security--as evidenced by the series of lethal suicide bombings in Israel's heartland--accounts, in large measure, for the electorate's verdict against Labor. If so, terrorist violence might have achieved the stated objective of both Palestinian and Israeli rejectionists: undermining regional peace, perhaps for a long time to come.

Notes

Analytical Assessment of Palestinian Rejectionism   293

1. Several analysts have called attention to the unfavorable nature of the terrain. Among these are the following: Y. Harkabi, *Fedayeen Action and Arab Strategy*, Adelphi Papers, No. 53 (London: The International Institute for Strategic Studies, 1968), pp. 18, 27 and 31; David Waines, *The Unholy War* (Wilmette, Il: Medina University Press International, 1971), p. 174; Barbara C. Aswad, "The Involvement of Peasants in Social Movements and Its Relation to the Palestine Revolution," in Naseer Aruri, ed., *The Palestinian Resistance to Israeli Occupation,* (Wilmette, Il.: Medina University Press International, 1970), p. 23; Ania Francos, "The Palestinian Revolution and the Third World," in *ibid.*, p. 43; and, Constantine Zuraik, "Today and Yesterday--Two Prominent Aspects of the New Meaning of Disaster," *Middle East Forum,* 1967, p. 19. In the past, Palestinian spokesmen have reacted to this unhappy reality by either denial or suggesting that the masses ("dense human forests") would overcome the deficiency. See, for example, *Free Palestine,* September 1970, p. 1; *Palestine Resistance Bulletin,* March 1971, p. 3; and, Edmund Ghareeb, "An Interview with Abu Amar," *Arab World,* May 1969, p. 28.

2. Giles Trendle, "Hizbullah's Guerrilla War in South Lebanon," *Middle East International,* November 3, 1995, pp. 19-20.

3. The *Hamas* slogan threatening Christians is recounted in *Al-Watan Al-Arabi* (Paris), March 29, 1991 in JPRS-NEA-91-030, May 23, 1991, p. 9. Distrust and, at times, tension and small-scale violence have characterized Christian-Muslim relations in the Palestinian community. See, for example, Yosef Elgazi, "Awaiting Salvation from Heaven," *Ha'aretz* (Tel Aviv), August 12, 1994 in FBIS-NES-94-158, August 16, 1994, pp. 11-13. Various meetings with Christian notables over the years left one of the authors (O'Neill) with the consistent and distinct impression that there was very significant distrust of the Muslims. On two occasions, one Christian mayor commented on the Muslim-Christian strife in Lebanon by suggesting that the United States should drop the dirtiest atom bomb it had on the Muslims. Although clearly hyperbole, the comments reveal something about the visceral feelings some Christian leaders have about the Muslim community. On another occasion, Christian businessmen indicated in an off-the-record discussion that, while Israeli rule was abominable, so was that of Jordan from 1948 to 1967.

4. The secular orientation of the Palestinians is noted by Ziad Abu-Amr, "Hamas: A Historical and Political Background," *Journal of Palestine Studies,* Summer 1993, p. 18. Another indication of the secular nature of the Palestinian community may be inferred from the work of Mas'ud Aghbariyah of the Giv'at Haviva Center for Arab Studies. Aghbariyah has pointed out that despite the support for the Islamic Movement, comparative surveys showed that it had

peaked in the early 1990's and fewer Israeli Moslems saw themselves as very religious compared to the past. A 1995 survey revealed only 22 percent viewed themselves as very religious and 27 percent as traditional, while 52 percent said they were not religious. See *The Jerusalem Post*, July 7, 1995.

5. Yezid Sayigh, "The Intifadah Continues: Legacy, Dynamics and Challenges," *Third World Quarterly*, July 1989, p. 29; Ziyad Abu-Amr, "The Palestinian Uprising in the West Bank and Gaza Strip," *Arab Studies Quarterly, Fall 1988*, p. 399; Re'uven Pedatzur, "Anatomy of a Materializing Leadership," *Ha'aretz* (Tel Aviv), February 12, 1989 in FBIS-NES-89-030, February 15, 1989, pp. 49-50.

6. *Ha'aretz* (Tel Aviv), June 23, 1995 in FBIS-NES-95-124, June 28, 1995, pp. 7-9. A good profile of the various components of the Palestinian community, which compares them in terms of a range of factors like education, infrastructure, health, economic, political and social conditions is Marianne Heiberg et al., *Palestinian Society in Gaza, West Bank and Jerusalem: A Survey of Living Conditions*, FAFO-Report 115 (Oslo, Norway: Norwegian Institute for Applied Social Science, 1993)

7. The relative quiesence of the Israeli Arabs and their disinclination to support violence is well-known. Hence, their relative inaction during the *Intifada* came as no particular surprise. See Qasim Zaid, "The Green Line's Red Line," *Al Ha'mishmar* (Tel Aviv), June 26, 1990 in JPRS-NEA-90-047, August 31, 1990, pp. 25-27. One expert who forsees the possibility of an Arab Intifada in Israel is Professor Sha'ul Mish'al of Tel Aviv University. See *The Jerusalem Post*, May 31, 1995. The growth and increased organizational efforts of *Hamas* inside the green line is discussed by Sara Friedman and Amir Gilat in the following two articles: "In Umm-al-Fahm Hamas Starts at the Kindergarten," *Ma'ariv, Shabat* supplement (Tel Aviv), February 3, 1995 in FBIS-NES-95-026, February 8, 1995, pp. 37-41 and "*Hamas*' Next Stop--the Knesset," *Ma'ariv, Shabat* supplement, February 10, 1995 in FBIS-NES-95-029, February 13, 1995, pp. 43-46. Also see the informative report by Steve Rodan and Jacob Dallal in *The Jerusalem Post*, Magazine supplement, August 19, 1994, pp. 6-10.

8 Dr. Eyad R. Sarraj quoted in Anthony Lewis, "Darkness in Gaza," *The New York Times*, May 6, 1996. As a reward for his contribution to Palestinian human rights, Dr. Sarraj was jailed by the PNA for this interview.

9. The membership of various Palestinian resistance organizations has changed over time and exact figures are not available. Nevertheless, general estimates of the size of the groups are fairly consistent. An excellent open source is The

Directorate of Intelligence, Central Intelligence Agency, *Palestinian Organizations*, LDA 92-12531, (Springfield, VA: National Technological Information Service, July 1992). Those interested in a more detailed listing of officials in the various organizations should consult *Palestinian Organizations and Officials,* FBIS-NES-95-030S, (Daily Report Supplement), February 14, 1995.

10. On the exiguous support for the Marxist groups see *Ha'aretz* (Tel Aviv) June 16, 1994 in FBIS-NES-94-117, June 17, 1994, pp. 5-6; *Al-Nahar* (Jerusalem), September 22, 1994 in FBIS-NES-94-185, September 23, 1994, pp. 11-12; *Ha'aretz* (Tel Aviv), June 23, 1995 in FBIS-NES-95-124, June 28, 1995, p. 9. Youssef M. Ibrahim, "Palestinian Religous Militants: Why Their Ranks Are Growing," *The New York Times,* November 8, 1994, cites a Palestinian official as indicating that *Hamas* is the only alternative to the PLO because the left-wing groups are irrelevant. Graham Usher suggests that organizational and ideological inability to deal with new realities are the main factors constricting the leftists. See his "The PLO Opposition: Rebels Without a Constituency, *Middle East International,* October 7, 1994, p. 16. The detriorating state of affairs in the PFLP, resulting from this situation, is reflected in a decision to terminate its main publication, *Al-Hadaf,* close offices, cut back on cadres, and end various cultual activities, according to *Al-Bayan* (Dubayy), January 17, 1995, FBIS-NES-95-013, January 20, 1995, p. 12.

11. Although its activities have diminished in the past few years due to internal dissention and its growing isolation in the Arab world, the ANO still poses a threat to Israelis, Jordanians and the PNA. As recently as January 1996, the Palestinian police reported capturing ANO members who were planning a bombing and assassination campaign. See Paris AFP, January 14, 1996 in FBIS-NES-96-010, January 16, 1996, p. 15.

12. *Ibid.* The senior IDF intelligence officer's estimate is cited in *Ha'aretz* (Tel Aviv), FBIS-NES-95-055, March 22, 1995, p. 43.

13. On the election see Serge Schmemann, "Palestinian Vote: Dawn for Most, Legitimacy for Arafat," *The New York Times,* February 22, 1996.

14. *Hamas* and the IJM commentaries abound with scathing depictions of Jews as cruel, harsh, devious, cunning, and faithless people who break covenants. See the comments of Sheik Bassam Jarar, a *Hamas* preacher, as quoted in Imanuel Sivan, "The Myth of the Children of Israel," *Ha'aretz* (Tel Aviv), March 15, 1994 in JPRS-NEA-94-019, April 20, 1994, pp. 30-31. The impermissibility of making peace with Israel is discussed in *Al-Mujtawa* (Kuwait), July 29, 1986.

The educational status of Islamic zealots is noted by *Globes, Shishi Weekly Supplement* (Tel Aviv), October 28, 1994, JPRS-TOT-94-045L, November 10, 1994, p. 29. Parenthetically, it is worth remembering that the perpetrator of the Hebron mosque slaughter, Baruch Goldstein, is, like his counterparts on the Islamic side, considered a martyr.

15. Chris Hedges, "A Language Divided Against Itself," *The New York Times*, January 29, 1995.

16. Serge Schmemann, "Terror Isn't Alone as a Threat to Mideast Peace," *The New York Times*, March 3, 1996.

17. The alienation of the Palestinians caused by Israeli repressive measures is so well-known that it hardly needs elaboration. Nowhere is it better epitomized than in the case of the Christian Arab town of Beit Sahur in the West Bank, where a passive population not given to anti-Israeli militancy was transformed into one that was reportedly swept up in seething anger and hatred as a result of Israeli security measures during the *Intifada*. See Youssef M. Ibrahim, "Israeli Army Pushes Town To Hatred in West Bank," *The New York Times*, March 15, 1989. The provision of social services by *Hamas* is also well-known. See, for example, Abu-Amr, "Hamas: A Historical and Political Background," p. 8; *The Economist*, December 19, 1992, p. 40. On the demonstrable increase in anger directed at Arafat and the PNA in 1994-1995 see, Youssef M. Ibrahim, "Support for Arafat in Gaza Replaced by Wide Enmity," *The New York Times*, December 3, 1994; Barton Gellman, "Palestinians Vent Their Ire Over Arafat," *The Washington Post (hereafter WP)*, February 27, 1995. As Gellman notes, despite his problems, Arafat retains his preeminence because, for many Palestinians, there is no alternative. Israel's former Chief of Military Intelligence, Major General Uri Sagi, reportedly indicated Arafat would win an election in the territories if it were held in Feburary 1995. Events a year later would, of course, prove him correct. See Jerusalem *Qol Yisra'el*, February 7, 1995, in FBIS-NES-95-026, February 8, 1995, p. 37.

18. Friedman and Gilat, "In Umm al-Fahm Hamas Starts at the Kindergarten," pp. 37-41; Roni Shaqed, "The Blood Account," *Yedi'ot Aharonot, Leshabat Supplement* (Tel Aviv) in JPRS-TOT-94-045L, November 10, 1994, p. 34.

19. Ha'aretz (Tel Aviv), June 16, 1994 in FBIS-NES-94-117, June 17, 1994 pp. 5-6; *Ha'aretz* (Tel Aviv) June 23, 1995 in FBIS-NES-95-124, June 28, 1995, p. 9.

20. Quoted in Joel Greenberg, "Palestinian 'Martyrs' All Too Willing," *The New*

Analytical Assessment of Palestinian Rejectionism 297

York Times, January 25, 1995.

21. A typical assertion of Islamic sanctioning of suicide operations may be seen in the following words of former *Fatah* official Munir al-Maqdah: "Islam's four creeds are clear on suicide operations when Muslim land is occupied. Our Islamic *shari'ah* permits it in this case. When a suicide fighter kills 20 or 30 Jews he goes to Paradise. Martyrdom in the cause of God is in line with the *shari'ah*, and there are several Koran[ic] verses and the Prophet Muhammad's traditions to support this. I do not believe that anyone has issued *fatwas* banning martyrdom in our time." See the interview of al-Maqdah in *Al-Diyar* (Beirut), March 21, 1996 in FBIS-NES-96-068, April 8, 1996, pp. 10-11.

22. The profile of suicide bombers is based on the insights of several academic specialists summarized by Smadar Peri, "They Kill Themselves for Allah," *Yediot Ahranot, 24 Hour Supplement*, (Tel Aviv), November 14, 1994 in JPRS-TOT-94-049L, December 29, 1994, pp. 22-24. The fact that Islamic esoteric appeals alone can be a powerful attraction is exemplfied in the case of 15-year old Musa Ziada, who was prepared to carry out a suicide bombing mission in February 1995 before a vigilant uncle intervened at the last moment. Unlike many young militants, Ziada came from a well-to-do familiy and was motivated by Islamic ideals and the noble promise of a martyr's place in paradise. See John Battersby, "A Boy Bomber Changes His Mind," *The Christian Science Monitor* (hereafter *CSM*), April 14, 1995. The views of Eyad Sarraj and the quote attributable to him are found in David Hoffman, "The Making of a Martyr," *WP*, March 12, 1996. Also see Neil MacFarquhar, "Portrait of a Suicide Bomber: Devout, Apolitical and Angry," *The New York Times*, March 18, 1996.

23. Ori Nir, "Forbearance and Several Interim Gratifications," *Ha'aretz* (Tel Aviv), January 5, 1995, JPRS-TOT-95001-L, January 19, 1995, p. 23.

24. John Battersby, "Self-Rule for Gaza Pays an Early Dividend: Hope," *CSM*, December 7, 1995.

25. On the upswing in support for Arafat and *Fatah* see the polling data reported by *Jericho Voice of Palestine*, October 22, 1995 in FBIS-NES-95-205, October 24, 1995, pp. 5-6.

26. As noted in the previous chapter, the 1948 refugee population has been the main support base for the armed struggle. As a result of Arafat's agreements with Israel and his channeling of money to the territories, the 1948 refugees perceive themselves as having been cast into a sort of political limbo, with little hope of compensation, to say nothing of returning to their original homes inside

the Green Line. A good summary of their thinking is reported by Jim Muir, "Palestinian Refugees in Lebanon Say Peace Deal Abandoned Them," *CSM*, July 5, 1994.

27. Directorate of Intelligence, Central Intelligence Agency, *Palestinian Organizations*; E. A. Wayne, "Strange Bedfellows in the Middle East," *CSM*, January 24, 1989.

28. A succinct account of the history of the Muslim Brotherhood and the emergence of *Hamas* from its ranks may be found in Abu-Amr, "*Hamas*: A Historical and Political Background," pp, 6-13. A more detailed exposition may be found in the same author's book, *The Islamic Movement in the West Bank and Gaza Strip* (Akko, Israel: al-Aswar House, 1989), JPRS-NEA-90-011-L, June 14, 1990, pp. 5-15.

29. Mohammad K. Shadid, "The Muslim Brotherhood Movement in the West Bank and Gaza," *Third World Quarterly*, April 1988, p. 662.

30. Abu-Amr, "*Hamas*: A Historical and Political Background," pp. 6-8.

31. *Ibid.*, pp. 10-11.

32. The complexity of the PLO organization can be appreciated by looking at *Palestinian Organizations and Officials*, Daily Report Supplement, FBIS-NES-95-030S, February 14, 1995. Many essays have been written about the structure and functioning of the PLO. Among the most useful remains Cheryl A. Rubenberg, "The Civilian Infrastructure of the Palestine Liberation Organization," *Journal of Palestine Studies*, Spring 1983. For Israeli comments on the discipline of *Hamas* and other useful insights into its organizational evolution see, Yossi Melman, "The Three Faces of *Hamas*," *WP*, March 10, 1996.

33. *Ha'aretz* (Tel Aviv), March 22, 1995 in FBIS-NES-95-055, March 22, 1995, p. 43; John Kifner, "Alms and Arms: Tactics in a Holy War," *The New York Times*, March 15, 1996.

34. Ibrahim, "Palestinian Religious Militants, *op cit.*;" Kifner, "Alms and Arms...," *op cit.*

35. Shadid, pp. 665-666.

36. Ibid., p. 665.

Analytical Assessment of Palestinian Rejectionism 299

37. *Ibid.*; Abu-Amr. *The Islamic Movement in the West Bank and Gaza Strip*, pp. 46-48; Ron Ben-Yishay, "Gloves Off," *Yedi'ot Aharonot, Leshabat* supplement (Tel Aviv), November 18, 1994 in FBIS-NES-94-225, November 22, 1994, 48-49. The commander of the *Hamas* military arm is reported to be Muhammad Qasim Sawalilah who resides in London. Sawalilah stands between Abu-Marzuq and the terrorist squads in the territories and thereby shields the former from direct involvement with the *al-Qassam* brigades. See *Yedi'ot Ahronot* (Tel Aviv), Jult 30, 1995 in FBIS-NES-95-146, July 31, 1995, pp. 48-49.

38. Steve Rodan, "Iran Seeks to Torpedo the Elections, *The Jerusalem Post*, May 17, 1996; Jerusalem Israel Television Channel 1, May 15, 1996 in FBIS-NES-96-096, May 16, 1996, pp. 3-4. Rodan depicts the new group as a rival rather than an appendage of the *al-Qassam* brigades and cites intelligence sources as saying Iran is its sponsor.

39. *Al-Sharq Al-Awsat* (London) November 1, 1994 in *FBIS-NES*-94212, November 2, 1994, p. 6.

40. Lamis Andoni, "Palestinian Islamist Group Signals Shift in Strategy," *CSM*, September 13, 1994. On the creation of the Islamic National Salvation Party see Serge Schmemann, "Ex-Hamas Group Forms Nonviolent Party With Arafat Backing," *The New York Times*, March 22, 1996. The offical statement establishing the INSP may be found in JMCC Press Service (Jerusalem), March 21, 1996 in FBIS-NES-96-057, March 22, 1996, pp. 5-6.

41. The reader interested in a detailed comparison of the PFLP and DFLP views should consult Leila S. Kadi, comp. and trans., *Basic Political Documents of the Armed Palestinian Resistance Movement* (Beirut: Palestine Liberation Organization Research Center, 1968), pp. 143-247. On the matter of the DFLP's condemnation of transnational terrorism see the interview of Hawatmeh in *An-Nahar* (Beirut), August 17, 1973 as excerpted in *Journal of Palestine Studies*, Autumn 1973, pp. 198-199 and the DFLP's pamphlet entitled *On Terrorism, Role of the Party, Leninism Versus Zionism* (Buffalo, NY: Palestinian Solidarity Committee, State University of New York, n.d.), pp. 2-5. Also found in *Al-Hurriya* (Beirut), September 12, 1969.

42. During the 1970s, the DFLP could be counted on to support Arafat's pragmatism, even if it continued to disagree with him on ideological and strategic matters. What landed it in the rejectionist camp in the 1990's was its repudiation of the agreements between the PLO and Israel, and its conclusion that they entailed too many concessions and did not address the settlements, Jerusalem and

refugee issues. That little had changed with respect to the DFLP's willingness to accept Israel was evident in a plan proposed by Hawatmah in February 1995 that, *inter alia*, provided for establishing two states for two peoples.See *Ha'aretz* (Tel Aviv), February 24, 1995 in FBIS-NES-95-037, February 24, 1995, pp. 4-5. On the split in the DFLP see Paul Lalor, "DFLP Differences Reflect the Debate Within the PLO," *Middle East International*, April 27, 1990, pp. 17-19.

43. The consistent refusal of the PFLP-GC to accept the existence of Israel is well-known to students of the Palestinian resistance. A typical reiteration of this may be found in comments by a military spokesman on its clandestine radio station, *Al-Quds*, on October 2, 1995: "We reaffirm that our guns will remain brandished until the Oslo agreement is toppled and Palestine and all the Arab territories are liberated." See FBIS-NES-95-191, October 3, 1995, p. 21. Not surprisingly, the PFLP-GC is emphatically opposed to amending or nullifying the Palestine National Charter which, in effect, calls for the elimination of Israel. See *Al-Quds* Palestinian Arab Radio (Clandestine), July 19, 1995 in FBIS-NES-95-139, July 20, 1995, pp. 5-6.

44. While the differences between *Hamas* and the IJM have been narrowed by the activities of the *al-Qassam* brigades, there have been few, if any, joint military operations. In fact, Fathi al-Shaqaqi, the late Secretary-General, told *Al-Safir* (Beirut) that the political views of the two groups were identical. See Interview with Islamic Jihad Secretary General Dr. Fathi al-Shaqaqi by Ali Jamalu in *Al-Safir* (Beirut), February 10, 1995 in FBIS-NES-95-032, February 16, 1995, p. 9. Whatever the truth of this matter, reports of differences within the groups continue to surface. In the case of *Hamas*, a senior official of the group stated flatly in early 1995 that the differences were having adverse effects on military operations. See *Al-Sharq Al-Awsat* (London:), February 8, 1995 in FBIS-NES-95-027, February 9, 1995, p. 11. In February and March 1996 there were clearly discordant notes struck by various *Hamas* spokesmen regarding the terrorist bombings against Israelis in Jerusalem, Tel Aviv and Ashqelon. Some were critical, while others applauded or took credit for the acts. Further complicating the situation was a report by the IDF Chief of Staff, who asserted that both *Hamas* and the IJM intended to disavow terrorist acts while secretly carrying them out. See Paris Radio Monte Carlo, February 27, 1996, Gaza Broadcasting Corporation Television Network, February 27, 1996, Paris AFP February 28, 1996, *Al-Sharq Al-Awsat*, February 27, 1996 and Jerusalem *Qol Yisra'el* February 27, 1996 in FBIS-NES-96-040, February 28, 1996, pp. 1-3 and 25. Also see *Al-Quds Al-Arabi* February 26, 1996 in FBIS-NES-96-039, February 27, 1996, p. 4. While expert speculation abounded and varied on the question of differences within *Hamas* over the use of terrorism and other matters, no convincing evidence was proffered regarding its extent,

Analytical Assessment of Palestinian Rejectionism   301

ingenuousness and actual effects. See, for example, Melman, "The Three Faces of *Hamas*, "*op cit*. Further confusing matters was a report by *Al-Hayah* (London), March 27, 1996, which cited an alleged *Hamas* document to the effect that all the seeming contradictions emanating from *Hamas* are part of a carefully contrived deception plan. See FBIS-NES-96-061, March 28, 1996, pp. 9-10. According to *Al-Bilad* (Amman), November 1, 1995, the splits in the IJM were foreshadowed at the inception of the group by al-Shaqaqi, who himself split from the pro-Iraq Islamic Jihad Movement, *Bayt al-Maqdis*, led by the strongly pro-Sunni Sheik As'ad Bayyud al-Tamimi. The later was strongly critical of al-Shaqaqi's link with Shiite Iran. In time, al-Shaqaqi would himself experience splits led by Sheik Abd-al-Aziz Awdah and Muhamad Abu-Samrah. See FBIS-NES-95-214, November 6, 1995, pp. 6-7; Ali Nun, "Split in Islamic Jihad Between the Awdah and al-Shaqaqi Trends," *Al-Hayah* (London), May 31, 1995 in FBIS-NES-95-105, June 1, 1995, p. 7. As for joint military operations involving *Hamas* and the IJM, they are, in a word, rare. One such case is reported by *Yediot Ahronot* (Tel Aviv), April 1, 1995 in FBIS-NES-95-069, April 11, 1995, p. 6.

45. On the various efforts to unify the PLO and the reasons for their failure see Bard E. O'Neill, *Armed Struggle in Palestine* (Boulder, CO: Westview Press, 1976), pp. 134-144; 152-153.

46. Interview of Imad Mukhtar, *Al-Safir* (Beirut), June 15, 1995 in FBIS-NES-95121, June 23, 1995, p. 7.

47. On the dismal state of affairs regarding the Group of Ten and the failure of new efforts to provide some semblance of unity between the popular fronts see, Ibrahim Humaydi, "The Popular Front and Democratic Front Against *Hamas* and *Jihad*. Talk About Unity Reveals Differences and Contradictions," *Al-Hayah* (London), December 12, 1994 in FBIS-NES-94-242, December 16, 1994, pp. 5-6.

48. *The Jerusalem Times*, October 27, 1995. Also see FBIS-TOT-95022, December 21, 1995, pp. 16-17.

49. See interview of Fathi al-Shaqaqi, *Al-Bayadir Al-Siyasi* (Jerusalem), September 10, 1994 in JPRS-NEA-94-054, October 20, 1994, p.11.

50. A recent example of yet another effort at unity on the rejectionist side was the announcement of a "national salvation program" by the erstwhile leftist adversaries, the PFLP and the DFLP, in the summer of 1994. Not surprisingly, the program remained a rhetorical fantasy to reality. See *Tishrin* (Damascus),

July 6, 1994 in FBIS-NES-94-135, July 14, 1994, p. 8.

51. External support for insurgents varies greatly with respect to type rendered and durability. The dispensation of aid by donor states is rarely due to altruism. In the vast majority of cases, regimes give aid because it serves their "national" interests, which in the Middle East means regime interests. Assistance to the Palestinian resistance groups over the years has been a classic example of this. An analysis of external support to the PLO in terms of donors and kinds of aid given may be found in O'Neill, *Armed Struggle in Palestine*, pp. 163-204. An indication of PFLP-GC fears of an eventual Syrian sellout may be inferred from reports that Jibril had approached Iran (and been refused) about moving there. See *Shihan* (Amman), January 21-27, 1995 in FBIS-NES-95-013, January 20, 1995, p. 13.

52. The call for Assad's assassination was made by Sheik Sa'd al-Din al-Ilmi, Chairman of the Supreme Islamic Council, at rallies at the *Al-Aqsa* Mosque in Jerusalem, according to Ziyad Abu-Amr. On this and the more general bad blood between the Palestinian Islamists and Syria, see his *The Islamic Movement in the West Bank and Gaza Strip* (Jerusalem and Akko: *al-Aswar* House, 1989), pp. 18; 28-29.

53. For Al-Shihabi's assurances to the rejectionists see *Al-Bilad* (Amman), March 12, 1996 in FBIS-NES-96051, March 14, 1996, p. 62.

54. Reports of sanctuaries for *Hamas* and the IJM in Syria (and by extension Lebanon), Sudan and Iran are well-known. Although bases and facilities in the latter two countries are useful, their strategic impact is minimal due to their distance from the principal arena of conflict. While the presence in Syria is more important, it hardly equates to a thriving, first-class sanctuary of the sort Polisario enjoyed in Algeria or the Viet Cong had in Laos, Cambodia and, especially, North Vietnam. Nonetheless, the fact remains that both Syria and Iran make life much easier for the rejectionists by providing safe havens from counter-terrorist operations. The same has been true in the case of Jordan, where *Hamas* spokesmen have long been active. Arafat and others have also contended that *Hamas* runs a banking operation out of the Hashemite Kingdom. The principal *Hamas* personage in Jordan, Ibrahim Ghawsaw, actually conducts affairs in the offices of the Islamic Action Front, the Jordanian branch of the Muslim Botherhood. Reports of material support for the Islamic groups tend to focus on financial outlays and training, rather than the provision of weapons. There is no reliably confirmed data that is precise with respect to its scope and extent. There is a plethora of reports, commentaries, and the like on the connections between Syria and the various Palestinian groups and *Hezbollah*.

Analytical Assessment of Palestinian Rejectionism   303

Among the more recent are Jerusalem *Qol Israel*, February 13, 1996 in FBIS-NES-96-031, February 14, 1996, p. 26; Paris AFP, December 9, 1994 in FBIS-NES-94-237, December 9, 1994, p. 34. One extensive report notes that, in addition to providing weapons and a sancturary for the militant Islamic groups, Syria has also made death threats against various peacemakers or supporters--eg., Arafat, Jordanian leaders and officials from the Union of Arab Emirates. Given the Syrian track record regarding assassinations, such threats are entirely plausible. See *Yediot Ahronot, Leshabat* supplement (Tel Aviv), March 15, 1996 in FBIS-NES-96-053, March 18, 1996, pp. 41-44. On the Jordanian connection see *Ha'aretz* (Tel Aviv), March 14, 1996 *in* FBIS-NES-96-052, March 15, 1996, p. 1; John Kifner, Money Is Chanelled to Hamas By Way of a 'Shocked' Jordan," *The New York Times*, March 21, 1996.

55. A reading of *FBIS-NES* daily reports over the past several years will reveal copious reportage of Iranian backing for the rejectionists. A convenient and focused summary may be found in "Teheran's Hostility Toward Israel, Peace Unabated," *FBIS Trends*, November 2, 1994, pp. 1-7. Sheikholeslam's comments are recounted in Kifner, "Alms and Arms," *op cit*. Iran's ties with both secular and Islamic rejectionists are described in Ali Nuri-Zadih et al., "Revolutionary Arab Shops Have Created 'New Cuba' in Teheran," *Al-Majallah* (London) December 8, 1992 in FBIS-NES-92-246, December 22, 1992, pp. 57-63. Recruitment among Palestinians is addressed in Tzvi Bar'el, "The Springs of Money From Teheran," *Ha'aretz* (Tel Aviv), August 26, 1994, JPRS-NEA-94-055, November 2, 1994, pp. 12-15. Support for *Hamas,* including military training, in the United States has been reported by *Al-Watan Al-Arabi*, a Paris weekly, according to *Yediot Ahronot* (Tel Aviv), November 3, 1994 in FBIS-NEA-94-214, November 4, 1994, pp. 2-3; Kifner," "Alms and Arms...," *op cit.*; Robert Marquand, "Clinton Tries to Plug Pipeline to *Hamas*," March 15, 1996. There are no confirmed figures on the amount of money for *Hamas* which comes from the United States. Estimates range from as low as 10-15 percent, to that of Palestinian Minister of International Cooperation, Nabil Sha'th, who estimates it is 75%. See James Brooke and Elaine Sciolino, "U.S. Muslims Say Their Aid Pays for Charity, Not Terror," *The New York Times*, August 16, 1995; interview with Nabil Sha'th in *Knack* (Brusssels), April 24-30, 1996 in FBIS-NES-96-084, April 30, 1996, p. 5. Most of what is provided goes to the socio-economic rather than the military activities of *Hamas.* While some see this as legitimate assistance, others see the distinction as irrelevant, since the flow of money in such political-military organizations is fungible.

56. Iran's sponsorship and continued strong backing of *Hezbollah* is common knowledge in the Middle East. See Robin Wright, *In the Name of God* (New York: Simon and Schuster, 1989), pp. 118-119; Carl Anthony Wege, "Hizbollah

Organization" *Studies in Conflict and Terrorism,* Vol 17, 1994; Mohammad Mohaddessin, *Islamic Fundamentalism* (Washington D.C.: Seven Locks Press, 1993), pp. 85-86 and 91. Acknowledging Iran's role as military hardware supplier, *Hezbollah* leader, Nawwaf al-Musawi, has freely admitted Teheran's provision of Katyusha rockets. As he put it, "everybody knows they come from Iran by way of Syria." See the interview in *Folha De Sao Paulo,* April 21, 1996 in FBIS-NES-96-084, April 30, 1996, p. 48. Also see the comments attributed to *Hezbollah's* secretary general in *The Jerusalem Post,* March 12, 1996.

57. One high-ranking *Hezbollah* official described the *Hezbollah-Hamas* relationship thusly: "*Hamas* is an Islamic movement in Palestine. *Hezballah* is an Islamic movement in Lebanon. And since they are both Islamic movements, every action carried out by one serves the other's cause too. But this does not mean that there is any operational or organizational cooperation. Each has its own identity, its own aims, its own leaders. There are no links." See interview of *Hezbollah* Political Council member Khadr Nur-al-Din in *La Repubblica* (Rome), April 21, 1996 in FBIS-NES-96-078, April 22, 1996, p. 65.

58. Paris AFP, March 18, 1996 in FBIS-NES-96-054, March 19, 1996, p. 70.

59. For Israeli accounts of the increased effectiveness of *Hezbollah* see Emanu'el Rozen, "The Security Zone: The Price Is Too High," *Ma'ariv* (Tel Aviv) August 27, 1993 in JPRS-NEA-93-017, September 21, 1993, pp. 4-6.

60. An analysis of the strengths and weaknesses of the Israeli counterinsurgency policies and activities may be found in O'Neill, pp. 66-102.

61. The official policy of the military government stressed three principles: minimal presence, minimal interference, and open bridges. See Peter Duval, "How Israel Feeds the Palestinian Revolution, *New Middle East,* June 1971, p. 32. On the implementation of these policies see Amos Elon, "The Israeli Occupation," *Commentary,* March 1968, pp. 43-44; Nora Levin, "Gaza and the West Bank," *Interplay,* July 1970, pp.34-37; Odeh Remba, "Israel and the Occupied Territories: Common Market in the Making," *New Middle East,* November 1970, p. 37; Interview of Na'bil Shath, *Free Palestine,* July 1971, p. 5; *Facts About Israel: 1971* (Jerusalem: Ministry of Foreign Affairs, 1971), pp. 22-23, 55-56, 62-73 and 171-174; *The Health Services of Judea and Samaria* (Jerusalem: Ministry of Foreign Affairs, 1974), pp. 3-49; *The New York Times,* September 1 and November 7, 1967, January 15 and June 17, 1968, June 28, 1973, *The Daily Star* (Beirut), June 6, 1971, and *The Jerusalem Post* (weekly), October 6, 1969.

Analytical Assessment of Palestinian Rejectionism 305

62. The problem of Israeli mobs attacking innocent Arabs after terrorist incidents, and the successes and blunders associated with Israeli population control policies in the late 1960's, especially the controversial neighborhood punishment policy, are assessed in O'Neill, pp. 65-74.

63. An informed portrayal and critical assessment of the Likud's social, political and economic policies in the territories may be found in Meron Benvenisti, *The West Bank Data Project: A Survey of Israel's Policies* (Washington, D.C.: American Enterprise Institute, 1984). Also see *1986 Report* (Washington, D.C.: American Enterprise Institute, 1986). Taken together, these reports provide clear insights into the context that gave birth to the *Intifada* in 1987. A strong argument that Israel deliberately committed itself to "de-developing" the Gaza Strip may be found in Sara Roy, *The Gaza Strip: The Political Economy of De-development* (Washington, D.C.: Institute of Palestine Studies, 1995).

64. The lack of IDF training for riot duty is discussed by Bernard E. Trainor, "Israeli Troops Prove Newcomers to Riot Control," *The New York Times*, February 19, 1989. The negative effects of the *Intifada* on the IDF were reported by Glenn Frankel, "Israeli Army Suffers Casualty: Confidence," *WP*, January 30, 1989. Official denials of mistreatment of the Arabs gradually gave way to tacit recognition of the problems associated with it and some efforts were made to sensitize soldiers about the consequences of brutality, according to Glenn Frankel, "Jarring Film Prepares Israeli Troops for Uprising," *WP*, March 3, 1989. Criticism of the excessive use of force by the Israelis was made by the U.S. Department of State in a report on human rights practices. See George D. Moffett III, "Do Israeli Officers Order Beatings?" *CSM*, February 15, 1989. The more restrictive rules of engagement that were adopted to address the problem of overreaction were published in *Ma'ariv* (Tel Aviv), May 29, 1989 in FBIS-NES-89-104, June 1, 1989, pp. 29-30.

65. Clyde Haberman, "Israel Resumes Sealing of Houses as Punishment," *The New York Times*, December 4, 1994.

66. The tougher anti-terrorism policies came in response to deadly bombings by *Hamas* and IJM operatives in 1994-1996. On the use of torture and claims by the Security Service that it saved lives see the report by Alon Pinkas in *The Jerusalem Post*, August 25, 1995.

67. On the al-Shaqaqi assassination see *Der Spiegel* (Hamburg), November 6, 1995 in FBIS-NES-95-216, November 8, 1995, pp. 45-48. The ingenious "hit" on Ayyash is briefly summarized in Joel Greenberg, "Slaying Blended Technology and Guile," *The New York Times*, January 10, 1996.

68. On the organization, decision-making and effectiveness of the Mossad hit teams see Ron Miberg, "This Is How Hit Men Operate," *Ma'ariv, Shabat* supplement (Tel Aviv), November 3, 1995 in FBIS-NES-95-214, November 6, 1995, pp. 25-27. For a succinct portrayal of past hit team activities, including their failures, see David B. Tinnin and Dag Christensen, *The Hit Team* (New York: Dell Publishing Co., 1977). The PNA has argued that the assassinations undermined an agreement it had with *Hamas* to suspend attacks against Israelis and led to the spate of suicide attacks in 1996. Whether or not such an agreement would have endured is anybody's guess. See John Battersby, "Palestinian Police Force Meets Goals To Disarm, Disband Hamas Militants," *CSM*, April 8, 1996.

69. In the words of PNA official Sofian Abu-Zaida, "*Hamas* is not living in another world. *Hamas* is living with us. Arresting members of *Hamas* could mean arresting our brothers and our cousins." John Battersby, "The Two Faces of *Hamas*: Terror and Philanthropy," *CSM*, October 24, 1994.

70. A succinct layout of the joint security structure may be found in *Ha'aretz* (Tel Aviv), October 27, 1995 in FBIS-NES-95-211, November 1, 1995, pp. 38-39.

71. The IDF document is summarized in *Ma'ariv* (Tel Aviv), December 27, 1995, FBIS-NES-95-248, December 27, 1995, p. 26.

72. *Qol Israel* (Jerusalem), December 27, 1995 in FBIS-NES-95-249, December 28, 1995, p. 25 and *Ha'aretz* (Tel Aviv), December 3, 1995 in FBIS-NES-95-232, December 4, 1995, p. 43.

73. John Battersby, "How a Cycle of Violence Entraps Arafat in Peace Talks," *CSM*, January 31, 1996.

74. The idea of assassinating leaders of the *al-Qassam* brigades was reportedly part of a document submitted to Arafat by the Joint Palestinian Emergency Committee, dated March 1996. Although ruling out such actions at the present stage, the document later indicated that in the strategic [i.e., longer] term a number of *al-Qassam* leaders should be physically eliminated. The reported document appeared in *Al-Majd* (Amman), April 22, 1996, an independent political weekly that is virulently anti-Arafat, but generally less sensational and more authoritative than its opposition counterparts. For the full text of the document see FBIS-NES-96-082, April 26, 1996, pp. 6-11. On the issue of assassinations see p. 8.

Analytical Assessment of Palestinian Rejectionism 307

75. Speech by Yasir Arafat at the inauguration of the first Palestinian Legislative Council in Gaza, Gaza Palestinian Broadcasting Corporation Television Network, March 7, 1996 in FBIS-NES-96-047, March 8, 1996, pp. 1-2; JMCC Press Service (Jerusalem), March 3, 1996 in FBIS-NES-96-043, March 4, 1996, p. 9. Different Palestinian views about the changes in the Covenant and the ramifications related to their eventual actualization are discussed in "Our Opinion: *Fatah* Publication No. 8, 32nd year, second half of April 1996:" The Palestinian National Covenant--Between Renewal and Being Frozen," (Internet) IRIS News Update, May 21, 1996 in FBIS-NES-May 30, 1996, pp. 10-13.

76. Graham Usher, "The Politics of Internal Security in Palestine," *Middle East International*, March 1, 1996, pp. 15-16; Nigel Parry, "The Hand-Over of Human Rights Violations," *ibid.*, pp. 17-18; Anthony Lewis, "Darkness in Gaza," *The New York Times*, May 6, 1996.

77. The PNA document may be found in *Al-Sabil* (Amman), *February 7-13, 1995 in* FBIS-NES-95-032, February 16, 1995, pp. 12-15. *Al-Sabil* (the Path) is the mouthpiece of the Islamic Action Front, which is dominated by the Moslem Brotherhood.

78. The *Hamas* reaction to the PNA plan appears in *Al-Sabil* (Amman), February 14-20, 1995, FBIS-NES-95-033, February 17, 1995, pp. 11-12. Earlier thinking regarding the establishment of a party may be found in Jamal Khashuqji, "Towards Formation of a Palestinian Islamic Party That Would Satisfy National Authority and Hamas Masses," *Al-Hayah* (London), June 9, 1995 in FBIS-NES-95-113, June 13, 1995, pp. 8-9.

79. *Davar Rishon* (Tel Aviv), May 13, 1996 in FBIS-NES-96-094, pp. 6-7.

80. The post-bombing actions are recounted in a concise and balanced rundown of the contributions and shortcomings of Arafat's anti-terrorist policies by Gail Pressberg and Linda Heller Kamm, "Arafat's Progress in Fighting Terror," *CSM*, March 15, 1996.

81. Interview with Nabil Sha'th in *Knack*, p. 3. Of course, what Sha'th conveniently ignores is the fly in the ointment--i.e., perceived financial corruption by Arafat's apparat, which has dissuaded donors from fulfilling their pledges.

82. To supplant the Islamic socio-economic institutions, the PNA needs money and resources, as well as a mechanism for preventing funds from being channeled to Islamic non-governmental organizations (NGOs). One proposal is to put all NGOs under control of the Ministry of the Interior, as is done in

Egypt. Another is to have all funds to NGOs channeled through a World Bank social fund. See Lamia Lahoud, "PNA Officials Terror Crackdown Making Progress," *The Jerusalem Post*, March 27, 1996. The lack of money reportedly led Arafat to backpedal his efforts to undermine *Hamas* institutions in 1996, according to Steve Rodan, "Iran Seeks to Torpedo the Elections," *The Jerusalem Post*, May 17, 1996.

83. A typical example of the PNA informational campaign critical of Jordan's tolerance of *Hamas*' activities is Interview with Nabil Sha'th, *Knack*, p. 5. Prior to the Israeli-Jordanian peace agreement, Rabin had charged that orders for terrorist strikes had originated in Jordan. See *The Jerusalem Post*, November 2, 1994.

84. A private American investigator indicated that Israeli agents from Mossad were dispatched to cooperate with the FBI in an effort to destroy or cripple networks supporting *Hamas* in the United States. See FBIS editorial report summarzing *Al-Watan Al Arabi*, November 4, 1994 in JPRS-TOT-94-047L, November 30, 1994, p. 16. The investigator was cited as saying that 40 percent of *Hamas*' financing comes from the United States and Britain.

85. *Hezbollah* activities, Israeli reactions and the anticipated impact of the peace process are summarized nicely in John Lancaster, "S. Lebanon Is Last Israeli-Arab Battleground," *WP*, January 22, 1996. Fadallah's doubts are reflected in the following comment: "The Resistance might think emotionally about Palestine, but it knows it is incapable of waging a war to liberate it. The issue is left to the Arab and Islamic world." Interview with Muhammad Husayn Fadallah in *Al-Nahar* (Beirut), April 26, 1996 in FBIS-NES-96-085, May 1, 1996, p. 25. For similar remarks by Mahmoud Koumate, deputy chief of *Hezbollah's* political bureau, see Douglas Jehl, "Lebanon Fighters Gain Stature, but for How Long?," *The New York Times*, April 21, 1996. Some believe that *Hezbollah's* participation in Lebanon's parliamentary affairs will have the long-term effect of moderating its policies. Others, looking at the experiences of the IRA and Basque Homeland and Liberty, see no necessary causal connection between participation in the political process and the cessation of violence.

86. Stephen C. Pelletiere, *Hamas and Hizbollah: The Radical Challenge to Israel in the Occupied Territories* (Carlisle Barracks, PA: Strategic Studies Institute, U.S. Army War College, 1994), p. 32.

87. Ze'ev Schiff, "The IDF Does Not Have An Operational Answer," *Ha'aretz* (Tel Aviv), March 22, 1996 in FBIS-NES-96-057, March 22, 1996, pp. 25-26. Also see Patrick Cockburn, "A War the Israelis Can All Support," *The*

Independent (London), April 18, 1996 in FBIS-NES-96-076, April 18, 1996, p. 10.

88. Interview with *Hezbollah* spokesman Na'if Qarayyin in *Die Tageszeitung* (Berlin), April 29, 1996 in FBIS-NES-96-087, May 3, 1996, p. 26.

89. In an astonishing report, *Yediot Ahranot* (Tel Aviv) reported on January 1, 1996 that the IDF "for the first time ever" had started holding counterguerrilla warfare training in preparation for routine duty in south Lebanon. The deficiency had been pointed out by an Israeli commander in the western sector two years before. See Emanuel Rozen, "The Security Zone: The Price Is Too High," *Ma'ariv* (Tel Aviv), August 27, 1993 in JPRS-NEA-93-017-L, September 21, 1993 p. 5; *Yediot Ahronot* (Tel Aviv), January 1, 1996 *in* FBIS-NES-96-002, January 3, 1996, p. 48. In an off-the-record discussion with one of the authors (O'Neill), a U.S. Army officer and specialist on the Middle East who served in Lebanon and observed Israeli movements in the security zone said he was amazed at the lack of operational security by IDF units about to go on patrol. Both their preparations and movements were easy to see and follow from outside the zone. To the extent that this occurred, it no doubt helps explain the costly ambushes which victimized IDF patrols in the zone. The reported infiltration of the South Lebanese Army, as well as an excellent general discussion of *Hezbollah's* success in the 1990s, may be found in Barton Gellman and John Lancaster, "The Undoing of Israel's Security Zone," *WP*, April 21, 1996.

CHAPTER SIX

THE DEADLY EMBRACE: IMPLICATIONS FOR THE PEACE PROCESS

CHAPTER VI

THE DEADLY EMBRACE: IMPLICATIONS FOR THE PEACE PROCESS

The bee and the serpent often sip from the selfsame flower.

Morte d'Abele, *Metastasio*

What this book is all about are two communities locked in a deadly embrace of primordial passions, feeding off and reinforcing each other's fears and enmities. It is also about a paradoxical convergence of evil--an evil epitomized in the murder of people at prayer in a synagogue in Istanbul, or in a mosque in Hebron. For, truly, there is nothing more heinous--or more paradoxical--than the killing of innocents in the name of God. Yet, this is precisely what zealots, on both sides, preach and practice.

As we have seen, the core issue underpinning the Israeli-Palestinian conflict is control of land. Security, borders, water, sovereignty, refugees, settlements, etc., are all derivative problems. The epicenter is land. Historically, the loss of territory has fed conflicts and sustained insurrections. The Middle East is no different in this regard. Arab uprisings in Palestine during the 1920's and 30's, and the emergence of the Palestinian resistance movement after the 1967 war were driven by the traumatic effect of losing land to Jewish acquisition, conquest and colonization.

More than anything, the peace process has turned the tables: While land remains the center of gravity, now it is Israel to be called upon to cede increasingly significant portions of the territory it controls. Thus, a new asymmetry is emerging wherein, for the first time this century, the Palestinians are on the winning side of the territorial equation. Correspondingly, as the Palestinians' key exoteric grievances are gradually being satisfied, loss of land is fast becoming the primary factor driving Israeli rejectionism. To make matters worse, the reversal has been occurring against the backdrop of an increasingly mystical--and unyielding--veneration of the God-given patrimony by Israel's fundamentalists.

The Israelis and the Palestinians are inextricably bound together by a myriad of geographical, historic, political, economic, and cultural links. As claimants to the same piece of territory, both have faced an essentially binary choice: fight over the land, or compromise and share it. Until the 1980's, however, rejectionism was effectively a unilateral phenomenon, reposed exclusively on the Palestinian side. This was only natural, since Israel's seemingly indefinite hold on the territories meant that all the esoteric and exoteric grievances that give rise to and sustain insurgencies festered in the Palestinian community.

As the notion of compromise and, specifically, Arafat's "heresy" of a mini-state, to be established in the West Bank and Gaza Strip, gained currency in the 1970's, the Palestinian movement underwent a violent bifurcation. Concurrently, as the idea of trading land for peace was embodied in the Camp David Accords, Israeli opponents of compromise were galvanized into action, albeit initially in the form of passive resistance. Within a few short years, however, what began as civil disobedience degenerated into violence, with Israeli peace activists and Arab civilians the targets of choice. Herein lie the roots of the deadly embrace.

As the peace process gathered momentum, so did the efforts to derail it. Like the proverbial scorpions in a jar, increasingly intransigent rejectionists sought to kill each other, so as to kill the budding rapprochement. Terrorism increased in terms of both frequency and lethality. The old adage that violence begets violence became a daily reality in Gaza, in the West Bank and in Israel proper. With both sides demonizing each other on religious/ nationalist grounds, each new outrage served to reinforce visceral hatreds. Concurrently, it added credence to the zealots' fundamental tenet of implacability, that is, the notion that the other side is inherently incapable--and unworthy--of rational human interaction, let alone coexistence. Consequently, Palestinian militants acquired new allies in their war against peace: Israeli rejectionists opposed

Implications for the Peace Process

to compromise on remarkably similar grounds.

As we have demonstrated, such Israeli organizations as *Kach*, *Kahane Chai*, *EYAL*, Terror Victims' Command (TVC), and Genesis are much smaller, less embedded and, especially, less notorious than their long-established Palestinian counterparts. More importantly, while explicitly committed to violence as a legitimate recourse, the Israeli groups' activities were initially limited in terms of scale and lethality, effectively masking their potential for escalation. In this sense, the 1994 Hebron massacre and the 1995 assassination of Prime Minister Rabin mark the point of convergence, thus further tightening the deadly embrace.

To understand the dynamics of this interaction one need not engage in a vain search for explicit coordination--or a joint conspiracy--linking Israeli and Palestinian rejectionism.[1] Rather, the focus of the inquiry should be on their mid-range goals. For, as we have shown, the foundation of the deadly embrace is the assumption--on each side--that the land, in its entirety, belongs exclusively to it. This axiom, reinforced by myriad religious, nationalist and strategic corollaries--effectively rules out any long-term collaboration or mutually agreeable compromise. It does not, however, preclude the two sides from working independently, but in tandem, to attain their shared intermediate aim of destroying the peace process. This, in turn, led to tacit cooperation in attaining such shared short-term objectives as toppling the Labor government--an aim explicitly espoused by both Islamic militants and the entire Israeli right.

Violence and its legitimizing rhetoric sustain the deadly embrace--and the tacit cooperation--but only as long as the interaction is mutually beneficial. Ultimately, however, each side's vision of the future presupposes the other's demise. Therefore, the struggle is bound to continue until one or both are ruined.

The fulcrum of the deadly embrace is the growing congruity of the most extreme elements on both sides. As our analysis demonstrates, the Israeli and Palestinian rejectionist movements are comprised of secular nationalists and religious zealots. While unbridled nationalism has shown itself to be a powerful motivator of strife, the addition of theology to the volatile brew of ethnic particularism, chauvinism and territorial maximalism, could easily spin the situation out of control. Under such circumstances, the already strong resistance to compromise will no doubt be transmogrified into a matter of dogma.

To aggravate matters still further, there has been a symmetric radicalization on both sides. The secular nationalists--that is, groups that are relatively easier to deal with--have been weakened in terms of their capabilities, as well as their popular and external support. This leaves center stage to the most intransigent, religiously-motivated elements which might well be beyond rational discourse.

The remarkable similarities between the militant Jewish religious fundamentalists and their Islamic counterparts lend a particularly apocalyptic cast to their interaction. Insofar as these groups believe in a transcendental source of authority, they are unlikely to be swayed by the empiricism that underpins any political dialogue. For, in the inevitable clash between *realpolitik* and metaphysically-based idealism, the latter will, by definition, take precedence with the true believers. Even more than in the political religion of traditional Marxism-Leninism, here the ends literally sanctify the means--all in the name of an omnipresent deity.

As we have posited in the preceding chapters, the religious rejectionists' irreconcilable ends boil down to the establishment of a political system based on the rigid imposition of infallible theological laws, as interpreted by modern zealots. The inescapable irony, of course, is that this vision is based on idealization of a past golden age that bears little resemblance to historic realities. For, as any student of history knows, with the first Jewish kingdoms and Islamic caliphates came the political infighting, violence, succession crises, assassinations, and wars which led to their ultimate demise: Centuries of exile and persecution for the former and an equally lengthy political, material and cultural stagnation for the latter. Yet, these facts are conveniently ignored--or blamed on others--as both sides seek to justify the future in the name of the past.

Implications for the Peace Process

It is important to note that, on both sides, the core issue is religious exclusivism rather than racism or ethnocentrism. Religious exclusivism takes its most severe form when theology infuses the interaction. For, unlike the proverbial "man on the street," whose biases usually go no further than instinctive dislike for members of groups other than his own, the prejudices of the true believers are anchored in lofty conceptualizations of their own superiority as either "the chosen people," or the articulators of God's last verdict. Such thinking, in turn, spurs action to carry out the divinely ordained mission of establishing God's rule on earth. Within the context of this millennial outcome, what is mutually exclusive is the very nature of the theocracy to be created. For this utopia can be either Jewish or Islamic; it can be based either on the *Halakha* or the *Sharia*. It can never be a shared entity, because the one delegitimizes the other. Simply put, God's truths are indivisible.

Given the explicit commitment to tolerance embodied in both traditional Judaism and Islam, serious Biblical and Koranic scholars might have justifiable misgivings on this score. The point is that the militant fundamentalists--on both sides--are fashioning their own doctrines, based on their unique exegeses of selected texts. Furthermore, they firmly believe that theirs is the only valid interpretation. Thus, the issue is not theological validity or rational argumentation, but, rather, a self-contained and self-evident belief system, designed to justify otherwise proscribed actions--such as murder--in the name of a sublime cause.

As our analysis makes clear, the Israeli-Palestinian interaction does not cause the rejectionism. What it does is perpetuate and fuel deep-seated hatreds, anchoring them in immutable verities. Insofar as both movements have aims beyond each other, they are likely to become self-sustaining and continue their rejectionism, precisely because their long-range agendas exceed their mutual animosities. Ultimately, each movement has a diametrically opposed vision of the desired end-state and its own internal dynamic, rooted in the psychological benefits inherent in active participation in insurgent movements--such as identification with a "noble cause," peer relations, a sense of belonging, self-esteem, and material benefits. In this sense, both movements have passed a crossover point, wherein the zero-sum nature of their struggle can continue, regardless of either the other's behavior or the vicissitudes of the peace process.

What's to be done? How might Israel, the PNA and the U.S. cope with such virulent threats to peace and stability? A coherent approach would begin with a reconsideration of the basic premises that underpin both analysis and decision-making. Accordingly, we shall recap our findings in the context of these assumptions and, on this basis, proceed to outline policy choices and recommend courses of action.

The first and most pervasive assumption, noted early in our analysis, is that the Israeli-Palestinian peace process is irreversible. Both the premise and its corollary assertion that peace cannot be undermined are rather remarkable in the context of a region where so little has proved to be permanent or predictable. One needs only recall the staggering number of fairly recent surprises to realize that linear, "rational" evolution is more often the exception than the rule.[2] Wishful thinking aside, nothing in the Middle East can be assumed to be immutable: allegiances, regimes, and policies can change literally overnight. Under such conditions, overconfidence and certitude often lead to embarrassment, if not policy failures.

In the final account, the assertion that, once commenced, a political process becomes unstoppable is as vain as its pessimistic counterpart that problems are never really resolved but bound to reappear in a new guise. Both are, at best, clever political slogans, rather than serious policy propositions, rooted in empirical analysis.

The Israeli-Palestinian rapprochement is a complex, fragile and, potentially, reversible process, taking place in perhaps the world's most volatile region. A significant erosion--or mere stagnation-- could quickly recreate the conditions that precipitated the *Intifada*, potentially igniting widespread violence. The prudent analyst or policy maker would, therefore, approach the issues at stake from a pragmatic point of view, rather than be driven by whimsical

Implications for the Peace Process

optimism or pessimism. Pragmatism in this context means the willingness and ability to anticipate new problems, to plan for the unravelling of solutions, and to offer flexible compromises that are neither panaceas nor reflections of wishful thinking. Such an approach is more conducive to sustaining a focus on managing the problem, rather than being diverted by the necessary ups and downs inherent in any political enterprise. By foreseeing possible regressions, one can strive to forestall and ameliorate their impact, without falling victim to unanticipated circumstances. That said, even the most pragmatic, far-sighted approach would be for naught, should either partner choose to renege on prior commitments, and/or thwart further progress. Simply put, will is the most critical--and least predictable--factor in the peace equation.

Closely related to the assumption of irreversibility is the intuitively contradictory premise that U.S. mediation is indispensable and that elaborate ceremonies play a key sustaining role in the peace process. In reality, any attempt to overcome a century of animosities is bound to involve a painstaking, long and, often, unglamorous effort. In the early stages of the negotiations, outsiders' participation and carefully staged pageantry are important in legitimizing the rapprochement, building confidence among the participants and creating an atmosphere conducive to the resolution of contentious issues. Thus, the September 1993 signing ceremonies on the White House lawn were well conceived and masterfully executed preliminary steps.

Such trappings of peace cannot, however, substitute for the hard work that must be done by the parties themselves to solve the very real problems still left open (such as refugees, the status of Jerusalem, water, the settlements, etc.). The danger is that continued emphasis on formalities that place interested outsiders in the lime-light will undercut--or at least delay--the institutionalization of direct cooperation between Israel and the PNA. To the extent that the partners themselves take credit--and shoulder the blame--for their actions, they will have a more lasting value where it counts most: in the region itself.

Thus, the priority must now shift away from U.S.-staged

ceremonies to the direct imprimatur of the participants. The onus of success or failure must rest with Jerusalem and Gaza, rather than Washington. Otherwise, it would be difficult to build and sustain the broad-based public support necessary to marginalize the opponents of peace.

Narrowing the focus from the peace process overall to those who would destroy it, our analysis should help dispel several additional misperceptions and facile assumptions. Key among these is the premise that an advanced stage of economic and political development somehow protects a nation from a serious insurgent threat, or, at least, better equips it to deal with internal perils. This argument naturally leads to the comforting conclusion that Israel is immune to subversion from within. Yet, the historic record offers little to support such complacency.

First, as a general matter, democracies confronting an insurgent threat simultaneously face an existential dilemma. For they must balance their core political values with the exigencies of security. Indeed, in a democracy, any extra-legal measures are likely to seem disproportionate, might alienate otherwise supportive citizens, and, at worse, undermine the very values the authorities are seeking to defend--thus playing directly into the insurgents' hand. In contrast, however repugnant one might find the ethics and morality of their methods, the fact remains that authoritarian regimes have proven quite effective in expunging insurgents, particularly small, easily identifiable groups.

More specifically, as our analysis clearly demonstrates, even the region's only democracy, with the most advanced economic system, can be highly susceptible to a phenomenon that has plagued its neighbors for years. Analysts and politicians who continue to deny this reality are not helping either Israel or the cause of peace.

Correspondingly, the threat posed by Israeli rejectionism can no longer be deemed inconsequential--nor ignored altogether. While the assassination attempts on Arab mayors and the Hebron massacre should have been seen as *prima facie* evidence of a clear and present danger, it took the murder of a Prime Minister to bring

Implications for the Peace Process

the issue into the open. Yet, even in the aftermath, the focus remains on the despicable actions of individuals, rather than the phenomenon as whole. This effectively precludes the emergence of a coherent, proactive strategy to contain the impact of rejectionism.

A related and equally misleading assumption is that secular political cultures are an effective antidote to religious extremism. The counter-intuitive reality is that predominantly secular populations can be swayed by promises to address their exoteric grievances--e.g., the loss of land and the political, military and economic advantages attached thereto--proffered by religious groups whose long range goals are anathema to the very notion of secularism. Moreover, political exigencies and congruity of short- and mid-term goals often lead secular compatriots to ignore, or dismiss, the metaphysical musings of the true believers. This is particularly true where--as is the case on both the Israeli and Palestinian sides--the religious core engages in deliberate obfuscation of their strikingly similar ultimate designs.

Analysis and policy are also clouded by the popular myth that all contemporary insurgencies are engaged in the sort of protracted popular war strategy devised by Mao and described, at some length, in Chapter I. In contrast, our analysis shows that most of the Israeli and Palestinian rejectionist organizations do not follow the Maoist blueprint. Often, they have no coherent strategy at all. Thus, while some of them might know where they are going, they have little or no idea how to get there. This conceptual deficiency does not lend itself to the accomplishment of long-range goals. It is, however, quite sufficient to advance short- and mid-term objectives, particularly those designed to destroy or disrupt evolving processes.

By the same token, to achieve such negative aims, insurgencies need not be homogeneous or cohesive. Like many insurgent movements noted in Chapter I, the Israeli and Palestinian rejectionists are quite diverse in terms of their composition, motivations, level of commitment, and vision of the desired end state. Thus, they may do no better than their equally divisive

Afghan counterparts did in achieving their ultimate aim of creating a united, theocratic state. But, just like the *mujahidin*, they could attain their intermediate objectives. The Russian withdrawal from Afghanistan proves the point; destruction of the peace process by Middle Eastern rejectionists would revalidate it.

Finally, we must once again depart from the reassuring platitude that, while Middle Eastern rejectionism might be an interesting phenomenon, its actual impact is negligible. This notion is popular even among the few experts who have studied Middle Eastern rejectionist groups and concluded that their relatively small scale and enduring inability to garner broad-based support doom them to irrelevance. In reality, size is not a reliable predictor of success. To wit, the Bolsheviks--a minority organization by any objective measure--were able to seize power and impose a political system for more than seven decades. By the same token, the Middle Eastern rejectionists' intermediate goal of reversing or destroying the peace process is attainable--as demonstrated by the near-term successes of such small groups as the Tamil Tigers, the IRA, the Cypriotes, and the Afghani *mujahidin*.

The rejectionists' ability to move beyond subversion and toward implementation of such teleological goals as the establishment of the Biblical Kingdom or the *Sharia* state is, of course, more heavily dependent on such criteria as popular support, resolve, cohesion, and long-term strategic coherence. Yet, here too it is important to distinguish between positive and negative aims--not in terms of a value judgment (i.e., good versus evil) but, rather, in terms of the critical difference between building anew and stalling, disrupting, or destroying what is.

As the experience of both revolutionaries and reformers demonstrates, the former is clearly the more difficult undertaking. Success in destroying an existing structure does not necessarily equate to the ability to construct a new edifice on its ruins. The gap between carrying out a negative aim strategy and designing and executing one with a positive aim is readily apparent in the difficulties encountered throughout post-Communist Eastern and Central Europe, as destroyers of the old face seemingly

Implications for the Peace Process

insurmountable difficulties in building the new. That said, the havoc the rejectionists could wreak in the near- and mid-term should provide a sufficient incentive to strive for their effective marginalization.

Comparative analyses of insurgencies make abundantly clear that dissident organizations are rarely eliminated altogether. They can, however, be rendered harmless, or insignificant, through a combination of political, economic and military measures that are skillfully tailored to address the root causes of the problem. The *sine qua non* of success is realistic expectations. Violence can be contained or reduced to manageable levels; it cannot be totally expunged. To expect anything more is to engender false hopes which, when unfulfilled, can have a paralyzing effect. What is called for is a series of specific measures whose cumulative impact, over time, will result in marginalization of these groups. This, in turn, requires the patient and determined pursuit of inherently limited objectives.

Such goals are achievable in the Middle East. Indeed, there is historic precedent on both the Israeli and Palestinian sides. As we have noted in Chapter II, Ben Gurion's success in suppressing and delegitimizing armed factionalism provides some important lessons for both Jerusalem and the PNA. More recently, the relative decline of the PFLP, the DFLP, the Abu Nidal Organization and, to a lesser extent, the PFLP-GC, serves as a useful paradigm. While the erosion might be attributed, in part, to the groups' own failings--that is, their ideological irrelevance, chronic factionalism and organizational shortcomings--Israeli political and military counterinsurgency initiatives were important in expediting and reinforcing this process.

The analysis that follows draws on past experience of marginalizing both Middle Eastern and other insurgent groups to suggest a concerted, highly differentiated effort to deal with the rejectionist threat to regional peace and stability. Make no mistake about it: Implementing these options would require difficult choices among competing courses of action and, at times, among equally distasteful alternatives. Key among these is the fundamental choice between a policy of inclusion or exclusion.

On the Palestinian side, the first step is to draw a distinction between the partial and total rejectionists. With respect to the former, small groups like the PFLP and the DFLP should be further marginalized by encouraging their open participation in the electoral process. While giving them an outlet to articulate their platforms, participation in mainstream politics should cause the final withering away of Marxist-inspired armed struggle. The obvious risk is a temporary increase in popular support for these groups, because of the opportunities afforded by open proselytization. In this particular case, however, the risk is minimal because, historically and culturally, the Marxist message has had an inherently limited appeal in the Arab world--particularly after the collapse of Soviet communism.

As for the total rejectionists, the issue of inclusion is rendered largely irrelevant by their longstanding opposition to anything remotely suggesting legitimization of their adversaries. The only exception would be to allow participation by parties or groups--like the Islamic National Salvation Party--which consistently eschew violence and adhere to democratic procedures. In our view, the risk that such inclusion would redound to the rejectionists' favor is outweighed by the gains that could accrue from tempering and splitting the movement.

On the Israeli side, of course, the issue is not political participation *per se*, since that right already exists but, rather, the possible inclusion of the far-right parties--both religious and secular--in the governing coalition. While there are clear merits in broadening the basis of support for the incumbent government's policies, the risks are significant. First, flexibility is often the price of consensus. Any broad-based coalition--or, for that matter, a national unity government--would likely be hamstrung by a series of crisscrossing agreements and back-room deals. The inevitable result would be policy paralysis and further erosion of the peace process. Second, Likud's ability and will to temper the radical rejectionists' proclivity to violence remains to be tested. By the same token, given the heterogeneity of the Israeli right,

Implications for the Peace Process

undifferentiated inclusion would only exacerbate mutual animosities and deepen the secular-religious divide, particularly if the true believers were to hinge their support on promotion of their parochial domestic agendas.

Regardless of coalition arrangements, any cooperation with the radical right must include an iron-clad commitment to shun violence. For democracy is based on willingness to abide by "the rules of the game"--that is, adhere to the procedures and laws that are the very essence of a democratic system. Political participation, therefore, must presuppose a modicum of respect for the norms of civilized behavior and the limits of legitimate dissent. The assassination of Prime Minister Rabin--universally condemned across the Israeli political spectrum--could be used as an object-lesson to dramatize the tragic consequences of political violence, thus compelling as many rejectionists as possible to publicly recommit themselves to the rule of law. For those who value their solemn word, such a vow might suffice. Otherwise, nothing short of literal excommunication, followed by a persistent, determined educational effort and leadership by example would be required. Despite the obvious risks, inclusion merits serious consideration--particularly on the Palestinian side--because of its potential to moderate the rejectionists in the short term and marginalize them in the longer term. Success would depend on both Israel's and the PNA's determination to stay the course of peace, despite internal pressures to the contrary. In other words, inclusion must be a means to an end, not an excuse for modifying or redefining policy objectives. To do anything less would be self- destructive.

The second policy choice is between deliberate exposure of rejectionists' excesses and the insouciance which effectively shields them from public scrutiny. Such indifference might be rooted in either sheer complacency or in the familiar psychological phenomenon of denial. The reluctance to confront the rejectionists head-on is understandable, given the inevitable acrimony and potential internecine violence that might ensue. Additionally, exposure might be perceived as detrimental to the prestige and international standing of the larger community that one represents.

Thus, a public admission that it is facing an internal threat might undercut Israel's image as a bastion of democratic stability. For the PNA, the risk entails reinforcing the perception that terrorism remains the Palestinians' hallmark and that the current authorities' ability to control or constrain it is too tenuous to be trusted.

Nonetheless, a concerted effort to isolate the total rejectionists is crucial. Moreover, the potential payoff more than compensates for the inherent risks. Such an effort requires a vigorous, sustained public education campaign to expose and condemn the grave dangers inherent in the programs espoused by these groups. Attention must be called to the such issues as: their uncompromising intolerance; their antediluvian practices and limiting lifestyle choices; curbs on political freedoms; and the ongoing strife which will inevitably result from their victory. Given the experience of Iran, one does not need to search far for an object-lesson of what is in store for those who live in a 20th century theocracy. Throughout the Muslim world, the initial attraction of religious rule has faded, as even moderate political opponents have been jailed or executed, religious minorities--like Bahais--have been exterminated, and women deprived of all but the most rudimentary rights. The Iranian example also demonstrates the utter failure of a theocratic system to deal with modern economic problems or to interact constructively in the international system. In the case of Israel, one could point to the destruction of the Second Temple--and the ensuing centuries of exile--as examples of the disastrous consequences of zealots taking charge.

Whatever the message, such a campaign cannot be conducted in fits and starts, nor in a low-key, episodic manner. Rather, to succeed, it must be robust, rigorous and sustained. Both the Israeli and Palestinian authorities should deliberately and consistently highlight the worst features of theocratic dictatorship, so as to strike resonant cords in their largely secular societies. The idea is to capitalize on the rejectionists' inherent weaknesses, mobilizing the public against them on the basis of self-interest, if not self-preservation. At a minimum, the goal would be to prevent tolerance of these groups' agendas, while energizing an active, broad-based

Implications for the Peace Process 327

opposition to their pursuits.

By the same token, both the PNA and the Israeli government could adopt the age-old strategy of divide and rule, exploiting the heterogeneity of their respective rejectionist groups. For example, the fact that the rank and file is usually moved by exoteric, rather than esoteric, issues provides an opportunity for a concerted effort to address their salient social, economic and political grievances, thus detaching the true believers from their base of popular support. With the leadership thus effectively isolated, the authorities could concentrate on undermining the theoretical/religious message, specifically the self-proclaimed monopoly on the truth. In the case of Palestinian and Israeli total rejectionists, the authorities must challenge the credibility of their theological arguments, invoking, when feasible, the best of Judaic or Islamic philosophical thought.

The third policy choice pertains to such palliative measures as the offers of a time-limited truce with Israel--ranging from 15 to a hundred years' cease-fire--proffered, for example, by *Hamas* spokesmen. The only way to verify the seriousness of such bids is to call the bluff. The risk is minimal and can be further reduced by conducting an indirect dialogue through the PNA. Should *Hamas* respond positively, both Israel's and the PNA's interests will be well served. The immediate benefits that would accrue from a cessation of hostilities are obvious. In the longer term, there is at least a chance that inactivity will sap both the psychological commitment and actual skills necessary to reignite an armed struggle. Indeed, the secular rejectionists themselves warned in 1974--at the time of the PLO split over acceptance of a mini-state--that the stagnation born of a truce would eviscerate the resistance and destroy its morale. Parallel offers by Israeli rejectionists--were they to materialize--should, of course, be treated in a similar manner.

Any attempt to divorce politics from economics is both demonstrably ludicrous and fraught with peril. The link between economic problems and political violence is well-known.[3] What is perhaps less appreciated is the fact that economic betterment is not a universal panacea, especially if it accentuates maldistribution of material benefits and, thus, aggravates the sense of relative deprivation among social groups. Further exacerbation of inequalities, in turn, plays into and is reinforced by existing animosities.

With these caveats in mind, the economic policy choices must be addressed on at least two levels. The first involves Israel's economic role in the region; the second pertains to Western assistance to Middle Eastern peacemakers.

Undoubtedly, Israel is the dominant regional economy. With that comes a special responsibility to exercise judicious restraint and take account of the sensitivities prevalent in the Arab world. The stark disparities between levels of economic development and technological know-how, separating Israel from its neighbors, cannot but create fears of abuse--particularly when superimposed on almost three decades of a neo-colonial relationship between Israel proper and the territories.

The excesses historically associated with unfettered private enterprise would only reinforce existing fears of neo-imperial exploitation, thus providing grist for the Palestinian rejectionists' propaganda mills. The choice here is not between economic engagement and non-involvement. Rather, the options involve humanistic capitalism--which allows for an accommodation to political realities and social sensibilities--and apolitical *laissez faire*, driven exclusively by profit. In a volatile region like the Middle East, sacrificing political exigencies on the altar of economic profiteering is not only short-sighted; it is bound to backfire.

As for Western economic assistance, the policy choice is between assertive support and outright neglect. The latter leaves Palestinian economic issues to the Palestinians themselves and is embodied in the attitude that "it's their problem." While economic betterment might, indeed, be "their problem," it will quickly become everybody's predicament because, absent a steady infusion of foreign aid, the PNA simply cannot carry out even the most essential functions of governing, not the least of which is securing law and order. While current Israeli policy recognizes these imperatives, witting or unwitting supporters of Israeli rejectionism apparently do not. Hinging vital economic aid on increasingly convoluted political conditions effectively dooms the PNA to failure, thus playing directly into the hands of rejectionists on both sides. By the same token, hollow promises not only raise expectations for a quick fix--thus feeding disillusionment, frustration and animosity--but also undermine the West's credibility as both an honest broker and a genuine partner for peace.

As for the ever-important security sphere, the Israeli government and the PNA face two basic types of threats: sporadic guerrilla warfare and terrorism. While the former is and will likely continue to be internal to the conflict area, spectacular attacks abroad are not to be discounted. As we have suggested throughout this book, terrorism remains the weapon of the weak, notoriously ineffective as a means to strategic ends. In the short term, however, it might be disproportionately successful in evoking over-reaction on the part of the victims. Herein lies the inherent impulse for escalation: Insofar as attacks--and counterattacks-- become routinized, terrorists are pushed toward ever more spectacular acts to cause the desired emotional rage which is destructive of compromise.

Since both sides realize that terrorist violence sustains the deadly embrace, they have already established unprecedented cooperation in the security area. Cooperative measures include intelligence sharing, joint patrols and border controls. What has been achieved thus far between longstanding enemies is remarkable by any standard. While a 100% effectiveness is unattainable, the policy choice is between resting on the laurels of past achievement or pushing for even closer coordination. The former is clearly the path of least resistance. However, given the growing ease with which weapons of mass destruction (WMD) can be obtained on the open market, the risks associated with this approach are horrendous.[4]

As the nerve gas attack by Aum Shinrikyo in the Tokyo subway clearly shows, such weapons are not beyond the reach of well-educated and technically skilled dissidents. While the threat of fratricide and the inherent uncontrollability of WMD might continue to deter their use, the taboo has already been broken and their "usability" demonstrated. Moreover, the technology of the future is likely to make these weapons more manageable, accessible and "user-friendly." Simply put, the benefit of attaining a critical objective--like destroying the peace process--might outweigh the costs and risks, particularly if the threat to one's own community is deemed minimal. Thus, a rational calculus might no longer exclude the employment of weapons of mass destruction. Of course, even if it does, we are still left with the irrational actors, who, unfortunately, are not in short supply in this region.

The looming threat of "information war," in both its lethal and non-lethal incarnations, is another critical argument for closer cooperation in the security sphere. As a technologically advanced society, Israel, like the U.S., is highly vulnerable to attacks--from both its own rejectionists and Palestinian militants--on its computer systems, banking, air traffic control, power grid, etc.[5] The PNA's vulnerability will grow commensurably, as it evolves a modern infrastructure. Here the choice is simple and direct: wait for the problem to occur or lay the groundwork for proactive, cooperative measures now. The latter approach presents a natural opportunity to further enhance Israel's image as a constructive regional player, ready to share its high-tech expertise with its neighbors.

Moving to the more traditional aspects of counter-terrorism, the courses of action Israel has taken over the years are quite familiar: passive defense, combined with such active measures as detention without trial, physical pressure, expulsion, hit teams, and cross-border operations against suspected staging areas. While the harshness of these measures will continue to run the risk of alienating important elites in both communities, these are choices that have already been made, and there is little or no prospect that they would be countermanded. The key has been and will remain their discriminate and even-handed use, as well as realistic expectations of success.

Consistent, dynamic cooperation with the PNA in such areas as intelligence and proactive detention is also crucial. The Palestinians, new to the business of counterinsurgency, will have

Implications for the Peace Process 331

to forestall rejectionist use of newly reclaimed areas as staging bases for anti-Israeli attacks. At the same time, they are also likely to face serious challenges to their nascent national institutions. We anticipate a dialectical relationship between old-style authoritarian politics--already in evidence in both Gaza and Jericho--and pressures to evolve genuinely democratic institutions. Such imperatives would emanate both from within the Palestinian community--witness the active role of human rights groups and such intellectuals as Dr. Hanan Ashrawi--as well as from potential donors in the U.S. and Western Europe. Yet, wishful thinking to the contrary, it is simply unrealistic to expect that centuries-old cultural and political proclivities would suddenly give way to a democratic nirvana.

The pragmatic choice is thus between unrestrained imposition of harsh security measures and a conscious effort to make them as discriminating as possible. Special care must be taken to avoid the detention and incarceration of legitimate political opponents, no matter how vociferous their rhetoric might be. The issue here is not so much upholding democratic values, as the practical necessity of avoiding the violent radicalization of the opposition.

This is not an easy course to sustain. Even in established pluralistic systems--such as the United Kingdom, Italy, and Israel--the imperatives of protecting innocent lives have sometimes come at the expense of civil rights. What is remarkable in these cases is that such encroachments in no way threatened the democratic edifice itself. The problem for the PNA is that it lacks the longstanding tradition of pluralism, respect for human rights and rule of law, which are needed to cushion the inevitable systemic shocks associated with counterinsurgency. Therefore, the less chance is left for improvisation on the part of loyal subordinates, the better.

While both Israel and the PNA should be expected to strive for such lofty norms as those set by Amnesty International, a realistic policy must allow for and be understanding of their immediate security concerns. In those few instances where there is a stark choice between procedures and life itself, the latter must, no doubt, continue to take precedence.

Last, but certainly not least, is the issue of external support. As we have suggested earlier, this can be a crucial determinant of the course and outcome of internal wars, particularly where the military and security forces have the situation well in hand, thus compelling the insurgents to rely on outsiders for their very existence.

This has always been the case for the Palestinians. Even in its heyday, the Palestinian resistance failed to establish a parallel hierarchy in the territories, let alone in Israel proper. Accordingly, material support from and sanctuary in contiguous states have been essential. Whereas in the past Jordan and Lebanon were indispensable in sustaining the armed struggle, now Syria and Iran are the centers of gravity. Of the two, Syria is by far the more crucial, due to both its proximity to the conflict area--threatening Israel, Jordan and the PNA--and its ability to circumscribe Palestinian violence, if it so chooses. Syria also serves as a sanctuary for the rejectionists--to include such erstwhile ideological adversaries of the Ba'th Party as *Hamas* and the IJM.

The policy choices here are inherent in the very term "center of gravity." As defined two centuries ago by Carl von Clausewitz, a center of gravity is "the hub of all power and movement" which, if destroyed, would spell the adversary's demise.[6] In our case, the "hub" is the sanctuary and the party capable of destroying it is Damascus. There is no insurmountable obstacle here, inasmuch as Syria does not support the ultimate rejectionist aims. For, it is not in its long-term interest to see the establishment of either a secular or an Islamic Palestinian state. And, while both would threaten Syria's hegemony, an Islamic state next door would also invalidate the very basis of the Ba'thist ideological legitimacy that upholds the Assad regime.

Insofar as all Arab leaders define regime maintenance as the preeminent national security concern, threats to its survival are, by definition, the most acute. These are particularly poignant exigencies for Assad, who presides over a minority regime, sustained, in large measure, by coercion. Accordingly, a peace process that takes account of such existential threats could be welcome under the right circumstances.

It is this imperative that makes an Israeli-Syrian accord so critical. Herein, the policy choice is between a narrow, tactical perspective and a broader, strategic approach which would satisfy both sides' vital interests. The latter course of action would leverage Assad's need to neutralize internal challenges to the Alawite regime, especially by Sunni extremists. The gain for Israel would be no less significant, attenuating both the conventional military threat posed by Syria and the terrorist threat posed by Damascus-sponsored rejectionists.

Yet, while a comprehensive Syria-Israel agreement is the linchpin of the regional security equation, the attendant risks are significant. First, the military significance of terrain, especially the high ground, remains relevant even in the age of missiles and weapons of mass destruction. This is particularly applicable to situations where there is stable mutual deterrence at the strategic level, effectively precluding the use of WMD and limiting combat to a conventional contest over terrain. Such was clearly the case during the ferocious battles for the Golan in 1967 and 1973. Therefore, any Israeli government is bound to seriously question the wisdom of returning the hard-won plateau to Syrian sovereignty. While robust U.S security guarantees might alleviate some of the justifiable concerns, any Israeli government would face serious internal opposition, if not outright resistance, to the magnitude of the necessary sacrifice. Given both Labor's and Likud's commitment to a referendum prior to territorial concessions--and considering that public opinion polls consistently show a sizeable plurality opposed to full return of the Golan--a potential deal could easily be rejected by a democratic vote. Moreover, because the vast majority of Golan settlers are secular, a confrontation over that land could help bridge the religious-secular divide and unite the Israeli rejectionists over an issue of national security. Such a short-term consensus might provide the extra margin of political clout to doom the accord.

For Syria, the risk is to both Assad personally, as well as to his minority regime. Old enemies who have been forced underground --such as the various Muslim Brotherhood factions--would likely link the "heresy" of compromising with the Jews with the overall "apostasy" of the Alawites. Whether this will translate into resurgence of violent opposition would depend, in part, on the regime's ability to retain the loyalty of the security establishment. As Rabin's assassination tragically demonstrates, all it takes is one zealot with a gun. The fundamental difference, of course, is that political succession in Syria is not anchored in democratic institutions and that, therefore, the cohesion of the political elites could be easily shattered. Thus, the ensuing struggle for power could center on--and be polarized by--the issue of "sell out," that is, the very idea of dealing with Israel. Naturally, Israel itself cannot but factor such eventualities into it own calculus.

Moving away from worst-case scenarios, Assad would still face two problems: First, he will need to suppress violent resistance by recalcitrant rejectionists in Lebanon and, perhaps, even Syria itself. Second, he will have to weather the storm of embarrassment that is sure to follow any attempt to close the offices and radio stations of such groups as the PFLP-GC, *Hamas* and the IJM, as well as those of his erstwhile allies like *S'aiqa* and the *Abu Musa* Organization. If the past is a guide, Syria's notorious secret police, the *Mukhabarat*, is fully capable of imposing the leadership's policies and neutralizing any opposition. Hence, maintaining the loyalty of the security services would remain a top priority for the Assad regime.

Finally, the strategic concord between Syria and Iran, dating back to the Iran-Iraq war, could be fractured. To comply with its agreement with Israel and to contain the internal threat, Syria will have little choice but to confiscate existing arsenals and forestall their replenishment by Teheran. The task would be made even more complex by the need to deal with the presence of the Iranian Revolutionary Guards and their *Hezbollah* clients in Lebanon. All this would further strain the fragile alliance of convenience between the secular regime in Damascus and the theocrats in Teheran.

Implications for the Peace Process

The complex policy options related to external support are not confined to the actors in the Middle East, since the flow of money from outside the region--most notably from the United States--also fuels rejectionist violence. This, in turn, makes the decisions inside the Middle East more difficult to make and carry out. Ameliorating this situation will require tough choices by both the U.S. government and the Jewish and Arab communities.

For the U.S. government, the options boil down to continued reliance on well-intentioned but ultimately ineffectual legislation, and a concerted effort to put some muscle behind the law and close at least a few of the most gaping loopholes. As we have argued, existing regulations are all too easy to circumvent through deliberate deception and obfuscation of the end-recipients. As long as the law permits the transfer of tax-exempt funds to foreign philanthropic, religious and educational organizations, the danger of diversion to the coffers of both Jewish and Palestinian rejectionists would remain.

The need to differentiate between legitimate charities and terrorist groups operating under a false flag is yet to be recognized, much less translated into an effective policy. At a minimum, more precise regulation must be instituted to prevent the flow of funds to any group directly or indirectly associated with Middle Eastern terrorism. If done right, this would compel legitimate Jewish and Arab charities to monitor their respective donor communities. An even tougher choice would involve legislation denying tax-exempt status to all foreign organizations operating on U.S. soil.

Given the inherent fungibility of financial transfers and the less-than-rigid enforcement of IRS regulations, the best one can hope for is a demonstrable reduction, rather than elimination, of the problem. Yet, the political perils for members of both the executive and the legislature branches are considerable, especially in election years. The extent of the risk would depend, in large measure, on the choices made by Arab and Jewish Americans, specifically, their readiness to place support for the peace process above any ties of kinship, religion, or political affiliation that account for these communities' witting or unwitting support for terrorist organizations. Such a stark choice must also involve putting an end, once and for all, to apologies for and public defense of activities violently opposed to such vital U.S. interests as democracy, peace and stability. The cost for Arab and Jewish American citizens is a strain on communal ties and individual friendships. Accepting such risks is what political courage is all about.

For Arab Americans there is the added incentive of countering--through actions rather than words--the unfairly biased association of Islam and terrorism. While popular images take a long time to dissipate, the process is unlikely to begin as long as the myopic and thinly-veiled sophistry effectively excusing--and, thus, condoning--Palestinian terrorism continues. In the perceptive words of the Kuwait's *Al Watan*:

> The activities of Arab-Americans have not made it easy for them to become assimilated in America. Their assimilation became more difficult, especially after American cities were turned into conflict centers used by Islamic movements and some Arab regimes for rallying supporters and recruiting activists. These Islamic movements then proceeded to establish various fundamentalist associations, leagues and organizations. All this will inevitably be disastrous for Arabs and Muslims in the United States, and in the Arab and Islamic worlds as well.[7]

In short, the time has come for Arab Americans to disassociate themselves from subversive activities that would not be tolerated anywhere in the Arab world. If the opportunity is not seized now, it might be lost forever, especially if today's apologists find themselves inextricably linked with a universally condemned future catastrophe.

The probability of such a devastating catastrophe will steadily increase as *Deus* and *machina* become increasingly fused. The new death machine, employed in the name of God by his self-proclaimed disciples, might spring from chemical formulae, laboratory vials, or cyber-codes. These forthcoming tools of the terrorist trade are particularly appealing, since they require relatively small operational and support structures. The highly-

Implications for the Peace Process

advanced levels of education and technological know-how, prevalent in both the Israeli and Palestinian communities; the growing accessibility of scientific data, now universally and immediately available on Internet; the permeability of international borders; and the uncontrollability of much of the arms trade--all combine to create a real opportunity for a handful of zealots to wreak havoc on a scale that hitherto only armies could attain. This is particularly true in a region saturated with the combustible mixture of self-righteousness, hatred and desperation--none of which is conducive to a rational calculus of costs, risks and benefits.

Therefore, unlike novelists, we cannot end on a happy note. The right policy choices are likely to reduce the impact of self-righteousness and hatred. Paradoxically, however, the desperation will remain, if not deepen. Brooding in their own, self-imposed darkness, the last rejectionists might emerge as a modern incarnation of the four horsemen of the apocalypse, to inflict untold suffering on their own communities, if not on the world at large. Thus, what the peacemakers are confronting is not just a set of political problems and alternative courses of action. Rather, they are engaged in an epic struggle against evil itself.

Notes

1. Significantly, in a November 10, 1995 interview with *Le Nouvel Observateur*, Yasir Arafat alleged direct collaboration between Israeli and Palestinian "fanatics" in carrying out such deadly terrorist attacks as the January 22, 1995 suicide bombing in Beit Lid, in which 21 Israelis died. Neither the alleged "facts" nor Arafat's claims to have passed "the highly detailed files" on the case to the Israeli government, as well as to the U.S., Russia, Egypt and the European Union, can be independently verified. However, the accusation dovetails with similar, albeit far less direct statements made by Labor officials, as well as with an Egyptian journalist's claim that there is an "unofficial alliance between Hamas and Likud", designed to return Likud to power, while destroying the peace process through terrorist violence. See, FBIS-NES-95-227, November 27, 1995, pp. 1-2 and Cairo *Al Musawwar*, March 1, 1996, FBIS-TOT-96-011-L, April 26, 1996, pp. 36-38.

2. Specifically, many Middle East specialists either could not imagine or chose to discount the possibility--often with high-sounding words such as "preposterous nonsense"--that such events as Israel's preemption in 1967, the October 1973 war, Sadat's visit to Jerusalem, the fall of the Shah, the eight-year war between Iran and Iraq, Iraq's invasion of Kuwait, and Israeli-Palestinian settlement could ever take place. By the same token, most European experts failed to foresee such seminal developments as the disintegration of the Warsaw Pact, the reunification of Germany, the collapse of the Soviet Union, and the end of the Cold War. Thus, the perils of linear thinking are by no means limited to the Middle East.

3. The relationship between economic disparities and high levels of political violence has been underscored by recent statistical analyses, using both logged ordinary least-squares (LOLS) and exponential Poisson regression (EPR). See Edward N. Muller and Mitchell A. Seligson, "Inequality and Insurgency," *American Political Science Review*, June 1987, pp. 425-451 and T. Y. Wang, William J. Dixon, Edward N. Muller, and Mitchell A. Seligson, "Inequality and Political Violence Revisited," *American Political Science Review*, December 1993, pp. 979-993.

4. There is a voluminous body of open-source literature, raising the specter of terrorists acquiring and employing radiological, biological, and/or chemical weapons. Among the best and most recent are: Robert G. Joseph and John F. Reichart, *Deterrence and Defense in a Nuclear, Biological and Chemical Environment*,(Washington D.C.: National Defense University Press, 1995), Keith B. Payne, "Deterring the Use of Weapons of Mass Destruction," *Comparative Strategy*, October-December 1995, pp. 347-359, and Robin Wright, "Be Very Afraid," *The New Republic*, May 1, 1995, pp. 19-27. See also, Jessica Mathews, "Inch-by-Inch Disarmament," *The Washington Post*, December 11, 1995.

5. As an example of a relatively benign employment of the tools of information warfare, one might cite the deliberate attempt by West Bank settlers to overload the national power grid by turning on all household electric devices simultaneously. The activity was publicized and coordinated via Internet in Fall, 1995. The fact that, throughout Likud's reign, there was a concerted effort to locate high-tech industries, especially computer-related enterprises,in the West Bank--effectively turning it into Israel's Silicone Valley--places the tools of information warfare in the heartland of rejectionism.

6. Carl von Clausewitz, *On War*, Edited and Translated by Michael Howard and Peter Paret, (Princeton, NJ: Princeton University Press,1976), pp. 595-596.

7. *Al Watan*, June 22, 1995, FBIS-NES-95-164, August 24, 1995, pp. 24-25.

INDEX

Abu Iyad (Salah Khalaf), 218, 230
Abu-Marzuq, Musa 222, 240
Abu Mus'ab, 227, 241
Abu Nidal Organization, (ANO), 218, 226, 229, 235, 242, 257, 258, 264, 295
Abu-Amr, Ziyad, 226, 239, 240, 294, 302
Adams, Jerry, 268
Agudat Israel (Aguda), 65, 66, 78, 122, 130, 131, 187
Aharai (Follow Me), 147
Al-Quds, 213, 240, 276, 300
Almond, Gabriel, 30
Aloni, Shulamit, 127, 168, 170
Altalena, 69, 70
Amal, 220, 228, 242,
Amana, 138, 142-145
American Civil War, 17, 264
American Friends of Yesha, 169
American-Israel Public Affairs Committee (AIPAC), 164, 168, 169
Amir, Yigal 150, 182
Arafat, Yasir, 218, 307, 315
Ariel, Israel, 100
Arlosoroff, Chaim, 68
Ashrawi, Hanan, 331
Awwad, Arabi, 269
Ayyash, Yahya, 285

Baader Meinhof, 24
Basque Homeland and Liberty, xv, 21, 267, 308
Batista, 19, 44
Begin, Menachem, 63, 69, 70
Ben Gurion, David, 63, 66
Benvenisti, Meron, 144, 145, 305

Ben Yosef, Shlomo, 155
Bereshit (Genesis), 79, 148, 149, 151, 315
Bernadotte, Volke, 70
Betar, 147
Bnei Akiva, 77, 140-142, 147
Bolsheviks, 12, 68, 152, 322
British Mandate, 41, 235
Burg, Abraham, 129
Bush, George, 91, 161, 163, 250

Camp David, 74, 84, 133, 161, 219, 220, 314
Castro, Fidel, 30
Chou En-lai, 272
Christopher, Warren, 168
Chu Te, 272
Clausewitz, Carl von, 332
Clinton, William Jefferson, 168, 171, 172, 290, 303
Cohen, Geula, 158
Cohler, Lawrence, 171
Corps of Volunteers, 40,

Debray, Regis, 18, 41, 54
Democratic Revolutionary Front (FDR), 41
Deri, Aryeh, 127
Dhofar Insurgency, 7
Direct Action (France), 21, 81, 86, 88, 90, 95, 119, 148, 154
DOV (Supression Of Traitors), 148, 149, 151,

Edri, Oren, 104
Egypt, xv, 4, 53, 74, 135, 153, 161, 215, 216, 219, 265, 289, 308, 315
Elba, Ido, 100

341

Eldad, Israel, 158
Elon, Beni, 149, 153
Endeavor, 43, 148, 149, 219, 226, 274
EYAL (Jewish Fighting Organization), 79, 147, 149-151
Eytan, Raphael, 158, 183

Fadallah, Muhammad Husayn, 291, 308
Fall, Bernard, 35
Faluji, Imad Al-, 213, 231, 243
Fanon, Francis, 85
Farabundo Marti National Liberation Front (FMLN), 41
Faraj, Muhammad Abdel Salam Al-, 260
Faris, Amin, 255
Fatah, 39, 215, 216, 223, 227, 229, 234, 237, 238, 242, 257-259, 276, 297, 307
Fatah-the uprising, 223, 227, 276
Fedayeen, 217, 218, 237, 254, 280, 281, 293
Feiglin, Moshe, 149
Fighting Communist Cells, 21
Frankel, Glenn, 70, 100, 305
Friedman, Robert I., 169-171

Gailani, Mohammed, 5
Gaza Strip, 144, 214-216, 220, 224, 231, 239-242, 244, 250, 251, 254-256, 261, 265, 282, 283, 285-287, 294, 298, 299, 302, 305, 314
Gemayel, Bashir, 220
Goldstein, Baruch, 61, 99, 100, 178, 185, 296
Green Line, 77, 93, 97, 98, 101, 104, 117, 118, 142, 143, 148, 149, 163, 166, 170, 177, 254, 255, 281, 294, 298
Greenberg, Uri Zvi, 83
Guevara, Che, 18, 19, 23, 54, 55, 229
Guillen, Abraham, 20, 55
Gush Emunim, 75, 77-79, 84, 87, 90, 94, 98, 138-146, 155, 157, 169, 182, 184
Guzovsky, Michael, 173

Habash, George, 225, 232, 237, 240, 252, 269
Hadassah, 166
Hafiz, Assad Al-, 274
Hagana, 68, 69, 71, 279
halacha (Jewish Law) 66, 82
Hamas, 61, 101, 134, 148, 158, 168, 176, 213, 222-226, 228, 230-232, 235, 236, 239-244, 249, 252, 258-262, 265-271, 275-279, 284, 285, 288, 289, 293-296, 298-308, 315, 327, 332, 334
Haredi, 65, 66, 123, 124
Harish, Mikha, 128
Harkabi, Yehoshafat, 65, 75
Hasan, Bana Al-, 241, 265
Hawatmah, Naif, 226
Hebron, vii, xiii, 61, 95, 96, 99, 100, 104, 148, 174, 175, 177-179, 184, 185, 286, 296, 313, 315, 320
Herev David (Sword of David), 78, 89, 150
Herut, 68, 72
Hezbollah, 6, 228, 236, 240-245, 250, 278, 290-292, 302-304, 308, 309, 334
Ho Chi Minh, 8, 23, 37, 230, 272

Index

Huk, 35
Huseini, Faysal Al-, 253
Hussein, King Ibn Talal, 219, 238, 274
Hussein, Saddam, 221, 274, 283

Intifada, 48, 81, 88, 97, 98, 100, 101, 117, 135, 145, 150, 165, 178, 181, 182, 220, 221, 223, 232, 237, 239, 242, 252, 253, 255, 265, 271, 283, 284, 294, 296, 305, 318
Irgun Zvai Leumi (ETZEL), 68, 69, 70
Irish Republican Army (IRA), xv, 21, 27, 132, 267, 308, 322
Islamic Conference Organization, 37
Islamic Group, xv, 4, 6, 150
Islamic Jihad, 61, 222, 235, 277, 300, 301
Israel Defense Forces (IDF), 69-71, 74, 88, 94, 96-100, 102-104, 125, 134, 137, 146, 147, 149, 150, 154, 167, 169, 171, 172, 175-179, 181, 182, 183-187, 224, 236, 266, 278, 280-284, 286, 287, 290, 291, 295, 300, 305, 306, 308, 309
istishhad (The Death of a Hero), 262
Italian Resistance, 40

Jabotinsky, Vladimir Ze'ev, 68, 69, 235
Jadallah, Muhammad, 272
Japanese Red Army, 21
Jewish Defense League (JDL), 83, 85
Jewish Underground, 89, 96, 100, 104, 182, 184, 279

Jibril, Ahmed 225, 230
Jihaz, Siri Al-, 267

Kach, 75, 78, 84-87, 89, 96, 135, 146, 147, 150, 151, 171, 172, 174, 175, 315
Kahane Chai, 78, 150, 151, 171, 172, 315
Kahane, Meir, 83
Khalistan Liberation Front, 6
Klein, Claude, 117
Kook, Abraham Isaac, 66
Kook, Yehuda Zvi, 78, 141
Koresh, David, 150
Kurds, 6, 26

Ladin, Usamah bin, 277
Lenin, 12, 19, 24, 31, 32, 54, 56, 140, 183
Levinger, Miriam, 139
Levinger, Moshe, 139, 141
Levy, David, 158
Likud, 62, 67, 78, 84, 88, 90, 91, 95, 102, 104-106, 121, 123, 126, 127, 129-131, 133-138, 142-144, 146, 148, 158-160, 162, 163, 167, 168, 176, 180, 183, 221, 225, 256, 282, 284, 305, 315, 324, 330, 333
Lohamei Herut Israel (LEHI), 68-70, 83, 150, 158, 279
Lustick, Ian, 75

MAFDAL (National Religious Party, or NRP), 65-67, 77, 122, 124, 125, 131, 137, 140, 141, 157, 170, 186
Magsaysay, Ramon, 46
Majid, Khalid Abd Al-, 269
Maliki, Riyad Al-, 272
Mao Tse-tung, 8, 13, 15, 16, 18,

19, 28, 30, 36, 53-56, 217, 230, 263, 272, 321
Marighella, Carlos, 20, 54
Marxist Popular Front, 4
Massoud, Ahmed Shah, 23
Milken, Michael and Lowell, 170
Miskito Indians, 4, 6
Mizrahi, 65, 66, 140
Moledet, 131, 146, 159,
mujahidin 75, 78, 86, 322
Mukhabarat, 334
Muslim Brotherhood, 5, 222, 223, 255, 265, 266, 276, 298, 334

Nasser, Gamal Abdel, 216, 274
Ne'eman, Yuval
Netanyahu, Benjamin, 130, 135, 137, 158
Neturei Karta, 65
Nuseiybah, Sari, 253

O'Neill, Tip, 119
Ofir, Gabi, 287
Omnibus Counterterrorism Act of 1995, 172
ORT, 166

Palestinian Liberation Organization (PLO), 39, 76, 95, 101, 127, 147, 168, 185, 186, 215, 216, 218-224, 229, 230, 235, 237-239, 242, 244, 253, 256, 265, 266, 271, 272, 274, 277, 278, 281, 282, 284, 288, 290, 295, 298, 299-302, 327
PALMACH, 69-71
Panjshir Valley, 23
People's Democratic Party of Afghanistan, 27

Peres, Shimon, 95, 121, 124, 127, 133-135, 150, 174, 175, 177, 181, 186, 187,
Pinto, Kobi, 104
Popular Front for the Liberation of Oman, 4
Popular Front for the Liberation of Palestine (PFLP), 39, 217-219, 223, 225, 226, 229, 230, 232, 234, 235, 238, 240, 252, 257, 258, 263, 264, 269, 270, 272, 275, 276, 295, 299-302, 323, 324, 334
Porat, Hanan, 141
Provisional Irish Republican Army (IRA), 21

Qabus, Sultan, 47
Qasim, Sheik Na'im, 243, 278
Quebec Liberation Front, 6
Qutb, Sayid Al-, 260

Rabin, Leah, 158
Rabin, Yitzhak, iii, vii, xii, xiii, 61, 70, 71, 74, 75, 81, 87-89, 99-101, 121, 126-131, 133, 135, 137, 146-148, 150, 151, 154, 157, 158, 163, 167-170, 172, 174-177, 180-182, 184-186, 249, 308, 315, 325, 334
Rafsanjani, Ali Akhbar Hashemi, 277
Reagan Administration, 161
Red Brigades, xv, 21, 24
Reichmann Family, 170

Saguia el Hamra, 6
Said bin Taimur, 4
Saison, 69
Sarraj, Eyad, 261, 297

Index

Savimbi, Jonas, 30
Sayarot, 280
Sendero Luminoso (Shining Path), 5, 32
Sepharadim, 62, 122, 124, 129
Shadid, Mohammed K., 267
shahid (martyr), 261
Shalom Achshav (Peace Now), 75
Shamir, Yitzhak, 69, 70, 90, 91, 161-163, 165, 176, 283
Shaqaqi, Fathi Al-, 227, 241, 242, 285, 300, 301
shariah (Islamic Law), 265
Sharon, Ariel, 176, 220
Sheikoleslam, Hussein, 277
Shemer, Naomi, 83
Shihabi, Hikmat Al-, 276
Shihadah, Raja, 253
Shiite, 220, 228, 270, 278, 290, 291, 301
Shinrikyo Aum, 329
Shomron (Samaria), 93, 144
shuba, 265
Sinyorah, Hanna, 253
Six Day War, 72, 73, 75, 81, 141, 161, 181, 183, 216
Smith, Ian, 25
Sorel, Georges, 85
Sprinzak, Ehud, 73, 75
Steinberg, Matti, 240, 262
Stern, Yair, 83
Syria, 5, 43, 136, 137, 153, 167, 215, 216, 219, 228, 229, 238, 239, 254, 263, 264, 269, 274-276, 278, 279, 289, 291, 302-304, 332-334

Tamil Tigers, xv, 6, 41, 322
Tehiya, 75, 78, 82, 158, 159
Terror Victims' Command (TVC), 148, 149, 315

Trendle, Giles, 250, 293
Tufayli, Sheik Subhi Al-, 228
Tzomet, 75, 78, 131, 158, 159

Ulster Defense Association, 7
umma, (Islamic Community) 226, 265
United Israel Appeal (UIA), 166
United Jewish Appeal (UJA) 166, 170, 171
United Zionist Command, 148

waqf (Islamic Trust), 252
War of Independence, 70, 96, 231, 215, 279
Weiss, Daniela, 139
Wolfsfeld, Gadi, 132
World Zionist Organization (WZO), 143, 171

Yamit, 74, 98, 103
Yasin, Sheik Ahmed, 265
Yasir Abd Rabu, 270
Yatom, Danny, 96
Yehuda (Judea), 93
Yemen Arab Republic, 5
YESHA, 138, 142, 144-146, 169, 170, 177
Yeshiva, 95, 100, 139, 141, 172, 181
Yeshivoth Hesder, 139, 181-183, 185
Yom Kippur War, 74, 81
Yugoslavia, 3

Zionism, 61-68, 70, 77, 84, 124, 143, 155, 236, 299
Zu Artzenu, (This is Our Land) 79, 148, 149
Zucker, Dedi, 95
Zvilli, Nisim, 169

ABOUT THE AUTHORS

Ilana Kass is a Professor of Military Strategy at the National War College. During 1992-93, she served on the Joint Staff, Strategic Plans and Policy Directorate (J-5), supporting the Chairman, Joint Chiefs of Staff, the Director, J-5, and the Office of the Secretary of Defense. Dr. Kass also taught at Georgetown University and the Hebrew University of Jerusalem, and served as a Major in the Israeli Defense Forces. She is the author of *Soviet Involvement in the Middle East: Policy Formulation* and has contributed numerous articles to such professional journals as Comparative Strategy, Strategic Review, International Defense Review, Defense and Diplomacy, and The Middle East Journal.

Bard E. O'Neill is Director of Middle East Studies at the National War College and Adjunct Full Professor at Catholic University where he teaches graduate courses in the Department of Politics. He is the author of numerous books and articles on the Middle East as well as internal wars and revolution. Among these are *Armed Struggle in Palestine* and *Insurgency and Terrorism*. Dr. O'Neill is also a consultant to various U.S. Government agencies and has been a guest analyst on a number of television and radio programs, including CNN and National Public Radio.